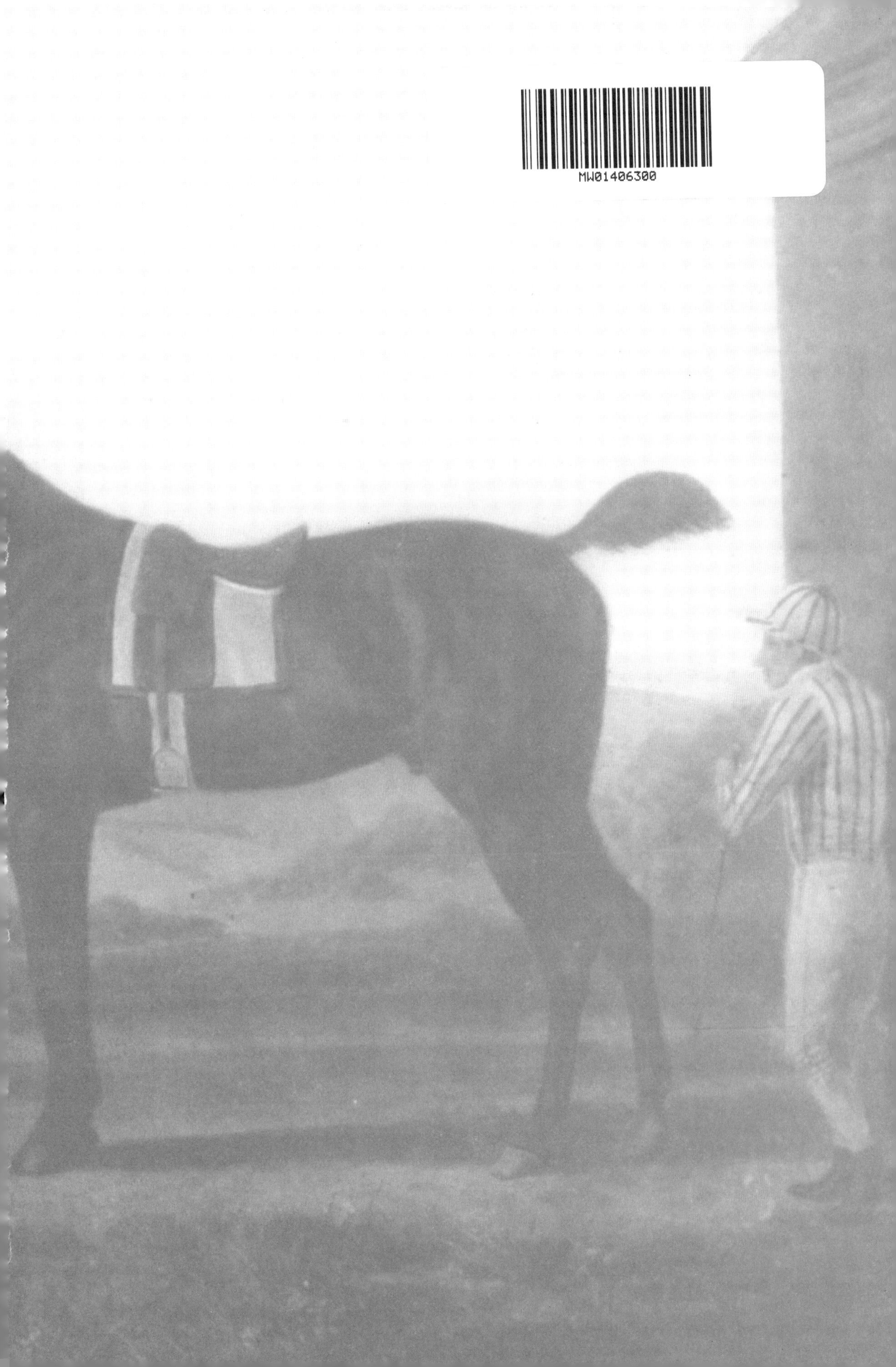

A KINGDOM

FOR THE HORSE

Robert Aitcheson Alexander The Master of Woodburn

Private Collection

A KINGDOM FOR THE HORSE

THE LEGACY OF R.A. ALEXANDER
AND WOODBURN FARMS

WILLIAM PRESTON MANGUM II

HARMONY HOUSE PUBLISHERS-LOUISVILLE

Executive Editors: William Strode, Joe Paul Pruett
Production Director: Boz Johnson
(Hardbound) ISBN 1-56469-037-7

©1999 William P. Mangum
First Edition Printed 1999
by Harmony House Publishers
P.O. Box 90 Prospect, KY 40059 USA
(502) 228-2010
Printed in the United States of America

All rights reserved. No part of this book may be reproduced or transmitted in any form or by any means, electronic or mechanical, including, photocopying, recording or by any information storage and retrieval system without written permission from Harmony House Publishers, except for the inclusion of brief quotations in a review.

Library of Congress Cataloging-in-Publication Data

Mangum, William Preston.
A kingdom for the horse : the legacy of R.A. Alexander and Woodburn Farms / William Preston Mangum II.
      p.   cm.
Includes bibliographical references (p.) and index.
ISBN 1-56469-037-7
1. Alexander, Robert Spreul Crawford Aitcheson, 1819-1867. 2. Horse breeders–Kentucky–Biography. 3. Race horses–Breeding–Kentucky–History–19th century. 4. Thoroughbred horse–Kentucky–History–19th century.　I. Title.
SF336.A58M35　1997
636.1' 2' 092–dc21
[B]　　　　　　　　　　　　　　　　　　　　　　　　　　　　　　97-39671
　　　　　　　　　　　　　　　　　　　　　　　　　　　　　　　　　CIP

DEDICATION

This book is dedicated with respect and admiration to the memory of
Robert Aitcheson Alexander
for his untiring, lifetime labor for the Sport of Kings

CONTENTS

Dedication v
Foreword ix
Preface xii

Chapter One: The Alexanders of Scotland 3
Chapter Two: Woodburn Farm-The Beginning 11
Chapter Three: The Cornerstones of the Kingdom 21
Chapter Four: Fellow Horsemen and Friends 39
Chapter Five: War Comes to Kentucky 45
Chapter Six: Quantrill's Arrival Into The Bluegrass 63
Chapter Seven: Disaster at Woodburn Farm 75
Chapter Eight: The Recovery of the Horses 83
Chapter Nine: Secret Sanctuary for the Horses 97
Chapter Ten: The Fate of the Raiders 107
Chapter Eleven: Racing Again Asteroid vs. Kentucky 115
Chapter Twelve: Death of the Master Breeder 129
Chapter Thirteen: Woodburn's Influence on the Western Turf 137
Chapter Fourteen: Frank James—Race Starter 159
Chapter Fifteen: Woodburn's Legacy 169
Chapter Sixteen: The Alexanders—Extended Family 185

Appendix 199
Footnotes 216
Index 256

The Armorial Beraings of Sir Claud Hagart-Alexander of Ballochmyle, Bt.

FOREWORD

The horse disappeared from the North American continent at some point in the mists of precivilization. It was reintroduced by the Spanish Conquistadors in the 16th Century. Since that time, it has adapted well as a companion for man, adjusting to a broad spectrum of disciplines. It has served as a beast of burden, a means of transport, a source of food, an engine of war, as well as a pet and companion. The dominant role that the horse fills in today's society is that of a competitor. From county horse shows to the Breeders Cup and the Grand Circuit, it is highly prized for its conformation, gait, jumping skills, strength, speed and competitive instincts. It has spawned a multibillion dollar industry, both in this country and around the world.

The ultimate result of this love affair with the racing of horses is the thoroughbred and the standardbred (both trotters and pacers). Their breeding began as haphazard pairings of animals both locally and from widely separated parts of the globe. While these matches occasionally produced individual horses which could win races consistently over their opponents, the organized breeding of racing stock developed slowly until Robert Spreul Crawford Aitcheson Alexander, an American born Scotsman, established a program of breeding blooded stock on his farm in Kentucky.

Dedicated to both the craft and science of producing the finest thoroughbred and standardbred horses possible, R.A. Alexander devoted his life from 1854 until his death in 1867 to the accurate recording of pedigrees. He focused upon the recognition of enduring qualities of both sires and broodmares. He carefully studied the particular assets achieved by the combination of superior gene pools (although he didn't use this term, the concept was clear in his mind). Nowhere is this better demonstrated than in the phenomenal successes he achieved by breeding his champion stallion, Lexington, to broodmares sired by Glencoe. He knew what pairings might produce endurance for the longer races of up to four miles, as well as the matches that could deliver early speed for the increasingly popular shorter contests of less than a mile. He was, to a significant degree, responsible for the establishment of the

American Stud Book authored by Sanders D. Bruce which was made possible by R.A.'s meticulous recording of pedigrees of the thoroughbred. He was still working on his records of pedigrees at the time of his death.

It seems only appropriate that this book should be dedicated to him and to the legacy which survived him. The horses which resulted from his perceptive and innovative approach to breeding grew to dominate the American turf in a manner that reflected not only his genius, but also his dedication to a dream of producing the finest horses possible, fueled by his persistence in the face of adversity, and the love of the horses he bred.

I first heard from William Mangum in June of 1983 when he wrote to me expressing an interest in a horse bred on Woodburn Farm that came to belong to Jesse James. I was able to be of little help, offering only that a story about the ownership of another Woodburn horse, Edwin Forrest, by Jesse's brother, Frank, appeared to be false. During the following decade over a score of letters and numerous phone calls from Bill indicated an increasing interest on his part in putting together a factual, historical account of the two Civil War raids on my family's farm that nearly ended its existence as a horse breeding establishment. He persuaded me to rummage through the dusty stud books, sales catalogues and letters that had been languishing in the attic of Woodburn House for generations in search of lost bits of history.

Through his own independent investigations, he was able to tell me facts about Woodburn that had been long forgotten by my family. The result of his 16 years of extensive research is the book that follows. He has honored me by inviting me to write a foreword to this scholarly and well written work that needs no introduction, but stands capably on its own merits.

Even the smallest events send ripples through time and take their place in the intricately woven tapestry of history. At a time when the nation was torn by civil war, two isolated guerrilla raids on a single horse farm in Central Kentucky seemed significant only to those directly involved. Yet, the results of these raids had far reaching effects on the nation's standardbred industry and to a lesser extent, on the future of the thoroughbred in this country. They also seemed to end the dream of a remarkable man who made an indelible impact on the breeding and racing of horses in America.

William Mangum brings history to life with his carefully researched accounts of such men as William C. Quantrill, Sue Mundy, Frank James and other individuals involved in the events described on the following pages. He also recounts the remarkable tale of a man, small in stature and in frail health, who built a dream, nurtured it and watched it grow, only to see it flicker in the winds of war and appear to die.

This man, Robert Spruel Crawford Aitcheson Alexander was my great, great uncle. Like

Moses, he caught a glimpse of the promised land, only to be denied admission into its realm. Had he lived beyond his 48th year, he would have seen the seeds he planted with the breeding programs he initiated on Woodburn Farm blossom into unparalleled success. Had the raids described in this book not taken place, he might have lived to see his dream flourish on an even grander scale. But in broken health and spirit he died alone on the farm to which he had devoted his life. Mr. Mangum tells this story with both compassion and historical accuracy, and in doing so, honors a man who was too soon forgotten.

    A.J. Alexander

    Lexington, Kentucky

PREFACE

William Preston Mangum, II
Chapel Hill, North Carolina

I am a horseman, and have been one since I can remember. My family's connection with harness race horses is through my mother's step-grandfather, Henry C. L. Miller, Sr., who owned harness horses including Mac Hanover of Hanover Shoe Farm. He would take his horses to winter at Pinehurst, N.C., and died during the 1940s on the train from Gettysburg, Pa., to Pinehurst. As a young man, I was fortunate to be chosen to work at "Airdrie Stud Farm," outside Midway, Kentucky. It was a hard job, but one that was fulfilling, rewarding and educational. I went to work at Airdrie, unaware of the influence it would play in my life. During my free time, I drove along the Old Frankfort Pike, which stretches northwest from Lexington to Frankfort through Fayette, Woodford and Franklin counties and passes through the heart of Kentucky's famous Bluegrass region, an area steeped in tradition and history. The pike is among the oldest roads in Kentucky and closely follows the old buffalo trace. Along it lie the picturesque fields and pastures belonging to the oldest and richest thoroughbred horse farms in the United States. These farms have produced some of the most famous names in racing history: Longfellow, Ten Broeck, Richard "Dick" Singleton, Early Light, Maud S., Jay-Eye-See, Enquirer, and Versailles. Early Kentucky Derby winners- Apollo, Baden-Baden, Fonso, Joe Cotton and Cannonade, the 1974 winner-were bred and foaled in this region. From a single source, the "Idle Hour Farm" in Fayette Country, owned by Colonel Edward Riley Bradley, have come Derby winners: Broker's Tip, Bubblin Over, Burgoo King, and Behave Yourself.

At Airdrie Farm, I became familiar with some of the farm's history and the bloodlines of Key to the Kingdom, (1970 by Bold Ruler–Key Bridge by Princequillo), Fifth Marine and Rich Cream (1975, by Creme de la Creme–Right Turn by Turn-to), the Worlds' record-holder for seven furlongs (1:19 2/5), and sire of the 1985 Super Derby, Jockey Club Gold Cup, and Belmont States winner, Creme Fraiche out of Likely Exchange. In 1980 I saw the great pacer and Worlds' record holder, Niatross (1:49.1), at "Castleton Farm." In 1981 I saw the gray pacing filly, Watering Can, driven by Stanley Dancer, win the Glen Garnsey Memorial at the Red Mile. I became obsessed with the bloodlines of the great thoroughbreds and standardbreds of the area and with the rich historical heritage of Kentucky and the legacy of Woodburn Farm.

The Bluegrass Region and its inhabitants played a significant role in the bloody years of the Civil War. With the exception of two battles in 1862, the Battle of Richmond in August and the Battle of Perryville in October, no large battles or campaigns were fought here. For most Kentuckians the War was a vicious, brutal and ugly guerrilla war. Numerous skirmishes occurred between the Union troops and Confederate guerrillas, but the raiders for the most part went unchecked.

A favorite target of the guerrillas were the horse farms of the region, where the raiders replaced their war-weary mounts with fresh stock. This stock was not the average contraband, but horses of the finest bloodlines and with the greatest endurance and speed of any horses in the nation at the time. They were a prize worth any risk.

Less than a mile west of the intersection of the Old Frankfort Pike and The Midway Road (Highway 62), is a stretch of road called "Shady Lane," undoubtedly one of the most beautiful places in Kentucky. Huge old trees form a green canopy over the lane, time worn stone fences border the road on both sides and seem to invite the visitor to the magnificent mansion called Woodburn House or Woodburn Manor. I would later learn that Quantrill's guerrillas and Sue Mundy used "Shady Lane" on February 2, 1865, to raid the home and farm of R.A. Alexander. What followed was the biggest raid on the horse farms of the district and a disaster for Woodburn Farm and Mr. Alexander.

Little has been written about the life of R.A. Alexander, but several sources document his farm, his stock and his great contributions to the racing industry. It piqued my interest. Who was R.A. Alexander? I began a search that would take 16 years and innumerable hours in libraries to accumulate a sizable amount of information. As I read and researched, I became obsessed with this remarkable man. A man, whose wisdom, foresight, love and tenacity built a kingdom for the horse.

I am proud and honored to share his story.

ACKNOWLEDGEMENTS

Walter Latzko and Phil Pines, Harness Horse Museum and Hall of Fame, Goshen, New York

Dr. A.J. Alexander, Lexington, Kentucky

William O. Boten, Duke University, Durham, North Carolina

Marla Conway, Hollywood Park, Inglewood, California

Vivian Montoya, Carleton F. Burke Library, The California Thoroughbred Breeders Association, Arcadia, California

Sandy Snider, Los Angeles State & County Arboretum, Arcadia, California

The Saddle Horse Museum, Kentucky Horse Park, Lexington, Kentucky

The Lexington Public Library, Lexington, Kentucky

The Filson Club, Louisville, Kentucky

The Missouri State Historical Society, Columbia, Missouri

Woodford County Historical Society, Versailles, Kentucky

The Kentucky Historical Society, Frankfort, Kentucky

King Library, University of Kentucky, Lexington, Kentucky

Davis Library, University of North Carolina, Chapel Hill, North Carolina

Zachary Smith Reynolds Library, Wake Forest University, Winston-Salem, North Carolina

Aurora Historical Society, Aurora, Illinois

Kane County Recorder Office, Geneva, Illinois

Library of Congress, Washington, D.C.

Court of the Lord Lyon, HM New Register House, Edinburgh, Scotland

Scottish Record Office, The National Archives of Scotland

Edinburgh, Scotland

Registry Office of the Turf Club, The Curragh, Co. Kildare, Ireland

Coat of Arms, by permission of Sir Cloud Hagart-Alexander of Ballochmyle, Bt., D.L., C.Eng., M.Inst.M.C., Kingencleugh House, Ayrshire, Scotland through Court of the Lord Lyon HM New Register House, Edinburgh, Scotland.

With special thanks to Cathy Cooper Schenck, Keeneland Association Library, Lexington, Kentucky, for her invaluable dedication and research.

A KINGDOM FOR THE HORSE

Painting of William Alexander II and family. At far left his son Robert IV and his wife Christian Aitcheson, circa 1766-1767.

CHAPTER ONE

The Alexanders of Scotland

The Alexanders originally came from Scotland and their ancestors are buried there at the 15th century Rosslyn Chapel, near the ruins of Rosslyn Castle. The Alexanders of Edinburgh were merchants and from an ancient and noble house, headed by the Earls of Sterling, although the family goes back much further.

Robert Alexander (1604-1687), a solicitor in Paisley, was the original purchaser of both Boghall and Blackhouse, in Ayrshire.[1] Robert (I)[2] passed Boghall on to his son, James (I), who became a Presbyterian minister. James (I), in turn, passed Boghall to his son, John (II), (ca. 1660-1712), a wealthy merchant and Burgess of Glasgow. John (II) married Janet, the daughter of Alexander Cuninghame of Graigends, Renfrewshire. He had two sons, Robert (II) and John (III), and a daughter, Anna. Anna married Peter Murdoch, Lord Provost of Glasgow, in 1731. Murdoch was by an earlier marriage, both father and father-in-law to other Provosts of the town and thus, through this marriage the Alexanders were connected to the leading "tobacco lords", of Glasgow. Anna and Peter Murdoch had two sons, the elder son, Robert of Blackhouse became principal Clerk of Session of Edinburgh, the highest court in Scotland.[3]

The younger son, William (I), was born in 1690. His early career is rather a mystery, but there is evidence that he was in Paris during the excitement of "The System" in 1719-20. In February 1720, while in France, he married Marianne de la Croix of Rochelle, from a prominent Huguenot family of Dutch origin. In 1722, or shortly thereafter, William returned to Scotland and established himself as a merchant and "the only banker in Edinburgh." William was to have had a distinguished public service career, as well as a financially successful commercial career. He served as Burgess and Guildmaster of Edinburgh in 1733 and in 1738 the government recognized him by naming him one of the 21 trustees for fisheries and manufacturers in Scotland. In addition William (I) had commercial connections throughout Scotland and England which also extended into Spain, France and the West Indies. He was the agent for the French tobacco monopoly in Scotland. One of William's regular activities was wine importation and he played a leading role in making French purchases in Scotland. At the height of his influence in the 1750s he served as Lord Provost of the City of Edinburgh from 1752-54 and represented

DESCENDANTS OF JOHN ALEXANDER

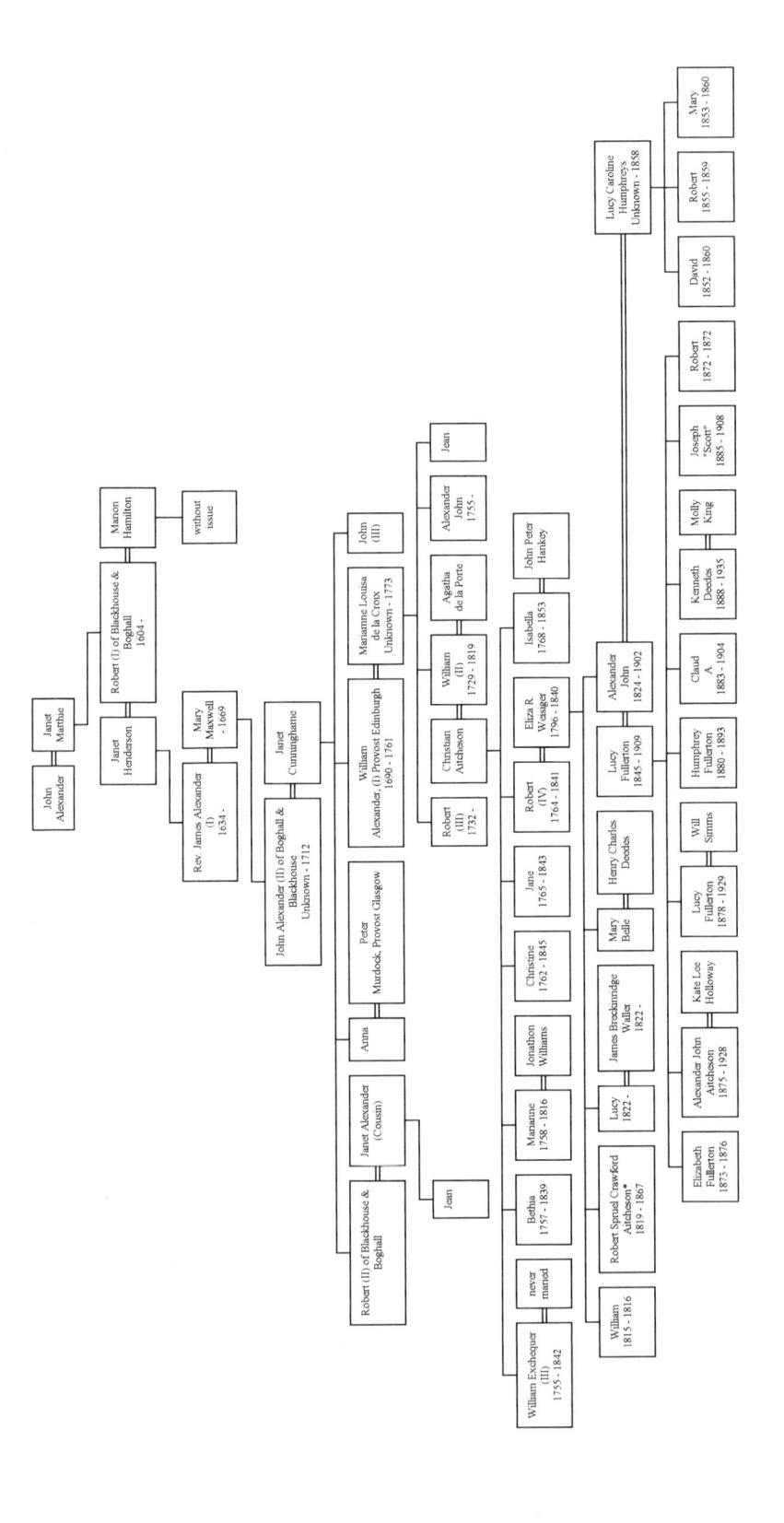

John Alexander — Janet Matthie

Robert (I) of Blackhouse & Boghall 1604 - — Marion Hamilton
- Janet Henderson — without issue
- Rev. James Alexander (I) 1634 - — Mary Maxwell - 1669

John Alexander (II) of Boghall & Blackhouse Unknown - 1712 — Janet Cunninghame

Alexander (I) Provost Edinburgh 1690 - 1761 — William Provost Edinburgh
- Peter Murdock, Provost Glasgow — Anna
- Jean
- Janet Alexander (Cousin) — Robert (II) of Blackhouse & Boghall

William (II) 1729 - 1819 — Marianne Louisa de la Croix Unknown - 1773
- John (III)
- Robert (III) 1732 -
- Christian Aitcheson
- Agatha de la Porte
- Alexander John 1755 -
- Jean

Robert (IV) 1764 - 1841 — Eliza R. Wassiger 1796 - 1840
- Isabella 1768 - 1853 — John Peter Hankey

William Exchequer (III) 1755 - 1842 — never married
- Bethia 1757 - 1839
- Marianne 1758 - 1816 — Jonathon Williams
- Christine 1762 - 1845
- Jane 1765 - 1843

Robert Spruel Crawford Aitcheson* 1819 - 1867
- William 1815 - 1816
- Lucy 1822 - — James Brockinridge Waller 1822 -
- Mary Belle — Henry Charles Deedes
- Alexander John 1824 - 1902 — Lucy Caroline Humphrey's Unknown - 1858

Elizabeth Fullerton 1875 - 1876
- Alexander John Aitcheson 1875 - 1928 — Kate Lee Holloway
- Lucy Fullerton 1878 - 1929 — Will Simms
- Humphrey Fullerton 1880 - 1893
- Claud A 1883 - 1904
- Kenneth Deedes 1888 - 1935 — Molly King
- Joseph "Scott" 1885 - 1908
- Robert 1872 - 1872
- David 1852 - 1860
- Robert 1855 - 1859
- Mary 1853 - 1860

Lucy Fullerton 1845 - 1909

William Alexander I, Lord Provost of
Edinburgh, Scotland

Marianne Louisa de la Croix, wife of Lord
Provost William Alexander

Edinburgh in the House of Commons during Parliament of 1754-1761. In addition, he was one of the commissioners for forfeited estates between 1755 and 1760.[4] He was a M.P., bank director of the Royal Bank of Scotland and the owner of William Alexander and Sons, his own banking firm.[5] William had four children: Robert (III), William (II), Alexander John and Jean.

At the beginning of the Seven Years' War, William sent his youngest son, Alexander John, to Boyd's Hole, Virginia on the Rappahannock River and later to the Caribbean to purchase tobacco for him and George FitzGerald of London to supply the Farmers-General. The French monopoly abandoned these purchases in 1757 and began the more normal purchases in Britain on commission. Alexander John Alexander stayed in Virginia on his own business although he claimed that he was "interested" in the family firm in Edinburgh.[6] When he died, his will identified him as a resident of Bath, England, and Grenada.

In 1759, William's banking firm came under crisis when George FitzGerald of London failed. William's oldest son, Robert (III), was one of the assignees in the bankruptcy. The ensuing financial strain broke William's health and the Lord Provost died in 1761.[7] Fortunately, his firm survived, later owned by his three sons, although none became directors of the Royal Bank, nor achieved the municipal or parliamentary positions of their father.

William (II) married Christian Aitcheson, whose father owned Airdrie House located outside the town of Airdrie in Lanarkshire near Glasgow, Scotland. There were six children from

Benjamin Franklin, minister from the American Colonies to France who befriended the Alexander Family in the 1760s. Robert Alexander, R. A.'s father, worked as Franklin's private secretary. The original portrait was commissioned by Robert Alexander III, painted by David Martin.

this marriage: William (III), Bethia, Marianne, Christian Aitcheson, Jane and Robert (IV).

Both William (II) and Robert (III) were drawn into the politics and society of the times. Robert (III) introduced Paris "literary suppers" into Edinburgh which were frequented by all the literary and fashionable people of the times. Therefore, it was natural that when Benjamin Franklin visited Edinburgh in the 1760s he was drawn into this intellectual circle and met the Alexanders.[8] By 1768 the friendship had grown between Franklin and the two brothers and during the financial panic of 1772, Franklin countersigned large loans of 5,000 pounds for the Alexanders to pay off their debts.[9] William (II) continued the Franklin-Alexander liaison after his brother's death in 1774. The last two thousand pounds, not an inconsequential sum, of the countersigned loan were repaid in 1775 or 1776 while William (II) was still in debtors prison. This further strengthened the friendship and trust between William and Franklin. After his release from prison, William (II) and two of his daughters moved to Dijon, France. From Dijon, William (II) continued his correspondence with Franklin who was at that time serving as Minister from the American Colonies to France.

"These two friends, although of different and hostile nationalities were so intimate that they often conferred on the subject of the great negotiation entrusted to Franklin, on the issue of which the destinies of both Europe and America seemed then suspended."[10]

How William (II) and the two daughters came to be in Paris in 1778-1779 was considered the "most secret of state secrets,"[11] and acted as a conduit to Franklin. In 1779 the Franklin-Alexander bond was strengthened when William (II)'s daughter, Marianne, married Jonathan Williams Jr., the great nephew of Franklin, who was a joyful guest at the wedding. Shortly after the death of his first wife, Christian, William (II) fled both from Scotland and France because of the heavy debts he had again accumulated. While in France William (II) became close friends with Armaund de la Port, a prominent French artist and Royalist, and his two teen-age daughters Maria and Agatha. According to family legend just prior to the beginning of the Reign of Terror (led by the French revolutionist Robespierre, the tribunal's public prosecutor) Armaund persuaded William Alexander to smuggle his daughters out of France. The 63-year-old William was able to accomplish this by marrying one of the girls, the 16-year-old Agatha. Armaund de la Port's concern for the safety of his daughters was not unfounded: he was beheaded in Paris in 1793. William's younger brother, Alexander John, became patron of his children, and William (II) emigrated to Virginia with his new bride.

Although Airdrie House and its estate should have passed naturally to William (II) at the death of his first wife, there was a falling out between him and the Aitcheson family. Therefore, Airdrie House was passed to his oldest son, William (III), who became the first Alexander to own Airdrie House. In 1782 William (II)'s son, Robert (IV), who had remained in England, traveled to Paris, and took a position with a Mr. Monduit as his chief preceptor, but later moved to Passy where he served two years as Franklin's private secretary. During this period, he developed a life long friendship with Jonathan Williams.[12] It was Benjamin Franklin who first encouraged Robert to come to America.[13] In 1787 Robert (IV) took his advice, booked passage from France and arrived in Virginia.[14] His father, William (II), had again managed to put himself deeply in debt and this was in part why Robert had decided to come to America. William's first child was born in Henrico County, Virginia, but he soon moved to the small community of Calf Pasture in Rockbridge County, Virginia, where he and his second family remained for many years. William (II), eventually moved his second family from Virginia to Woodford County, Kentucky, in 1813 and was given farm land by his son Robert next to what became Woodburn Farm. William (II) died in Kentucky on January 10, 1819, at the age of 90.[15]

Although born a British subject, Robert (IV), became an American citizen in 1791 and while still in Virginia obtained the original land grant in Kentucky that would later become Woodburn Farm. He purchased the land "sight unseen" from the estate of General Hugh

Robert Alexander. He was the first President of the Bank of Kentucky.

Eliza Richardson Weisiger Alexander of Frankfort, Kentucky. She was the daughter of Daniel Weisiger.

Mercer, a hero of the French & Indian War, who had been given this property through a military land grant.[16]

Robert (IV) later met and married Eliza Richardson Weisiger of Frankfort, Kentucky, and from this marriage came five children: William (died in infancy), Robert Aitcheson (R.A.), Alexander John "Alec" (A.J.), Mary Belle and Lucy.[17] In the years between 1796 and 1826 Robert (IV) sold other tracts of his estate, totaling about 1,900 acres reducing his original estate to 921 acres.[18] In 1811 Robert (IV) sold a portion of his estate, the land where Woodburn House stands today, to William Buford.[19] Robert (IV) later became the first President of the Bank of Kentucky in Frankfort and also served as a member of the Kentucky State Legislature.

His son, R.A., was sent to England at age 13 to enter Trinity College at Cambridge on July 8, 1840.[20] While not in school, he lived with his uncle and later guardian, Sir William (William III) in Scotland and in London. Sir William had never married, but had gained a high reputation as an equity and real property lawyer for 20 years and member of Parliament for two years.[21] He was:

> "...raised to the head of the Court Exchequer, being constituted Lord Chief Baron (Chancellor) of the Exchequer of Britain on January 9, 1824, and thereupon made a Privy Counselor and knighted."[22]

R.A.'s brother: Alexander John Alexander, as a young man. (Pastel)

In 1831 Sir William gained a large addition to his fortune when iron ore was discovered on his estate at Airdrie.[23] Sir William's estate now included the extensive estates of Airdrie House and Cowden Hill and the profits from the mining operations at both.

R.A.'s father, Robert (IV), died in 1841 from complications of an unfortunate carriage accident in Frankfort, Kentucky, and at his death the estate was divided among three of his four surviving children.[24] R.A. would, however, later purchase the shares of the estate from his siblings to obtain sole possession of what remained of Woodburn Farm. Through R.A.'s purchases the original 921 acres grew and the number fluctuated throughout his life as he bought and sold land until his death.[25]

In 1842 his uncle, Sir William, left the family estates of Airdrie and Cowden Hill in Scotland to R. A. In order to acquire this inheritance, however, he had to return to Scotland, renounce his American citizenship and become a British subject. R.A. Alexander later named his properties and businesses after the Airdrie House estate in Scotland, including Airdrie Mill in Montgomery, Illinois. Airdrie Ironworks and Airdrie Mill both located in Muhlenburg County, Kentucky and Airdrie Stud Farm on the Old Frankfort Pike get their name from the same source.[26] R.A. changed his name legally to Robert Spruel Crawford Aitcheson Alexander and his documents occasionally bear this signature or the initials of this name.[27] R.A., who remained a British citizen until his death, graduated from Trinity College in 1846 with the degree of Bachelor of Arts, but did not return to America until 1849.[28]

"Woodburn" as it appeared when R. A. Alexander owned it. The house was built by his father Robert Alexander shortly after 1790. R.A. was born and died at Woodburn, the farm to which he had devoted his life.

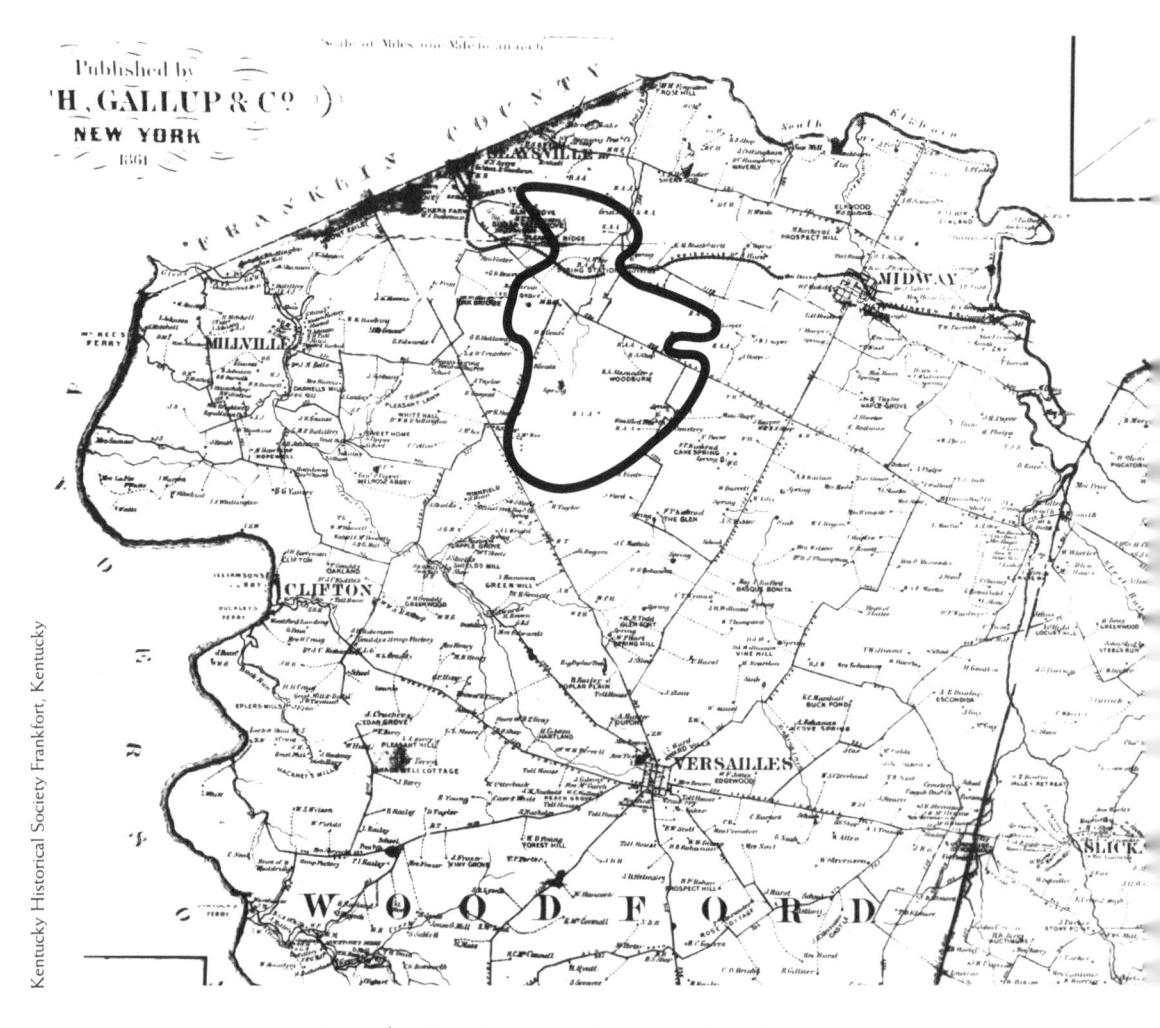

An 1861 map showing the Midway and Versailles area and how large Woodburn was at the time of the Civil War. Woodburn is located in the center of the map and extends North of the railroad track near Seaysville at the Franklin County line.

CHAPTER TWO

Woodburn Farm ◆ The Beginning

Sometime between the years 1851 and 1854 R.A. Alexander bought about 17,000 acres of land in Muhlenburg County which lay along the Green River and established the town of Airdrie. R.A. built the Airdrie Ironworks (also known as the Airdrie Furnace), a mill, a large stone house (destroyed in a fire in 1907), a hotel and several houses for the iron workers whom he had brought to America from Scotland. The venture proved unprofitable and R.A. abandoned the furnace in 1857 or 1858.[1]

In Woodford County Alexander began to buy back much of the land which had been sold by his father, in addition to surrounding acreage. One of his major acquisitions, sometime between 1855 and 1860, was the tract where Woodburn House stood which was still owned by the Bufords. As part of the purchase agreement, Mrs. Buford was allowed to live in Woodburn House until her death sometime in July, 1866.[2] Under the Buford ownership, Woodburn House had been called Free Hill Farm (also published as "Tree Hill Farm"). William Buford married Francis Walker Kirtley who bore him three sons, Abraham, Tom and Henry.

After the death of William Buford, R.A. Alexander made various claims against his estate, including one for the sum of $3,350. According to R.A., the sum represented interest owed on a mortgage, although William Buford had told his sons, Tom and Henry, that the interest in question had been paid in full. Since there was no documentation to validate either party's claim, Tom contested R.A.'s claim and filed a suit, but the case never went to court and the sum was later paid by the estate.[3]

Sometime between 1855 and 1860 R.A. purchased Woodburn House and the land from the Buford family. As part of the purchase agreement, Mrs. Buford was allowed to live in Woodburn House until her death sometime in July, 1866.[4]

R.A. never lived in Woodburn House. He lived in the house built by his father which began as a log cabin (built after 1790 and part of which is believed to have burned in the 1920s) on part of the original land grant across the road from Woodburn House on what is now Lanark Farm, the home of Mr. and Mrs. James E. Bassett, III.[5]

Alexander was described as courteous, kind, polite, gentle and unassuming in manner. On the race track he was described as "affable, a gentleman in winning as well as defeat."[6] *Turf, Field and Farm* described him as the "purest-minded and kindest hearted of men. He was one that could not well be spared because his influence was calculated to promote the best interest of the country."[7]

R.A. was as a small, slender man, with a high forehead, thinning hair, a "hue approaching a light brown," with blue eyes and fair complexion. His face was "a compromise between the humorous and the grave" and "light whiskers gave a fullness to his cheeks." Alexander's plain, neat fitting clothing made him appear "small and more Quaker like" and he wore a black felt hat "pushed back from his brow." His step was light and his movement was easy and graceful and everything about him was "plain to simplicity" but there was "nothing austere in his bearing." He "looked more like a scholar than a horse-breeder or stock-farmer." R.A. was described as an "unostentatious gentleman, honored, respected and beloved by all who made his aquaintance," and "unassuming in manner, treating men of all conditions alike."[8]

Although Alexander frequently suffered from bouts of ill health, he was extremely active and energetic.[9] R.A. was an entrepreneur, innovator, stock-breeder, and above all, a gentleman. He was a man with diverse interests and it was reported that his talents "were of no ordinary character...." He [combined] a sound understanding, a rich, vigorous mind with a logical precision of thought. His information was extensive and varied, and all his thoughts clear and well-cast, but all of these attainments were held subordinate to the one grand passion of his nature—the improvement of the stock and agricultural interests of his native state."[10]

Although more commonly known for his horse breeding, Alexander's breeding accomplishments in the United States also include Shorthorn and Jersey cattle, Cotswold and Southdown sheep, and Berkshire pigs.[11] Alexander studied agricultural science comparable to the studies in England and France which included soil fertility, drainage, tillage, forestry, and the feeding and housing of livestock.[12]

R.A.'s interests were not limited. In a letter to the manufacturer of Ballard's Breech Loading Rifle in 1863, he suggested modifications to convert the military weapon into a hunting rifle. His modifications included reducing the caliber, shortening the barrel, extending the stock and modifying the trigger-locking mechanisms and breech mechanism.[13]

R.A.'s personal notebooks contained plans, comments and ideas. The notebooks

DESIGNS FOR A MANSION HOUSE,

ARRANGED BY THE INSTRUCTION OF

R. A. ALEXANDER ESQR.

OF

AIRDRIE,

&c. &c.

Dr. A. J. Alexander

Designs for a mansion house, arranged by the institution of R. A. Alexander, Esqr. of Airdrie by J. P. Gillespi Graham, Architect, Edinburgh, 1852. It was never built, although a front gate entrance was constructed, which still stands at Airdrie Stud.

Mansion design, "Entrance Front."

Mansion design, "South Elevation."

were filled page after page with 1860s European style chemical formulas for the dyeing of fibers and the preparation of flax for spinning into thread. The first written formulas logged precipitates from simple chemicals that might be locally available. It appeared that Alexander was "exploring a number of materials that he thought might be useful as mordents, which fixes some dyes tightly on the surfaces of various fibers." The second part, titled *Chevalier Claussen's Method of Preparing Flax* was a procedure for "treating flax with a basic solution to separate fibers and alter the surface, somewhat akin to the treatment of cotton fibers with lye, in the mercerization of cotton."[14]

His notebook also contained floor plans for his future mansion, designed and sketched, but unfortunately, never built. Designing future buildings was R.A.'s common practice and his sketches and drawings have been found on his letters as well. On one letter, from the Passaic County Agricultural Society, dated June 9, 1864, he sketched in pencil the building, floor plans and elevations for a new horse barn.[15]

Alexander's many interests forced him to travel frequently. Since he was away from the farm for long periods of time, he delegated the day to day operations to those dependable men who had earned his trust. Alexander, however, personally handled all breeding selections and made executive decisions about finances and other business matters. Turf writer John H. Wallace described Woodburn Farm as:

> "... a mammoth establishment for the breeding of all varieties of domestic animals of the highest type and excellence.... The founding of an establishment so immense, and for the grand purpose of the breeding and improving the varieties of domestic animals, was the agricultural sensation of the period, and everybody, from one end of the land to the other, soon knew of and applauded the great enterprise. There had been great enterprises on similar lines before, and there have been even greater ones since, but Mr. Alexander's Woodburn Farm, of Kentucky, may always be looked upon as the real pioneer in stock breeding on a large and methodical scale, and without limit to resources."[16]

It was cattle that first established Woodburn Farm as a great breeding establishment. R.A. had a strong influence on the Shorthorn cattle business in the United States. His importations were considered by some to be the most notable individual importations to the West. This, combined with his large wealth made him a benefactor to the cattle interest of America.[17]

His prosperity in the United States and England in 1850 increased rapidly and in 1852 and 1853 R.A. and his brother, A.J., returned to England to begin a tour of the herds of that country.[18] R.A. returned to the same area during the summer of 1855.[19] R.A.'s intentions to import cattle into America were documented in his 1854 stock-farm-catalogue:

"Being an admirer of fine stock, I had a two fold object in view when I proposed to myself to import Shorthorn viz, to indulge my own fancy and supply (what at the time seemed much needed) some new crosses for the stock of this country, of which the breeders here might avail themselves either by breeding to the bulls of my importation or by purchasing the produce of my herd."[20]

The *History of Shorthorn Cattle* later supported R.A.'s effort and clarified the issue by reiterating:

"We may read here the noble public spirit which always actuated this noble gentleman, and also the general view, which he had of breeding. He had no thought of introducing new tribes to supplant the old, he only wished to afford a much-needed fresh cross...."[21]

R.A. wrote a *Short Account of Shorthorn Cattle* in his 1856 Catalogue which further elucidated his views, and undeniably clarified his standard of excellence as determined by "intrinsic merit." R.A. preferred the Shorthorn breed because of their superior excellence "whether for the purpose of crossing other stock, or (being bred pure) for the purpose of grazing and feeding."[22]

According to James Sinclair's *History of Shorthorn Cattle*,

"In 1854 he [Alexander] issued a catalogue containing the pedigree of ninety cows.... These animals had been selected with great care and judgment without regard to cost.... For two of them–Duchess of Athol and Second Duke of Athol–he paid Colonel Towneley 500 guineas, which was at the time considered a large price."[23]

In 1854 Mr. Alexander paid $3,500 for the two-year-old roan bull, Sirius, at an auction.[24] In 1855, he shipped another bull, Sebastopol, to Bourbon County, Kentucky, where the bull was owned jointly by Brutus J. Clay, George Bedford, Charles T. Garrard and a man named Duncan.[25]

In 1856 R.A.'s herd numbered 153 cows, which was described as "a more evenly excellent lot of so large a number."[26]

"Mr. Alexander undertook by three methods to make his herd of real value to Kentucky–first, by exhibiting widely; second, by annual sales; third, by letting his bulls. The latter plan unfortunately was never popular. The other means led to great results."[27]

By 1856 R.A. was known to be "the most extensive breeder of fine stock in the United States...." In September Alexander's second annual stock sale was noted:

"...when 20 bulls and 12 heifers were sold–the former for an aggregate of $5,640, and the latter for $3,665–averaging $281.81 each. In addition to the cattle, there were 31 sheep sold, bucks and ewes, pure bred Southdown and Cotswolds, which brought $851—an average of $27.46—one of the bulls brought $805."[28] In 1857, R.A.'s Shorthorn cattle sale was also noted: "There were 28 head of young bulls which brought $9,980. There were 31 head of heifers which brought $6,555. The Duke of Airdrie let to George M. Bedford of Bourbon County., Kentucky for $1,250, Lord John was let for the year to Morris Thomas of Shelby [County] for $515. A lot of Southdown and Cotswold bucks were sold in pens ranging from $21 to $135 each."[29]

On May 25, 1860 the *Frankfort, Kentucky Tri Weekly Commonwealth* carried an advertisement for the 6th annual sale at Woodburn on June 13th of Shorthorn bulls, cows, heifers and Southdown sheep. The advertisement stated:

"It is unnecessary for us to say anything about Mr. Alexander's stock, as his reputation as a successful stock raiser is well known throughout the United States."[30]

By 1860 his herd numbered 200 head. Paul Henlein noted in his book, *Cattle Kingdom in the Ohio Valley, 1783-1860*, that R.A.'s herd (and later his brother's herd) was "cared for as almost no other herd in the United States was at the time, and stood as the great exemplar of the period of 1852-7."[31]

Alexander's life at Woodburn Farm was typical of the plantation life in Kentucky and *Wilkes' Spirit of the Times* observed that business on the vast estate went on with the "regularity of clock-work...."[32] Business transactions were duly recorded in R.A.'s farm journals which listed such activities as the slaughter of farm animals, the subsequent sale of beef and mutton, livestock inventories as well as sales of livestock as far away as Texas, Louisiana, Ohio, Indiana and California. His "cash accounts" reflected a steady purchase of stores and cash output to a number of various accounts including individuals hired to work on the farm. In 1858 R.A.'s "ad valorem," *Woodford County Revenue Tax and County Levy* listed "3,851 acres in 3 counties, 160 horses, many mules or Jennies, 405 head of cattle, one carriage, a gold plated watch, a silver plated clock and 74 total slaves."[33] Although a British subject, R.A. was allowed to own slaves because of Kentucky's Slave Codes. Other slaves labored at Woodburn Farm prior to the Civil War, but were not owned by him. They were obtained legally through the common practice of "slave leases."[34]

An advertisement in a Kentucky newspaper for "twenty-five Negro boys, from thirteen to fifteen years old to work in a woolen factory" reflects the demand of the times for hired slaves to work in industry as well as the land. Gristmills, sawmills, cotton factories, hemp factories, iron foundries and tobacco factories used them extensively, especially the smaller enterprises with limited capital. Therefore, it was quite profitable for those who owned numerous slaves to lease them to those who either could not afford them, or did not wish to own them outright. In 1860 about half of the slave laborers in Virginia tobacco factories were hired.[35]

An 1867 newspaper article reported that free blacks remained at Woodburn Farm after the end of the War:

"...a mulatto woman who nursed him [R.A.] as a child, who has grown old in growing from slavery into freedom, is his housekeeper, and her faith is firm and abiding in "Massa Robert." Black servants buzzed through the hall and about the rooms, polite to a fault and only too eager to win the approval of their master. Unless a guest, not a single white face, except that of our host, meets us in any of the rambling apartments of the Woodburn mansion."[36]

An 1860 newspaper article described Woodburn Farm and the family mansion as: "a simple one story and a half building, but it is long and wide and large enough to accommodate almost any number of visitors. It is built of wood, and is neatly and comfortably furnished, while the library and paintings are rare and valuable. Each of the superintendents and the trainer (six or more in all) has a comfortable residence; the stables, cattle sheds, etc., are of the most comfortable and substantial description, and his milk house surpasses anything of the kind we have ever seen.... Mr. Alexander has stone-masons, brick-makers, carpenters, blacksmiths, etc., constantly working upon his estate.... Last, but not least in our esteem, is the family church, a neat brick building standing nearly in the center of this princely domain, built by Mr. Alexander for his own people, and such of his neighbors as choose to go there."[37]

According to Dan M. Bowmar III's *Giants of the Turf*, the church referred to in the article was the Old Woodford Church, a community church supported by Alexander, but not built by him. The *1860 Census* contains the names of numerous workers at Woodburn and lists them as emigrants from England, Ireland and Scotland.[38] It is possible that when Alexander lost interest in the mining venture at Airdrie Furnace around 1858, some of the skilled workers were brought to the farm.

An 1867 newspaper article described R.A.'s house as "furnished with elegance, though not gaudy," stylish and orderly which reflected his solitary, bachelor lifestyle. On the walls hung oil portraits of his race horses, "chiefly from the easel of [Edward] Troye."[39] Like many of the wealthy landowners prior to the popularity of photography, R.A. commissioned Edward Troye, a noted Swiss artist, to paint portraits of his distinguished stock. In the summer of 1854 Alexander commissioned Troye to paint several

Alderney and Shorthorn bulls which included 2nd Duke of Atholl, Lord John and Grand Master, whom he had imported from Scotland.[40] This endeavor led to Troye's commission to paint Lexington in 1857.[41]

When Alexander commissioned Troye to paint the Woodburn horses, he invited the artist to stay at Woodburn Farm for the time that it took to complete his commission. Alexander's decision was taken in part because it was the custom of the time and in part, because Troye had the reputation of indulging himself from time to time in the spirits that made Kentucky famous. This opportunity allowed Troye convenient access to his subjects and his stay at Woodburn covered a span of three years.[42] Today many of the paintings hang in private collections, and the National Museum of Racing in Saratoga Springs, New York, has a very large collection of these commissioned paintings, including the famous one of Lexington.

Alexander's knowledge of all kinds of stock was clear and accurate, but the thoroughbred horse was his greatest love.[43]

Keeneland Library

The great stallion Lexington at age seven. Owned by R. A. Alexander and painted by Thomas Scott. Lexington was Woodburn's foundation sire.

CHAPTER THREE

The Cornerstones of the Kingdom

Although Alexander was interested in the breeding of all livestock, his love for horses fueled his dream to create the finest stable of racing stock ever known. In 1853 or 1854 R.A. started to collect the largest and best herd of broodmares in America, and by 1856 R.A. began to build his trotting stud.[1] His decision to invest in trotters showed Alexander's independence and courage, since most Kentucky "hardboot" horsemen looked at trotters as a "Yankee sport" and considered them "an anathema."[2] R.A.'s decision to build a trotting stable caused great resentment and outrage among Kentucky breeders, but his wealth (quite possibly the second greatest fortune in Kentucky at that time) and social status allowed him to ignore their narrow opinions and lack of foresight.[3]

Determined to add a trotting stable to his Woodburn Stud, "he set energetically about collecting broodmares and stallions with the ranking of his thoroughbred class."[4] R.A. was able to establish a stud of trotters, which was "among the very first of any magnitude in the States."[5] Alexander's dream was to establish a breeding farm in Kentucky of both racing breeds and to refine both equally.[6] Alexander selected his trotting broodmares by the same criteria used in selecting his thoroughbred mares. He purchased only those mares who were "proven producers, proven performers or sisters or half-sisters to proven producers and performers." It was the first attempt of any breeder to do so.[7]

One of his first selections was Madam Temple, the dam of Flora Temple, "The Bob-Tailed Mare" (made famous by the Stephen Foster song, *Camptown Races*.)[8] Other mares included Madam Dudley; Black Rose, who later proved to be one of Woodburn's best broodmares; Grey Goose; Bay York; Juliet and Missouri.[9] R.A. organized his trotting stud with the purchase of Pilot Jr., Edwin Forrest and Norman.[10] His farm was "the first establishment devoted to systematic, thoroughly planned, and carefully conducted race horse production of both thoroughbreds and harness types in America."[11]

LEXINGTON

In June 1856 R.A. Alexander went to England, accompanied by Nelson Dudley of Fayette County, to buy and import the finest stallions money could obtain to start his thoroughbred stud. Ironically, R.A. would find his foundation sire, Lexington, at his neighbor's farm. While in England Dudley insisted that Alexander purchase Lexington from Richard Ten Broeck. Lexington, according to Dudley:

> "was the best racehorse in the world, and if he did not purchase him, situated as he was, he would be a thorn [literally] in his side...whatever else he bought he must not leave England until he purchased Lexington."

Richard Ten Broeck happened to be in England at the same time as R.A. and in deference to Dudley's advice and judgment, Alexander sought him out.[12]

According to Kent Hollingsworth's book, *The Great Ones*, Ten Broeck had initially acquired Lexington by forming a syndicate which included Kentucky horsemen "Abe" Buford; the uncle of General Abe Buford of "Bosque Bonita Farm"; Junius R. Ward and Captain Willa Viley, who had nominal charge of Lexington on behalf of the syndicate. Lexington had raced all that season for the syndicate and they decided to allow him a rest. Ten Broeck wanted Lexington to race against Lecomte since a large sum of money had been offered for the race, and, to satisfy his desires, Ten Broeck bought out the others' interest for a reported $5,000.[13]

Shortly after his defeat by Lecomte at New Orleans on April 14, 1855, Lexington's eyes failed. Ten Broeck was forced to retire the stallion from racing and turned the stallion over to the care of William Frank Harper at "Shadowlawn Farm." R.A. purchased Lexington in 1857 for $15,000, the highest price ever given for an American horse of any breed up to that time. This single purchase would later be recognized as the sale that would make Woodburn Farm, "the most famous and successful stud in America."[14] The original contract read:

> "R. Ten Broeck has sold to R.A. Alexander his horse, Lexington, at the price of fifteen thousand dollars, one half payable by ck [check], on London [bank], on his return to Ky., if the horse is well, except his eyes, & the other in same manner by ck, on London [bank] on the 1st of Apr. 1857,-should Lexington be alive as this date–R. Ten Broeck the privilege of bringing three mares each yr. free of charge-[signed] R. Ten Broeck."[15]

R.A. paid Ten Broeck the requested $7,500 in cash while in England and the remainder when he returned to America. Although Ten Broeck had stipulated in the contract that he retained the right to bring three mares each year to Woodburn to be bred to Lexington "free of charge," Ten Broeck later dropped this stipulation to settle a substantial debt due Alexander for boarding, breeding, and other miscellaneous debts. Alexander cancelled Ten Broeck's debt on April 10, 1858.[16]

Although this was the first transaction between the two horse breeders, it would not be the last. In August 1860 *Wilkes' Spirit of the Times* reported that Alexander sent the bay filly, Annette, by imported Scythian, out of Alice Carneal, Lexington's dam, and the bay colt by Lexington, out of Ducatoon, by Wagner, out of Picayune, to Ten Broeck's racing stable in England.[17] Although Lexington was blind, Alexander exhibited him at the St. Louis Fair in 1859.[18] Except for a temporary stay at Williamsville, Illinois in 1865, Lexington remained at stud at Woodburn Farm from the 1857 season to the day of his death on July 1, 1875, at age 25.[19]

"Lexington made twenty-one seasons in the stud, for he remained virile to the last and had covered about a dozen mares the spring before he died, over 50 percent of which he got with foal."[20]

The Lexington blood line would become famous:

"...[Lexington's] blood has combined and mingled most harmoniously with all the different racing strains; and either directly from him, his sons, daughters and grand-daughters have descended the best horses that have ever adorned the American turf. A cross of his blood upon native or imported strains has been the great keystone of success. As a race horse, he stands pre-eminently the best this country has ever produced, and as a stallion he takes rank as the foremost in the world. He was far superior to all the horses that have gone before him, as the brilliancy of the sun is superior to the glimmer of the most distant star."[21]

Imported Leamington was bred to a few Lexington mares. The result his first season was an immediate success. He got Longfellow, Enquirer and Lynchburg. Leamington was himself from a great family, his sire being Faugh-a-Ballagh, brother to Irish Birdcatcher, who was by Whalebon, a son of Waxy. Leamington's dam was a daughter of Pantaloon and Daphne. He transmitted the characteristics of this celebrated cross to all his progeny. Leamington was brought from England in 1865 and died at Chestnut Hills in New York on May 6, 1878.

SCYTHIAN

One of the most famous of Alexander's thoroughbreds was the English import, Scythian, winner of the Newmarket Stakes, the Dee Stakes, the Goodwood Stakes, the Chester Cup and a half-dozen other races. He was hailed by the *London Times* as "one of the best stallions ever produced in Great Britain."[22]

Alexander purchased Scythian at the same time he purchased Lexington from Ten Broeck and brought Scythian to America in 1856. Although Scythian had been an outstanding racehorse, he was initially unsuccessful at stud. R.A. took to driving him in his personal gig, but

War refugee, Australian, stood second only to Lexington as a sire and with Lexington carried the reputation and fame of Woodburn Farm in the production of thoroughbred race horses.

The great son of Lexington, Asteroid, who was taken in the October 22, 1864, raid along with five other horses by Confederate guerrillas led by Sue Mundy. Asteroid was considered by R. A. Alexander as the best horse he ever owned.

reinstated him into the stud when his get, Lizzie W. and Sympathy, proved themselves at Saratoga and Paterson, New Jersey.[23] By 1867 Scythian was dead.[24]

AUSTRALIAN

The thoroughbred stallion Australian, initially called Millington, was bred by W.E. Duncomb and foaled in 1858 in England. Alexander Keene Richards imported Australian along with his dam Emelia to Georgetown, Kentucky, that same year. During the winter of 1861, R.A. purchased Australian along with other stock from Richards for the sum of $5,000.

Australian stood his first season at stud at Woodburn in 1863 and because he produced "speed horses," he was considered "second to the renowned Lexington as sire and between these two the reputation of Woodburn [was] carried to the top of the tree in the production of racehorses."[25] The Leamington cross is also through Australian, most notably with Iroquois, a full brother to Harold, being out of Maggie B.B. by Australian, out of Madeline by Boston, second dam Magnolia by Glencoe. She won the Sequel Stakes at Saratoga in 1870, and was a very fast mare. Iroquois was foaled in 1878 and died at Belle Meade Stud in September 1899.

ASTEROID

Asteroid, a son of Lexington, considered by Alexander the best horse he ever owned, was the best three-year-old of his year and far superior to his stablemate Norfolk. Asteroid did not race as a two-year-old, but ran five races as a three-year-old and seven as a four-year-old. He won them all. Asteroid was scheduled to race Kentucky in 1866, but went lame prior to the race. He broke down at five years old and was retired, unbeaten. Asteroid won only a total of $12,880, small stakes purses compared to today's standards. One should remember, however, that his racing career took place during the war when purses were quite small.[26]

As a stallion Asteroid was not considered a success, due to an undescended testicle (cryptorchid or ridgling), which caused him to be an uncertain sire. After only a few years at stud, Asteroid became impotent and remained so until his death in 1886. Despite this, however, Alexander kept him at Woodburn and saw to it that he was well cared for because of his "mighty deeds" on the race track. R.A. was frequently offered large amounts of money for Asteroid. Once he was offered "$30,000 for the great horse," but R.A. declined all offers.[27]

NORFOLK

Norfolk, a son of Lexington, bred and foaled at Woodburn in 1861, was sold after his win in the first Jersey Derby in June, 1864 for $15,001, a dollar more than Alexander had paid for

Norfolk: sold for $15,001 to Theodore H. Winters, owner of Rancho del Rio. He was taken to California where he became a top sire.

Lexington. On August 2, 1864, Norfolk beat Kentucky (the winner of the first Travers Stakes and the Saratoga Cup Stakes) in the only race that Kentucky ever lost.[28]

"Mr. Alexander raced horses of his own breeding with marked success. He brought out Maiden, the dam of Parole, the first mare to win the Travers Stakes; Asteroid, who was never beaten in a race during his turf career; Norfolk, one of the best horses ever on the American turf and the winner of the fastest race ever run at three-mile-heats, 5:27 1/4, 5:29 1/2, and one of our most successful and popular sires."[29]

Norfolk was sold to Mr. Theodore H. Winters, nicknamed "Black T" because of his large mustache which resembled a cross tie on a telegraph pole, who owned Rancho del Rio in Yolo County.[30] Winters sent Norfolk to California early during his three-year-old season, and therefore, Norfolk never had the opportunity to race against his stable mate Asteroid.[31]

A letter, dated June 9, 1864, from Mr. E. Boudinot for the Passaic County Agricultural Society at the race track at Paterson, New Jersey, stated that the new owners of Norfolk had gotten into trouble with the Committee and the colt "ruled off and not in the Derby which he was in great style [for]. The letter also exonerated "Ansel [Alexander's trainer] and his boys" of any guilt and stated that they were "much praised by all of our Committee."[32] Norfolk was:

"banned from major racing in the East and California tracks were written to specifically to exclude him. The greatest son of Lexington was literally forced into retirement. Like so many of Lexington's sons, Norfolk possessed the double gift of speed and stamina and he, like no other, passed these attributes on to his offspring.... After a long, productive life Norfolk died at age 29 on November 25, 1890, and [is] buried beneath a giant oak tree at Winters' El Arroyo Ranch in Sacramento where he spent the last quarter century of his life. Norfolk stands as California's unbeaten 19th Century racehorse." Noted turf writer T.B. Merry described him as "the only race horse I ever saw, except his sire, Lexington." [33]

NORWICH

Norwich was a son of Lexington and a full brother to Norfolk. His racing career was brief, only the year 1866, but his three starts, two at Paterson, N.J., and the other at Saratoga, produced one win, one third and one sixth place.[34] He was a gelding.

PILOT JR.

In 1858 R.A. purchased the 14-year-old trotting stallion Pilot Jr., who today is regarded as having founded his own family because his influence through his daughters was so immediate and far-reaching.

"They [the daughters] are among the glories of the *Trotting Register*, and two of them especially rank among the most eminent matrons of all time—Midnight and Miss Russell."[35]

Pilot Jr., although not taken in the second raid, is considered a "victim of the raid." He died shortly after being removed from Kentucky to Illinois. His blood has had a great influence in helping to form the American trotter.

Pilot Jr. was the first Kentucky-bred trotting sire to gain a national reputation. In his day he was the King of all Bluegrass trotting stallions. He had eight offspring in the 2:30 list, all in or before 1860. Two stallions, Pilot Temple (2:24 1/2) and Tattler (2:26), who would stand at Woodburn in 1868, placed "him at the head of all Bluegrass progenitors for the time."[36] Tattler died on August 14, 1878, at Trenton, New Jersey. He is the sire of Indianapolis (2:21), Voltain (2:21 1/4) and Gossip.

Allegedly, in his prime Pilot Jr. could trot a mile in about 2:35. He never raced, however, although there was some talk about matching him against Mambrino Chief when Mambrino Chief first arrived in Kentucky. There was a considerable rivalry between the two because they were the leading trotting stallions in Kentucky before Alexander's Abdallah arrived.[37] According to the *1864 Woodburn Stud Farm Catalogue*, Pilot Jr.'s stud fee was $30.[38]

For a brief time in 1860 R.A. loaned both Pilot Jr. and Scythian to Colonel George Elliott's farm, "Wall Springs," just outside of Gallatin, Tennessee. Elliott was an intimate friend of General Andrew Jackson whom he had served under "at New Orleans and the Creek war." In 1810 Elliott started his stud with the purchase of the great thoroughbred stallion Topgallant, whom he sold six years later. He also owned Pacolet by Citizen, Tippo Saib, Brimmer, import-

Edwin Forrest, once believed to have been taken in the Woodburn Raid by Frank James, was one of Woodburn's foundation trotting sires.

ed Silver Eye, imported Valiant, imported Jolly Roger (whom he owned from 1820 until his death in 1825), Napoleon by Sir Archy, Leviathan (who was syndicated), St. Giles, Lapdog, Sovereign, and Albion.[39]

EDWIN FORREST 49

Edwin Forrest 49, also known as Alexander's Edwin Forrest, was a bay trotting stallion, with black points, foaled in 1850, by Bay Kentucky Hunter, dam Doll by Young Highlander. He was a trotter with the best time credited with miles 2:35 to 2:40. It was said of Edwin Forrest that "he could trot like hell and run like a son-of-a-bitch."[40] Edwin Forrest got only two performers in the 2:30 list.

Alexander purchased Edwin Forrest in 1856 largely because he was from the same male line as Flora Temple.[41] One fifth of the standard performers by Mambrino Patchen "carried the blood of Edwin Forrest" despite the fact that Mambrino Patchen was claimed to be by the saddle horse Gaines' Denmark, and not the trotting sire Mambrino Chief.[42] General John Breckinridge Castleman, the first President of the American Saddle Horse Association,

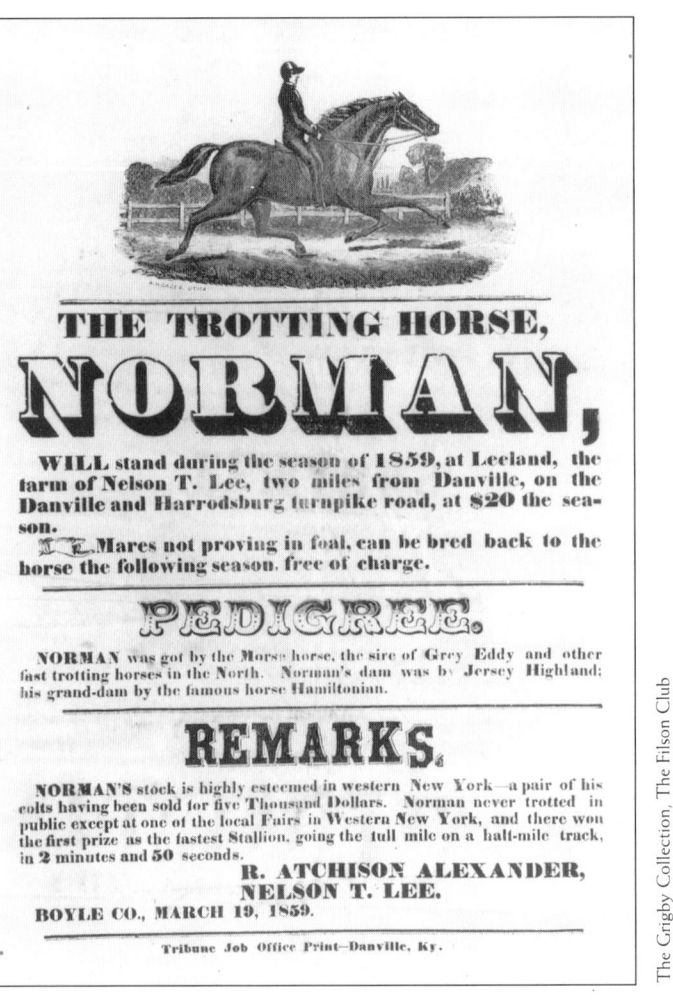

> **THE TROTTING HORSE, NORMAN,**
>
> WILL stand during the season of 1859, at Leeland, the farm of Nelson T. Lee, two miles from Danville, on the Danville and Harrodsburg turnpike road, at $20 the season.
>
> Mares not proving in foal, can be bred back to the horse the following season, free of charge.
>
> **PEDIGREE.**
>
> NORMAN was got by the Morse horse, the sire of Grey Eddy and other fast trotting horses in the North. Norman's dam was by Jersey Highland; his grand-dam by the famous horse Hamiltonian.
>
> **REMARKS.**
>
> NORMAN'S stock is highly esteemed in western New York—a pair of his colts having been sold for five Thousand Dollars. Norman never trotted in public except at one of the local Fairs in Western New York, and there won the first prize as the fastest Stallion, going the full mile on a half-mile track, in 2 minutes and 50 seconds.
>
> R. ATCHISON ALEXANDER,
> NELSON T. LEE.
>
> BOYLE CO., MARCH 19, 1859.
>
> Tribune Job Office Print—Danville, Ky.

This is from an original 12" x 16 1/2" broadside advertisement for the stallion Norman. This would have been placed on the street corners on kiosks or public bulletin boards around the cities.

The Grigby Collection, The Filson Club

insisted this claim was true. Castleman based his argument on the erroneous claim that Mambrino Chief "never sired any black colt and no horse or mare credited to him in the stud books credited [him] with having produced any black or chestnut except Mambrino Patchen 58."[43] Castleman even had this claim inserted in the *Saddle Horse Register* in 1903. Darkness, however, known as Big Black, was by Mambrino Chief out of Black Rose. Other writers besides turf writer John Hervey believe that Mambrino Patchen was by Mambrino Chief and not by Gaines' Denmark. It appears that this subject is still open for debate.[44] (See Chapter Eight for the Edwin Forrest controversy.)

Alexander's Abdallah, died of pneumonia as a result of being forced to swim an icy river in February by his guerrilla rider. He was left in Mr. Bush's barn in Lawrenceburg, Kentucky, and died on February 6, 1865.

ALEXANDER'S NORMAN

"Norman was a brown horse, foaled about 1846, got by the Morse Horse, son of European; dam one of a pair of brown mares purchased by John N. Slocum of Samuel Slocum, a Quaker of Leroy, Jefferson County, New York, and represented to be by Magnum Bonum. These mares passed to Mr. Russell, and from him to Titcomb & Waldron, who bred the better of the two to the Morse Horse, and the produce was Alexander's Norman. This colt passed through several hands till he reached Henry L. Barker, of Clinton, New York, and about 1860, Barker sold him to R.A. Alexander, of Woodburn Farm, Kentucky. He died in 1878.... He was not retained long at Woodburn Farm. He does not seem to have been a uniform transmitter of speed, but when it did appear it was apt to be of a high order. He left but two representatives in the 2:30 list Lula, (2:15), with 56 heats, and May Queen, (2:20), with twenty-five heats. He left four sons that became the sires of fifty-eight performers and thirteen daughters that produced nineteen performers. Such sons as Swigert and Blackwood speak well for his transmitting powers."[45]

Daughters of Alexander's Norman were:

> "...more successful as speed perpetuators than his sons. May Queen (2:20) mated with Electioneer, produced May King (2:20), sire of the popular stallion Bingen (2:06 1/4). Lula (2:15) mated with George Wilkes (2:22) produced a daughter that mated with Electioneer, produced Advertiser (2:15 1/4), a fast trotter and quite a successful sire of speed. One of his get was Adbell who held the World's Champion record for yearling trotters (2:23). This family has become absorbed by and assimilated with the Hambletonian family, but it is a valuable factor in a trotting pedigree...bred on through May King (2:20) and Advertiser (2:15 1/4)."[46]

ABDALLAH 15; ALEXANDER'S ABDALLAH

Abdallah 15 was a bay colt, bred by Lewis J. Sutton of Warwick and foaled in 1852 in Goshen, New York. He was by Hambletonian 10, dam, Katie Darling by Bay Roman (2:42 record). Abdallah was the sire of Goldsmith Maid who "lowered the World's Record seven times, (2:14 record)."[47] He was the first son of Hambletonian 10 to go to Kentucky, but died before a single one of his sons or daughters appeared on a racetrack.[48] Abdallah showed evidence from the start of being a natural born trotter.[49] Not only did he show good trotting action, he exhibited speed. Joseph Love and James "Uncle Jimmy" Miller of Cynthiana, Kentucky, in Harrison County purchased Abdallah from Sutton and Miller literally drove him from New York to Kentucky in March 1859. In August 1862, Alexander purchased Abdallah for $2,000 in cash and the trade of the stallion Forest Temple 136, a son of Edwin Forrest and Madam Temple. Abdallah made the 1863 and 1864 seasons at Woodburn with a stud fee of $30.[50]

BAY CHIEF

Bay Chief was a bay trotting colt, foaled in 1859 by Mambrino Chief 11 (trotter), out of Keoku, by Keokuk, son of imported Truffle; "second dam claimed to be a thoroughbred daughter of the Arabian stallion Stamboul."[51] *The Trotting Register* states that Bay Chief had once trotted a half mile in 1:08, an outstanding record for that era. According to renowned trainer Hirum Woodruff's *The American Trotting Horse* published in 1868:

> "when it is considered that their [Kentucky] trotting-stallions have been very often well bred, and then put to thoroughbred mares it must go far to account for the extraordinary feats performed there by colts that were only four years old. I see no absolute reason to deny the statement made, that Mr. Alexander's colt, Bay Chief, by Mambrino Chief, out of a thoroughbred mare, trotted half a mile, at four years old, in one minute and eight seconds, and repeated in 1:08 1/2."[52]

R.A. published the first known American stock farm catalogue in 1857. It was devoted exclusively to thoroughbreds.[53] The catalogue was designed to list Woodburn's stallions,

The great stallion, Lexington, painted by Edward Troye.

broodmares and yearlings which were for sale, but it also served as a complete record of the horses at the farm. Subsequent thoroughbred catalogues followed in 1859 and 1860, a publishing tradition that continued at Woodburn Farm until the end of the 19th Century.[54]

The May 1879 issue of *Wallace's Monthly* claims the earliest catalogue for trotters was January 1861.[55] One authority stated that the August 22, 1860, catalogue listed twelve trotting mares: nine bred to Edwin Forrest and another to Norman. It also listed three trotting colts and fourteen fillies: one foaled in 1856 by Mambrino Chief, three foaled in 1857 by Edwin Forrest, four foaled in 1858 by Edwin Forrest, three foaled by Eureka, Star Davis, and Garrett's Horse, and five foaled in 1859 by Pilot Jr.[56]

The trotting stallions listed in his 1864 catalogue include Abdallah, Edwin Forrest, Norman and Pilot Jr. Also listed were 72 broodmares, 29 of which were fillies reserved for breeding purposes, leaving only 43 actual matrons. In addition, the catalogue listed 40 head of colts and fillies. According to this list, Alexander owned a total of 116 head of trotting stock, more than had ever been assembled under one ownership up to that time.[57] One writer profoundly described Alexander's system of selection:

33

"He was not looking for a pedigree in the son of a Cannuck pacer [Old Pilot] any more than he was looking for good eyes when he bought the blind Lexington. He wanted the horse that could do it, pedigree or no pedigree, eyes or no eyes."[58]

It is evident that Alexander searched for specific traits in the breeding stock and expected those traits to manifest themselves through the horses he bought and placed into the Woodburn Stud. In his catalogues under the section, "Terms of Breeding," R.A. inserted the formal request that all patrons sending mares to his stallions also "send their Pedigrees, that they may be recorded."[59] This was the first time a stallion owner had ever made such a provision, although today this is standard procedure.[60]

Alexander was an innovator who experimented to develop and improve various breeds. Through selective crossbreeding, he improved the American standardbred race horse. His practice of breeding thoroughbreds with broodmares which produced notable trotters, as well as Morgan horses and other horses which showed trotting traits, resulted in increased speed. His hope was that these traits would be transmitted and manifest themselves to the next generation and they did. Producing speed was the main factor in this breeding theory and the result was an athlete built to trot and pace fast, and the transmission of these traits from offspring to offspring produced champion after champion. Alexander advanced the introduction of the standardbred into Kentucky and helped to secure its place in racing and breeding. He was also the founder of *The American Trotting Horse*, although unfortunately no surviving issues can be located at the Harness Racing Museum and Hall of Fame in Goshen, New York.[61] In 1859, the Lexington Trotting Club was organized and Alexander was elected as its first President.[62] Woodburn truly earned its title, "Mother Farm of the Standardbred," and Alexander lived long enough to see Kentucky horsemen place the Standardbred in an honored position.[63]

"Mr. Alexander was a pioneer and a foundation-layer. Woodburn was the first great American stud farm which was organized upon thoroughly intelligent and systematic principles.... Alexander was the pioneer worker upon a wholly different plan. He set out to bring together animals deliberately chosen because they represented the most successful lines and crosses, to mate them carefully and methodically, giving great care to everything connected therewith, and he was the first American breeder to adopt the English system of holding annual sales of his yearlings at which all offerings were sold without reserve or by-bidding of any kind, for just what they would bring."[64]

What guided Alexander? We may never know, but what we do know is that Woodburn Farm gave to the American racing industry its roots. From the stud "Woodburn [produced] some of the most famous race horses...either bred or [were] the produce of matrons bred in it."[65] "The establishment of Woodburn Farm by R.A. Alexander...with a trotting department on

The Great Diomed "Father of the American Turf" had a profound influence on American Thoroughbred, Standardbred and Saddlebred bloodlines, and Woodburn Farm stock.

a grand scale, proved the decisive factor insofar as the trotters' future in Kentucky was concerned...."[66]

INFLUENCE OF THE GREAT DIOMED

Trotting and saddlebred-type horses were being bred and shown in Missouri, Kentucky, Tennessee, and New York long before the Civil War, but not on the magnitude of Woodburn Farm. These animals carried much thoroughbred blood with outcrosses to Morgans and harness-type horses, for all three breeds are closely related. These crosses are in such basic saddlebred and trotting families as the Cockspurs, Copperbottoms, and Canadian Hals. The blood of Gibson's Tom Hal and Copperbottom (both being natural pacers) was influential in the establishment of the pacing strains in the standardbred breed. In the 1800's they were the most famous of those horses known as the Canadian Pacers. Ethan Allen 50, foaled in 1849 by Vermont Black Hawk, was probably the most prolific of the Morgan stallions and famous in his day. He died at age 27 at Lawrence, Kansas, on September 10, 1876.

One such sire of thoroughbreds, saddlebreds, and influence in harness type horses, whose blood was supreme, was the great Diomed, (by Florizel, a daughter of Spectator,–grandson of

King Herod and a great grandson of the Godolphin Barb. Through Herod, Diomed is traced directly to Byerly Turk). Brought to America in 1798 he did more to improve the speed of American horses than all other stallions to have been imported up to his day.[67] He is "found in all the pedigrees of all the record breakers in this country, (who's blood lines are known) whether runners, trotters or pacers."[68]

Only a few years after Diomed reached America some of his get had proved to be the very best horses that this country had produced, and his descendants, both male and female, transmitted race qualities with greater uniformity and of higher order than had the descendants of any other horse ever brought from England to America. He and his descendants accomplished more in the way of improving the speed, gameness and endurance of the racing stock of America than all the imported thoroughbred horses that preceded him.[69]

"His unequaled merit and remarkable power to transmit the qualities upon which speed depends made Diomed [the epitome] of any stallion in England in his day, and the most successful sire of race horses ever brought to America."[70]

Diomed is the sire of the great horses Gray Diomed, Young Giantess, Sir Archy and Top Gallant.[71] Living until he was 31 years of age, Diomed made a:

"...deep and lasting impression on the turf, founding the first great racing family in America through his son, Sir Archy (1805), who so overshadowed his contemporaries as a racehorse that he was forced to retire for lack of opposition [as was Norfolk]. Sir Archy was the start of the Timoleon (1814)–Boston (1833)–Lexington (1850)–Norfolk (1861)–Emperor of Norfolk (1885)–Americus (1892) sire line."[72]

"The noted trotters that have been mostly strongly impregnated with the Diomed strain have been the descendants of Miss Russell, Midnight, [dam of Jay-Eye-See, 2:10] Mambrino Patchen 58, and Seely's American Star 14."[73] "The finest in quality of the sons of Hambletonian were those out of the American Star mares, such as Dictator [2:29 3/4], Jay Gould [2:21 1/2], etc., but they were as a rule on the small side as was also Abdallah 15."[74]

Jay Gould died at 35 years old and had sired 26 trotters with records below 2:30. American Star died in February 1861 near Goshen, New York. Miss Russell was more strongly inbred to the Diomed strain than any other trotting mare of her day. She inherited one strain through the dam of her sire Pilot Jr. and her dam, Sally Russell, was more intensely inbred to imported Diomed than any other animal whose name appears in the *American Stud Book*.[75] Eventide, the dam of Maud S. (bred and foaled at Woodburn), and Lord Russell (only full brother to Maud S.) were strongly inbred to the best of Diomed strains:[76]

"The Messenger influence through Hambletonian 10 gave the trotting conformation and the inclination to adopt and stick to that gait, while the inheritance from Diomed gave great speed ability and other racing qualities.... There are a few thoroughbred strains that seem to blend harmoniously with the trotting strains, and the result is an improvement in speed and racing qualities over animals that are bred wholly in trotting lines. The Diomed strain has proved the best of these, but the Trustee, the Margrave, the Australian, the Consternation, the Knight of St. George [owned by A. Keene Richards], the Expedition, through Williamson's Belmont and a few other strains have been a great value in increasing the speed ability of the descendants of Hambletonian 10 and Mambrino Chief 11."[77]

Diomed was imported into Virginia in 1799, by Col. John Hoomes, when the horse was 22 years old. He lived until 1808, but it is believed that he got no foals after the 1805 season. What this stallion did in those few years in the way of improving the racing stock of America, is unsurpassed:

"By 1843, the best records of mile heats for thoroughbreds, up to that time, had been won by direct descendants in the paternal line of imported Diomed. Twenty-one of 31 records in two mile heats were held by animals that trace directly to imported Diomed. Out of 24 records in three mile heats, 16 of the winners are direct descendants in the male line of Diomed, and of the 17 records in the four mile heats 10 of them trace directly to Diomed through their sires. Out of the 90 best records, the winners of 61 of them trace directly through their sires to Diomed, and the dams of 13 of the others were descendants of his, most of which were inbred to him."[78]

Diomed is the winner of the first Derby Stakes at Epsom, England (1780), and became the "Father of the American Turf." As a sire of Saddle horses Diomed was supreme. "The two most conspicuous Virginia horsemen of his day, Thomas Jefferson and John Marshall, habitually rode Diomeds and the same was true of Andrew Jackson on the Tennessee frontier."[79]

One Morgan pedigree in which Diomed appears is that of Daniel Lambert by Ethan Allen 50 out of Fanny Cook who was by Abdallah 15, out of a chestnut mare, name unknown, by Stockholm's American Star by Duroc by Diomed.[80] Sir Archy and Potomac were perhaps the two most famous sons of Diomed.[81] One surprising bloodline is Atalanta's dam, Flirt. Her sire is Iowa by the thoroughbred imp. Glencoe, and her (Flirt's) dam, was by Veto, a son of Sir Archy. Atalanta produced the great 1894 Worlds' champion trotter, that "sweet little mare," Alix (2:03 3/4). Other proof of the Diomed blood influencing the Woodburn stock, is the stallion, Ringgold, son of Boston. Alexander purchased this horse, who was in advanced age, in 1861. Ringgold was inbred to Diomed through his son, Sir Archy and Ball's Florizel. Ringgold's dam, Flirtilla, by Sir Archy, was out of old Flirtilla, by Sir Archy. Although Ringgold did not live long, he did get at Woodburn Onward, out of My Lady and Deleware, out of Ariel, by Sarpedon.[82]

General Abraham "Abe" Buford was born in Woodburn Mansion on January 18, 1820. Buford owned Bosque Bonita, which today is part of Lane's End Farm.

CHAPTER FOUR

Fellow Horsemen And Friends

Abraham "Abe" Buford was born in Woodburn House on January 18, 1820. He graduated from the U.S. Military Academy at West Point in 1841. He later served with General Zachary Taylor in the Mexican War and was decorated for gallant and meritorious services in the battle of Buena Vista and promoted to Captain.[1] In February 1854, Captain Buford purchased 420 acres for the sum of $21,396 and named his farm "Bosque Bonita" or "Pretty Woods." Today, this land is part of William Farish's Lane's End Farm located on the Midway-Versailles Road.

Captain Buford resigned his U.S. Army commission on October 22, 1854, and retired to his beloved estate. There he built the original house (which was destroyed by fire in the 1890's) and began to raise thoroughbreds and Shorthorn cattle.[2] One of Buford's first purchases was the stallion, imported Sovereign, which would become his foundation sire. Bosque Bonita Farm would later produce such famous names as Crossland, Nellie Gray, Selena, Enquirer, Hollywood, Marion, Versailles, Goodnight, McWhirter, McHenry, Lizzie Whipps, Lynchburg, Revenue, Ontario, Sudie McNair, and Lizzie G. by War Dance and Faustus. Understandably, Buford later became one of the state's prominent turfmen during post-war racing. For a brief time in 1866, Leamington stood at Bosque Bonita. From this sole season came Enquirer, Longfellow, Littleton, Lynchburg, Anna Mace and Miss Alice.[3] General Buford served in the American Turf Congress and in May 1866 was appointed by the Chair as a delegate to Saratoga along with R.A. Alexander and Alexander Keene Richards.[4]

Buford became President of the Richmond & Danville Railroad and represented Woodford County in the State Legislature from 1877-1878. Many hardships (the death of his only son, William A., in 1872 and of his wife, Amanda Harris, in 1879, the murder of Judge Elliott in Frankfort by his brother, Tom, plus financial failures and debts ultimately ending in the loss of his estate in 1880) led him to suicide at Danville, Indiana, on June 9, 1884.[5]

Woodburn House, built by the Buford family, is today known as "Woodburn Mansion." Picture was possibly taken before or during the Civil War.

The Nantura Farm, also nearby, was owned by the Harpers: Adam, John, Jake and sister, Betsy. The Harpers' ancestors were originally Dutch, although they had lived in Germany prior to coming to the United States. The Harpers first settled in Virginia but later moved to Kentucky where their father, Jacob Harper, purchased 700 acres from the heirs of General Hugh Mercer between 1795–1797. Jacob Harper later expanded the farm to about 1,500 acres and began to breed race horses.[6]

Nantura Farm's horses, such as Longfellow, Ten Broeck, Jills Johnston, Germantown, Early Light, Bowen, Easter and others helped to establish Nantura's well known reputation.[7] It was recorded in 1885 that Nantura Stock Farm consisted of 576 acres which lay on both sides of the Old Frankfort Pike and was adjoined and separated by Woodburn Farm. William Harper, first cousin to Adam and John Harper, eventually lost his farm and died in bankruptcy.[8] John Harper died in 1874.[9] Frank B. Harper, John's nephew, later inherited the farm after the Civil War where he lived until April 4, 1905.

Major Warren Viley (the title "Major" may have been honorary or earned in the state militia), "regarded as one of the county's most dependable and upright citizens," was the owner of Stonewall Farm located near Woodburn Farm. Warren had been born in Scott County in 1817 and was a descendant of prominent Huguenot ancestry. He and his father, Willa, were not only neighbors but were considered Alexander's best friends.[10]

Willa Viley was among the founders of the Kentucky-Association Race Course at Lexington in 1826 (also published as 1823).[11] Willa owned Richard "Dick" Singleton, Alex Churchill, Dick Johnson, a full brother to Dick Singleton, Black Eyed Susan, dam of Dick Singleton[12] by Tiger. Tiger was bred by George Burbridge but owned by Willa. Viley also owned the dam of Plato, Mistletoe, and Catharine,[13] McDuffy, Maria by Hamiltonian, Railway, Alexander, Buck Elk, Murat, Belle Anderson, dam of Zenith, Scarlet, Adam Huntsman, Jim Allen by Sir Archy of Montorio, Gobbler, Catherine Ogle, Theobalion, Lady Moffit, Queen Mary, Ralf, Mary Brennan, West Florida, Mary Portor, Mercer, Emily Johnson, Dick Menifee, Sally Hardin, Oglenah and Gildersleeve.[14] Willa was also a member of the syndicate that owned Lexington prior to his purchase by R.A. Alexander.

Warren was also recognized as one of the early breeders of thoroughbreds and had raised Capitola by Vandal, (who stood at Belle Meade) the dam of Uncle Vic, and King Alfonso, who was later sold to the Woodburn Stud. Other horses bred at Stonewall Farm included Hospodar, Miss Naylor, Miss Gallop, Bab, W. Overton, Tenpenny, Silurian and Commissioner Foster. The farm stallions were imported Meltonian, Belvidere and Linden.[15] It was Warren Viley who gave the famous mare Black Bess to General John Hunt Morgan.[16]

John Harper who owned Nantura Farm, pictured with his great racehorse, Longfellow; Bobbie Swim, up. Harper's brother, Adam, was killed by Sue Mundy's guerrillas, November 1, 1864. Longfellow, a son of Leamington, was foaled in 1867 and died at Nantura on November 6, 1893, at age 26.

Alexander and Alexander Keene Richards "had much in common [and were] intimate friends ever ready to assist each other and although both were dedicated to improving the breed of the thoroughbred, their approach was that of the scholar, rather than that of sportsman." Richards owned the beautiful, blood bay stallion, The Knight of St. George by Irish Birdcatcher out of Maltese. The Knight:

> "served at Rawcliffe Stud Company of England until the 1st of May 1859 and on the 4th of the same month was shipped from Liverpool to Montreal, where he arrived in fine condition on the 17th of May, and was thence transported to Kentucky."[17]

Richards built up a stable of fine pure bred Arabian horses and traveled to Arabia to purchase the horses from the Anayzas, the Tarabine tribe of Bedouins and other tribes. His first trip was made in 1851 to 1853. Richards' second trip was in 1855-1856, during the Crimean War. He was accompanied by his friend, Edward Troye.[18]

Richards, who was born in Scott County, Kentucky, on October 14, 1827, was an active Southern sympathizer, an ardent Secessionist and participant during the Civil War and, therefore, was particularly vulnerable. In the early days of the War, Richards evacuated most

Stonewall House located on the Versailles-Midway Road, home of Major Warren Viley.

of his Arabian and thoroughbred stock to the Louisiana plantation Wellswood, which was owned by his friend General Thomas Jefferson Wells, but the stallion Australian was not included in this move.[19] Prior to the Civil War:

> "Mr. Richards was ranked as the richest man in Kentucky.... The main source of his wealth being the vast interests in the cane and cotton fields of the Deep South. It was there that he fled, for that is where his heart lay." When Richards left Kentucky, R.A. became the state's wealthiest resident and "foremost property owner."[20]

Richards equipped and mounted an entire company of Confederate cavalry at his own cost and served as a Colonel on the Staff of General John C. Breckinridge.[21] Richards presented Confederate raider General John Hunt Morgan with one of his finest thoroughbreds, a son of Glencoe, which Morgan used as his personal mount. The horse, named Glencoe Jr., was painted by Edward Troye in the equestrian portrait of General Winfield Scott which is now in the National Gallery Collection in Washington.[22] After the end of the War, Richards rebuilt his racing stable in Kentucky.

Major Warren Viley, owner of Stonewall Farm, volunteered to recover Asteroid from Sue Mundy. Upon Asteroid's recovery and return to Versailles, both he and his rescuers received an ovation from the citizens.

CHAPTER FIVE

War Comes to Kentucky

Although Kentucky was a border state and openly expressed its neutrality, many Kentuckians chose allegiance by county.[1] On January 19, 1861, the Frankfort newspaper, *The Daily Commonwealth*, printed a notice from the people of Woodford County and sent to the U.S. Senate and House of Representatives which expressed Woodford County's allegiance to the Union:

"...regarding disunion as disastrous to our best interest, would alike denounce this secession movement at the South and at the north that spirit of resistance to the laws of our country relative to our rights in slave property, which is recognized both by the Constitution and the laws of Congress...to give us, who desire to stand by the Union, such assurances as we require, that our rights will be respected and secured to us."[2]

Alexander's personal sentiments about the War were expressed in a letter to his sister, Mary, on May 31, 1861:

"I find all pretty well[,] the political affairs, however, are so gloomy that it is enough to make one heartsick to think of them and yet it is a matter of utter impossibility to discard them from one's mind[.] This State is attempting to maintain a neutrality position and the Government has given some of our leading men to understand that it will be satisfied if she can only maintain her neutrality—but our own people are divided in opinion, some are joining the South at once at every risk[.] Such a course would make Kentuck[y] one of the greatest battlefields that the world ever saw in case this war goes on[,] as I fear it will[.] The other & larger party are for keeping aloof from the struggle as much as possible & if possible maintain our position of neutrality[,] & so keep fire and sword from our own doors[.] This position would assist the South nearly as much as if the State were to join them[;] for as the Government of the U.S. has promised not to interfere with our State in any way if we keep quiet & do not assume a hostile attitude[.] We shall serve as a protection to the State immediately South of us, should[,] however[,] the secession parts call for the assistance of the South & troops from

Main Street Illiopolis, Illinois, where Alexander went to scout out land for the possibility of moving his horses there.

The small town of Elkhart, Illinois, where Alexander boarded the train to continue on to Chicago in September 1861.

Tennessee cross over our boundary they would be attacked by the Union party & government assistance asked for if necessary[.] God grant that this may not be the case he alone knows what a few days or weeks may bring forth."[3]

This open pro-Union stance was not adopted by all in Woodford County, but the sentiments of the majority made the county vulnerable to Confederate guerrilla raids. Alexander recognized the issue of vulnerability and in September 1861 traveled by railway from Louisville to Chicago.[4] His personal journal reveals that he detoured from the designated destination to stop at Illiopolis, Illinois, to scout the land for a possible sanctuary for his horses should the War threaten Woodburn. From Illiopolis (near Williamsville), he traveled to Elkhart and caught the train to Chicago. Although his visit was brief at Illiopolis (September 20th-21st), he met with Mr. Thomas Taylor and a Mr. Humphrey who showed him potential land investments. He returned from Chicago on September 24th to Chetham, south of Springfield, to meet with G.W. Taylor, a relation of T.B. Taylor of Williamsville. In preparing a contingency plan, R.A. showed foresight and his dedication to protecting his horses.[5]

The Union Forces perceived guerrillas as criminals cut off from the Confederacy for which they were fighting. Military efforts against the guerrillas had little effect. Although

Federal forces maintained small cavalry units in all the towns, the patrols sent out to intercept guerrilla activity usually ended with little success. The guerrillas destroyed Federal communications, laid ambushes and made lighting raids on small towns.[6] The guerrillas roamed in small organized bands, mainly supported by the civilian population. This support which was initially obtained through sympathizers to the Confederacy, was later perpetuated and expanded through a combination of terror and force which set the terms of war in this theater. Clearly, guerrilla forces could not exist without this widespread civilian network.

Brigadier General Stephen Gano Burbridge, appointed commander of the Military District of Kentucky on February 5, 1864, found Kentucky absolutely overrun by guerrillas.[7] In an attempt to stop the guerrilla threat, he instituted the infamous retaliation policy.[8] The retaliation policy was simple, based strictly on revenge and generally far exceeded reaching a financial settlement or the usual eye for an eye. He ordered captured men who had been engaged in guerrilla operations taken to a spot where Unionists had been killed and executed.[9] The Federal army generally dealt harshly with guerrillas and towards the end of the War, Federal authorities passed a partially unconstitutional law designed to deal with the guerrilla problem. In 1864 the Kentucky Legislature established fines up to $5,000 and one-year imprisonment for "treasonable practices." The act of February 22, 1864, "allowed double indemnity through civil action for depredation losses."[10]

Hatred towards guerrillas, however, was not restricted to the Federal army, but shared by their victims as well. A Frankfort newspaper editor expressed his approval of the 1864 act by writing: "We have but one amendment to make to the proclamation, and that is every guerrilla and marauder who is caught, ought to be hung upon the first tree."[11] The opinion of W.F. Wickerman certainly expressed how some Kentuckians felt about guerrillas when he told his family: "...if you catch one of them I want you to kill the infernal scamps of the earth, they are not fit for no place but hell."[12]

On July 14, 1864, General Burbridge ordered two prisoners-of-war, identified as John May Hamilton of Richmond, Virginia, part of Sidney Cook's guerrillas who had been captured in a raid on Johnson County on March 6, 1864, and Richard Berry from Glasgow, Kentucky, removed from a compound in Lexington. The guerrillas were sent to Bloomfield under Union escort, taken to "Buckner Hill" and executed by firing squad for the death of a John R. Jones.[13]

On October 25, 1864, Captain Rowland E. Hackett and 50 men of the 26th Kentucky were ordered to take four men, Wilson Lilly, Sherwood Hatley, M. Bincoe, and Lindsey Duke Buckner, a Confederate Captain in Colonel Chenoweth's regiment, to Jefferstown (in

Jefferson county) and execute them. This was done in retaliation for the shooting of a Federal soldier by Sue Mundy's men.[14] On November 7th three men "believed" to have been guerrillas, Jas. Hopkins, John W. Sipple and Samuel Stagville, were shot to death seven miles from Bloomfield by order of the military authority in retaliation for the killing of two black men, supposedly by Sue Mundy's men, the week before.[15]

Burbridge's retaliation policy and the laws on "treasonable acts" seemed to have little effect on the guerrillas and did very little to reduce the raids in Central Kentucky. On October 13, 1864, guerrillas raided Bethal in Bath County and whipped the county judge with a strap. On October 23rd guerrillas raided Tilton and on October 25th Sidney Cook's guerrillas raided Flemingsburg, in Fleming County, robbing the bank there. Sidney Cook also raided Ashland, located in Boyd County, and Oak Hill.[16] On October 26th the guerrillas raided Hillsboro, also in Fleming County. The guerrilla operations continued in this area and on December 4, 1864, guerrillas raided Owingsville in Bath County.[17]

At the outbreak of the War Alexander made a brave attempt to carry on his breeding operations uninterrupted by the conflict. Since it was commonly known that Alexander was a British subject and that the sympathy of Great Britain early in the war was with the Confederacy, R.A. believed that this affiliation would protect Woodburn Farm and keep it safe from raids by the Confederate forces.[18] Legend recounts that he flew the Union Jack at the farm.[19] But in any case his British citizenship ultimately proved ineffective. Compared with other farms in the region, however, Woodburn was unusually fortunate in the early years of the war, but this would change dramatically as the war continued.

There is some evidence that Alexander did have a confrontation with Confederate guerrillas early in the war. "One Arm" Sam Berry and his band were well known in the region and it is believed, although not proven, that Berry attempted a raid on Woodburn Farm. Allegedly Alexander thwarted the raid and drove the guerrillas away, but not before he had shot and wounded Sam Berry in the heel.[20]

As the War began to draw to an end, however, Confederate guerrilla operations increased in Central Kentucky. Alexander seemed unperturbed by this increased presence. The guerrillas displayed a thorough knowledge of farms around Midway and Versailles and constantly harassed other breeders. Many breeders suffered severe losses from their depredations. Alexander's belief in his immunity from Confederate raids led him not only to continue operations at the farm, but to enlarge its scope. In spite of mounting hostile action in the area both branches of the stud were enlarged whenever Alexander was presented with the opportunity to acquire first class stallions and mares. During the War the thoroughbred part of the stud grew to 113 head, while the trotting part grew to 116, making a total of 229 horses on the farm which is remarkable in itself.[21]

War refugee Gaines' Denmark 61 bred only a few mares while at Woodburn Farm. He was not taken in any of the raids.

Woodburn was considered a safe haven by Kentucky breeders. Throughout the War Woodburn served as a refuge for several valuable horses which were believed by their owners to be in danger from Confederate guerrillas or from Federal forces. Among the most notable war refugees sent to Woodburn for safekeeping were Australian, owned by A. Keene Richards,[22] Nebula, the dam of Asteroid, owned by Jack Pendleton Chinn[23] and the celebrated saddlehorse progenitor Gaines' Denmark 61, owned by Willis Field Jones.[24]

GAINES' DENMARK 61

As he prepared to leave for service in the Confederate Army, Jones sent Gaines' Denmark along with Aerolite, a full sister to Idlewild, Reveille and possibly other valuable horses to Woodburn.[25] Jones, who was a horse breeder, also returned several mares in his possession to their rightful owners, including Monogram, owned by "Mr. Boice of South Carolina," after she had been bred to Mambrino Chief.[26] Most published records concerning Gaines' Denmark overlook the time that the stallion was in Alexander's care. Denmark arrived at Woodburn on September 8, 1862, under the protection of a black stud groom, Durastus, who had been left in charge of both Gaines' Denmark and Mambrino Chief 11.[27]

Unfortunately, Woodburn did not prove to be a safe haven for Gaines' Denmark and he was pressed into service as a Confederate mount. Although no one can be absolutely certain what date or under what circumstances Denmark was removed from Woodburn, one fact seems clear: there is nothing to indicate that the horse was taken from the farm by force or as booty from a guerrilla raid.

According to Lynn Weatherman, editor of the *American Saddle Horse Magazine* and an authority on Gaines' Denmark, Denmark allegedly served as Confederate General John Hunt Morgan's personal mount.[28] General Morgan, a native of Lexington and a true Southern hero, was considered a Partisan Ranger and not a guerrilla. General Morgan did raid railroads in the Midway area, but there is no evidence that he personally raided Woodburn Farm.

In July 1863 General Braxton Bragg authorized General Morgan to undertake a raid into Kentucky and "to move where ever he chose," but Bragg disapproved of Morgan's request to raid north of the Ohio River.[29] General Morgan decided to raid across the Ohio River anyway and to carry out his plans he needed horses for this mission. Weatherman advocates that Morgan acquired Denmark, possibly through the efforts of Mrs. Jones, for this venture, and the dates of Morgan's raid do coincide with the time that Denmark was absent from Woodburn farm.

During Morgan's raid through Indiana and Ohio, his cavalry was on one occasion required to ride more than "90 miles in 35 hours" and at times his troops put an average of "21 hours in the saddle."[30] Even if Denmark was not part of Morgan's raid, the raid exemplified the incredible endurance and stamina required by both men and horses and clarifies why saddlebred horses were favored by the cavalry and guerrillas. Confederate General Basil Duke praised the saddle horse as a cavalry mount:

> "...the saddle-bred horse is very valuable for cavalry service because of other reasons than merely his superior powers of endurance. His smoother action and easier gaits render the march less fatiguing to the rider; he succumbs less readily to privations and exposures and responds more cheerfully to kind and careful treatment. He requires more promptly and perfectly the drill and the habits of the camp and march and his intelligence and courage make him more reliable on the field."[31]

On July 26th Morgan was forced to surrender, but 300 of his men escaped and made their way to Abingdon, Virginia.[32] Weatherman believes that Willis Jones, assigned to the Army of Northern Virginia, recognized Denmark among the cavalry mounts and traded for him. By this time Denmark was in "terrible condition and never recovered from the abuse

Daniel Swigert, who came to Woodburn in 1862 and was related to R. A. Alexander through marriage, would become one of the state's great post-war breeders. He served on the original Board of Directors of Churchill Downs.

to which he had been subjected."[33] Willis Jones later served on the staff of General Charles William Field and was killed on Darbytown Road in August 1864 during an engagement at Deep Bottom Run, Virginia.[34]

There is considerable controversy over the length of time Denmark actually served as an army mount. Some believe that he was taken shortly after his arrival in 1862 and not returned to the farm until after the War, but certain known facts refute this claim. Woodburn records indicate that Denmark could not have left Woodburn before May of 1863. Daniel Swigert's notes recorded in his personal copy of the *1864 Woodburn Stud Farm Catalogue* and in his own handwriting stated that: "R.A. Alexander's gray saddle mare foaled March 18th 1864, Gray filly by Denmark, few white hair's in curve of forehead, and right ankle white."[35] The farm's "stud" ledger book also lists "a gray filly by Denmark foaled in March, 1864, as well as a colt by Denmark foaled April 25, 1864," which indicates that Gaines' Denmark was there for the breeding season and could not have left before May 1863.[36]

Woodburn records also indicate that Denmark's military service could only have lasted one year since entries in the *Woodburn Stud Book*, such as "45 mares bred to Denmark in 1864" indicate that Denmark had been returned to the farm by that time. Alexander's ledger book also shows that Gaines' Denmark was bred to Alexander's "gray saddle mare on May 7, 1865." The *Woodburn Stud Book* lists five mares bred to Denmark at Overstreet Farm, located in Garrard County, that fall.[37] Although there have been many stories about his death, it is now believed that Denmark died a tragic death by drowning near Cynthiana in Harrison County, Kentucky, in 1866.[38]

Although Morgan never raided Woodburn Farm, Morgan's men, however, were accused of killing some Woodburn mares at a location other than Woodburn. On June 10, 1864, Morgan's men allegedly stole the 11-year-old thoroughbred broodmare Margaret Morris, (listed in Daniel Swigert's personal copy of the *1864 Woodburn Stud Farm Catalogue*) from nearby Georgetown.[39] Again on July 2, 1864, *Wilkes' Spirit of the Times* reported raiders believed to have been Morgan's men took the horses Bay Flower and Maria "Mattie" Gross from Woodburn Farm. Daniel Swigert, Woodburn's superintendent and cousin to R.A. by marriage, pursued them and paid a ransom to get the horses back.[40] In a June 22nd letter to his brother, R.A. gives the following account of the two raids by Morgan's men:

"I returned home this day a week ago and found myself minus 5 head of horses viz. a thoroughbred mare Margaret Morris stolen from Keene Richards slave where she had been sent to be bred to the stallion Australian, making a season there as I had so much stock that I could not well keep him & those mares he was to cover here[.] Dan [Swigert] went over to Georgetown as soon as he heard that the Rebels had come into that quarter & just arrived in time to save the rest some 22 in No.; he brought these home with the horse Australian. Whilst he was gone these men came to my place & found Henry in the Guinea [hen] house. Ordered him to show them the training stable & when there ordered out the mares Bay Flower & Mattie Gross (a filly I bought of Spencer Graves[,] a Lexington 4 yr. old out of the dam of Dick Doty). These they took off with Henry to attend to them. These same men went to the Harpers and were about taking Sue Lewis, the Lexington out of Nebula, but John Harper begged her back allowing them to take another mare belonging to a Mr. Barnes of Tennessee instead[.] Dan & [Samuel] Thompson followed these men to the neighborhood of Frankfort & thence to Cynthiana where they arrived just after Morgan had taken [General Edward H.] Hobson & his party [prisoner.] After some trouble, Morgan ordered the mares to be delivered to Dan[,] gave him[,] Thompson & Henry a pass out of their lines & thus they left just in time to avoid the fight between Burbridge and Morgan which came off immediately after[.] By riding all night they got to Newton Craigs by sunrise in the morning having ridden about 90 miles[.] Dan had ridden the Bay Mare I bought of Mr. Humphreys & had her taken from him just before he got to Cynthiana. A Rebel soldier coolly ordering him to dismount which he enforced by no gentle threats[.] Dan got in exchange a broken down horse he was obliged to leave behind & when he got the mares he mounted Bay Flower[,] Henry being on Mattie Gross & so the two returned home. The other horses I lost were two thoroughbred gelding[s], a Lexington and a Scythian that were ridden by Peggot...."[41]

During the last two years of the war, when Kentucky was almost entirely in Union control and Union victory seemed imminent, a revival of horse racing was undertaken on a grand scale. Alexander participated in this revival and organized a racing stable, placing a slave trainer named Ansel Williamson in charge. Alexander's racing stable:

"swept through the campaign almost invincibly, with two unbeaten sons of Lexington, Asteroid and Norfolk, at its head. Norfolk and several other horses were sold, and Asteroid and the remainder returned to Woodburn with flying colors."[42]

Although there were many guerrillas fighting in Kentucky, none were feared as much as Sue Mundy, whose real name was Marcellus Jerome Clark. (See Appendix for a list of Kentucky guerrillas.) On Saturday, October 22, 1864, the guerrilla Sue Mundy[43] made his first raid on Woodburn Farm shattering the aura of invulnerability.[44]

SUE MUNDY'S FIRST RAID

In the middle of the day, between 2:00 and 2:30 p.m., while Alexander was eating his meal a black woman came running into the house. Alarmed, she reported that "there was a

Infamous guerrilla leader, Jerome Clark alias "Sue Mundy," who rode Asteroid off the farm and later received the ransom from Major Warren Viley. Mundy would participate in the second raid on Woodburn on February 2, 1865.

great commotion at the stables, a party of men being engaged in seizing and carrying off the horses."[45]

Since it was daylight and guerrilla raids against the horse farms usually took place after dark, R.A. could not believe at first that a raid was in progress. His doubts were quickly dispelled when a boy ran into the house to confirm the report.[46] Apparently the guerrilla leader with six of his men[47] had walked into the training stable and seized the prize racers Asteroid and Bay Dick by Lexington as well as three of the "choicest" two-year-olds sired by Lexington.[48] Two of these three racing colts taken from the training stable were later identified by R.A. as Norwich and Ansel. R.A. also listed a "filly by Ringgold out of Emma Wright" and Bay Dick,[49] who had triumphed in a prodigious year in 1864 and had become quite a money maker on the race course. There was no *Racing Calendar* for that year, but in the *Racing Calendars 1861-1869*, Bay Dick is listed has having four starts in 1865, winning three of them, and placed second in the other. In 1866 he had only one start and ran second.[50]

Alexander and his employees hurried to the stables only to find the guerrillas gone and with them five valuable thoroughbreds, including the unbeaten colt Asteroid. Alexander, his employees and several neighbors "started in pursuit and followed the guerrillas as far as the Kentucky River."[51] At the river, some ten miles from the farm, the guerrillas halted and the groups exchanged shots. Alexander's party made a charge "which threw [the guerrillas] into confusion" causing them to scatter.[52] One of the raiders (believed to be the leader), riding Asteroid, plunged into the river. The colt swam across under a hail of bullets. The pursuit continued and five of the horses were recovered.[53]

Newspaper reports varied as to the total number of horses taken. Woodburn accounts listed only five thoroughbred horses. Daniel Swigert's notes, however, on each horse in his *1864 Woodburn Stud Catalogue*, such as: "hip number 67, a bay brood mare, foaled 1861, by Edwin Forrest was stolen in October 1864" indicate that at least one trotting mare was taken, which would bring the total to six horses.[54]

After the skirmish at the river R.A. gave up the chase and returned to Woodburn with the five recovered horses. The pursuers later reported that they had wounded the guerrilla leader, but there is no evidence to support this claim. The *Spirit of the Times* reported that the raiders at Woodburn had been led by the Confederate guerrilla Sue Mundy.[55] It is significant, however, that Alexander later offered "one thousand dollars for the return of Asteroid and five thousand dollars for the capture of Mundy." Since the horse was worth at least $30,000, clearly Alexander wanted to avenge his loss.[56]

No Federal army correspondence exists regarding the October 22 raid on Woodburn since the army was not called upon to recover the animals. It is doubtful that R.A. even considered calling for Federal troops, since they were generally as unsuccessful in chasing and capturing raiders as they were in preventing guerrilla raids. The increasing number of guerrillas in the region prevented the army from offering much protection to civilians and often the civilian populace was forced to take matters into their own hands. Federal troops often failed to protect their own equipment and personnel against attacks. On October 23, the day after the raid on Woodburn, Brigadier General Hyland B. Lyon's guerrilla band derailed a train of Army supplies on the Nashville Railroad near Woodburn Farm and burned the cars and freight.[57]

Alexander asked his neighbor, Major Warren Viley, to "undertake the thing for me" and it is not surprising that Alexander would "authorize Viley to ransom the famous colt at any price...."[58] Allegedly the rifle carried by Major Viley on this expedition had been presented to Viley by R.A and was the same weapon that Alexander had used to wound "One-Arm" Berry. The rifle was displayed for years afterward in the hall of the house on Rose Hill in Versailles, owned by Viley's daughter, Mrs. Lydia May Lansing, who married Paul Lansing.[59]

According to R.A., "Mr. V. set off next morning and I understand, met Zac Henry on the road and he asked him if he would go with him."[60] At dawn the following morning, October 23, Major Viley was joined by Captain Zachariah "Zach" B. Henry and Colonel "Zeke" Clay as he rode through Versailles.[61]

Zachariah B. Henry, the son of Eliza McGuffin and Mason Henry, was born in 1838 on the family farm which "lay between the Clifton and Glenn's Creek roads, three miles from Versailles."[62] Henry had served in the Confederate army and had met Frank and Jesse James before they engaged in guerrilla warfare. Henry maintained that "they were fine fellows who had been goaded into that life."[63] It is important to note that Henry had a cousin, Tom Henry, a known Confederate guerrilla, who allegedly rode with Quantrill.

Colonel Ezekiel Field Clay was the oldest son of Amelia Field and Brutus J. Clay of Bourbon County. He had a national reputation as a breeder of blooded stock and had served as the president of the Agricultural Fair Association of that county for many years. Ezekiel was also the half brother of the Hon. Cassius M. Clay Jr., because his father had married Ann Field, Amelia's sister, after she died in July of 1843.

Clay enlisted in the 1st Kentucky Mounted Rifles of the Confederate Army. In 1862 he personally organized the 1st Battalion and was promoted to the rank of Lieutenant Colonel. In April 1864 he was wounded and blinded in one eye at Puncheon Creek, Kentucky, and

Ezekiel F. Clay, accompanied Major Warren Viley and "Zach" Henry, on the expedition to recover Asteroid. Clay later established Runnymede Stud on the Paris and Cynthiana Pike, which is still in existence.

captured. Clay was sent to the Federal prison on Johnson's Island in Sandusky Bay in Lake Erie. He served about six months before he was paroled and returned to Bourbon County, Kentucky, where he established Runnymede Stud on the Paris and Cynthiana Pike and raised the great race horses Miss Woodford, Hanover, Sir Dixon and many others. Colonel Clay served for several years as the President of the Kentucky Racing Association.[64]

The three men followed the raiders for nearly 40 miles and finally overtook them near Bloomfield in Nelson County.[65] As a ploy to elicit more information about the men they were pursuing, one of the men claimed to be "the uncle of the man who had been wounded and who much desired to see him."[66]

The three weary men soon happened upon two mounted guerrillas and quickly recognized one of the horses as Asteroid. In response to Major Viley's salutation both guerrillas drew their pistols and, for a moment, it appeared that the long chase would end in tragedy. Then Viley began to "parley with Asteroid's rider" telling him that the horse he was riding had been a pet and asking him to relinquish it. The guerrilla stoutly refused, declaring the horse to be the best he had ever ridden. Viley then offered a ransom and the raider finally agreed to surrender the horse. According to Viley, the raider, not knowing Asteroid's value, asked for $250 (or $300 depending on which account one reads), which was the approximate value of the horse the guerrilla had lost, and also demanded that Viley later furnish him with another horse, "as good a mount as he was riding."[67] Viley wrote the man a check and surprisingly the guerrilla turned Asteroid over to him unharmed. Viley later identified Asteroid's rider as Sue Mundy.

Asteroid was returned to Woodburn on or about November 1, just ten days after he had been taken. When the rescuers passed through Versailles on the way to Woodburn with the prized Asteroid they were given an ovation.[68] According to R.A., when Viley returned, he refused payment for his service and R.A. wrote:

> "...he had undertaken the thing out of consideration for me & from the fact that I had done so much for the stock interest in the state. I asked him what I shall do as regards [to] Henry [and] he said I had better ask him[.] I took Henry aside and asked him how I could compensate him. He said that he did not want me to give him anything[,] but if I would lend him $2000 he would take it as a favor, that he owed money which he did not like his Father to know of. I thought the sum more than I could give as I believed that I should never get a cent back from him. I told him, I would think the matter over & say what I would do as I did not have that sum there by me. I saw Jim [Zac] Henry some days after & told him that I had concluded to give him $1000 for services rendered in order to getting back Asteroid, he seemed to think I was rather ungrateful & said he was very much in want of $2000, but I left him with the understanding that I was to give him $1000= which I did in the course of a few days by [way of] Mr. [Daniel] Swigert."[69]

In total, R.A. paid $1,300 for the return of Asteroid, a small amount indeed for a horse whose value was reported by the *Chicago Tribune* as $10,000, but many considered the stallion worth that and much more.[70]

On November 5th Mundy and his men were involved in a skirmish with infantry forces in and around Bloomfield in Nelson County. While the guerrillas were having their horses shod (while raiding and pillaging the town) Major Samuel Martin and members of the 37th Kentucky Infantry rode into town. Martin's company surprised the guerrillas and they scattered. The Federals pursued the fleeing raiders and wounded "the notorious Sue Mundy" who escaped with "One Arm" Sam Berry. Although Mundy made a successful escape, the Federal troops did, however, manage to capture his pipe. Three of the dead guerrillas were later identified as Tindle, John Parkhurst, alias Jack Rabet, and Henry Warford.[71] Obviously, Sue Mundy was not seriously injured, because in early December Mundy with some of his men went to the house of John Wetherton and murdered him. They then traveled to the home of a man named Lee and murdered him, shooting him in the head.[72]

Cognizant of the danger that continued to hover around the farm and committed to protect his horses, Alexander decided to post armed guards around the property. Alexander's preparations were noted in a letter to his brother Alec on January 27, 1865.[73] In March 1865 Alexander again referred to the raid, the subsequent recapture of Asteroid and preparations against future raids in a letter to Henry Charles Deedes. Deedes had married Alexander's sister Mary Belle, who resided in England:

> "I believe you heard of the first guerrilla raid made upon me by five rascals who took a no. of my horses, who were pursued and from whom we took all but my racehorse Asteroid. I got a couple of my neighbors, very resolute men, to go into the hills and get the horse which was alone with little cost, though at some risk, my friends paying the price of a good hack for my horse which the rascals had stolen."

On that occasion all of the horses had been recovered, but Alexander had:

> "armed my men and kept six armed watchmen, besides the laborers who could be called into service making in all eighteen to twenty well armed men when all collected. My watchmen were placed at three points to give the alarm, two at the stables, my training stable and stallins [stallions] stable and two at my house."[74]

At dusk on November 1 shortly after the rescue of Asteroid, Sue Mundy and his band boldly called at Stonewall to claim the horse that Major Viley had promised. The guerrillas were wearing gray uniforms and Major Viley at first believed they were Confederate soldiers. There is no written documentation proving that Viley kept his word to the guerrilla, however, the fact that Mundy left Stonewall without incident indicates that the bargain was kept. The guerrillas then demanded supper and Major Viley obliged them. Unknown to him, the guerrillas had a malevolent plan in mind, a raid on his neighbors at Nantura Farm.

Nantura Farm had been targeted because the Harpers were well known Unionists and considered enemies by the Confederate guerrillas. Nantura Farm, unfortunately, was also located on one of the main routes used by guerrilla forces passing through Central Kentucky. Most of the attacks credited to Sue Mundy occurred on or near the road leading from Louisville to Bardstown. This road would be called "Mundy's Way" for years after the war.[75] In late June 1864 John Harper had been successful in preventing raiders from stealing his horses Sue Lewis, Loadstone, and Rhinodine.[76] On Tuesday night, November 1, 1864, Confederate guerrillas surrounded the Harper house. The Harpers attempted to defend themselves and a brief, but heavy exchange of gunfire followed. Adam Harper was shot and killed at the farm's front gate and one guerrilla was wounded.[77]

Burbridge acted quickly after the raid on Nantura, and on Friday, November 5th, ordered four guerrillas taken from the prison at Lexington under guard and executed at the Harpers' residence in retaliation for Adam Harper's murder.[78] (This incident may have taken place in Midway rather than at Nantura.) Today a marker in the Midway cemetery commemorates the four who were shot. On the marker are the following names: M. Jackson, J. Jackson, G. Rissinger and N. Adams.[79] The War had come to Woodburn Farm.

Signed "Carte de Vista of William C. Quantrill" during the Civil War. Quantrill went to Kentucky in 1865 with 48 of his band.

Carl Breihan Collection

CHAPTER SIX

Quantrill's Arrival Into The Bluegrass

Shortly after Mundy's raid on Woodburn, the infamous William Clarke "Charley" Quantrill who had been in hiding since General Sterling Price's raid and subsequent retreat on December 2, 1864, decided to regroup members of his old command to include Frank James. In August 1864 General Edmund Kirby Smith, in an effort to recapture Missouri, ordered Major General Price to leave Princeton, Arkansas, and cross the Arkansas River. Price crossed the river between Little Rock and Fort Smily unmolested and marched to Pocahontas, where he joined forces with Brigadier General Jo O. Shelby. The combined force of 12,000 men entered Missouri on September 19, 1864.

On September 25th Price concentrated his forces at Fredricktown, but was unable to advance towards St. Louis because of increased Federal resistance. Price then moved eastward towards Pilot Knob, but was repulsed in a bloody six-hour fight on September 27th with a loss of 1,500 men. Instead of retreating he turned westward towards Kansas City.[1] As Price's army made their way west large numbers of guerrillas came out from the woods to ride with the army. Guerrilla warfare in Missouri had been active since the beginning of the conflict, but the regular army knew little of what had transpired or what was to take place.

"The sight of these half-wild creatures was a jolt to regular soldiers and a graphic, sickening comment of the condition of the War in Missouri. Proudly displayed around the necks of their horses or dangling from bridles were trophies of human ears and freshly torn scalps."[2]

On September 26th guerrillas under the leadership of Captain George Todd engaged in a skirmish at Goslin's Lane and killed a "dozen Yankee soldiers and captured a wagon train of provisions...." That night Todd's guerrillas, which included Frank and Jesse James, joined forces with Captain William "Bloody Bill" Anderson, Quantrill's second in command, in the Perche Hills.[3]

A. D. "Donnie" Pence went to Kentucky with Quantrill. Pence later became the sheriff of Nelson County.

QUANTRILL'S ARRIVAL INTO THE BLUEGRASS

Frank and his brother had joined Quantrill in the beginning of the struggle prior to the infamous raid on Lawrence, Kansas, where 126 men and boys were massacred and the town burned to the ground. Quantrill had already gained notoriety by his exploits and according to Frank James in a magazine interview in 1914:

> "we knew he was not a very fine character, but we were like the followers of [Pancho] Villa or [Victoriano] Huerta: we wanted to destroy the folks that wanted to destroy us, and we would follow any man that would show us how to do it. Besides, I was young then. When a man is young his blood is hot; there's a million things he'll do then that he won't do when he's older. There's a story about a man at a banquet. He was offered champagne to drink, but he said, 'I want quick action. I'll take Bourbon whisky.' That was the way I felt. That's why I joined Quantrill: to get quick action. And I got it too. Jesse and I were with Quantrill until he was killed in Kentucky."[4]

In 1901, at the reunion of Quantrill's men, Frank related how he had come to join Quantrill's band:

> "I followed Quantrill all during the war,' said Frank, reminiscently gazing across the cultivated fields of prosperous farmers. 'I was but a boy when I joined his command. I had been in the Confederate army. While at my home in Kearney I heard that Quantrill was in Jackson County, so I decided to enlist under his flag. I met Bill Gregg, Quantrill's first lieutenant, in Clay County, and with him rowed across the Missouri River to this county [Jackson] and joined Quantrill at the Webb place on Blackwater ford of the Sni [River] just a few miles from here. This was May 1863."[5]

Quantrill used unconditional battle tactics and it was known that he would never "attack or fight a squad of soldiers of equal numbers with his own,…never fight equal numbers when dismounted,…never stand a charge unless he had every advantage in numbers, arms and situation of ground." Quantrill surrounded himself with men who were willing to execute his orders at any cost.[6]

According to Frank James, on the morning of September 27th Captain Anderson took about 30 of this company and entered Centralia where they captured a passenger train. More than 20 Union soldiers were taken from the train, hurriedly placed against a wall and summarily executed. Anderson then robbed the passengers, killed two men who attempted to hide valuables, set the train on fire and escaped with approximately $3,000 from the Express car.[7]

About two hours later, three companies of the 39th Missouri Cavalry under Major A.E.V. Johnson arrived at Centralia. Although details of what occurred next vary tremendously, most accounts agree that Major Johnson's troops halted three miles outside of Centralia on a hill and dismounted. Frank James said, "John Koger, a funny fellow in our

Two raiders, wearing Federal uniforms, who rode to Kentucky with Quantrill. On the right, John McCorkle with Tom B. Harris. Taken at Lexington, Missouri, 1864.

Frank James (sitting) wearing Confederate officers coat. On the right, his brother Jesse, and on the left, Fletcher Taylor.. Photograph taken after the war, believed to have been taken in Nashville.

ranks, watched the Yankees get down from their horses and said: 'Why the fools are going to fight us on foot!' and then added in seriousness, 'God help 'em.'" The combined mounted forces of Todd and Anderson, about 225 men, charged up the slopes and slaughtered the terrified Federal soldiers. The guerrillas killed, scalped and mutilated 124 of the 147 Missouri soldiers and according to Frank, Jesse James was credited with killing Major Johnson.[8] The fight was unilateral, barbaric and considered a bloody massacre.

On October 11th Todd, Anderson and Quantrill met with General Price who gave them orders to clear the path for his advance.[9] The Battle at Westport on October 22 was the biggest Civil War engagement west of the Missouri River and a disaster for the Confederate forces.[10] Price retreated 61 miles to Marais Des Cygens, Kansas where he halted and engaged in yet another costly battle on October 25. Defeated, Price retreated through the Indian Territory and on December 2 reentered the Confederate lines at Laynesport, Arkansas, with only 6,000 survivors.[11]

Todd was killed near Independence on October 21 in a skirmish with Captain Wagner's 2nd Colorado Cavalry,[12] and Bloody Bill Anderson was killed at Orrick, Missouri, on October 26 while leading a charge against Union forces. Soldiers dragged his body through the streets and put him on display. His body was finally decapitated and his head placed on a spiked telegraph pole. "Bloody Bill" was only 25 years old.[13] Quantrill realized that the war in Missouri was over and decided to move. He regrouped his guerrillas at the Wigginton Place, near Waverly, Missouri. They rode south from Jackson County to Pocahontas, Arkansas, where Dave Poole and George Shephard split from the main party with a large contingent of men. The Poole and Shephard group eventually made their way to Texas, where they joined General Jo O. Shelby who eventually went into Mexico with remanents of his "Iron Brigade."

Some believe that Quantrill's purpose for leaving Missouri was to travel to Washington to assassinate President Lincoln, but others refute this and argue that he realized the war was lost and perhaps he went to surrender with General Robert E. Lee.[14] Most historians, however, agree that these claims are romantic embellishments and that his move and subsequent exploits in Kentucky were simply his continuation of the guerrilla war in a different theater.[15]

Quantrill led a contingent of 48 raiders into Kentucky.[16] The group included Frank James, Jim Younger, Dick Burnes, Bud Pence (all of later outlaw fame) and A.D. "Donnie" Pence who would become Sheriff of Nelson County.[17] The guerrillas wore Federal uniforms and passed themselves off as part of the 4th Missouri Cavalry (a fictitious unit) sent to Kentucky to hunt guerrillas. Quantrill, posing as a "Captain Clarke," was dressed in a captain's uniform.[18] Quantrill had killed a Captain Clarke of the 2nd Colorado Cavalry in 1863 and had stolen the commission.[19] By 1863 the Union uniform had been standardized with minor alterations; one cavalry captain's uniform could easily be substituted for that of another cavalry company.

On January 1, 1865, the small force crossed the Mississippi River at Charlie Morris's "Pacific Place" near Devil's Elbow, 16 miles north of Memphis. The band then traveled through Big Creek, Portersville, Covington, Tabernacle, Brownsville, Bell's, Gadsden, Humbolt, Milan, McKenzie, and Paris and finally it crossed the Tennessee River into Kentucky.[20] According to John McCorkle, he, along with George Wigginton and Tom Harris, separated from the main band and traveled through Canton, located on the Cumberland River in Trigg County. Here they rejoined Quantrill and made their way to Greenville in Muhlenburg County.[21] The Kentucky route took the guerrillas through Cadiz and Hopkinsville and by January 28 the entire group had reached Chaplintown (now Chaplin).[22]

On January 29th at 9:00 a.m. Quantrill and 35 of his men entered Danville on the Hustonville Turnpike seeking horses and supplies and to destroy the telegraph office. Several of them wore:

"new Federal overcoats and the leader had a regular coat with two bars on the shoulder under his overcoat... while Captain Clark[e] (for so he called himself) was in the saloon, his men still sitting in line on their horses talked freely with citizens-They said they were Missouri troops, I think they said, 'The 3d Missouri Cavalry' [actually the 4th]." When Quantrill was accosted by Federal Lieutenant Thomas P. Young,

"Clark[e] opened his overcoat and pointing to his shoulder straps answered 'are they not enough!' 'No!' replied Young, 'any damned guerrilla could wear shoulder straps, let me see your papers.' Captain Clark[e] smiled quaintly and after glancing at Young in a pitying way called out to one of his men, 'John, come here.' John obeyed. When Clark[e] said, 'This gentleman wants to see our papers.' John lifted out a very long revolver from under his overcoat and shoving the business end of it in Lieut. Young's face, said 'God damn you, here's our papers.' Then Capt. Clark[e] gave a command in a loud tone, when all his men dropped every bit of their amiability, drew their pistols and savagely ordered all the citizens into line - Captain Clark[e] then addressing Young said, 'Behave yourself, Sir and you will not be harmed, but I will have no more of your foolishness....' He came to where the citizens were in line and said, in a well modulated pleasant voice, 'We are not guerillas [sic] gentlemen, we are Confederate troops and our object is to get quietly out of the state; if any of my men take anything from you report him to me....' Living in Danville at the time was Mr. N.R. McMurray who had resided for a number of years in Independence, Mo. After the troopers had been in town perhaps a half hour and were satisfied the citizens would not fire upon them, they relaxed their vigilance and no longer required the citizens to stand in line. It was then that Mr. McMurray approached your correspondent [Alex Anderson] and whispered, 'Do you know who commands these men? It is nobody but Quantrill, I have seen him often in Missouri, and I have just had a talk with Chat Renick [killed later that day] his Lieutenant... and he tells me that Capt. Clark[e] is nobody but Capt. Quantrill....' This band was in town nearly an hour, and the only property taken was a pair of boots, which the man who took them surely needed."[23]

One account of the raid described how the guerrillas "helped themselves to boots and then shot several of their own horses."[24] Quantrill then ordered the telegraph office destroyed and Captain William L. Gross, Assistant Superintendent of the Military Telegraph, reported that the raiders gutted his office "pretty effectually."[25]

The band left on the Perryville Pike at 11:15 a.m. and headed north. According to guerrilla John McCorkle, the band divided into squads after the raid on Danville and then continued their ride to Harrodsburg "to get their suppers."[26] Dividing into small squads was a frequent tactic utilized by guerrillas when on the move to a target or in an escape. Riding in

The Judge Alexander Sayers' Home located between Samuels' Depot and Deatsville. This home was used by the guerrillas as a rendezvous.

small groups made it harder for the Federals to track them and forced the Federals to separate their larger forces into smaller units.

Captain James H. Bridgewater, with 70 or 80 Federals, pursued the guerrillas and overtook them about four miles from Harrodsburg in Mercer County, where a fight occurred.[27] Captain Bridgewater's troopers were considered a band "nearly as irregular on the Federal side as were Quantrill's men on the Confederate side."[28] During the skirmish that night 12 of the 48 original raiders were killed or captured. Two of Bridgewater's men were wounded in the skirmish, but none of them were killed. One report stated that four guerrillas, which included two of the Noland brothers, Bill and Henry, along with Chat Renick, were killed, but four or five were wounded and several taken prisoner. The group captured included Jim Wiggington, Dick Glasscock, George Robinson, Jim Younger and Andy McGuire. The prisoners were taken to Louisville, but later escaped. George Robinson was recaptured and later hanged at Louisville in retaliation. The remaining guerrillas made their way towards Taylorsville in Spencer County.[29] After the night skirmish at Harrodsburg Union forces tried to intercept the guerrillas before they again lost them in the rolling countryside. Major Thomas Mahoney's report in the *Original Rebellion Records* relates that Captain Wiley Searcy had a fight with Quantrill at Chaplintown on the 30th, and although one raider was wounded, the rest escaped because they had "better horses."[30]

After the skirmishes at Danville, Harrodsburg and Chaplintown, Quantrill and his men quartered at an unknown farm in the vicinity of Taylorsville. Although the farmer was never identified, it could have been the home of Judge Alexander Sayers.[31] Judge Sayers and his wife, Finetta, were Confederate sympathizers and close friends of Frank James. They were once believed to have been the aunt and uncle of Frank James, although a closer investigation has proved this to be untrue.[32] The white two-story, brick house, located on the road leading to Taylorsville between Samuel's Depot and Deatsville, was often used as a rendezvous and safe house by the guerrillas, and Frank James continued to use the Sayers' home as a hideout throughout his outlaw years. The band could also have camped at the home of Richard Haskins in the broken country of Nelson County known as the "Knobs," (today the Knobs State Forest).[33] The guerrillas may have used the home of Judge Jonathan Davis in Spencer County who later admitted that Quantrill had often stayed at his home.[34]

Having lost part of the original contingent, Quantrill resolved to "quit playing Federal," and Quantrill's band dropped all pretense and no longer claimed to be troops of the 4th Missouri Cavalry. Aware that Mundy was in the area, Quantrill inquired about him; the farmer who had been harboring Quantrill agreed to negotiate a meeting with Mundy the next morning, January 30, at Taylorsville. Quantrill, however, actually made the rendezvous somewhere in Nelson County near Bloomfield.[35] Mundy had been on reconnaissance and operating in northern Shelby County and southern Henry County.

The rolling countryside of Spencer and Nelson counties provided the guerrillas with excellent hiding places. Towns in these counties were really villages. These counties were favored by the guerrillas because they contained pockets of Confederate sympathizers who protected them and supplied them with information, food and other assistance necessary for their survival.

Guerrilla activity continued to increase in the area and heavy action was reported throughout December and January. The *War of the Rebellion Original Records* show that guerrilla raids were reported near Lexington, Frankfort, Bardstown, Eminence, Covington and Elizabethtown. Although guerrilla actions were viewed as independent, random raids, the guerrillas were well organized and were working cohesively with a large scale plan. On December 30, Acting Major John L. Shirke and Captain R.M. Newberwick, of the 7th Pennsylvania Cavalry were murdered in the parlor of Mr. Grigsby's house near Bardstown by 16 of Henry Magruder's guerrillas.[36] Magruder's band also captured a train near Lebanon Junction on the afternoon of January 7 and murdered four discharged soldiers of the 15th Kentucky.[37] William ("Billy") Henry Magruder and Henry Metcalf were also identified as among the band who burned the Fox Creek Bridge on January 18 near Shepherdsville in Bullitt County.[38] On January 12 it was reported that Sue Mundy had murdered five members of the 15th Kentucky Infantry near Lebanon, and destroyed a number of box cars of the Louisville and Nashville Railroad.[39] On January 20 the citizens of West Point in Hardin County skirmished with guerrillas led by Ben Wiggington.[40] On Wednesday, February 1, *The*

Chicago Tribune reported that on January 27, Captain "One Arm" Sam Berry and five guerrillas were fired upon by Federal troops while approaching within a short distance of Bardstown.[41] On February 1, *The New York Times* reported that Captain Edward Terrell of the Union Guards had caught and executed the notorious Ike Ludwig on Saturday, January 28. That afternoon Captain Terrell's men had a fight with Captain Colter's guerrillas several miles from Bloomfield, "dangerously [wounding] Colter."[42] On the 29th Sue Mundy and Henry Magruder, along with 60 guerrillas, attacked 117 soldiers of the Federal Home Guards in Bloomfield in Nelson County.[43] Also on the 29th there was a skirmish at Bardstown between a detachment of Colonel Harvey M. Buckley's 54th Kentucky and Mundy's guerrillas.[44] On January 30 Major Sam Jones with 200 men were reported within nine miles of Elizabethtown in Hardin County.[45] Although it may never be clear exactly what objectives the guerrillas were pursuing it is clear that the numerous raids led Federal troops away from the Quantrill-Mundy band, thus creating the opportunity to invade the Midway area and attack Woodburn without interference.

Tracking the movements of Quantrill and Mundy from January 29 through February 3 shows that the route completed a large loop from Danville, through Henry and Owen Counties, then they turned south to Georgetown and Midway. The route continued through Versailles to Lawrenceburg and south to Danville. The destruction of the telegraph at

Historical highway marker in Midway telling of the February 2, 1865 raid. The number of horses is incorrect, 16 were taken.

Kentucky's "Guerrilla Country": map shows the large loop of the route taken by Quantrill and Sue Mundy to enter the Midway area, and by which they escaped.

Danville by Quantrill on the 29th crippled communications and rendered Federal troops in the area ineffective as the guerrillas continued their raids northward. The guerrillas easily eluded the Federal troops and by the afternoon of February 1 had disappeared. Colonel Harvey M. Buckley reported to Brigadier General Edward Henry Hobson, Commander at Lexington, that he had:[46]

"chased Quantrill all day yesterday [January 31] from Spencer [County] through Shelby [County] toward [the] Louisville and Frankfort Railroad; am still after him."[47]

Still other reports asked if the guerrillas had been seen beyond Elizabethtown. General Hobson then ordered General Daniel W. Lindsay to pursue Quantrill and his men into Henry County.[48]

Quantrill and Mundy were spotted again on February 1. All civility gone, they launched small raids on the unsuspecting countryside in the area of Smithfield. Mundy was reported to have passed through the town at 2:00 a.m. headed in the direction of New Castle. About two miles outside Eminence Mundy attacked a detachment of the 17th Army Corps and four or five of Mundy's men were reported wounded in the fight.[49]

There were a few brief skirmishes. The hit and run tactics indicate that the primary objective was not to engage with the enemy, but to move quickly toward their target at Woodburn. The guerrillas rode at night and early morning to avoid being seen. Colonel Buckley heartily pursued the Quantrill-Mundy band into Henry County and in his report from Shelbyville stated: "horses are worn out; we can't do anything without fresh horses. Please send some, if only fifty. Quantrill is with the gang."[50]

After receiving word from Mount Sterling that guerrillas had burned the depot and freight cars at Lair Station during the night of February 1, General Thomas Howes sent a mounted force to scout the country toward Cynthiana.[51] Howes assumed that this was the Quantrill-Mundy band as they made their way toward Pond Gap and warned Federal check points in the surrounding area. This was a diversion, however, since there were four or five groups of guerrillas throughout the area and Union scouts mistook them to be one force. Meanwhile, the Quantrill-Mundy group made its way east from northern Henry and Owen counties. Major Andrew G. Hamilton, 12th Kentucky Cavalry, reported that guerrillas had crossed the Kentucky River at Worthville in southern Carroll County, but the Federals were ordered to remain at their posts at Eminence to protect their horses.[52] Toward evening on February 2 it began to rain lightly. The Quantrill-Mundy guerrillas continued their ride toward Georgetown in Scott County. Colonel Simeon B. Brown reported from Mount Sterling that squads of guerrillas had ridden through Georgetown early that evening and were believed to be headed for Pond Gap.[53] *The New York Times* identified the guerrillas as bands led by "Quantrill, Sue Mundy and [Henry] Magruder...[which] had been driven from Georgetown by the Federal forces."[54]

The guerrillas had not been driven from the town. After being sighted at Georgetown they again slipped away from the Union forces. The terrain around Georgetown consisted of wooded hills, hollows, sinkholes and ravines crossed by winding roads. This rough landscape continued southward to Versailles and beyond. It provided good cover.

The Federal soldiers had no idea what Mundy, Quantrill and Henry Magruder were planning. It was not until after the raid that it became clear that they were seeking fresh horses and heading for Woodburn Farm.

"Feb 2-25 [up to 35] guerrillas under Capts. Sue "Munday" ([a.k.a. Marcellus] Jerome Clarke) and Quantrill dash into Midway, Woodford co., rob the citizens, and burn[ed] the railroad depot; the[y] visit[ed] the farm of R. Aitcheson Alexander, [and] robb[ed] him of [16] fine blooded horses."[55]

William "Billy" Henry Magruder, guerrilla leader and friend of Sue Mundy, participated with Mundy and Quantrill in the February 2, 1865, raid on Woodburn.

Tom Watson Collection

CHAPTER SEVEN

Disaster At Woodburn Farm

All the precautions initiated after the first raid proved ineffectual when at 6 o'clock on the evening of February 2, two files of soldiers "clad in federal overcoats" rode into the kitchen yard of the main house and started toward the stables. A watchman had given the alarm in time for the house to be secured and windows bolted, but Alexander was caught unprepared by the duplicitous game of cat-and-mouse by which the disguised men had gained access to his valuable animals.

With "gun in my hand and a pistol in my belt," R.A. walked to the kitchen doorway and cried, "halt" just as the column had ridden halfway past the door. They halted at once and Alexander asked, "What will you have gentlemen?" At first they pretended to want only "provender for 200 horses." Alexander protested that it was a "pretty large order" and that although he had provender, he did not have a "place to feed so many horses." Realizing that the deception would not work the guerrillas changed their story.

The men then identified themselves as a detachment that had been sent to "press" horses, but Alexander then asked the men to show him their orders. Upon this request the Captain and the entire line drew their pistols and the Captain stated, "This is our order." It was then that R.A. recognized the men as guerrillas. R.A. was not a man accustomed to taking orders even when staring at the barrels of the raiders' guns. Because he was more than willing to risk his life to protect his horses and farm, he began to stall for time and continued this tactic throughout the raid.

Alexander first threatened the men with a fight with his own handful of watchmen by telling the Captain, "Well I suppose if you are bound to have the horses there is no necessity for a fight about it, but if you are disposed to have a fight I have some men here and we will give you the best fight we can." Unknown to R.A., however, the guerrillas had planned the raid carefully and had a card of their own to play. Sue Mundy knew of the Viley's relationship with R.A. since the ransom of Asteroid by Warren Viley in November.

Captain Willa Viley, father of Maj. Warren Viley, was taken hostage by Quantrill and Mundy prior to the raid on Woodburn. The 77 year old Viley was quoted to have pleaded with Alexander, "Alexander, for God's sake, let them have the horses."

William C. Quantrill, circa 1865, taken in Louisville, Kentucky. Quantrill, along with Sue Mundy and Henry Magruder, raided Woodburn Farm and stole 16 valuable horses on February 2, 1865.

To ensure that R.A. would surrender the horses at Woodburn without resistance, they had a hostage with them-Captain Willa Viley.

During the ride through the Midway area prior to the raid on Woodburn the guerrillas had stopped at the home of Thomas Payne and taken Payne's buggy horse from the stable. Captain Willa Viley who had been visiting Payne at the time was..."exasperated at the outrage, as he deemed it (then 76 [actually he was 77] years of age) he mounted a bareback horse, in his morning-gown, and boldly went in pursuit."[1] Unfortunately, his noble effort failed. The raiders took him hostage and forced him to go with them to Woodburn. Viley, who had "always shown himself my friend," begged Alexander to surrender the horses, telling him:

> "Alexander, for God's sake let them have the horses. The Captain says he will be satisfied if you let him have two horses without a fight or any trouble."[2]

R.A. saw that the "scamps" had every advantage. Realizing the situation was to his disadvantage and his friend's life was in danger, Alexander acceded to Viley's request. R.A.

gave his word to surrender the two horses, because he considered himself a man of his word and that his word was as good as his bond. After concluding that the matter was settled, he offered to "shake hands in the bargain." R.A. walked through the first rank and shook hands with the Captain, who gave his name as "Marion," (a fictitious name), to confirm the bargain. Alexander's account of the raid and the *Rebellion Records* strongly suggest that "Marion," was Quantrill.[3]

As Alexander climbed the steps to return to the kitchen door, Quantrill demanded that Alexander march his men out and deliver up his arms. Alexander asserted that they had made a bargain and if, "I am to give you two horses, you shall have the horses, but I will neither march out my men or give up my arms." Alexander explained that he needed his arms for his own protection, but offered to have them moved into the house. Quantrill warned R.A. that if a shot was fired, he would "torch the whole place." Alexander replied to the threat, that "if a gun were fired, it would be his [Quantrill's] fault."

Only then did Alexander, Daniel Swigert, the servants in the house and the watchmen lay down their arms. As R.A. returned to the kitchen door Quantrill asked, "Where are those horses? I am in a hurry." Alexander pointed to the stable near the house and replied, "They are in the stable there." He reluctantly accompanied Quantrill and the band to the brick barn which held only "a pair of thoroughbred mares well broken to harness, a thoroughbred horse...used as a saddle horse...and some 2 or 3 others of less value."

Upon arriving at the stable Alexander told Quantrill that he would find one of the horses that he proposed to give him. Quantrill inquired if it was a "good one," and Alexander replied, "Yes, as good as could be found." Quantrill was not fooled by Alexander's offer of his lesser stock. He had obtained detailed knowledge from Sue Mundy concerning Alexander's blood stock, for he asked specifically for the "bald horse, meaning a horse with white in his face."

Alexander said that he had several such horses answering to that description and then Quantrill said, "I mean a horse known as the bald horse." R. A. knew that the "rascal" was "well informed" and answered truthfully that he had such a horse. Alexander could see that he had been bested by Quantrill. In spite of his protestations that the "bald horse was a good trotting horse, valuable to me, but of comparatively little use to him and that I had twenty horses that I could give him better suited to his use," Quantrill demanded the horse. Having argued that the horse was valuable as a trotter, Alexander said, "I could get a good price for [it] as a fast trotting horse." Quantrill, insisted on having the horse stating, "if the horse is valuable to you, he is valuable to me." Alarmed, Alexander realized that Quantrill had every intention of stealing his valuable racehorses as well. Alexander then recognized that he could be taken hostage and held for ransom since he had been warned in a letter sent to him some two or three weeks earlier about this possibility. Therefore, he directed the men to his trotting stable on a nearby hill opposite the house.[4] Alexander claimed that F.V.R.L. Hull, one of his men, had the key and volunteered to go to search for it. Leaving the guerrillas at his riding stable, he went directly to the crib house where his men stayed and found Hull there.

Hull, a native of Albany, New York, had driven Almont in the only two races that the great sire ever raced.[5] Hull came to Woodburn in 1859 and worked in the trotting horse stable under H.S. Avery, who was its superintendent in 1860.[6] Hull was later promoted to superintendent after Avery. Hull's personal *1864 Woodburn Farm Catalogue* is now in the collection of the Keeneland Association Library in Lexington. In an interview at Woodburn in 1898, Hull also described firsthand the events of the raid.[7]

Alexander hurriedly explained to Hull that Quantrill had asked for the bald horse and was so insistent on having him that he feared that they would "be obliged to give him to them." R.A. then instructed Hull, that if possible, he should give them any other horse in his place. The two men then entered the kitchen yard and Hull started for the stables shouting to R.A. that "Henry" had the key to the trotting stable. In reply Alexander stated that he would "look up Henry" and headed toward the main house. It is believed, although never proven, that this "Henry" was H.S. Avery.

Alexander passed two of the raiders sitting on their horses outside the kitchen door holding two other horses with empty saddles. They did not speak, but R.A. realized that the two empty saddles indicated that the guerrillas had entered the house. R.A. assumed they had gone inside for some water and, hurrying by the two mounted men, entered the kitchen. He proceeded up the long passageway from the kitchen to the dining room, where he found one of the raiders with a cocked pistol standing at the fireplace next to Mrs. A. Swigert, who was holding an infant in her arms.

The other occupants in the room were a nurse, who also had a child in her arms and "little Mary Swigert." (Daniel Swigert and his family had been staying with R.A. at Woodburn since the former raid.) The other guerrilla was standing at the far end of the room and had already collected a number of guns throughout the house, including the rifle of Alexander's father, which he had brought from Virginia. According to R.A., the guerrilla "seemed quite loaded down with guns." The women were "nearly frightened to death" by the two men and when R.A. heard one of them order Mrs. Swigert to get the rest of the arms, he stepped into the room. R.A., standing between the two guerrillas, turned and faced the man with the pistol and firmly stated, "The Captain says, if I give him two horses without a fight or any trouble, I can keep my arms and I am going to keep them."

In response the man turned, and presenting his pistol at Alexander's breast said, "Damn you, deliver up the rest of those arms or I'll shoot you." Although R.A. could tell that the man was drunk and quite capable of anything, he knocked the pistol away from his body and struggled with the man. R.A. tried to push him into the hall so that he could bolt the kitchen and hall doors, but when Alexander tried to trip him, both men fell into the hallway. Alexander pinned the raider to the floor. As the guerrilla tried to free himself from Alexander, he called for his companion to shoot Alexander for he "was killing him." In answer the fellow replied, "He is not armed. He cannot hurt you much." As the two men rose together, Alexander retained his hold "encircling him just at the elbow joint so as to pinion him." During the guerrillas' efforts to get away, he again called out to the other raider to shoot R.A. The second guerrilla then called out, "Let him go Mr. Alexander." Alexander protested, "I will not let him go. He will shoot me as I have no arms." Realizing that the man could get away Alexander struck out, "giving him the benefit of my knee a second time."

As the two men fell again to the floor the raider's pistol went off when his hand struck against an iron safe in the hall. (R.A. does not mention the fact that he could have been killed in his letter to Deedes.) The man yelled out that he had broken his arm, but unfortunately, this was not the case.[8] Alexander could not hold the guerrilla down and as the two rose to their feet, again the second raider shouted, "Let him go!" The guerrilla gave Alexander his word that he would protect him. Alexander reluctantly let the man go, but as he did so gave him a shove so that "he [the guerrilla] went through the door towards the kitchen." The second guerrilla, still carrying "two guns and four pistols," stepped between the two men and kept the other guerrilla moving toward the kitchen.[9]

As they disappeared from the passageway, R.A. quickly followed and bolted the two doors in the hallway. He returned to the dining room and told Mrs. Swigert not to open the door "on any account...if the fellows should return and inquire for me...say that I have gone out." Having said this, R.A. went to the front part of the house and out onto the upper part of the garden. From this vantage point he could see the guerrillas at the trotting stables. It had begun to grow dark, but Alexander could see that they had built a fire in front of the stables and were removing the horses. He raced to the remote stable where his prized Lexington was housed and told his man there to remove his most valuable stock. He then dispatched a boy to the training stable to tell Ansel, the trainer, to remove Asteroid and the other prize horses. After the guerrillas (Frank James among them) entered the trotting stable, they "informed Mr. Hull who was at the trotting stable [who had just arrived at the barn, after leaving Alexander in the kitchen yard] that they must have a few horses, and good ones. At the same time they notified him that if he made any objection they would kill him."[10]

The guerrillas took their pick of the valuable horses from the stalls while Alexander's men stood by helplessly. The trainer and others pleaded in vain with the man who took Abdallah to select another horse since,

> "Abdallah, at the time, was fat, bare footed, and only a few days before his feet had been trimmed and pared down. No horse on the place could have been selected so little-fitted to endure a long hurried ride over flinty roads. But the more Mr. Hull tried to convince his unwelcome visitors of this fact, the more determined were they to take the stallion, which they did and rode the magnificent son of Katie Darling to his death."[11]

Considerable money was offered by Alexander's men to protect the horses; Quantrill was offered $10,000 not to take Bay Chief, but all offers were refused.[12]

Meanwhile before the boy could reach the training stable with the message, the guerrillas had already removed four horses. One of the guerrillas asked for Asteroid by name. Because it was dark the shrewd trainer, Ansel, pulled a switch and substituted an inferior horse. The substitution was a brave act because the guerrillas had demanded possession of the horses at gun point, but in Alexander's words Ansel's actions "saved the best horse in the stable."[13] The "counterfeit" horse was the 1862 colt by Star Davis out of Lindora.[14]

Although Asteroid had been saved by the quick thinking trainer, the guerrillas removed two colts and two other horses, including the three-year-old colt, Norwich (the full brother to Norfolk). They took the three-year-old filly Nannie Butler by Lexington and an unidentified four-year-old mare. They also removed four horses from the trotting stable, four from the riding horse stable and three more "from various places, making 16 horses in all."[15]

Both the *Richmond, Virginia Daily Examiner* and *The New York Times* carried the news of the raid on Midway. Lewis Collins would later document that this band of guerrillas was the same that would ride to Woodburn. In Collins' book, *History of Kentucky*, he quoted an unknown source which identified Mundy and Quantrill. This quote is credible because it is the only source which closely identified the number of horses taken from Woodburn and the book was the source for the inscription on the historical highway marker in Midway.[16]

The *War of the Rebellion Original Records* reveal that Mundy and Quantrill had joined forces by the evening of February 2.[17] Therefore, one can deduce that Quantrill and Mundy rode together to the farm that night. The total number of guerrillas in the bands led by Magruder, Quantrill and Mundy at the time of the raid is not known, however, reports of "squads of guerrillas riding through Georgetown" suggests that all of the guerrillas under the three leaders were in the area. Only Quantrill and his men, accompanied by Magruder and Sue Mundy, actually rode to Woodburn. The remaining guerrillas may have acted as a rear guard as they waited for Magruder and Mundy to return to Midway.

The use of Viley as a hostage by the guerrillas appears to confirm that Mundy was at the Woodburn Farm raid. The fact that Mundy knew Viley and had previously visited the farm could explain how the guerrillas knew so much detailed information about the Woodburn horses. Other supporting evidence that Quantrill and Mundy raided Woodburn together came at the 26th reunion of the survivors of Quantrill's Band on September 14, 1923, at Wallace's Grove near Kansas City, Missouri. George N. Noland was quoted as saying, "After the war they disfranchised us, so for years I registered at Independence as 'George N. Noland, one of Quantrill's horse thieves.'"[18] All of the Nolands (Bill, Henry and Ed) rode with Quantrill's guerrillas and were with Quantrill in Kentucky in 1865. Bill and Henry were killed during the skirmish at Harrodsburg only four days before the raid. By 1923 the Woodburn Raid had become famous and George Noland's "horse thieves" statement was a boast that insinuated that he rode with Quantrill to Woodburn that night.[19]

By 1902 the Viley hostage story had been greatly embellished, part of which has been accepted as fact. This apocryphal legend, however, was published in *The Woodford Sun*, at the time of Major Warren Viley's death in its entirety. According to this legend, the high tempered Viley:

> "had flown into a rage" when the guerrillas stole a valuable mare from his farm. The article stated that Viley, with supernatural strength, got out of his deathbed, put on his clothes and a pair of bedroom slippers, forced the lid of his desk open with a gun stock (his wife had secured his guns to keep him at home because he would "die in the road from sheer weakness"), "secured his pistol, went out and mounted his Grandson's pony that was hitched at the door with a child's saddle on its back and started after the guerrillas." Viley rode from Scott County to Woodford County and "finally overtook the horse thieves who agreed to surrender the horse if Viley showed them the way to the Kentucky River."[20]

If this story were true, then the speed and durability of the mighty little pony rivaled the best thoroughbreds of the time, and R.A. should have bought him and incorporated this bloodline into his breeding stock.

Brigadier General Edward H. Hobson, Commander of Union Forces in Central Kentucky, led the pursuit of the guerrillas who raided Woodburn. Inexperienced with guerrilla tactics, his confusion and uncertainty initially proved ineffective during the Quantrill-Munday raid.

CHAPTER EIGHT

The Recovery of the Horses

After the efficient and productive raid on Woodburn the guerrillas headed to Midway on their new mounts taking Viley with them. When the group reached the farm of Frank P. Kinkead, listed as "Cane Spring" on the 1861 map of the Midway area, the exhausted Viley fell from his horse.[1] The guerrillas left him where he fell and rode on.[2]

"Viley was later carried to his son's home, [Stonewall Farm]. He died there a short time afterward on March 18, 1865, shortly after his 78 birthday... his death being hastened by the exposure of that ride."[3]

The guerrillas burned the railway depot and the telegraph office at Midway to delay pursuit. While these buildings burned, the band robbed the stores and citizens on the streets, taking their watches and money. The raiders started down Versailles Pike (Highway 62) at full gallop, riding past Stonewall Farm.[4]

Since Quantrill and Mundy were able to leave Georgetown, raid Woodburn and burn the Midway depot and telegraph office unmolested, the Federals had no clear idea where the guerrillas were or what their plan of action might have been. Meanwhile, a messenger from Woodburn Farm had been sent to Lexington to sound the alarm and to report the stolen horses. Having learned that guerrillas were in Midway, a company of the 12th Ohio Cavalry which was encamped in Lexington adjacent to the old Lexington Association race track, gave pursuit.[5]

The *War of the Rebellion Original Records* document in detail what next occurred. After the raid at Midway Mundy and Quantrill rode through Versailles and headed in the direction of Lawrenceburg. The band traveled along the Lawrenceburg Road for a few miles and then probably cut across country into Anderson County to avoid the Union scouting parties. Efforts to track the wily pack were in vain and indeed, at times, Union efforts appeared comical, since unit commanders seemed unable to decide where reinforcements were needed. Nevertheless the chase continued.[6]

The Versailles-Midway Road, in front of Stonewall Farm, very much the way it looked during the Civil War. Having burned the Midway Depot, the guerrillas galloped up this road to escape pursuing Union cavalry.

General Edward Henry Hobson, commander at Lexington, assumed that the guerrillas would "return through the country to Bloomfield" and sent the 12th Kentucky from Eminence to intercept them.[7] He then ordered the commanding officer at Crab Orchard to take part of his mounted force "to Danville, since [the guerrillas] had moved in the direction of Versailles," and to pick up troops along the way.[8]

He also sent a message to Major Thomas Mahoney at Lebanon stating that the guerrillas were taking the "back track," and ordered him to look for the guerrillas at Bloomfield.[9]

General Hobson sent word to Brigadier General Speed Smith Fry at Camp Nelson, General Daniel W. Lindsey at Frankfort, Lieutenant Colonel Robert Henry Bentley at Richmond and Major George F. Barnes at Elizabethtown to inform them that Mundy and "Clarke's guerrillas" had burned the Midway depot.[10] Hobson ordered their companies to move toward Danville and advised them to be alert and ready to move if the guerrillas were spotted.[11]

On February 3rd Union reports indicate that the guerrillas had not been sighted. Captain John S. Butler had scouted between Flat Rock and Middleton, but had stopped eight miles short of Mount Sterling.[12] On the night of the 3rd, companies of the 12th Ohio moved from Crab Orchard to Danville and Lebanon, and the rest of the 12th Kentucky prepared to move from Camp Nelson.

Major George F. Barnes reported, that although he had been delayed by companies belonging to the 13th Kentucky stationed at Raywick and Hodgenville, a force of 300 guerrillas were threatening the towns in the area.[13] Major Barnes identified these guerrillas as

"Colonel [Sam] Jones, Major [Dick] Taylor's, Press Williams and others," but also reported that the guerrillas who had crossed the Louisville and Frankfort Railroad were Quantrill's band.[14] He reported that he was moving west with his force of 2,110 men to scout the area. Subsequently, the companies of the 13th were sent back to Raywick and Hodgenville to protect the town.

One reason the raiders eluded capture so easily was that the guerrillas had split up. The Quantrill-Mundy band separated to quell bickering and fighting among its members. One of Quantrill's men, Peyton Long, left with Sue Mundy and Magruder and was later killed in a skirmish with Captain Jim Bridgewater's forces at Bewleyville on the border of Breckinridge County and Meade County.[15] Although it is not clear where the guerrillas separated, it is believed that the break occurred in the vicinity of Versailles or Lawrenceburg and official correspondence seems to suggest that they broke up into several groups.

The guerrillas moved swiftly through the rolling countryside and managed to go "to ground" for the night. Expertise and expediency served them well, at least temporarily. Quantrill made camp about twelve miles from Woodburn in the area of Lawrenceburg and spent the night on the "farm of Mr. Bush in a rough and hilly country."[16] Shortly before morning, on February 3 the band was attacked by the Woodford County Home Guards in Anderson County. Tom Henry was wounded.[17] Quantrill managed to mount Bay Chief, and quickly became a "conspicuous mark for Federal bullets during the skirmish." During the fray Bay Chief was shot

> "through the muzzle, through both thighs and one hock. In this condition he carried his rider two miles in the retreat, when the horse was so weakened by loss of blood, a Federal cavalryman overtook them. His [pistol] being empty, the soldier aimed a blow at [Quantrill], but missing him lost his balance and fell from his horse. The guerrilla leader quickly saw his opportunity, jumped from Bay Chief, mounted the soldier's horse and escaped."[18]

Four of Alexander's horses were recaptured, including Bay Chief. Bay Chief's wounds were so severe, however, that he died ten days later despite all efforts to save him.[19] Bay Chief was six years old.[20] Abdallah was also in this fight, but his rider escaped by plunging him into a nearby river. Abdallah was left at Lawrenceburg where he was later found. In his report to General Lindsey, General Hobson took relish in the news that the guerrilla raids had been finally halted; he hoped that he would soon have the guerrillas killed or scattered.[21] Hobson had already been informed about the fight in which Bay Chief was shot from under Quantrill and Abdallah had been forced to swim across the river.

The victory was pyrrhic, however, for by February 6 it was reported that the "Press Williams' gang of guerrillas" had visited Leitchfield in Grayson County a few days before and the following morning "twenty to thirty of Quantrill's mounted men" under the command of "Captain" Sam Jones had ridden into Leitchfield where they "appropriated a quantity of boots and shoes and whiskey, but left without doing much damage."[22]

By the 8th some 45 to 50 guerrillas, allegedly under Quantrill, Mundy and Magruder, killed three men from the 13th Kentucky at New Market and took four others to Bradfordsville, Marion County, where they murdered them.[23] During a desperate fight at Bradfordsville the guerrillas charged Major Thomas Mahoney's "Invalid Corps" and then rode off in the direction of Hustonville. At Hustonville the guerrillas captured a wagon train of five teams. Guerrilla Allen Parmer who would later become Frank James' brother-in-law (he married Susan Lavenia James), killed a Union Major. The officer grabbed the bridle of Parmer's horse during the fight. Parmer coldly placed his revolver against the Major's forehead and fired, "ripping off half the top of the Federal's head." [24]

Quantrill and "about fifty men," were spotted around 10:00 a.m. at Saint Mary's station in Marion County moving toward Campbellsville.[25] Guerrillas, including Frank James, Henry Magruder, Bud Pence, John Ross and William Hulse, were involved in an attack on the road leading from Lebanon to Campbellsville in Taylor County.[26]

After several days the Federals recovered their balance and were soon in hot pursuit. Initially, the Federals attempted to concentrate forces by moving detachments from the various regions; they failed, and gaps in the lines allowed the guerrillas easy escape routes. Reports sent from Lexington indicate that the Federal "master plan" called for corralling the raiders in the area of Danville. As the net tightened south of Danville the gaps were closed and the remaining guerrillas were caught in the trap.

At 2:00 a.m. on February 9th, after a harried and difficult chase, Captain Jim Bridgewater finally "smashed up" the guerrillas at the "Little South Fork west of Hustonville" in northern Casey County. Four guerrillas were killed and 35 horses were captured, but Quantrill and the rest of the band escaped "barefooted" into the woods. Seven guerrillas escaped on horseback fleeing in the direction of Parksville or Haysville. Three more men were captured in the woods and another was killed when he tried to escape.[27]

Detachments from Stanford, Crab Orchard, Campbellsville, Columbia, Danville, Lebanon, and Lawrenceburg scouted the area south of Parksville and captured three of Quantrill's men in the woods near Hustonville; the guerrillas were later taken to Danville.[28] In order to return to Nelson County the remaining guerrillas split up into small groups and took to the bush with every man for himself. Eventually most of the guerrillas regrouped in Nelson County.

By the afternoon of the 11th the guerrillas had again returned to the Midway area near Woodburn Farm. Quantrill had backtracked to Woodburn to try to avoid another fight with the Federals, so therefore little action was reported around Woodburn Farm and the vicinity until the guerrillas were spotted again. General Hobson ordered Major John Clowney at Frankfort to send a courier to Lawrenceburg and notify the Commanding Officer there that "200 guerrillas were reported at Alexander's farm near Midway," although there is no evidence to suggest that the guerrillas ever trespassed on Woodburn. Hobson ordered the Lawrenceburg commander to cooperate with detachments from Lexington and hunt for the guerrillas.[29]

On Saturday night, February 15, there was a skirmish between Captain Bates's Home Guards and a band of guerrillas said to have been part of General Lyon's command. The guerrillas were routed, leaving six men dead, while Bates' command suffered minimal losses: With one killed and one wounded.[30] The February 25 edition of *Spirit of the Times* reported the recovery of several of Woodburn's stolen horses:

> "Seven have been recovered. Abdallah was recaptured, but has since died. Bay Chief was recovered but died from his wounds....Nannie Butler was the only thoroughbred that was among those that have been returned, Norwich has not yet been recovered."[31]

Details of the raid were published by several newspapers, but failed to describe the poignancy and the pathos of the raid both for Alexander and his household.

In a lengthy letter R.A. painstakingly wrote this account of the recovery of three mares and Norwich by Zach Henry. Henry, who had helped Warren Viley with the recovery of Asteroid after the October 22, 1864 raid, was considered a friend by Alexander. This account, however opens numerous doors of speculation concerning Henry's motives and integrity, his cousin's role in the raid and what part, if any, Zach Henry played in either of the two raids. Since nothing can be proven, the complete account is provided:

> "On the following Monday, Court Day at Versailles, I went to Versailles thinking to be able to induce some of the citizens to join in an organization to defend our doors from such robbers. Whilst there Mr. Warren Viley came to me & said that a certain person who did not wish his name mentioned wishes to know what I would give to get back the brother of Norfolk. I said to him that if the horse could be captured from the scoundrels who took him I would give $1000 for his recovery, but I would not give a cent if the money was to go to thieves. Mr. Viley afterwards informed me that the man who made the inquiry as to what I would give was Zac Henry[,] but that when he went to look for him to tell him what I said[,] he could not find him & so he did not inform him as to my answer to his question. I learned afterwards that Henry[,] hearing that a cousin of his was one of the band who robbed me was badly wounded at Mr. Bush's farm in Anderson Co[.] near the river[,] had gone[.] He had set off in a hurry to see him as he believed he could learn through him where the rest of the band were likely to be

found and could thus get back the horse Norwich (brother to Norfolk) for which he hoped & expected to be paid. I also learned that Z. Henry spent some time with his cousin from whom he gained all the information he desired which enabled him to find the guerrilla band to whom he gave full information as to Henry[,] his cousin[,] whom they rescued a few nights after through this information. Whilst Henry was gone I had a visit from some old gentleman Squire E.H. McKay of Bloomfield who informed me that Capt. Clark[e] [Quantrill] a Confederate officer, through a friend of his (who was a Southern sympathizer) had requested him to come to me, whom he (Clark[e]) supposed to be a man of wealth and influence & request of me to use my influence to save the lives of some of his (Clark[e]'s) men who had been captured by the Federal soldiers & who he feared might be hung as guerrillas. I told Mr. McKay that I could not do anything in the matter that I was here respected by the Federal and Confederate authorities as a British subject & all that I could do would be to see that these men had legal advice. Mr. McKay said that Capt. Clark[e] had stated to him that some of his men were with the guerrillas that made the raid on me; that he had been obliged to let them go to keep on good terms with the guerrillas who knowing the country could aid him in eluding the Federals. That he had in his possession two mares belonging to me & that he intended restoring them to me & that he much regretted that he had even allowed his men to accompany so lawless a band as the one that made this raid & added that he could send the 2 mares to Louisville. I gave him (McKay) directions as to sending them & he returned home. I afterwards heard from McKay that Capt. Clark[e] had handed over the mares to a man who stated that he was looking up my stock. Zac Henry returned a few days later afterward bringing the two mares & stated that a third was at a certain point but to lame to be brought back; that he had got these three mares by promising to replace them & that Capt. Clark[e] stated that he must have a saddle in addition with 3 others. I had two horses left at my place by the guerrillas and bought a mare from Z[.] Henry to make the three horses and furnished a saddle which he took off & returned with the lame mare soon after[,] but stated that he could hear nothing of the brother to Norfolk about 16 Feby[.] After his return from his first trip I paid Z. H. $100 for expenses as he said he was out of money and intended going back to try and get some of the stolen horses and seemed confident that he would be able to get Norwich. Some time after his return from his first or second trip to Nelson Co. he came to me and showed me a letter he had received from Capt. Clark[e] (the Confederate officer who had written to me about his men and who handed over to [me] the two mares promised me & a third that was lame at the time) stating that a mare belonging to me had been left at certain point in Clark Co[.] & could be had if I sent for him, he added that she had been injured in a hind leg. I sent my herdsman for the mare a few days after & got her."[32]

Alexander's lengthy description of the events of the final raid in his letter to Henry Charles Deedes leaves little doubt that the raid had a devastating effect from which he never fully recovered:

"...I have become careless in almost everything that requires exertion. Ill health and the condition of affairs in Kentucky had so depressing affect on me that I feel little interest in any sort of business and unless I am obliged to attend to it I generally try and trust the duty to someone else."[33]

The horses represented a large investment and their loss resulted in a financial setback. Bay Chief, the horse Quantrill had demanded, was by Alexander's account worth at least fifteen thousand dollars and thus represented his greatest single loss. This was the price he had paid for Lexington. Alexander later stated: "[Bay Chief] was worth fully as much as any horse I own except Lexington himself....I doubt if I would have touched fifteen thousand dollars in greenbacks for him."[34] Had Bay Chief lived the number of descendants of Mambrino Chief with standard records would doubtless have been considerably larger.[35]

Abdallah 15 was the second most valuable trotting stallion taken and recovered at Lawrenceburg, but died only days later in the stable where he had been found. There are several accounts about Abdallah's death, and it still has not been determined from the surviving accounts what happened. Therefore, all the accounts must be considered, since some of the information in each story is true. Although it is not known how Alexander came about the information about the death of Abdallah or who told him the story, Alexander mentions in a letter that "a Federal soldier rode him to death." Since the guerrillas had been dressed in Federal uniforms at the time of the raid, however, a guerrilla could have been mistaken for a Federal soldier. One account states that Abdallah was recaptured after his physical condition had deteriorated beyond repair. In this account, the raider refused to give him up unless Abdallah was ransomed, but was forced finally to abandon him alongside the road.[36]

The most factual account states that Abdallah and Bay Chief and the other Woodburn horses were involved in the fight in Anderson County with the Woodford County Home Guards. To make his escape, Abdallah's rider forced the hot and steamy horse to swim across an icy river. Abdallah was ridden as far as Lawrenceburg, just south of Frankfort and approximately 16 miles from Woodburn, where he finally gave out and could travel no further. Mr. Hull was quoted as saying that Abdallah "was left in a deplorable condition...in a barn where there were 16 other horses exhausted from being over ridden."[37] This account supports evidence that Abdallah was discovered with other horses in a barn and not by the roadside as other writers have claimed.[38] When he was found Abdallah's hooves were bruised and bleeding, but he might have recovered if he had not been so hot when he swam across the river. Pneumonia set in and he died on February 6, 1865 in "Mr. Bush's barn" where he had been found.[39] He was 13 years old.[40] Abdallah's death was one of the "heaviest losses the breed of American trotter ever sustained. Despite his tragic early death his blood is carried today by the majority of our best harness race horses."[41] Abdallah was the "founder of one of the very greatest of the Hambletonian sub-families, and he stands in the records as a progenitor of the first rank."[42] He epitomizes the best stallions this country has produced and his needless loss was a great tragedy.[43] Abdallah was "one of the most prepotent males that the standard breed has ever produced, a victim of the horrors of war."[44]

According to Alexander, the third most valuable horse taken was the bay gelding Norwich by Lexington, whose dam, Novice, was by Glencoe.[45] R.A. wrote in his letter on March 4 that, "...[Norwich] was still in the hands of the guerrillas when I last heard from home."[46] The March 18 edition of *Wilkes' Spirit of the Times* published the news of Alexander's departure for Illinois and noted that Alexander "has heard of Norwich but [has] not recovered [him]. Said to be hid away in Anderson County."[47] Norwich was finally recovered on June 3 at Shelbyville.[48] The recovery again involved Zach Henry, but the following letter indicates that this time R.A. understood that Henry was just trying to get money from him. This incident probably changed their friendship. According to R.A.:

> "In passing through Louisville on my way home from St. Louis on 1st June following (1865) I heard from Mr. Avery of Louisville that my horse Norwich had been captured by Capt. [Edward] Terrell & was at Shelbyville[.] I got him the following day & found that D. Swigert[,] having heard of the capture of the horse[,] had set off at once & soon after my arrival Swigert and Terrell arrived bringing the horse. I paid Terrell $500 for capturing & returning the horse to me[.] At the Louisville races in the Spring Zac Henry comes to me & said that he would like a little money[;] I did not quite understand his way of asking for money & said do you wish me to lend you some? [H]e said, 'no, you owe me some;' I asked for what,[.] [H]e answered, 'for getting back your horse[.]' [R.A. thought Asteroid?]. I told him that I thought I had paid well for all the horses that I got back; he said, 'I owed him for the horse[,] Norwich[.]' As the horse never would have been got back had he not exerted himself in the matter; that through his influence his cousin, a guerrilla Tom Henry[,] had traded with [the guerrilla Ben] Froman & got the horse & through Tom Henry's capture[,] Terrell had got hold of him. I told him I had paid Terrell for capturing the horse & that I did not think anyone else had any claim[.] Henry then urged that he understood that I had offered to pay $1000 for the return of this horse & that I had paid Terrell but $500. I should pay him the balance[.] I told him

that this was ridiculous; that if he had attempted to get the horse for the reward he had failed & having had his expenses paid was more than he had a right to expect."[49]

On March 4th R.A. estimated that "six horses and mares are still missing including two which are dead and their value is not less than $32,000."[50]

Nannie Butler was a bay thoroughbred filly, foaled 1861, by Lexington, dam, Tokey by Yorkshire.[51] According to Daniel Swigert's *1864 Woodburn Stud Farm Catalogue*, Nannie Butler had been sold for $3,500, but remained on the farm.[52] By March 18 Nannie Butler had been recovered.[53] She was part of R.A.'s 1866 racing stable.

Another stolen horse was Lindora's 1862 unnamed brown colt, by Star Davis, by imported Glencoe, dam, Margret Wood by imported Priam; a runner. Lindora's breeding record establishes that this 1862 colt was not recovered from the guerrillas after the raid and Keeneland Association Library has no name for this colt which indicates that he never raced. Therefore, it is safe to say that the colt was not recovered and one of the raiders ended up with him.

R.A. did not own the stallion Star Davis, but Woodburn records indicate that Star Davis bred several Woodburn mares. In a listing of the foundation broodmares several are by Star Davis. According to the *1860 Woodburn Catalogue* Alexander bred Star Davis, a thoroughbred, to his trotting stock. Star Davis, foaled in 1849, was owned and bred by John M. Clay, son of U.S. Senator Henry Clay, and may have been a war refugee. He was the sire of Day Star, winner of the 1878 Kentucky Derby.[54] He died in December of 1876 and was buried at Clay's Ashland Stud.[55]

Darkness, a.k.a. "Big Black" and "Woodburn American," was foaled in 1858. He was a black stallion by Mambrino Chief 11, out of Black Rose, by Tom Teemer. Darkness was a trotter with a best time of 2:40 and was recaptured and became a trotting mate of Jessie Wales whose best time was 2:30 and Jessie Wales' race records mention Darkness.[56] Darkness participated in the great Double Team Trot (Darkness and Jesse Wales versus Honest Allen, son of Ethan Allen 50, and Kirkwood, captured in the Currier & Ives print of which the author has a copy), and was a three-quarter brother to Bay Chief.

EDWIN FORREST/FRANK JAMES CONTROVERSY

Another horse which may have been taken and recovered was Edwin Forrest, although a thorough investigation of available documentation cannot substantiate this as fact. It has long been a popular belief that Edwin Forrest was taken by Frank James during the raid. At the intersection of the Old Frankfort Pike and Highway 62, (the Midway Road), stands an old, white, wooden-and-brick structure called the "Black Horse Tavern," which was later sold to Frank Harper of Nantura Farm. The birth of Zerelda (Cole) James, mother of Frank and

Jesse James, in this house had a significant influence on events that occurred in this area during the Civil War. Stories from his mother provided Frank James with knowledge about the terrain, the location of towns and farms and names of prominent people of the region. During the Civil War Frank James visited this countryside where his mother was born.[57] Frank's knowledge of the area undoubtedly proved to be very useful to the guerrillas and gave them an indisputable advantage over the uninformed Federal soldiers chasing them.

There is no question that Frank James participated in the second raid at Woodburn, but whether Edwin Forrest was taken remains a point of contention between historians. Although there is a published newspaper article claiming that Edwin Forrest was taken in the raid, there is no mention in Alexander's account of the raid that the stallion was taken nor any account of his recapture.

There is, however, a caption on a print of a painting of the stallion by Edward Troye which states that Frank James acquired the horse "as a result of a raid on Woodburn in early 1865 by elements of Quantrill's guerrillas and rode him [as his personal mount] for many years afterward."[58] The latter part of the caption is an unusual claim since the horse was a trotter. It may be true that Frank James owned a horse named Edwin Forrest, but there is too much contradictory evidence to validate any claim that Frank owned or rode Alexander's Edwin Forrest 49. The *American Stallion Register* listed nine horses with the name of Edwin Forrest living between 1827 and 1871. Six were sons of Alexander's Edwin Forrest.[59]

An absurd account of the recovery of the horses is one that appeared on April 29, 1874 in *The Louisville Courier-Journal*. It suggests that Quantrill sent the "sixteen" stolen horses back to Alexander whereupon Alexander, "presented him [Quantrill] with a fine horse and Frank James with Ed Forrest as a present."[60] Quantrill (Capt. Clarke) negotiated for the recovery of two mares at Louisville and one other who was so lame she had to be retrieved later. Alexander had to exchange horses to get the three mares back.[61] Mr. Alexander did not, nor would he have ever "given" Edwin Forrest away to anyone, let alone Frank James!

One cannot extrapolate from the simple fact that Frank James participated in the raid and may have owned an "Edwin Forrest" that Frank took the stallion from Woodburn for his personal mount. If Alexander's Edwin Forrest was taken, he would had been recaptured with the other horses at Lawrenceburg. Documents prove that he was sent to Montgomery, Illinois, where he stood from April 29 to September 27, 1865, for a stud fee of $20.[62]

Edwin Forrest was brought back to Woodburn in the fall of 1865. Dr. A.J. Alexander possesses a receipt for a stud fee to Edwin Forrest at Woodburn dated 1867 and a stud book which shows that Edwin Forrest last serviced a mare at Woodburn on July 16, 1867. This indicates that Edwin Forrest remained at Woodburn for that season.[63]

In 1868 Edwin Forrest was sold to W.H. Sample for the Keokuk, Iowa Stock Breeding

Offut-Cole Tavern, historical road marker, at intersection of Old Frankfort Pike and Midway-Versailles Road.

Photographs by William P. Magnum II.

Frank James, circa 1870s, participated in the February 2 raid; there is some question if he did in fact ride Edwin Forrest off Woodburn Farm that evening.

Kentucky Historical Society

Association and later sold to G.W. Furguson.[64] In 1874, Edwin Forrest burned to death in a stable fire at Marshalltown, Iowa. The *American Stallion Register* gives Edwin Forrest's death as 1883.[65]

Alexander's losses were not as great as they might have been since Lexington, who eventually "led the American sire list an unsurpassed 16 times and stands with Stockwell and St. Simon in England as the greatest stallion in the nineteenth century," had been spared.[66] If the raiders had: "chanced to loot the thoroughbred stable and not the trotting stables, it might have been Lexington and Australian instead of Abdallah and Bay Chief that perished—a loss that would have staggered computation."[67]

Lexington had become blind by 1856 and this saved the great stallion from the raiders. A blind horse would have been useless to guerrillas looking for fast horses. A January 2, 1864 article in *Wilkes'*, however, revealed that Lexington was not as handicapped as one might believe:

> "...the old horse is in magnificent order. He was frisking about in his paddock like a colt, throwing up his head and coming to a sudden stop within ten feet of a tree, when he came near one. As he is quite blind, it is the exquisite sense of smell which enables Lexington to discover when he nears the trees in his gambols."[68]

Even though Alexander had escaped the war with considerably more for which to be thankful than most southerners, the deaths of Abdallah and Bay Chief represented not just a pecuniary loss, but also the loss of two great breeding stallions. We can agree, however, with Alexander when he observed: "we can console ourselves with the idea that it might have been far worse."[69] One optimistic note is that the colt, Monroe Chief, record of 2:18 1/4 in 1882, a son of Abdallah, out of a daughter of Bay Chief, "united the blood of the two great [stallions] that perished in the guerrilla raid upon Woodburn Farm in 1865."[70] This final raid would prove to have a great influence on R.A. in the brief years to come. See Chapter 14 for Frank James' career in the racing industry.

Airdrie Mill in Montgomery, Illinois, bought by R. A. Alexander on March 3, 1863, for $26,000. His trotters were moved to Illinois in February 1865.

Photograph by William P. Mangum II

The Black Hawk Mill on the Fox River in Aurora, Illinois, 1859-1860. The mill was purchased by R. A. Alexander prior to moving his horses to Illinois to protect them from guerrilla raids in Kentucky.

Aurora Historical Society

CHAPTER NINE

Secret Sanctuary for the Horses

There can be little doubt that the mistreatment of his horses upset Alexander as much, if not more, than his financial losses. He was so distressed that he immediately decided to move his remaining stock to Illinois and Ohio. In March R.A. felt compelled to explain to Henry Deedes the circumstances surrounding the raids and his reasons for moving the horses.[1] In his letter to Deedes, R.A. gave a description of the raid and authorization to mobilize his financial investments and assets in Great Britain. He described the necessity to free some funds from his holdings there, which was complicated by his loss of confidence in his English representative, an attorney named Melville. R.A. badly needed the money to defray the costs of moving his most valuable horses from Woodburn and to maintain his stock in four separate locations.

Alexander's decision to choose Illinois as a safe haven for his horses was based in part on the fact that he owned land and two flour mills there, Black Hawk in Aurora and the Airdrie Mill in Montgomery, both on the Fox River. These properties would provide the basic needs for the horses. On March 3, 1863, R.A. purchased the Daniel S. Gray-Watkins flour mill, which he later renamed "Airdrie Mill," from Vine A. Watkins, Catharine Watkins, Amelia Gray, Agnes Gray and Margaret Gray for the sum of $26,000.[2] The mill was located in Montgomery, two miles south of Aurora in Kane County and about 40 miles from Chicago on the Burlington and Quincy Railroad. On November 18, 1864, R.A. purchased the land directly across the river from Airdrie Mill, known today as Montgomery Park, for the sum of $3,300 to use as a temporary farm.[3]

During the month of February, 1865, Alexander sent Pilot Jr. and 42 head of trotting breeding stock to Montgomery.[4] He shipped the horses secretly by night on the Louisville & Nashville Railway from Spring Station, located one and a quarter miles from Woodburn Farm.[5] Upon arrival, the horses were unloaded at the depot, led down Mill Street, a direct route from the railroad depot to the bridge, past Airdrie Mill, across the Fox River and onto the farm.[6]

The Fox River which runs through Montgomery and Aurora, Illinois. The horses were led from the railroad across the bridge and onto Alexander's land at right.

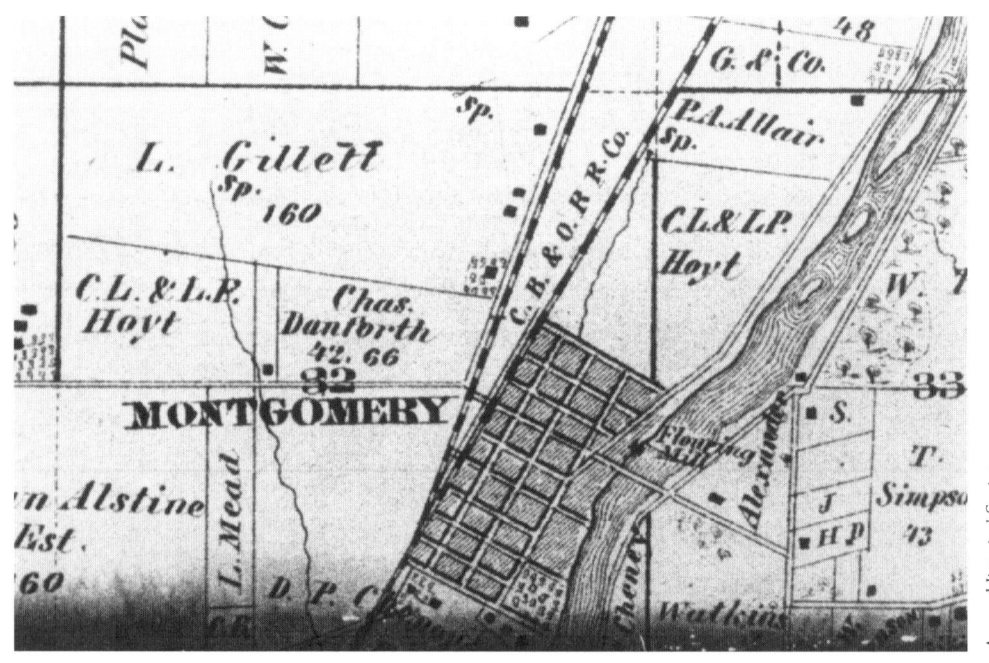

Map of Montgomery, Illinois showing the Airdrie "Flouring Mill" and Alexander's property across the Fox River.

On April 30 Alexander shipped Lexington, Australian and 48 to 50 of his best thoroughbred breeding stock to a farm near Williamsville, Illinois, in Sangamon County, north of Springfield. According to R.A.'s diary, in September 1861 he traveled to Chicago to survey several pieces of property. It is believed that he rented land from T.G. Taylor, (to date no deed or contract has been found), or kept the horses in a large barn near the old depot in Williamsville which is no longer standing.[7]

According to one published story, Lexington was unwilling to board the stock car at Spring Station:

> "All the stock had been loaded except Lexington. Blind since the end of his racing career, [he] was never known for his good temperament. The stallion refused to enter the train on his own accord, and slaves finally had to surround the raging, screaming stallion and literally lift him into the boxcar."[8]

Also on the 30th Alexander shipped the trotting broodmares, Black Rose, Madam Dudley and Gray Goose, to Montgomery. On May 2nd he sent three more thoroughbred broodmares to Montgomery. Alexander moved over 100 horses in all to Illinois, his racing string to the Buckeye Race Track in Cincinnati, Ohio, and yet another group of horses to "maternal relatives who lived in that state," which left only his less valuable horses and young stock at Woodburn.[9] See Appendix for horses moved to Illinois.

Black Rose appears on this list, but according to a record journal titled, "Trotting Foals from 1859 to 1869 Inclusive," Black Rose is listed as foaling a "bay filly, large star, left fore and hind ankle white" on February 24, 1865. This would indicate that she foaled at Woodburn and was moved to Montgomery with the foal at her side.[10]

The runners sent to Cincinnati included Asteroid, Asterick, Bay Flower, Ansel, Bay Dick, Netty Viley, Merrill, Lancaster, Norway and others which made up Alexander's racing string for the summer of 1865. He continued to race his stable throughout the 1865 season (from May to October). These race horses, as listed in the *1865 Racing Calendar*, appeared at tracks in St. Louis, Missouri; Louisville, Kentucky; Cincinnati, Ohio; Paterson, New Jersey; and Lexington, Kentucky. Alexander ended his racing season for the year at Louisville with a string of 16 horses led by Asteroid.[11]

Alexander suffered another poignant loss indirectly connected to the raid when the great gray trotting stallion, Pilot Jr., by Old Pilot out of Nancy Pope, by Havoc, the grandson of Sir Archy, died of hemorrhaging due to the rupture of cerebral blood vessels, called apoplexy.[12] Pilot Jr. died on April 14, 1865 at the age of 21, having been moved from Woodburn to Montgomery, Illinois. His name occupies a prominent place in the trotting horse history and the blood of this outstanding horse held great sway in helping to develop the trotting horse breed.[13] Others of his get include John Morgan, known as Medoc,

"Montgomery Park" the land across the Fox River from the Airdrie Mill where the trotting stock were moved to in 1865. Alexander bought the land on November 18, 1864 for $3,300.

Small house across from "Montgomery Park." The house is believed to have been also purchased by Alexander, because it is shown on the map of Montgomery, Illinois.

The old railway station at Williamsville, Illinois, where Alexander's thoroughbreds were brought in May 1865. The horses were likely unloaded here.

Photographs by William P. Mangum II

2:24, and Bayard, 2:31 3/4, whose dam was Bay York.[14] He was a great sire and got eight trotters (from 2:30 to 2:24) and his death was a great loss to the Woodburn Trotting Stud.

The gray thoroughbred, Nebula, ranked as one of the "best of Woodburn's broodmares," also became a victim. Nebula, by Glencoe out of Sue Lewis, was foaled in 1852. She foaled the gray colt, Hotspur by Lexington on March 29, 1865. Injured during transport from Kentucky to Illinois, she died from the effects of this injury; her death was a great personal loss to R.A.[15] See Chapter 5, "Colonel Jack" P. Chinn.

In reference to Abdallah 15, turf historian, John Hervey criticized R.A. Alexander when he stated:

"the lack of foresight of his owner, who after the tragedy sent all of his most valuable animals out of state into Ohio and Illinois, locking the stable door after the horse had been stolen."[16]

Hervey's criticism was a narrow view and opinion and did not take into consideration the strenuous task of preparing the farms to receive the horses nor the inherent difficulties of transporting stock by train during war time. All of the horses could have easily been confiscated by the Federal army in route to Ohio and Illinois.

It is not known exactly how or when Alexander's horses were returned from Illinois and Ohio to Woodburn Farm, but it is generally believed that most of the breeding stock were returned in mid to late August of that year. In a letter from R.A. to his brother, Alec, dated August 5th, R.A. stated:

"Dan [Swigert] left for Williamsville to bring back some of my stock. He was delayed some days by the illness of his little boy...."[17]

One can surmise that they returned by train in the same manner that they had traveled to Illinois. Edwin Forrest, however, was not returned until after September.[18] A letter to the editor of *The Turf, Field and Farm* who listed his name simply as "Horsey," reported that he had visited Woodburn Farm "the other day" and had seen Lexington, Australian and Asteroid which indicates that all the horses had returned home by November 1865.[19]

Alexander had done everything in his power to protect his horses and the fact that he saved as many as he did is greatly to his credit. Although outlaw bands of ex-guerrillas still existed, Alexander did not apparently fear future raids. He no doubt considered that winter was approaching and wished to move the horses home before the first snow. In an article on June 24, 1865, *Wilkes' Spirit of the Times* summarized the four years of hardship by simply stating that, "Kentucky had been severely shaken by the War and needs repose."[20]

Near the end and shortly after the War R.A. traveled extensively throughout the North. In March, he traveled to Chicago where he met his brother-in-law, James Breckinridge Waller, his sister, Lucy, and his brother, A.J., who lived there. By April he

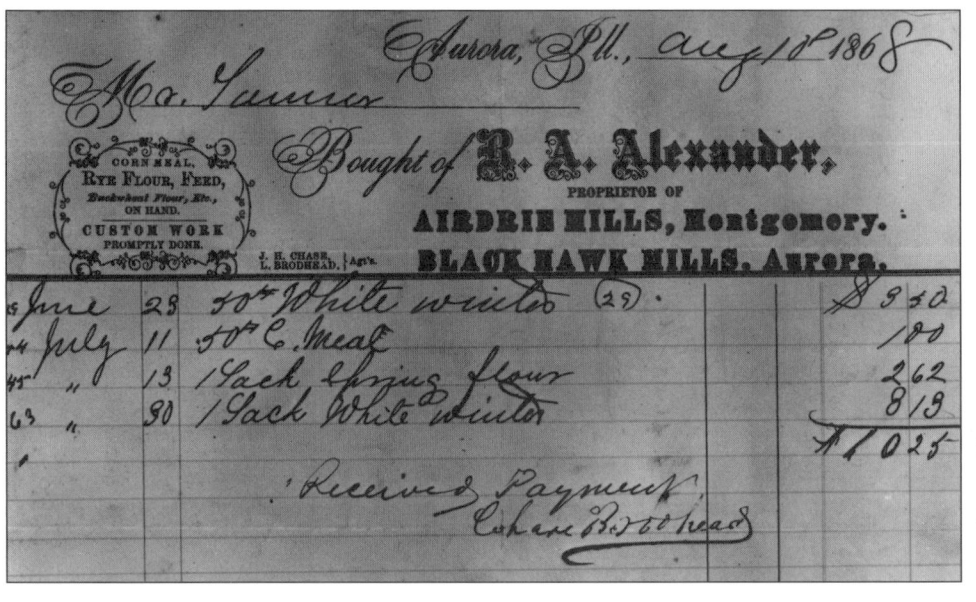

Receipt for Airdrie Mills, Montgomery, Black Hawk Mills, Aurora, Illinois, dated August 1868 showing the proprietor as R. A. Alexander and the two mills incorporated.

apparently made a decision to sell some of his best horses. The raids had been too costly; he was watching his dream die before him.

News of the sale was chronicled by the *Wilkes' Spirit of the Times* on April 15 and also appeared in the August 5 edition and again in the September 23 edition of Sanders D. Bruce's *Turf, Field and Farm*.[21] It appears that the advertisement was only placed in sporting newspapers since a thorough search of *The Chicago Tribune* and *The New York Times* failed to uncover any advertisements of this sale. The advertisement read:

"Proposed sale of Alexander's horses. Horses for sale: Lexington, Scythian, Australian, Pilot, Jr., Edwin Forrest and others. Thoroughbred stock are at Williamsville, Sangamon County, Illinois. Trotting stock are at Montgomery, Illinois. Horses in training are at the Cincinnati Track."[22] It is a mystery why this ad even appeared at all since none of the stallions advertised were ever sold.

R.A. did, however, advertise a sale at Woodburn in 1866 which included his:

"entire lot of thoroughbred foals of 1865, being twenty-five head, mostly by Lexington, many of them out of tried mares. Also 40 trotting brood mares, a portion of them thoroughbreds. Also all my trotting horses, except my yearlings and a few kept for breeding purposes," but it did not include any of his stallions.[23]

> A LARGE NUMBER OF THOROUGH-BRED AND TROTTING HORSES FOR SALE.
> The unsettled condition of Kentucky having compelled me to remove from thence, I now offer at private sale all my horse stock, consisting of Stallions, Brood Mares, horses in training, and young stock.
> The Stallions include Lexington, Scythian, Australian, Pilot, Jr., Edwin Forrest, and others.
> The Brood Mares embrace some of the most noted Mares in the United States. Among them are the dam of Norfolk, with foal by her side; the dam of Asteroid, with foal by her side; also the dam of Bay Flower and Beacon, with foal by her side; the dam of Maiden, with foal by her side; dam of Florida and Rhinodine; dam of Mollie Jackson; dam of Thunder and Lightning; dam of Mammona and Magenta, and many others, bred and to be bred to Lexington, Australian, and Scythian.
> Also Idlewild, Asteroid, and several brothers to Norfolk, Asteroid, and Bay Flower.
> The horses in training are at the Cincinnati track, the thoroughbred brood stock are at Williamsville, Sangamon County, Ill., and the trotting brood stock are now at Montgomery, about forty miles from Chicago, on the Burlington and Quincy Railway.
> The young stock are still on my farm in Kentucky. Any one desiring to purchase any of the above-named stock may address D. SWIGERT, Williamsville, Sangamon County, Ill., or to the undersigned, care of Waller & Co., Chicago, Ill.
> R. AITCHESON ALEXANDER.

Advertisement that appeared for the sale of Alexander's horses in 1865 when the valuable horses were removed from Woodburn.

A much repeated story that allegedly occurred about this time concerned Napoleon Belland Jr. and his accomplishments that "helped save Woodburn." The story originated in an interview between the elderly Belland and John Hervey and was later reprinted in Hervey's book, *Racing in America, 1830-1865*. There are numerous errors throughout the 1921 interview and many claims by Belland that are simply not true. Documentation from the archives of Keeneland Association Library invalidates many of Belland's statements:[24]

a) Belland claimed that he rode Thunder, son of Lexington out of Blue Bonnet, at Paterson, N.J., in 1862 and beat the Woodburn mare, Bayflower, ridden by Gilpatrick, in the three mile heat. Bayflower never ran at Paterson, N.J. Thunder did not run at Paterson, N.J., in 1862, but did race there in 1863. He was ridden, however, by E. Rafferty in both races. Thunder did run against Bayflower in two races but at St. Louis in 1864, placing third in each race.[25]

b) Belland claimed that Jacob Pincus was at Woodburn in 1862, but Pincus started training for Alexander in 1866.[26]

c) Belland stated that he raced Leatherlungs who was owned by August Belmont, but in fact, although Leatherlungs was owned by several different people including J.W. Weldon, Bowie & Hall and C.F. Elwes, he was never owned during his racing career by August Belmont.[27]

Napoleon Belland Jr. was the son of the famous French jockey, who had been brought to New York by Richard Ten Broeck after seeing him race in England. Belland Jr. arrived with his father in New York in 1856 still "in knee britches." Belland Sr. had met R.A. Alexander at the sale of Lexington in 1856 and in 1858, R.A. persuaded the father to allow the young Belland to come to Woodburn as an "exercise lad" where he remained for "four years, except in winters, when he returned to New York to attend school."[28] According to Belland Jr.:

"The breaking out of the Civil War naturally had a very bad effect upon Woodburn. Things became so precarious that Mr. Alexander decided it would be unsafe to keep all his horses there, where they would be exposed to pillage and confiscation, so he sent a large draft of them to his brother who was living at Montgomery...and these horses were kept in Illinois two or three years; three at least, I think, for it was in 1862 they were sent there and they did not return until hostilities had ceased in 1865. Having sent the best of his breeding stock to Illinois, R.A. Alexander finally decided to send a lot of young stock to Canada in my charge.... Also a large part of the population up there were of French blood and spoke French, which I still spoke better than I did English. So in the late fall of 1862 I left Woodburn with two carloads of thoroughbreds, thirty-four horses in all.... As you know, the Civil War did not close until the spring of 1865, and my Canadian trip lasted no less than three and [a] half years. I did not meet Mr. Alexander again until in the spring of 1866 in New York City and during that time I had little communication with him.... During all that time no settlement of any kind had taken place between Mr. Alexander and myself and he knew little of how I fared.... Several of the horses had died, but all but three of the others I had sold, as a rule for high prices. I had raced many of them,...they almost always won. You can imagine his astonishment when I turned to him something over $300,000; my memory is not exact as to the sum, but I think it was $334,000.... He said to me, 'You have saved Woodburn Farm. The war has almost ruined me and I was nearly out of funds. This will put me on my feet again!'"[29]

It is hard to believe that R.A. Alexander, being a prudent business man, would just turn over 34 of his valuable racing stock to a young man whose only known skill was that of an exercise rider. It is even more difficult to believe that he would then allow him to leave the country to race and sell the horses without regular communication or monetary reports.

Obviously, Belland was also confused about the dates concerning the move to Illinois, since documentation verifies that the move took place in 1865. If Belland left Woodburn in 1862 and had little communication with R.A. during the time that he was gone, he would not know what took place at Woodburn Farm after that date. Belland, probably heard about the move after the fact, and probably assumed that the event took place after his departure in 1862 and that the horses remained in Illinois until the end of the war.

Belland also stated in the same interview that he was "riding for Mr. or Sir Roderick Cameron at the time he imported Glenelg, the colt then being in the belly of his dam, Babta." Therefore, Belland must have been riding for Cameron in 1865, since Glenelg was foaled in 1866. If he was riding for Cameron in 1865, he could not have been in Canada racing for Alexander.

Although there were no names of horses mentioned in the 1921 interview, Hervey said in his book *Racing in America, 1830-1865* that the stallion, Ruric, was among this group.[30] Ruric was bred and raised by W.A. Dudley and was foaled on May 24, 1853, by imported Sovereign. Ruric was purchased from W.A. Dudley by R.A. Alexander in 1857 for $5,000.[31] The June 17, 1863 *Woodburn Stud Farm Sale Catalogue* listed several mares, Dolly, Belle Lewis, Charlotte Buford, Ada Cheatham and Brunette as either "with foal by Ruric" or "stinted to Ruric" which indicates that Ruric was at Woodburn Farm in Spring 1863. The *1867 Woodburn Stud Farm Sale Catalogue* provided further documentation concerning Ruric's location in 1864 when it listed the bay colt foaled 1865, "by Ruric" and another "trotting filly, foaled 1865, got by Ruric." It is evident by these records that Ruric was at Woodburn during the time he was claimed to be in Canada with Napoleon Belland Jr.[32]

Sue Mundy after his capture on March 11, 1865. He was hanged in Louisville on the afternoon of March 15, 1865, before a crowd of 10,000 spectators.

CHAPTER TEN

The Fate of the Raiders

The *War of the Rebellion Records* reveal the fate of Sue Mundy and the other raiders involved in the Woodburn Farm raid. Sue Mundy remained with Henry Magruder throughout February, and had teamed up with guerrilla Henry Metcalf by the end of the month. The three men regrouped their bands and then traveled together as far as somewhere near Brandenburg in Meade County where they separated.

On February 18 Major Charles B. Leavitt, 12th U.S. Colored Heavy Artillery at Colesburg, reported to General Hugh Ewing at Louisville that Fort Jones was under attack and that he could "hear the artillery." Major Leavitt took six 60 men to reinforce the fort and rode to Lebanon Junction. He later reported that Magruder's band, numbering 31 men, came within three-quarters of a mile of Colesburg, and killed three of his men who were on their way from Fort Jones to draw rations. Major Leavitt also reported that Sue Mundy's men, some 60 in number, came within 200 yards of the fort. Another guerrilla force was reported west of Lebanon Junction where they had robbed a number of citizens.[1]

By February 28 Sue Mundy's guerrillas, accompanied by some of Quantrill's men, had moved back to the Mississippi River.[2] They pillaged and burned part of Hickman, Kentucky, in Fulton County, a town located directly on the river.[3] These guerrillas included Frank James and Donnie Pence. The two were later involved in a skirmish at Bewleyville near Stephensport in Meade County, where Frank saved Donnie Pence's life.[4] Mundy, however, was not among them, because he had separated from the band earlier. *The Chicago Daily Tribune* reported that on the morning of February 29 Major Hamilton's command from Hawesville and Clay's command from Cloverport had "routed Davison and Magruder's guerrilla band" near Hawesville. The article claims that they had captured Davison and wounded Magruder, although this fact was never verified.[5]

This historical highway marker tells where Quantrill was mortally wounded on May 10, 1865.

On March 3 a small group of guerrillas were ambushed in Hancock County by the Home Guard. Major Sam Jones was killed and Henry Magruder severely wounded in the left lung and shoulder. Sue Mundy and Henry Metcalf, who had joined the guerrillas at Brandenburg prior to the skirmish, managed to escape with the wounded Magruder. The party made their way to the home of Dr. Lewis, who for several days attended Magruder's wounds. On Monday evening, March 6, approximately 20 unknown guerrillas attempted to make an incursion into Brandenburg, but were repulsed by Federal troops stationed there.[6]

On March 9 a skirmish took place at Howard's Hill and on March 11 Federal troops were sent to Owensboro to chase bands of guerrillas reported in the area. Also on Saturday, March 11, a troop of about 50 soldiers, under the command of Captain Lewis O. Marshall of Company B, 30th Wisconsin Infantry, surrounded a tobacco barn at the Cox Place near the small village of Webster in Breckinridge County, ten miles south of Brandenburg.[7]

The following morning the troops attacked the barn and knocked in the barn door. After a brief but furious fight the notorious guerrillas Sue Mundy, Henry Magruder and Henry Metcalf surrendered. The guerrillas were taken to Big Springs and held in the cellar of the old General Store and later that evening transported by the steamer, "Morning Star," up the river to the military prison at Louisville.[8] When Mundy learned that he was to be transferred there, he reportedly said, "there was enough published against him to kill him in Louisville."[9]

Mundy's trial before a military commission commenced on Tuesday, March 14. The prisoner was quickly found guilty of the charges and specifications adduced and sentenced to be hanged the next day, Wednesday, March 15, at 4 p.m.. Mundy was to be hanged "on an open ground" directly west of the old Crittenden Hospital, facing Broadway, between Sixteenth and Seventeenth streets. By the afternoon of the 15th, a crowd of ten thousand or more had gathered around the gallows.[10] Mundy was driven to the gallows by carriage, surrounded by a military escort. Rev. Talbot of the Episcopal Church, Captain Swope of the 5th Indiana Cavalry, the provost-marshal, and several other officers escorted Mundy to the scaffold. Mundy, who stood about six feet tall with long dark hair that fell to his shoulders, briefly related his career in the Confederacy and claimed that he was just a "regular Confederate soldier, and as such he should die."

The noose was adjusted and a white cap placed over his face. The provost-marshal gave the signal and the drop fell. Mundy's neck was not broken by the fall, and he "struggled convulsively for two or three minutes, after which all was still...." Jerome Clark, alias Sue Mundy, was 20 years old.[11]

The trial of Henry Metcalf started the day after Mundy went to the gallows but was postponed at the request of his attorney.[12] He was convicted, but General Palmer commuted his death sentence to five years imprisonment.[13] Henry C. Magruder, recovering from his wounds, did not go to trial until September 16th.[14] He was too weak to attend court, the court met in his cell and Magruder, propped up on his cot, heard his conviction and sentence of death.[15] He was hanged in the yard of the military prison at Louisville on the afternoon of October 20.[16] He was 22 years old.

The War ended in April 1865, but it was not until May 1865, that Quantrill was tracked down in Spencer County, Kentucky, where he had been hiding. On May 10th Quantrill and his small band of about 25 men left the home of Bedford Russell in Nelson County and made their way west to Salt River.[17] To escape a heavy rainstorm the guerrillas took shelter in a large barn on the farm of Major James Wakefield. Wet and tired, some of the men went to sleep in the hay on the barn floor. Unknown to the group, a detachment of Federals under the command of Captain Edward Terrell had earlier spotted the small band and tracked them to the barn. A furious fight ensued and Quantrill was shot in the back near the shoulder blade, which paralyzed him. In addition, the tip of his forefinger on his right hand had been shot off. The Federal troops removed him from the field near the barn where he fell and took him to the Wakefield home.[18] Captain Terrell placed Quantrill under the care of Mr. Wakefield until he could return with a wagon for the prisoner. According to Wakefield:

> "In the spring of 1865...a man who went by the name of Captain Clark[e] came to my place with a squad of men.... Captain Clark[e] treated us very well & [his men] behaved themselves so that we got to liking them. They came often to my place, but never stay[ed] long at a time. After we got pretty well acquainted, Captain Clark[e] told [us] his real name was Quantrill but he did not want it known."[19]

In 1910 the *Confederate Veteran* magazine claimed that Quantrill was neither shot nor captured, but was still alive. Frank James refuted the claim in a letter, and furnished the details of his death. According to Frank, he and two other comrades were the only ones of the command to see Quantrill alive after he had been wounded at Major Wakefield's farm. Frank had been hiding at Judge Alex Sayer's home near Samuels Depot and Deatsville, "about twenty miles from the scene" of the skirmish. Around sundown two of the men who had been with Quantrill at the Wakefield farm had managed to escape, rode to the Sayer's home and reported what had happened. After procuring fresh mounts and eating supper at the Judge's home, the small party, identified as Frank James, "One-Arm" Allen Parmer, John Ross and William Hulse, returned to Major Wakefield's farm.[20] John McCorkle, however, later claimed that the party consisted of Frank James, John Ross, Bill (William) Hulse and Payne Jones.[21] Wakefield later claimed that another group of guerrillas arrived the next night which would explain the difference in the names, but the fact remains that Quantrill was moved the next morning.

Frank found Quantrill lying wounded in a trundle bed. Quantrill said to his friend, "Frank, I have run a long time, but they got me at last." Frank urged Quantrill to let them move him to the rough and broken country called the "Knobs," located near Samuels Depot, but Quantrill replied, "No, I will die, and it is no use." Frank said his good-byes and left the house. The other two men who had been standing guard then "went in and said their farewells."

The next morning Captain Terrell, with a troop of cavalry, returned and moved the mortally wounded guerrilla by wagon to the Louisville Military Prison Hospital. According to Wakefield, Quantrill claimed that he was Captain Clarke of the 4th Missouri Cavalry, and denied that he was Quantrill.[22] *The New York Daily Tribune* carried a report of Quantrill's capture, but remained guarded as to the identity of the guerrilla:

"Louisville, Saturday, May 13, 1865. A guerrilla supposed to be Quantrill of Lawrence,[Kansas] massacre notoriety was wounded by Terrell's scouts near Taylorsville on Wednesday and lodged in the military prison today."[23]

At Quantrill's request he was moved from the Prison Hospital and placed in "a Catholic hospital." The only Catholic hospital in Louisville at that time was St. Joseph's, the very hospital where Henry Magruder was recovering from his chest wound.[24]

Mrs. Nev Ross, a refugee from Jackson County, Missouri, went immediately to see Quantrill and remained with him until his death on June 6. A day or two after his death, Mrs. Ross returned to her son and the remainder of the guerrilla band at Samuels Depot, to give them the news.[25] Quantrill was a young man; only 28 years old.[26]

Guerrillas were forced to negotiate for their own surrender terms, since they had been refused the right to surrender with regular Confederate soldiers. On May 18, 1865, Brigadier General J.V. Pratt telegraphed St. Louis to report that guerrilla bands had offered to surrender themselves to the U.S. authorities if they could surrender as other Confederate forces. Some of these guerrillas had been under the leadership of noted Missouri guerrilla leaders Clifton D. Holtzclaw, James H. "Jim" Jackson, Dave Poole and

William C. Charley Quantrill.

The *New York Tribune* published President Johnson's reply to the guerrillas' request. Referring to the surrender terms agreed to by Generals Sherman and Joe Johnston at the Bennett farm in Durham, North Carolina, it stated:

"the proposition of such outlaws as Holtzclaw, Jackson, Pool, and Quantrill, to surrender upon the terms granted regular organized troops 'is not debatable.' No such surrender ought to be thought of. To accept the surrender of such a murderer as Quantrill, the fiend who sacked Lawrence, [Kansas] and caused the streets of that town to run with blood, is too ridiculous a proposition to discuss. We want the surrender of no such scoundrels. We want their bodies, dead or alive."[27]

Most considered these men as murderers and thieves, and felt that they should be... "hunted down [with] bloodhounds, if no other way of taking them were possible..." but negotiations continued with General John M. Palmer, commander of the Union forces in Kentucky. While negotiations were underway the guerrillas set up their headquarters in the area of Deatsville and Samuels Depot under the command of Captain Henry Porter.[28]

On July 26, 1865, General Palmer accepted their surrender terms. The guerrillas, representing most of the remaining members of Quantrill's guerrilla band, included Captain Henry Porter, Bill Hulse, John Harris, John Ross, Randall Venable, Dave Hilton, Bud Pence, Allen Parmer, Lee McMurty, Ike Hall, Bob Hall, Payne Jones, Andy McGuire, Jim Lilly, and Frank James. They surrendered to Captain Young at Samuels Depot. All were given pardons which had been countersigned by General Palmer.[29] John McCorkle later claimed that Frank James had told him that Captain Mead with a few of his men, "met them near Bardstown" and told them to keep their arms and horses and to remain with him until he could hear from General Palmer.[30]

In an interview with William W. Scott, Bob Hall stated that 16 men under the command of Captain Henry Porter also surrendered at Samuels Depot and gave the above names.[31] Two other Quantrill raiders, William Basham and Tom Evans, surrendered at Smiley (known then as Smileytown) Kentucky, located about six miles from Bloomfield, later that same year, and John McCorkle and George Wigginton, along with "two companions", surrendered at Winchester, Kentucky.[32]

Frank James remained in Kentucky for a time and later joined his brother, Jesse, in Nashville, Tennessee. The two eventually returned to Kentucky and Missouri and became the leaders of the infamous James-Younger gang. For the next 17 years the brothers would rob and terrorize the country as they waged their own private war against the banks and railroads.

"One Arm" Sam Berry was captured on or about December 10, 1865, near Bloomfield and taken to Louisville.[33] He was placed on trial for the murder of Tom Hall of Washington County on November 26, 1864, and "robbing Henry Deihl of a hundred and nine dollars" in Jefferson County on February 9, 1865.[34] Berry, found guilty by the Military Commission, was sentenced to death on February 10, 1866. President Johnson commuted his death sentence to ten years solitary confinement in the Albany, New York, penitentiary. Berry served "seven years [until his death], during which period he never saw the light of day."[35]

John Morrissey who was involved in the Asteroid-Kentucky Controversy to bully Alexander into a match race.

CHAPTER ELEVEN

Racing Again ◆ Asteroid vs. Kentucky

R.A. continued to send entries and nominations of Woodburn horses for races throughout and after the war.[1] In May 1865 Daniel Swigert and R.A. went to St. Louis for the Spring Meeting of the Laclede Association races. R.A. assisted occasionally with Captain W.L. Minor, at the request of the President of the Association, to perform the part of Timers.[2] Between June 6th and June 10th R.A. raced at Woodlawn, near Louisville, with Asteroid beating John Harper's Lodestone in two one-mile heats.[3] R.A. stated in a letter to his brother Alec, that he had entered five horses, "one being the 'Graty colt,' in the Michigan Stakes at Cincinnati in late June.[4]

Despite the devastation from the raids, Alexander's 1865 racing season was very successful. R.A. had earlier organized a racing stable (1863-64) which he had placed under the slave Ansel Williamson. It is not certain how Ansel acquired the name Williamson, because he had been owned by a T.B. Goldsly of Alabama, and sold to A. Keene Richards in 1855.[5] Prior to the War Richards "loaned Ansel to Alexander." Ansel is credited with training Alexander's Norfolk and the colt Ansel (named for his trainer) as well as Nellie Gray and Hollywood for General Buford.[6] Ansel and another slave named John were responsible for the training and racing of Asteroid during this period. In January 1866 both Ansel and John returned to Georgetown as free men and employees of their former owner, A. Keene Richards, to help rebuild his racing stable.[7]

The performance by Asteroid at Woodlawn coupled with (the race horse) Kentucky's consistent wins created an extraordinary interest in matching the two horses against each other in the Saratoga Cup. Asteroid, Kentucky and Norfolk were all half brothers. (Technically a "half" brother has to have the same dam, not the same stallion. Claiming the three horses as half brothers may have been used to fuel the controversy.) Kentucky's dam, Magnolia, Asteroid's dam, Nebula, and Norfolk's dam, Novice, were all by Glencoe who was bred and owned by Lord Jersey, on the island of Jersey, which belongs to England. In 1848 W.F. Harper purchased the 17-year-old Glencoe for $3,000. In the summer of 1857 Harper sold Glencoe to A. Keene Richards. Unfortunately, Glencoe never produced anything for Richards, since he died two months later on August 25, 1857, at the age of 26. Glencoe was buried at Blue Grass Park in Georgetown, Kentucky.[8]

Kentucky and Asteroid, both bay colts, were sons of Lexington and foaled in 1861. Although Kentucky was considered an Eastern horse, he was in fact bred by John M. Clay, son of Henry Clay, at Ashland Stud in Lexington, Kentucky.[9] On July 1 the New York based *Wilkes' Spirit of the Times* released a scathing article in an effort to bully R.A into considering the possibility of matching Asteroid against Kentucky at the Saratoga Meeting in August, although R.A. had refused to take Asteroid to Saratoga or even further East than Columbus, Ohio. In part it read:

> "Mr. Alexander is too sensible a man to fail to appreciate the responsibility which attaches to his previous success, and likewise to the patronage which he has received for his stock, from the turfmen of all sections, to refrain from risking his share of a test which has become requisite to the breeders of the country. They are entitled to know which is the fastest stallion in America, and this can be determined in no other way, than by running Asteroid against Kentucky."[10]

This article started a campaign to force R.A. to bring Asteroid to Saratoga which would run through the summer and then die down, only to come up again the following year. Alexander's refusal to transport Asteroid to Saratoga was strongly criticized by *Wilkes'*, which stated:

> "...we do not see how he can justify it under his claims to be considered a liberal patron of the turf; nor do we see how he can expect to retain the assumed prestige of his colt, if by forfeiting 'The Cup' he shrinks the only opportunity he has ever had of measuring Asteroid against a horse of known merits and first-class reputation.... The conclusion will necessarily be that Mr. Alexander is afraid to produce Asteroid against Kentucky...[.] At Cincinnati it was offered to run this other Lexington [colt] of the same age against him for $10,000 aside and to give for Asteroid $22,500 if he won. Here is a price of $32,500 for Asteroid, if Asteroid be what has been assumed and everyone will say, that a owner who is worth millions of dollars, and who seems to believe in his horse, should not have turned his back upon such an offer. This is not the way to support the interest of the turf, nor make a fair return to the public for years of patronage and profit."[11]

Wilkes' continued to challenge Mr. Alexander in print and on July 15 published an offer to set the date for the meeting of the two horses at Saratoga between August 1-6, for sum of $25,000 dollars, which would determine the championship of the American Turf.[12] *Wilkes'* stated that Alexander:

> "[since]has profited by racing, he should contribute his full share to the interest of the turf; and that he cannot justify himself to the breeders of the country, who have so largely purchased of his stock, nor to the general racing community, whose interest in the turf has indirectly patronized his stud, if he permits the season to go by, without accepting the offered opportunity to prove which is the best stallion of his produce.... In this connection we have a right to repeat that though Mr. Alexander has made large entries to the prominent Atlantic race-meetings of the last four seasons, he has not sent a single horse to run in them and his connection with the turf, therefore, so far as being beneficial, has only served to create undue expectations, which have resulted in private discouragement and public disappointment."[13]

Wilkes' also published an article that argued that R.A. Alexander "was morally bound" in some liberal manner to return public revenues since R.A. indirectly derived profits,

> "from the public love for racing which fills the race stands and makes a market for his colts[and] a very great portion of his annual income...; a larger portion of the profits of the race tracks of the United States, by breeding and selling racers to run upon them, than do the united proprietors of all the running courses in the land...; being possessed of the best stallion in the country...."[14]

JOHN MORRISSEY

This cry would soon be taken up by others eager to see the two great horses matched including Irishman John Morrissey. Morrissey had been a deck hand on a Hudson River steamer, a Forty-Niner, a saloon-keeper, ex-World Champion pugilist, gambler, and Congressman. In New York during the post-Civil War days, "he was a belligerent celebrity secure in the patronage of Commodore Vanderbilt who had taken a fancy to him and given him helpful tips on the stock market."[15] Morrissey was now the chief proprietor of the Saratoga race track and the grand Union Club casino. Morrissey, John Hunter, who owned Kentucky, William R. Travers, President of Saratoga, and Charles R. Wheatley, Secretary of Saratoga, also challenged R.A. to race Asteroid against Kentucky at Saratoga.[16]

> "In 1863 Morrissey made his main contribution to sports and gambling in America. That summer having prospered greatly from his casino and from real estate deals,

Morrissey built a grandstand and laid out an adjoining oval track, roughly a mile around for the running of [thoroughbreds]...."

William R. Travers, John Hunter and Leonard W. Jerome formed a racing association with Travers as President.

"In 1864 the association took over the track and relocated it across the road form Morrissey's original site.... Though Morrissey no longer owned the track outright, he shared in the profits, [acting] as Chief Betting Commissioner for the meeting. He must also have remained at least a silent partner in the ownership of the track.... At his death in 1878 his holdings in Saratoga were listed as including a three-eighths share in the gambling casino and a one-third interest in the race track...."[17]

Not all believed the hype and R.A.'s actions were also defended. In a simple letter to the editor, one party calling himself, "EGG," stated that *Wilkes'* was:

"guilty of injustice towards Mr. Alexander in connection with the Asteroid and Kentucky controversy. Simply that he declines traveling his horse to Saratoga to meet Kentucky that they would meet upon equal terms there, is nonsensical to talk about, as Asteroid would have to travel four times the distance than Kentucky would, by rail...."[18]

In a letter from Woodburn, dated July 27, 1865 (printed on August 5 in *Wilkes' Spirit of the Times*), R.A. finally put into words his thoughts concerning match races and made a counteroffer to put an end to the tirade when he wrote:

"I have always been opposed to making or encouraging big matches, for various reasons: In the first case, it partakes more of gambling than I like. In the second case, it not infrequently creates no little ill feeling between the parties engaged, and as men are more often carried away by their sympathies for one or other of the horses in match races, than in others, more money is usually won or lost, and often to an injurious extent. These are some of my reasons for disliking to engage in any heavy match, but as your proposition has been considered by many as a direct challenge to run Kentucky against Asteroid, and my engagements having been such as to have determined me, ere your challenge appeared, not to take my horse to Saratoga, I beg to say that I will run Asteroid against Kentucky, two races, for $10,000 aside each race; half forfeit.... As some of our friends have ascertained that traveling is no disadvantage to a race horse, I hope you will come West and let Kentucky snuff his native air once more. I think our tracks are as good as those in the East, and a horse owned East of the Alleghenies will be as great a curiosity on a course in this section of country as one of my entries would be were he to appear to run for the Jersey Derby, St. Lager, or the Saratoga Cup. The War being over [however] we may be able to support one another better; and I now tell you, that I not only hope to beat Kentucky, should he come West, but hope also to win more than one Derby at St. Lager with colts not only entered in my name, but run as my property; unless, indeed, I shall be ruled out for non-appearance within a certain time of which I think, in strict justice, I should have due notice. P.S.–As you will have due time to think the matter over by Monday, 7th August, I may here say that I expect the proposition to be accepted, or rejected, at latest by that time."[19]

In an August 4 letter to Alexander, Hunter rejected the offer since he was preparing Kentucky for the Saratoga Cup, but stated that after the Saratoga Cup was over, Kentucky would "be in such condition as will warrant further engagements on his part for the approaching fall...."[20] Kentucky won the Saratoga Cup on August 8, 1865, and according to *The Turf, Field and Farm*, R.A. dictated from his sick bed the "laconic reply, 'The proposition does not suit.'"[21]

On August 5, R.A. wrote a letter to his brother from Woodburn. In this letter he stated:

"As I had arranged to join Asteroid [for] a four mile trial on Thursday (yesterday) I went down to the racecourse on Wednesday evening and on Thursday had a good track & had a trial of a lot of 3 year olds & also of Asteroid= I think him the best race horse in the U.S. by long odds & if I keep him well & right I can beat Lexington's time by several seconds under similar circumstances. I ran him 4 miles in a better time than was ever made except in Lexington's time match & carried more weight being a 4 year old than Lexington did through a 5 year old=. I have been rather bullied into proposing to match Asteroid against Kentucky [another] Lexington [colt] owned by some New Yorkers & if they accept to proposition & Kentucky is anything like the horse I suppose him to be you will hear of some extraordinary racing this Autumn."[22]

The next day, *Turf, Field and Farm's* editor, Sanders D. Bruce, printed a rebuttal to the *Wilkes'* articles by pointing out that Hunter had entered Kentucky for the Lexington Stake, but forfeited, and that Kentucky could have as readily made the journey to Lexington as Asteroid could to Saratoga, since it was the same distance and the same changes that Asteroid would have to make. Bruce went on to detail R.A.'s losses during the War:

"...owing to the outrages committed on him by guerrillas, entailing a loss over sixty thousand dollars in stock, some that cannot be replaced, among them Nebula, the dam of Asteroid, and his own life and safety jeopardized, he had to remove all his stock from Kentucky...to have them trained away from him under such disadvantageous circumstances that when he got through his western engagements he had but one horse–Asteroid–fit to travel with. [Bruce also pointed out that R.A. had only one trainer and could not neglect] eight or nine 3-year olds, some engaged in stakes at Lexington twice the value of the Saratoga Cup, nineteen first-class 2-year olds for the fall stakes at St. Louis, Cincinnati, Louisville and Lexington, unbroken, undeveloped and that especially demanded the attention of his trainer."[23]

Alexander's counter offer, published in September, put forth an agreement between the two men to meet and run two races at Cincinnati's Buckeye Course. Alexander also offered to match the two horses at a race meeting at any course in Kentucky, with a second race to be held in New York. Although an answer was requested by August 29, John Hunter decided to take no notice whatsoever.[24]

By the end of August other race tracks had begun to get involved and started to make offers for a match race. The Laclede Association of St. Louis offered $10,000 for three one-mile heats with a $2,000 entrance fee, the Buckeye Course in Cincinnati offered $5,000 for three one-mile heats with a $1,000 entrance fee as well as several other proposals which included one in December from California, which backed a race between Norfolk, Asteroid and Kentucky.[25] In essence, the controversy had become a sweepstakes for the tracks.

In January 1866 R.A.'s racing stable was disrupted again when Asteroid's trainer, Ansel, and his rider, John, returned to Mr. Richards' racing stable. Alexander Keene Richards reestablished his "magnificent stable of racing stock" after having had to disperse his stock during the War.[26] By 1864 A. Keene Richards had been ruined "through the loss of his slaves with which to work his great 'Transylvania' plantation in Louisiana." Richards made every effort to recoup his fortunes and on August 25, 1865, received executive clemency signed by President Andrew Johnson. For a short while it appeared that he would succeed in his attempt to rebuild his fortune, but two months after R.A.'s death, on February 29, 1868, Richards was declared bankrupt by the Federal Court of Winchester, Kentucky. He died on March 19, 1881, of pneumonia at the age of 54.[27]

In 1855 Ansel "was sold to A. Keene Richards to whom he belonged when his [Richards] colors [silver gray and white stripes] first appeared on the turf in 1856. Under Alexander he [Ansel] received his freedom."[28]

Brown Dick was the name of the famous race horse whom Ansel had trained for T.B. Goldsby in 1869, but Brown Dick was also the nickname of the slave, Ed Brown, who was born in 1850 in Fayette County and also owned by A. Keene Richards. Ed Brown was leased to Alexander when he was seven years old.

"He early became one of the top jockeys in the country—in fact, he was fourteen years old when Troye painted his portrait. Because he was the fastest foot racer of the neighborhood, he was given the name of the race horse...[and] he was the top jockey in the Woodburn racing stable."[29]

In late Summer 1865 it was reported that R.A. had been trying to get a second trainer to "take part of his stable, intending to keep a stable permanently [in the] north, and one [in the] west, interchanging his horses as he thought best so that he might be represented at both places."[30] In January 1866 R.A. publicly announced his plan to divide the stable:

> "Mr. Jacob Pincus would have superintendence of the northern or eastern division, while the southern or western division will be under charge of Mr. John Alcock. We presume that Mr. Pincus will make the headquarters of his division near this city [New York], while Mr. Alcock will remain at Woodburn Farm."[31]

This announcement again stirred up interest in the match between Asteroid and Kentucky which could not be settled until the two would agree to meet.

In February and March R.A. is found at Woodburn. In a letter dated February 1 to the Secretary Charles R. Wheatley at Saratoga Springs, he entered Norwich, Ansel and Bay Dick in the 1866 Saratoga Cup. In the same letter he entered Lancaster, Baywood, Merrill, Norway, Watson and two unnamed bay colts in the Sequel Stakes for 1866. He also included Norwood, Aneroid, Liverpool, La Polka, Kalida and five other two-year-olds to enter the 1867 Saratoga Stakes, and his entries Aneroid, Liverpool, La Polka, Kalida, Bayonet and 12 others for the 1868 Travers Stakes for three-year-olds.

On March 1st R.A. wrote a letter from Woodburn to W.E. Mitton to make his entries for the Spring Meeting at Woodlawn Race Course. He entered six colts in the Sweepstakes for three-year-olds, mile heats. He also entered six colts in the Sweepstakes for three-year-olds, two mile heats, and also made his entry for "the Challenge Vase, a dash of four miles." On March 30th Alexander wrote to Mr. S.F. Purdy to enter Asteroid, Norwich, Idlewild and Bay Dick in the Inauguration Stakes in September 1866 at Jerome Park in New York. He also entered Merrill, Norway, Watson, Lancaster and Baywater in the Jerome Stakes for three-year-olds, and entered Newry, Marion, Baywood, Balmorral and Alhambrah in the Nursery Stakes for two-year-olds.[32]

On March 17th *Turf, Field and Farm* reported from Cincinnati about the issue of a prospective meeting of Asteroid and Kentucky in a match race. The question was presented by Western turfman as to whether or not the East was entitled to the "two great magnets?" The East had not made an "inducement" and had not been "held out for Asteroid to make a journey from the interior to the Atlantic coast."[33] In May 1866 Asteroid was injured at the Woodlawn Meeting in Louisville and according to R.A. was "thrown out of training" and would not be able to run during the Spring of 1866. The type of injury or how it occurred was not detailed, but R.A. was quoted to have said that the accident was not serious.[34]

The great Idlewild was part of Alexander's 1866 racing stable and went on to become a great broodmare at Woodburn Farm.

"In consequence of having hit himself, either in 'walking over' for the Woodlawn Vase, or in taking an exercise gallop, Asteroid has been thrown out of training."[35]

Because of Alexander's actions at this meeting, a controversy arose; R.A.'s actions were defended by *Turf, Field and Farm*:

"It appears that the success of Mr. Alexander's stable on the first day was not received with the manly frankness that the public expected from men proverbial for high-toned feeling and generous bearing in the hour of defeat. Mr. A. saw how deeply they were chagrined, and with delicate instinct refused to enter any of his horses for the following day in order that other rivals might stand a better chance to win a victory. But even this...his motive was misunderstood, or if understood, not appreciated, for the four hundred dollar purse was permitted to pass from the Association without the public receiving the equivalent of the excitement attending the races. With forty trained horses on the ground the two mile race resulted in a simple walk over. For the third day, but one entry for each race was made, and both of these were Mr. Alexander's, who claimed that he was mainly influenced in taking this step to prevent any more walk overs, and that he might be able to save the purses for the Association. He stated that he did not race for money, and that the amount of the purses, which were justly his by the laws of racing, would be returned to the Association. It is needless to add that the Woodlawn Course was deserted on Wednesday."[36]

The following month, *Turf, Field and Farm* reported:

"...the accident to Asteroid...is more serious than was apprehended at first, yet it is hoped that by careful attention he will be able to meet Kentucky, Fleetwing, Loadstone and other notables in the great four mile race at Fordham in September."[37]

Despite Asteroid's injury *Turf, Field and Farm* reported:

"...A portion of Mr. Alexander's powerful Kentucky stable arrived last week [in New Jersey], in charge of that clever young trainer, Jacob Pincus.... The lot comprises the three Derby and [St.] Lager three year olds, Merrill, Watson and Baywater, and the four year old Brother to Norfolk, Norwich."[38]

On May 7th Mr. Alexander's horse, Lancaster (by Lexington), won the first race, winning both heats, and Ansel (by Lexington) won the second race.[39] Mr. Alexander's horses were favorites at large odds. Merrill (by Lexington), and Watson both won. Nannie Butler and Lady Dan Bryant, both by Lexington, were beat by Kentucky. Norwich won the Consolation Stake defeating the favorite.[40] In June R.A. Alexander, A. Keene Richards and General Buford were the delegates from Woodlawn to the American Turf Congress.[41]

Three months following Asteroid's accident on August 25, *Turf, Field and Farm's* report on his condition stated that he "has recovered apparently from his injuries excepting the appearance, which is now very slight of the break of the tendon on his right foreleg. With gentle, but constant exercise, he may yet be seasoned and prepared for a race this Fall...."[42] The August 25 edition of *Turf, Field and Farm* also reported that Alexander had arrived in Saratoga Springs, New York.[43]

By September *Turf, Field and Farm* reported that Asteroid was "Eastward bound" and that the impending race between Asteroid and Kentucky was "looked upon as a settled fact."[44] On September 8 *Wilkes' Spirit of the Times* announced "Asteroid on the Road to Fordham." The article reported that: "Asteroid, who is coming like the Campbells [Alexander being Scottish], to oppose Kentucky, Onward, Fleetwing, Julius, Eugene, etc., in the great Inauguration Stakes."[45] On September 22 Alexander arrived in New York "for the purpose of attending the American Jockey Club races at Jerome Park." The article also referred to the upcoming race at Fordham, Westchester County, New York on the 25th, 26th, 27th and 29th. It was billed as "the great race of the year and the greatest turf contest of modern time."[46]

On Thursday, September 20, and again on Friday, Asteroid galloped training trials in the mud. On Saturday he showed signs of lameness and on Sunday morning Asteroid "sprung the tendon on the right foreleg severely." It was believed that the injury originated from the trials on Thursday and Friday and Asteroid was declared lame and reluctantly withdrawn from the race.

This was a great disappointment to everyone, including Alexander, who was quoted to have said that "he would rather have suffered a $50,000 loss than to have the horse break down at this time."[47] Asteroid was permanently retired undefeated to Woodburn Farm. Despite Asteroid's injury and subsequent retirement Alexander's racing stable continued its successful season. On October 15, the first day at Woodlawn, Merrill won the three-year-old Willard Hotel Stakes, and Idlewild ran second in the Jockey Club Purse of $800. On the second day Asterisk won the first race with a $500 purse.[48]

Despite the fact that R.A. was headed for New York in September, there was no delay of the annual Woodburn Farm Sale of 1866:

> "Mr Alexander offers his entire lot of thoroughbreds of 1865, as well as fifty or sixty head of trotting broodmares, together with some Shorthorns and a few Alderneys, on the 5th and 6th days of September."[49]

Earlier in May R.A. had sold a bay stallion, foaled in 1862, by imported Knight of St. George at public sale at Lexington.[50] The end of the war and the return of his horses to Woodburn renewed Alexander's spirits and for a short while his life returned to normal. R.A. published his

1866 equine catalogue listing available breeding stock and yearlings for sale. Unlike his previous ones Alexander's catalogue was printed in New York City and listed Lexington, Australian, and Scythian and 89 broodmares "which was by far the largest number ever up to that time assembled by one breeder in this country...."[51]

A December 14, 1866, letter from R.A. Alexander was published in *Turf, Field and Farm* which stated:

> "Having been informed that not withstanding my repeated declarations of my intention to retire from the turf after the next year, it is believed by some that my object is merely to deceive the public and thus to induce them to purchase such young stock as I do not desire to train and run myself. I beg through your columns to inform such persons as may be interested in the matter, that for some time at least, and probably during the remainder of my life, I shall content myself with breeding, leaving the more arduous and exciting task of training and racing the young stock bred here, to those who, in their love of excitement and their desire to excel their competitors, are willing to sacrifice the ease and comforts of a quiet life, to which, in the present condition of my health, I now attached more importance than formerly."[52]

Despite R.A.'s frail health, his horses raced throughout the 1867 season. The circuit included Mobile, Ala.; Lexington, Ky.; Cincinnati, Ohio; Louisville, Ky.; Paterson, N.J.; Jerome Park and Saratoga Springs, N.Y. and St. Louis, Missouri.[53] The racing string consisted of Asterisk, Bay Dick, Norwich, Ansel, Watson, Jonesboro, Anvil, Red Dick, Norway, Peggerty, Lancaster, Merrill, Baywater, Baywood, Bay Leaf, Marion, Newry, Adelaide, Dickens, Woodstock, Canada and eight others which had not yet been named.[54] At the Fall meeting at Laclede in St. Louis, Jonesboro won the Sweepstakes Hurdle of two miles over eight hurdles for $500, winning it in four minutes 3 1/2 seconds. Woodstock won the first heat of the third race, running third in the third heat. Woodstock also won the first race on the opening day of the Woodlawn Fall races on October 14.[55]

In May 1867 Milton H. Sanford, who owned the Preakness Racing Stable (and "Preakness Stud"), traveled to Woodburn Farm to purchase six yearlings which included: two bay fillies by Lexington, a bay filly by Australian, a chestnut filly, a sister of Norfolk by Lexington, a chestnut filly by Star Davis and a chestnut colt by Lexington.[56]

On June 12th, 1867, R.A. conducted his annual stock sale. The farm sale catalogue listed "70 head of both thoroughbred and trotting stock." The advertisement also commented that:

> "...among the trotters are Pilots, Mambrinos and Ned Forrests, all out of thoroughbred mares. This combination of blood is all the rage among horsemen, and nobody wants even a common roadster now, unless he has an unsullied pedigree."

The great stallion Planet bought by Alexander in July 1867 did not go to Woodburn until he was 14 years old.

This statement certainly confirmed that Alexander's dream of producing exceptional trotting stock by cross-breeding thoroughbreds had been realized.[57]

In July 1867 R.A. purchased the renowned horse, Planet, from Colonel Doswell of Virginia, which he considered an "important addition" to his racing stud. Planet not only possessed "good running qualities he also possessed good trotting action."[58] Planet was considered a speed sire and passed this trait consistently to his offspring. Although R.A. had purchased Planet for Woodburn, he did not make his first season there as a stud until he was 14 years old.[59] He died at Woodburn in 1875.[60] On October 17 R.A. purchased some blood stock from John Campbell at Woodlawn Race Course which included Lizzie McDonald and a chestnut filly by Joe Stoner.[61] This great revitalization of activity shown by R.A. from April 1865 through October 1867, however, would be short-lived.

The Woodlawn Vase, created by Tiffany & Co., was commissioned by R. A. Alexander and presented by him to the Woodlawn Race Association in 1860. Today it is the trophy presented to the winner of the Preakness Stakes.

CHAPTER TWELVE

Death of the Master Breeder

"Whereas the empire established by the Master of Woodburn still endures and scarcely a horse of the first class passes the post today in this country, unless bred exclusively from ancestors recently imported, [that does not carry] the blood of the sires and dams that he collected in its paddocks and sent forth from there to conquer and enrich the American turf and stud, literally from Ocean to Ocean and Lakes to Gulf."[1]

By the summer of 1867 Alexander's health began to alarm his friends and family. He had been a slender, somewhat frail-looking man all his life, although he "never spared himself and was incessantly active."[2] In 1865 R.A. had begun to lose his health. In his March 4, 1865, letter to Deedes, he had complained about his health; stating: "My throat has been dreadfully sore and my jaw aches. Some call it neuralgia. I have no doubt but that the nerve is affected, but I think bad teeth are the cause of the pain."[3] Although the cause of the pain was unknown, it certainly could have originated or been aggravated during the struggle in the house with the guerrilla during the second raid.

He seems to have become depressed and discouraged; his spirit had been broken. The stress of the war, the anxiety of the raids, the loss of his prize horses, and the vast financial worries of moving the horses to Illinois and Ohio and back to Kentucky began to take their toll. It was later reported that:

"...for two years past his friends have seen a marked change—never well, but still on the move. He seemed absorbed in his pursuits, and he followed them with an unsparing energy, as if life was too short to reach the goal he had assigned himself. He seemed to be aware, and often said, that his life would not be a long one, and that he would never reach fifty, and he seemed anxious to crowd within its short space all he desired to do. He never spared himself, always on the move...."[4]

R.A. was reported to have been very conscientious and one reporter recorded that he believed that "this was the cause of his bachelorhood." R.A. was quoted to have remarked to a friend that "with his poor health, a weak frame, he could not think it right to impose such a burden upon a lovely woman; but as he never married, next to a woman he loved the noble horse."[5]

In November 1867 he became seriously ill and died suddenly on December 1st at his beloved Woodburn Farm at the age of 48. He was reported to have died of "no disease...but of prostration." His last words were reported to have been: "There is nothing true, but Heaven."[6] He was laid to rest in the beautiful family plot in the Frankfort Cemetery which overlooks the river in Frankfort, Kentucky. He lies at rest beside his father beneath a simple headstone which reads "Robert A. Alexander; Born: October 23, 1819; Died: December 1, 1867." A.J. Alexander inherited Woodburn Farm in accordance with the "express dying wish of his brother."[7]

> "When the coterie of New York magnates that had assumed control of the turf, following its reorganization after the war, declined to have anything to do with the efforts of Colonel [Sanders D.] Bruce to bring out the *American Stud Book*, it was R.A. who made its publication possible by becoming the chief financial supporter of the enterprise."[8]

Although he had never married, he still left a heritage that has endured through his breeding of race horses. He had worked long hours on a reliable compilation of thoroughbred genealogies, which ultimately became the official *American Stud Book*. The first double volume of the *American Stud Book* was dedicated to him when it appeared in 1873. The dedication read:

> "As an Humble Mark of Respect/ For the Improvement of the Blood Horse and who/ Earnestly Strove to Place the Sports of the Turf Above Reproach/ this/ Work, That has Required the Labor of a Lifetime/ Is dedicated/ To the Late Robert Aitcheson Alexander/ of Woodburn, Kentucky."[9]

He owned stock in race tracks, most notably the Buckeye Course in Cincinnati and stock in the *Louisville Association for the Improvement of the Breed of Horses* which was the name of the stockholders association for the Woodlawn Association Race Course.[10]

A willingness to experiment and foresight to develop the trotting race horse showed Alexander's courage and devotion to the improvement of racing stock and racing in America. Proof of this cross are the world's champions, the foundation sires, and the world's record breakers that have come from this breeding and have helped in the development of the standard breed. By this practice, Alexander helped to inject speed into the trotting horse. Without inserting opinions or politics, one could argue that Mr. Alexander could be ranked as a modern breeder. His advanced practices and his outstanding breeding record speak for themselves; which is not to say he was above controversy for his breeding ideas.

R.A. Alexander was an innovator with concepts of breeding ahead of his time and far advanced compared with breeders of the era. *Wallace's Monthly* speculated that had R.A. Alexander lived longer, "his advanced ideas...would have demonstrated their soundness and safety before all the world."[11] Perhaps too, Woodburn's influence would have been more far reaching, but Alexander still left Woodburn as one of the largest, most successful and most influential breeding establishment in America. "The extraordinary success attained by R.A. Alexander is all the more remarkable when we pause to consider that his career as breeder really extended over... a decade."[12] In January 1866 when rumor of excluding Mr. Alexander from the race course was circulating, Mr. Alexander's influence upon the turf and his breeding reputation were used in his defense by one writer, who speaks highly of his reputation. Noted by the *Turf, Field and Farm*:

> "We trust to the sound judgment and good sense of turfmen to correct the evil. Nor can we believe that any serious thoughts are entertained of excluding Mr. Alexander from the race course. Lexington is his individual property, purchased at a large figure for the improvement of his stock. He is much advanced in years, and can serve but few mares each season, therefore his owner is justified in reserving his services for his [Alexander's] extensive stable. Mr. Alexander has done more to improve the blood-horse of America than any other man in this country, and if his success has been great, his early investments were no less hazardous. He has devoted much thought to the subject of breeding, and his extensive stud farm has monopolized his attention. We should not feel jealous of his success, since the peerless colts of Lexington, bred under his immediate eye, have given new fame and popularity to the race course, thereby adding value to the blooded horses of the entire country. Upon Mr. Alexander's success the good fortune of hundreds of other breeders depend. He has brought the thoroughbred prominently before the public, and created a demand for him. As the price of an animal is always regulated by the demand for it, breeders and turfman should look upon the proprietor of Woodburn Farm with eyes not blinded by jealousy. They should take a higher view of the matter, and while they envy Mr. Alexander, let the feeling not be characterized with vindictiveness but with generosity, tempered with justice, and let them firmly resolve to emulate his example. Exclude Mr. Alexander's stable from the race course and a rapid decline will be marked in the prosperity of turf associations."[13]

"He bred with judgment and care—the prosperity and high standing of the American turf today are largely due to his influence."[14] Throughout Woodburn's early years under R.A.'s guidance, the Kentucky thoroughbred contingent was outraged by his cross-breeding "experiments" with his thoroughbreds; his complete domination of racing from during the

The only building standing that was connected with the old Woodlawn Race Course.

Historical highway marker that tells of the Woodlawn Race Course and the Woodlawn Vase.

Photographs by William H. Strode.

Civil War (1865) to his death in 1867, and his raising the prices of his yearlings offered at the annual Woodburn Farm Sales. Despite this, however, here was a gentleman completely devoted to elevating the sport of the turf in the United States, who continued to run the Woodburn Stud with little care to those who opposed him. *The Chicago Tribune* wrote of him at his death:

> "[He] devoted his powers and his wealth to agriculture, particularly to that branch of it which relates to the breeding and perfection of animals. In this he was successful beyond any man of his time. His estate (Woodburn) in Woodford County, five or six thousand acres in extent, was perhaps the model farm of the country; certainly the flocks and herds that were fed upon it far surpass in number and value those of any other breeder in the United States or England. His horses, cattle and sheep on hand at one time have not infrequently been valued as high as a million and a half dollars; and from them the larger part of the imported breeds in the West have been derived...."[15]

Although he died in the prime of his life, and was taken much too soon, he was a man who identified himself with the future. By 1901 the entire Woodburn Stud had been dispersed, but its influence and legacy has proved to have been crucial in the development of the horse racing industry in America.

Today the trophy presented to the winner of the Preakness Stakes, the second race of the Triple Crown, is the famous Woodlawn Vase, the oldest trophy in American sports. Alexander had buried the vase on the grounds of Woodburn during the Civil War to keep it safe from marauders.[16] The vase is one trophy that remained hidden from the raiders, Quantrill and Mundy, that rainy night at Woodburn. Appraised at $1 million in 1985 by the Kirk-Stief Company of Baltimore, this 36 inch silver vase, (surmounted by a full figure of the great horse Lexington mounted by a costumed jockey), is the most valuable trophy in American sports. Its provenance reaches back to the 1861, when R.A. Alexander commissioned the celebrated jewelers, Tiffany & Company, to create the Challenge Vase for the old Woodlawn Association Race Course which flourished in Louisville before and after the Civil War. To win this trophy is one of the highest honors in thoroughbred races.

The vase took its name from the 201–acre Race Course located on the Louisville and Frankfort Railroad (today the C.S.X. Railroad), east of St. Matthew's just off Westport Road and covered today by the city of Woodlawn Park. The track opened in 1859, and was sometimes called the "Saratoga of the West." The March 1988 issue of *Town And Country Magazine* featured an article on the award trophies that Tiffany & Company had made throughout the years. This four–page article featured a full-page picture of the Woodlawn Vase, but did not mention Robert A. Alexander. At the time the vase was made

(1860,) and presented personally by Alexander to the Woodlawn Race Course Association (1861), it was valued at $1,500.

Benjamin Gratz Bruce, founder of the *Thoroughbred Record* newspaper, was deeply moved by Robert A. Alexander's death and wrote of him at his passing:

"Of great will and determination, whatever met the approval of his judgment was undertaken with a will, and his whole soul entered with enthusiasm into its accomplishment. He never waited to be led by others he led the throng himself. By his actions and his works he should be judged, and it will be found that he has left his mark upon the age as her greatest breeder, a mark only for good. Some men pass through life like meteors and leave as slight an impression, while others seem to impenetrate themselves with the living and identify themselves with the future. This is eminently the case with Mr. Alexander, for his name is indelibly stamped with all the future stock in this country."[17]

Alexander was a man who "labored earnestly and hard to elevate the condition of the best types of the animal kingdom, believing that their elevation would have a refining influence upon mankind."[18] "Mr. Alexander stood alone, worked alone, and achieved alone. The only things that favored his enterprise was his wealth and his determination. He was a man of great breadth of mind...."[19] In his efforts "he did more to elevate racing not only in Kentucky, but throughout the United States, than any other.... He was, certainly, the brightest star in the racing firmament.... One of the purest, best men whose presence ever graced a race track."[20]

"In writing the history of the breeding studs of America, Woodburn must be classed as the oldest, largest and most celebrated. It was the first of all the breeding establishments...to make annual sales. It covers, with the sole exception of Belle Meade [in Nashville, Tennessee] and studs on the Pacific slope, the largest number of acres of land, and has a greater variety of choicely bred animals, than any singular establishment in the world–but not a large number of thoroughbreds, but it has one of the largest and best bred studs of trotters and a large and very superior herd of Shorthorn cattle, a fine flock of pure-bred Southdown sheep and a small but select herd of Jerseys, in addition to the stud of distinguished thoroughbreds, which have won fame both in America and England...."[21]

On July 4, 1993, Robert Aitcheson Alexander was inducted into the Immortal Room of the Harness Racing Museum & Hall of Fame at Goshen, New York, being recognized for helping to introduce the trotting horse into Kentucky and for his important breeding contributions to the trotting-horse breed. Today a photograph of his portrait hangs in the Hall of Fame.[22]

American racing (both standardbred and thoroughbred industries) is forever indebted to Robert Aitcheson Alexander; his important influence is still felt today. Those who love the sport of the turf and the breeding of race horses should remember and revere this man who, in adverse times and in a relatively short life, contributed so much to the excellence of the breeds he loved.

And so it is that Robert Aitcheson Alexander's dream did not die with him but burned brightly in the decades following his death, settling into a gentle flickering flame that abides today among the gently rolling pastures of the Bluegrass.

Advertisement from *The Chicago Tribune* announcing Jay-Eye-See trying to beat the trotting record.

The great trotting world's champion Jay-Eye-See, 2:10 bred and foaled at Woodburn Farm.

CHAPTER THIRTEEN

Woodburn's Influence on the Western Turf

"Blind he peers about, but sees not. Now and then he pricks his ears,

Lis'ning for the judges' summons, waiting vainly for the cheers

That were wont of old to greet him when he trod the track a king,

When met and told each other of his greatness in the ring.

Whispers fly about the race tracks when some mighty deed is done—

Tis no more than we expected from the blood of Lexington."

Hyder Ali [1]

After the Civil War, the breeding of trotters was taken up more freely by Kentucky (with the primary influence coming from Woodburn Farm) and New York. Morgan horses were then in their heyday of fame, the speed limit was gradually lowered until 2:30 was considered about the proper credentials for a horse fit to go to the races in select company. At that time 2:20 horses were a rarity–not enough of them at one time to make a respectable race, and it was not until late in the 1870's that the 2:20 list was large enough to be considered seriously as a top speed for trotters. The 2:30 line was still the standard by which horses were judged, but since the advent of the bicycle sulky (race bike) in 1892 the 2:30 and 2:20 trotters became obsolete so far as racing purposes are concerned, and by the turn of the century no horse could hope to win a respectable purse unless capable under favorable conditions of trotting in 2:15, and even that rate of speed would still not do. Organized breeding of these race horses greatly influenced the results achieved on the race track and in this respect Woodburn Farm proved to be an influential giant. Our industry owes a great debt to R.A. Alexander.

Maud S. 2:08 3/4. The fastest trotter of 1880s was bred and foaled at Woodburn Farm.

The great trotting champion Nancy Hanks, 2:04 whose bloodlines are traced back to Woodburn Farm.

TROTTERS

According to John Hervey's *The American Trotter*:

"While in time the practice of interbreeding thoroughbred with trotting blood at first hand was discontinued as the Standard breed assumed its own separate status and distinctiveness, at the same time its use from Woodburn sources produced results of lasting fame and influence. As instances we may quote Midnight, dam of Jay-Eye-See 2:10, the pioneer 2:10 trotter, bred at Woodburn and by Pilot Jr. out of Twilight, (Thoroughbred), by Lexington; also Miss Russell, the dam of Maud S. 2:08 3/4 [owned by William H. Vanderbilt in 1883], the first to beat 2:10; and of the eminent progenitor Nutwood (both bred at the farm), she by Pilot Jr. out of Sally Russell, (Thoroughbred), by Boston, sire of Lexington.... The blood of Lexington, through many different channels, enters a host of our great trotting genealogies, and these animals all trace to him through sons and daughters begotten at Woodburn. His companion sires there for years were those other two renowned Thoroughbreds, imported Australian and Planet, [Australian] sired Estella, bred at Woodburn, she the grandam of the two brothers Alcantara 2:23 [foaled in 1876 out of Alma Mater and she by Mambrino Patchen out of the thoroughbred Estella] and Alcyone 2:27, [foaled in 1877 and died in 1887, sire of Martha Wilkes 2:08, (made in September 1892) the first trotter to race a heat in 2:10 or better, and Harrieta 2:09 3/4] two of the most potent sons of George Wilkes. Estella was out of Fannie G. by imp. Margrave, and by breeding another daughter of that mare to Planet Mr. Alexander obtained Dame Winnie, sold from Woodburn to Governor [Leland] Stanford [owner of Palo Alto (the Tall Pine) Farm, established 1875], who by breeding her to Electioneer obtained Palo Alto 2:08 3/4, the "half-bred" champion trotting stallion and still holder of the high-wheel record for entire horses [died at Stanford's Farm near Redwood City, California on July 21, 1892]; and his own sister Gertrude Russell 2:23 1/2, she the grandam of Belwin 2:06 3/4, one of the most successful sires of modern times. Moreover, as Belwin was by McKinney 2:11 1/4, [whose dam was Belle Winnie out of Gertrude Russell] and that progenitor by Alcyone, he was inbred, through both sire and dam, to this family of Woodburn-bred Thoroughbred mares. We might cover with similar citation, but will only add that just as the first 2:10 trotters came from Woodburn sources, so the first 2:05 trotter, Nancy Hanks 2:04, had for grandam Sophie, by Alexander's Edwin Forrest; while Bingen 2:06 1/4, the illustrious family builder, was by May King 2:20, he out of May Queen 2:20, by Alexander's Norman."[2]

Alcazar 2:20 1/2, owned by Leonard J. Rose stood at Rosemead Stock Farm in Southern California.

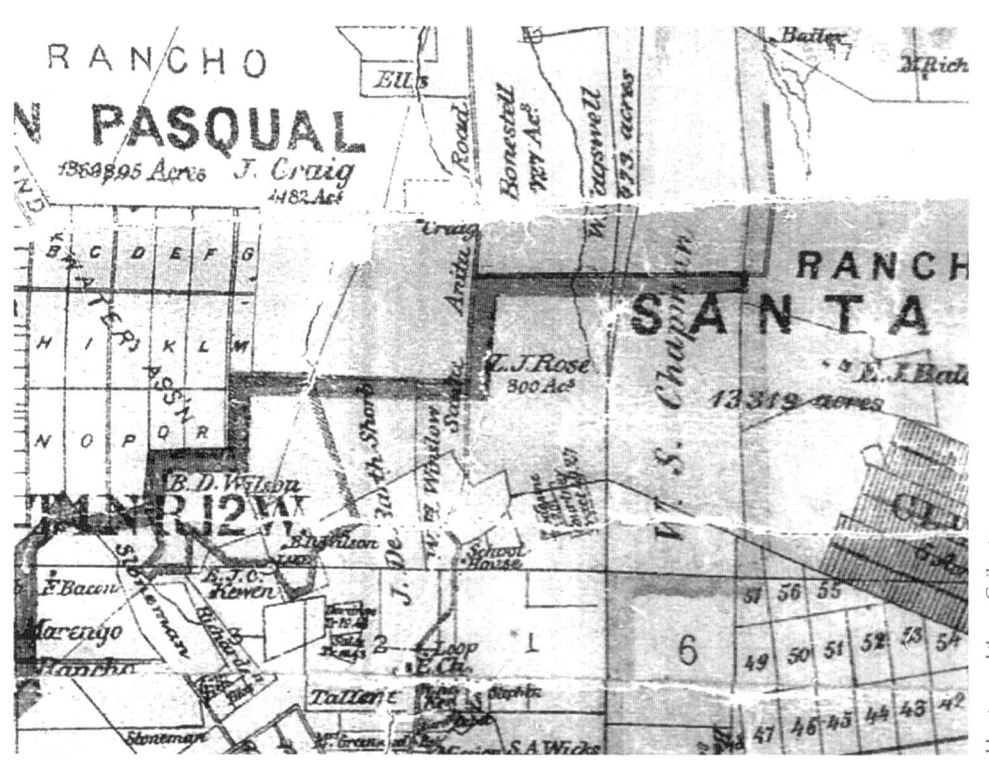

Section from Map of the County of Los Angeles, California, comp. by J. H. Wildy (1877), showing L. J. Rose ranch to the left of the W.S. Chapman property near center of map, and E. J. "Lucky" Baldwin's property all at the foot of the San Gabriel Mountains.

GEORGE WILKES/AUSTRALIAN

As stated before, Australian's impact on this influential trotting family is through his daughter, Estella, the grandam of the two great brothers, Alcantara 2:23 and Alcyone 2:27, "two of the most potent sons of George Wilkes."[3] Alcantara had a wonderfully long career in the stud. When one contemplates what Alcyone accomplished by the time he was 10 years old, and considers what his chances would have been had he lived to the age of Alcantara, the conclusion is that not only would he have outranked all stallions as a sire of 2:15 and 2:10 horses, but that he would have left a troop of sons whom McKinney (2:11 1/4) would have been but one.[4] By 1887

> "...it [was] sufficient to say that the trotters and the introduction of the thoroughbred element to enable the animal to maintain speed over a distance of ground, have been clearly demonstrated in the performances of Maud S. having the fast mile [to this date] on record, 2:08 3/4 and Jay-Eye-See, 2:10. The granddams of both are strickly thoroughbred."[5]

STEVEN'S BALD CHIEF

Bay Chief got few colts, and none of his sons or daughters made a record in standard time, nor did they sire or produce a standard performer. His son, Stevens' Bald Chief (dam, Commodore), however, went to Wisconsin, (bought by George C. Stevens his farm being located at West Allis). Steven's Bald Chief sired the noted broodmare, Minnehaha, the dam of eight trotters that made records in standard time, one of which was the broodmare, Beautiful Bells (2:29 1/2). Minnehaha was sent to California having been bought by Leonard J. Rose.[6] Steven's Bald Chief, dam Dolly Spanker, by Hunt's Commodore, second dam by Potomac, a son of Diomed. Hunt's Commodore was inbred to Messenger, and Minnehaha's dam was Nettie Clay of the immortal Clay family, she by Strader's Cassius M. Clay Jr.[7] Minnehaha became "the empress of broodmares," one of the greatest broodmares of trotters, the dam of eight trotters that made records in standard time and the grandam of many great horses. "Minnehaha was the dam of Beautiful Bells 2:29 1/2 and Eva 2:23 1/2, from each of whom has come a family of champions and sires and dams of champions."[8]

Leonard John Rose, an early California pioneer in breeding trotting horses, settled in the San Gabriel Valley located east of Los Angeles in 1860. In 1866 he established Rosemead Stock Farm, which the city of Rosemead is named for, following the sale of his large estate Sunny Slope.

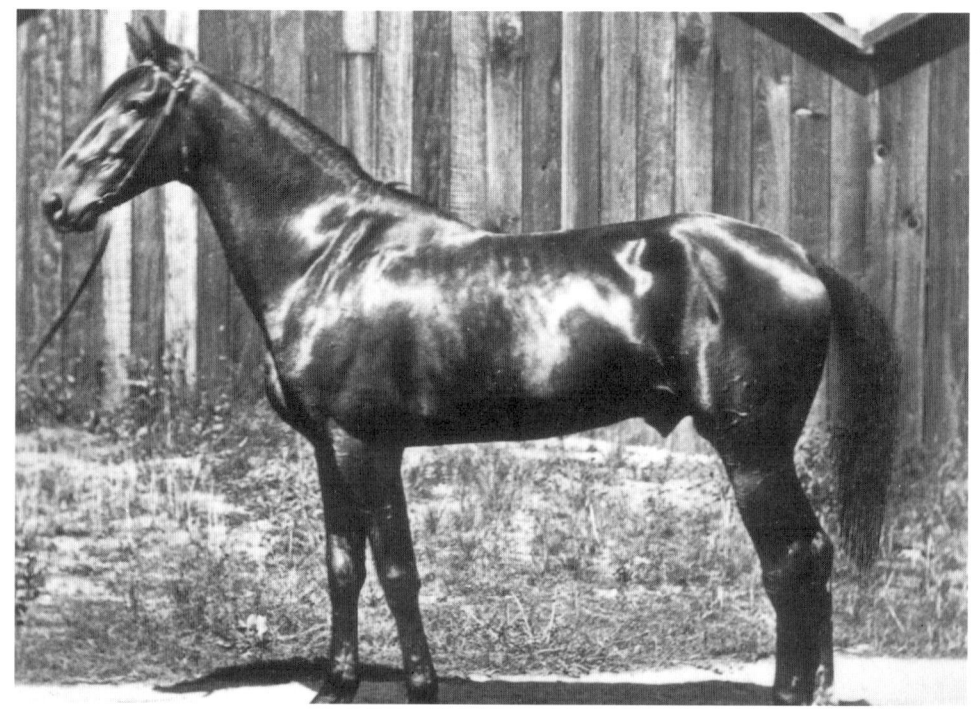

Sultan was the sire of Stamboul and The Moor was the sire of Sultan.

Stamboul the Great, 1887, champion trotter (2:07:1/2) and three-time winner of best in show at Madison Square Garden. He was the grandson of The Moor and is buried at Historic Track in Goshen, New York.

In 1869 on a return trip from New York City he visited Milwaukee, Wisconsin, and bought six trotting colts and fillies from George C. Stevens. "They were the first horses ever shipped to California by transcontinental railroad."[9] Rose later confessed,

"that he had bought the horses sight unseen and strictly on pedigree, two of them—a colt named The Moor and a filly called Minnehaha—went on to establish important bloodlines of their own. The Moor, who died of a lung fever at age 10, did not sire more than 50 colts during his lifespan, more than half of those produce of mustang mares. Yet he sired five that trotted a mile in 2:30. Minnehaha, one of the greatest standardbred broodmares of all time, had four foals in that mystic 2:30 circle.

Beautiful Bells, a cantankerous filly produced from a mating between The Moor and Minnehaha, set several trotting records and then sold to Sen. Leland Stanford's 'Palo Alto Stock Farm.' She became the dam of 17 champions including sub-2:30 performer Hinda Rose. Sultan, another son of The Moor, trotted in 2:24 and became the most talked-of stallion in America. Rose kept him until he was 11 and then sold him to a pair of Kentuckians for $15,000.

To succeed Sultan [sold for $17,000 and sent to Kentucky] as the head of his breeding operation, Rose kept Stamboul, a grandson of The Moor. In the spring of 1889 Rose wagered $5,000 that Stamboul would break the trotting record of 2:12 before the year was over. Although he lost his bet, Stamboul was later clocked in 2:11 and eventually set a world record of 2:07 1/2. Rose ultimately sold Stamboul to Walter S. Hobart of San Francisco, for $50,000."[10] On December 20, 1892 he was resold for $41,000 to E. H. Harriman.

Mr. Rose bred all of Minnehaha's foals who produced some of the harness industry's finest to ever be seen on the Western turf include: Beautiful Bells, Atalanta, Mabel, Philocea, Sweetheart (2:22 1/2), Eva (2:23 1/2), Almeh, California, Alcazar, San Gabriel, Daisy Rose, Mascot, Baron Rose, and Pawnee. Minnehaha's produce alone brought Rose well over $100,000 and she was the first mare to produce ten trotting performers in the 2:30 list.[11] In 1890 at a New York auction, Rose received $238,800 for 86 race horses. In March 1889 Rose sold 46 head for a total of $117,700, mainly the get of Stamboul and Alcazar, and in March 1891 he sold ten horses for $27,950.[12]

One of Minnehaha's grandsons was Chimes foaled at Leland Stanford's California Palo Alto Farm, who made his record in the Kentucky three-year-old trot at Lexington. He was sold at two years old in 1886 to Village Farm for $12,000, where he was bred into another Kentucky line of trotters, that of Mambrino King, from which came The Abbot 2:03 1/4.[13] Leonard J. Rose's famous stables and orchards at Rosemead contained:

"880 acres of the best land in California, and here he placed The Moor, Fleetwing,

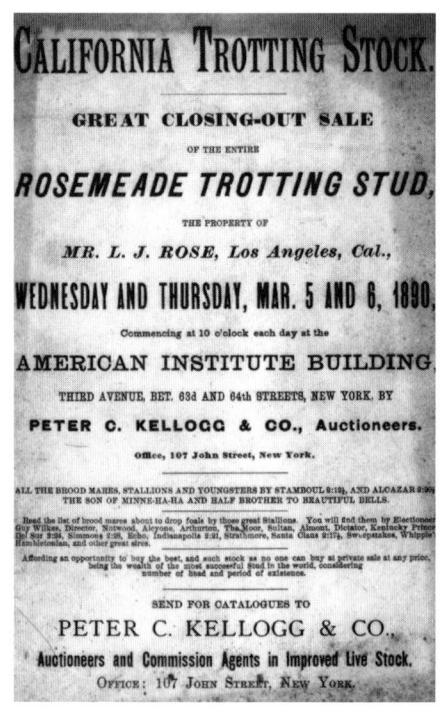

Sale catalogue of L. J. Rose's close-out sale of 1890.

Maggie Mitchell, and Minnehaha. Here he bred Stamboul (2:07 1/2), Alcazar (2:00), and many other great trotting sires and matrons."[14] On May 17, 1898, at his beautiful home in Los Angeles, Leonard J. Rose died by his own hand; he was 72 years old. With "his fortune being gone, his property mortgaged for all it was worth, he grew despondent and took an (overdose) of morphine."[15]

Leonard Rose's trotting stock has another connection to Woodburn Farm through The Moor.

"Almont was bred at Woodburn Farm, was foaled 1864, and was by Alexander's Abdallah, out of Sally Anderson, by Mambrino Chief; grandam Kate, a wonderfully fast pacer by Pilot Jr. Kate, whose dam was called the Pope mare, pedigree unknown, had several foals, among them the "catch filly" that was the dam of Clay Pilot, sire of The Moor, that got the great broodmare, Beautiful Bells, 2:29 1/2 [Minnehaha's first foal] and Sultan, 2:24, the sire of the world famous Stamboul, 2:07 1/2, [record made at Stockton, California November 23, 1892]. Thus the blood of this pacing Pilot Jr. mare figures in three sub families of the Almont family, the Beautiful Bells family, and the Sultan family. ...The Moor himself a fast trotter and successful sire. He died at 10 years old, leaving...38 other performers and 13 producing sons and 20 producing daughters. The Moor founded an excellent family."[16]

As a youngster The Abbot (by Chimes, a son of Electioneer and Beautiful Bells, 2:29 1/2) did not show any promise of being a sensational trotting performer. He was bred by C.J. Hamlin on the Village Farm located at East Aurora, New York, and foaled in 1893. His dam was Nettie King 2:20 1/4, by Mambrino King (son of Mambrino Patchen); second dam Nettie Murphy, by Hamlin Patchen; third dam by a son of Kentucky Whip. Those who are familiar with this breeding may know that The Abbot (who was foaled in 1893 and died at the Scannell Stock Farm at Fishkill Landing, N. Y. on February 19, 1904) was a full brother to The Abbe, a pacer, (who took the trotting record of 2:10 3/4 as a three-year-old in 1903, and the following year paced a record of 2:03 1/2). He is today prominent in starting one of the great male lines of pacers, one being the great Adios, he the sire of Good Time, Bret Hanover and Meadow Skipper, ("who in 1977 was the leading sire of 2:00 performers with 100 sons and daughters.")[17]

THOROUGHBREDS

Woodburn's and Lexington's influence was not limited to the East Coast.

"Norfolk, Grinstead and Joe Hooker stood on the West coast and sired many fleet and game racehorses that crossed the mountains and invaded the East and could win important races in the best of company. To mention a few of the thoroughbreds descended from the Lexington male line that came out of the far West and won many important stakes and noted races were: Volante, Emperor of Norfolk, Yo Tambien, C.H. Todd, Molly McCarthy, El Rio Rey, Rey del Caredes (Americus), etc.

Norfolk was practically buried alive on the West coast. He stood where there was only a very limited number of high–class mares that could be mated with him at that time. The best of his mates were Marian, dam of Emperor of Norfolk, and Hennie Farrow, dam of Flood, which was also dam of Molly McCarthy, so Norfolk proved that he was capable of siring high class horses when he was given good mares.... With the exception of Marian and Hennie Farrow it is not likely that any of his mates produced high class horses by other stallions."[18]

Under Elias Jackson "Lucky" Baldwin's direction Rancho Santa Anita, located in Arcadia, blossomed in the 1880's into a successful full breeding and racing establishment. In 1885 Baldwin purchased a son of Norfolk, Emperor of Norfolk, from Theodore Winters for $2,500. Emperor of Norfolk went on to win 21 of 29 starts and placed in six others, and reigned in the United States as champion of his division each year he ran.[19] As a stallion he produced Cruzados out of Atalanta 2nd (by Grinstead out of Blossom by Virgil out of

Grinstead grandson of Lexington and a cornerstone of Rancho Santa Anita, here with farm manager Lowen Tucker. Original picture owned by Vesta Tucker Reeves.

Blunder by Lexington), who also became a great champion, and it is through him that the male line of Lexington survived into the 20th Century.[20]

The cornerstones of Baldwin's stud were the purchases of the five-year old Kentucky-bred, brown bay stallion, Grinstead (son of Gilroy, full brother to Kentucky and a grandson to Lexington),[21] and the Woodburn-bred Rutherford (son of Australian and brother to Spendthrift). Grinstead was bred by J.A. Grinstead of Walnut Hill Stud in Kentucky and foaled in 1871. His dam was a sister to Ruric, by imported Sovereign.[22] He bought both of them at Saratoga in 1874 (although another source gives 1876). Both horses "...ultimately exerted a profound influence on early Western breeding, both as sires and [as] broodmare sires."[23] In 1875 Baldwin accompanied his racing mare, Mollie McCarthy (bred by A. Maillard, but Baldwin bought her from Theodore Winters), to Louisville to race her against Frank Harper's Ten Broeck at Churchill Downs. Fortunately, she was defeated, because this defeat only "strengthened Baldwin's determination to breed champion runners" and he wanted only the best horses money could buy.[24]

Unlike most early California breeders who imported foreign animals, Baldwin made his purchases from New York and Kentucky. That same year at the Saratoga sales he bought the Kentucky-bred fillies, Josie C. (foaled 1873, by Leamington out of a dam by Lexington and bred by John O'Donnell of New York)[25] and Maggie Emerson (foaled 1874, by

Baywood out of Lag by Loadstone out of La Bruna by Scythian, and bred by Milton H. Sanford, owner of Preakness Stud).[26] Enroute to his home, he visited Woodburn Farm and there purchased six more fillies: "Ophir [by Baywood out of Lag by Loadstone and bred by M.H. Sanford],[27] Blossom [by Virgil out of Blunder by Lexington],[28] Santa Anita [foaled 1875 by Virgil out of Mary Martin by Lexington and bred by Milton .H. Sanford],[29] Jennie D. [foaled 1875, by Glenelg out of Regan by Lexington and bred by M.H. Sanford],[30] Glenita [by imported Glenelg out of Lark by Lexington and bred by M.H. Sanford][31] and Clara D.," (whose dam was The Nun by Lexington out of Novice and a full sister to Norfolk). It was these eight broodmares that "comprised the foundation band at the Arcadia rancho." To these eight mares he added the following fillies, but only one is listed with the 12 fillies that were offered in the Woodburn sale in 1877. All are, however, from Woodburn stock, but Baldwin more than likely bought the others at M.H. Sanford's Preakness Stud Farm, as were the above mentioned. Sister Anne (foaled 1876, by Glenelg out of The Nun by Lexington, Sister Anne being a sister to Clara D. and Norfolk, and bred by M.H. Sanford),[32] Experiment (foaled 1876, by Monarchist out of Cornflower by Virgil out of Cordelia by Lexington and bred by M.H. Sanford),[33] and Althola (foaled April 21, 1876, by Glen Athol out of Annette by Lexington and bred by A.J. Alexander,[34] listed in the *1877 Woodburn Farm Catalogue* as hip number 22), and Jennie B. (by imported Glenelg out of Regan by Lexington and bred M.H. Sanford).[35] Virgil was foaled in 1864 by Vandal, son of Glencoe out of Hymenia by Yorkshire, and died on September 8, 1886 at Elmendorf Stud Farm. Virgil is the sire of Hindoo and the phenomenal Tremont.

At the height of its glory in 1891, the ranch comprised of about 54 broodmares and Baldwin's stallions included: Gano (by Grinstead out of Santa Anita),[36] Amigo (by Joe Daniels out of Partisana),[37] Verano (by Grinstead out of Jennie D.),[38] The Hook (by Fishhook),[39] Cheviot (by Traducer),[40] Rey el Santa Anita (by Cheviot out of Alaho by Grinstead)[41] and Cruzados (by Emperor of Norfolk out of Atalanta 2nd).[42] In December 1880 it was reported that both of Baldwin's horses, Jennie B. and Clara D., were barred from all the races at Oakland Park California; the reason given was that if they were allowed to race they would "have walkovers." Up to that December Jennie B. had run ten races winning the last nine. Clara D. won eight times out of 11 starts, winning the last seven straight.[43]

"Baldwin stocked the Santa Anita Ranch with the finest thoroughbreds and engaged in stock breeding on a magnificent scale" which "enabled him to build a stable that soon became one of the strongest on the western turf."[44] With these outstanding animals "it did not take Baldwin long to develop an excellent breeding program, one which stressed speed rather than rugged durability."[45] His ranch was "...one of the most successful racing stables

Cruzados, son of Emperor of Norfolk.

The fastest son of Emperor of Norfolk was Cruzados, who also went into Baldwin's stud at Rancho Santa Anita.

for the size of its stud ever developed in America; one of a mere handful that actually were made to pay."[46]

The ranch made Baldwin:

"one of the most successful horsemen in American turf history" and for the next 30 years "some of the fastest horses ever seen in America during the latter part of the 19th century were raised in the pastures of Baldwin's Rancho Santa Anita." [47]

Woodburn had a direct and profound influence on the Santa Anita Stud. "In a single season Baldwin's [racing colors], the red Maltese Cross, were first across the finish [line] in 15 races out of 25 starts at Saratoga."[48] Woodburn-bred stock had a profound influence on California (and western) racing and breeding, which carried into the 20th-Century.[49]

At his Baldwin Hotel in San Francisco it is said that in "Lucky" Baldwin's "personal suite of rooms poker was played for formidable stakes and the destinies of Baldwin's matchless racing stable were shaped over oceans of Kentucky Bourbon."[50] His ranch today is the Arboretum of L.A. County and there Baldwin built the Queen Anne Cottage. The Queen Anne cottage was constructed in 1885-86 probably as a honeymoon gift for Baldwin's fourth wife, 16-year-old Lillie Bennett. The two were married in May of 1884; however, they separated one year later. The house was converted to a memorial to Baldwin's third wife, Jennie Dexter, who had died in 1881. An oil painting of her hangs in the house. The cottage, designed by Albert A. Bennett, Lillie Bennett's father, became the Santa Anita Ranch guest house, (the designation "Queen Anne" was added years later in reference to the architectural style).[51]

Two good friends of Baldwin's and his daughter Clara, were Josephine and Wyatt Earp who lived at The Baldwin Hotel. Wyatt worked and trained his trotters at Rancho Santa Anita. According to Josephine Sarah Marcus Earp's book, *I Married Wyatt Earp*, Verona Baldwin, "Lucky" Baldwin's young cousin, accused him of "ruining [her] "mind and body," shot and only wounded him. Lillian Ashley's sister shot him while in the courtroom where he was being tried for seducing Lillian. Beyond this he ran through five wives...."[52]

Emperor of Norfolk was the best horse bred in California before the turn of the century. A champion both years he raced. Baldwin bred at least eight stakes winners by Emperor of Norfolk, and of these, seven raced under his Maltese Cross racing colors.[53] The Maltese Cross is also carved in the outside base of his Coaching Barn and in the Queen Anne Cottage.

"Emperor of Norfolk spent practically his whole life on the E.J. Baldwin ranch in California, where his mates were mostly those that were bred and owned [by] Baldwin.... The infirmities of old age prevented Mr. Baldwin affording Emperor of Norfolk an opportunity to assert his full powers as a sire. He was not able to give personal supervision to his breeding and racing interest and for several reasons the offspring of this great horse did not get to the races in the best of condition and consequently did not win the races that they should have won. When racing was practically stopped by adverse legislation in California [1909], Emperor of Norfolk and his sons and daughters were afforded but very limited opportunities either on the track or in the stud.

Rey del Caredes (Americus), was a high class son of Emperor of Norfolk bred by Baldwin and bought by Richard Croker [after he won the Culver Handicap on October 1, 1895] who then took him to England. He had but very limited opportunities in the stud there, owing to propaganda staged by the British turf authorities against the American horses. In spite of this fact, his name appears in the pedigrees of several of Englands and Irelands sensational thoroughbreds. Cruzados was considered a high caliber colt and was heavily backed for the American Derby at Washington Park [Chicago] before the Derby Trial. [This] was run prior to the American Derby, in which race he fell coupled with McChesney that ruined and almost terminated his racing career."[54]

In 1894, Chant won the Kentucky Derby, however, in 1895 Americus was exported to England taking both the bloodline of Lexington and Woodburn's influence to Europe.

Rey del Caredas was foaled in 1892 and bought on October 22, 1895, by Richard "Boss" Croker of New York's Tammany Hall for $40,000. Rey del Caredas was exported that Fall to England and his named changed to Americus. Americus raced there and in Ireland until 1901. See Appendix Americus.

"He sired 38 winners and his name appears in the extended pedigrees of many of England's greatest modern race horses, and through his Irish-bred daughter Americus Girl, he has kept the bloodline of Lexington alive into the twentieth century…in the extended pedigrees of some of the world's finest horses, including Nasrullah, Tudor Minstrel and Mahmoud, Fair Trial, Court Martial, Mumtaz Mahal and Royal Charger."[55] Americus Girl is the dam of Lady Josephine, she the dam of the foundation mares Mumtaz Mahal, Lady Juror, Lady Diamond, Celoso, Bernadello, Magdelemas, Cruzdos and Americano.[56]

Norito and Cruzados were mated with only a few of the mares that were left on the Baldwin ranch by the heirs after Mr. Baldwin's death. Not many of their offspring ever got to the races, but one, Lantados, sired by the latter, was a colt possessed with tremendous speed which he proved in his trials that he could carry over a distance of ground with weight up. He was considered a sensational colt the winter he was in Tijuana, but owing to sickness and other adverse conditions he was not able to display his high form when racing.[57]

LEXINGTON'S LINE THROUGH NORFOLK

Norfolk (1861)

Emperor of Norfolk (1885)

Cruzados (1899)

Lantados (1918)

El Relicario, winner of the 1929 Miami Juvenile Stakes.

Rey el Rio (foaled 1933)

Rey el Tierra (1945)[58]

Baldwin won the American Derby four times with his horses Volante 1885 (by Grinstead out of Sister Anne),[59] Silver Cloud 1886 (by Grinstead out of Experiment),[60] Emperor of Norfolk 1888 (by Norfolk) and Rey el Santa Anita 1894 (by Cheviot out of Altho).[61] All are buried together under a large Maltese Cross tombstone within Santa Anita Park. Considering the size of his stud, the "American turf history credits Baldwin with being the most successful racing man in the country during the gay 90's."[62] Baldwin also built the first Santa Anita racetrack which opened in December 1907, not the large and impressive present track of today, which stands as a monument to Baldwin. On the following morning, the second day of racing, Emperor of Norfolk died at age 22. Baldwin's track was only open until the end of the 1909 season. Baldwin died on March 1st of the same year at the age of 81. Although his champions were from Woodburn blood lines, E.J. "Lucky" Baldwin made a profound influence on California and Western Racing.

"Baldwin Lake" in front of the Queen Anne Cottage.

Interior of the Queen Anne Cottage built by "Lucky" Baldwin in 1885-86.

The Queen Anne Cottage built by "Lucky" Baldwin note the Maltese Crosses in the tower.

The Arboretum of Los Angeles County.

"Lucky" Baldwin's Coach Barn with California Redwood interior, note the Maltese Crosses.

Interior of the Queen Anne Cottage.

Interior of the Queen Anne Cottage. It was built by E. J. "Lucky" Baldwin for his 16-year-old wife, but became the Rancho Santa Anita guest house.

The Arboretum of Los Angeles County.

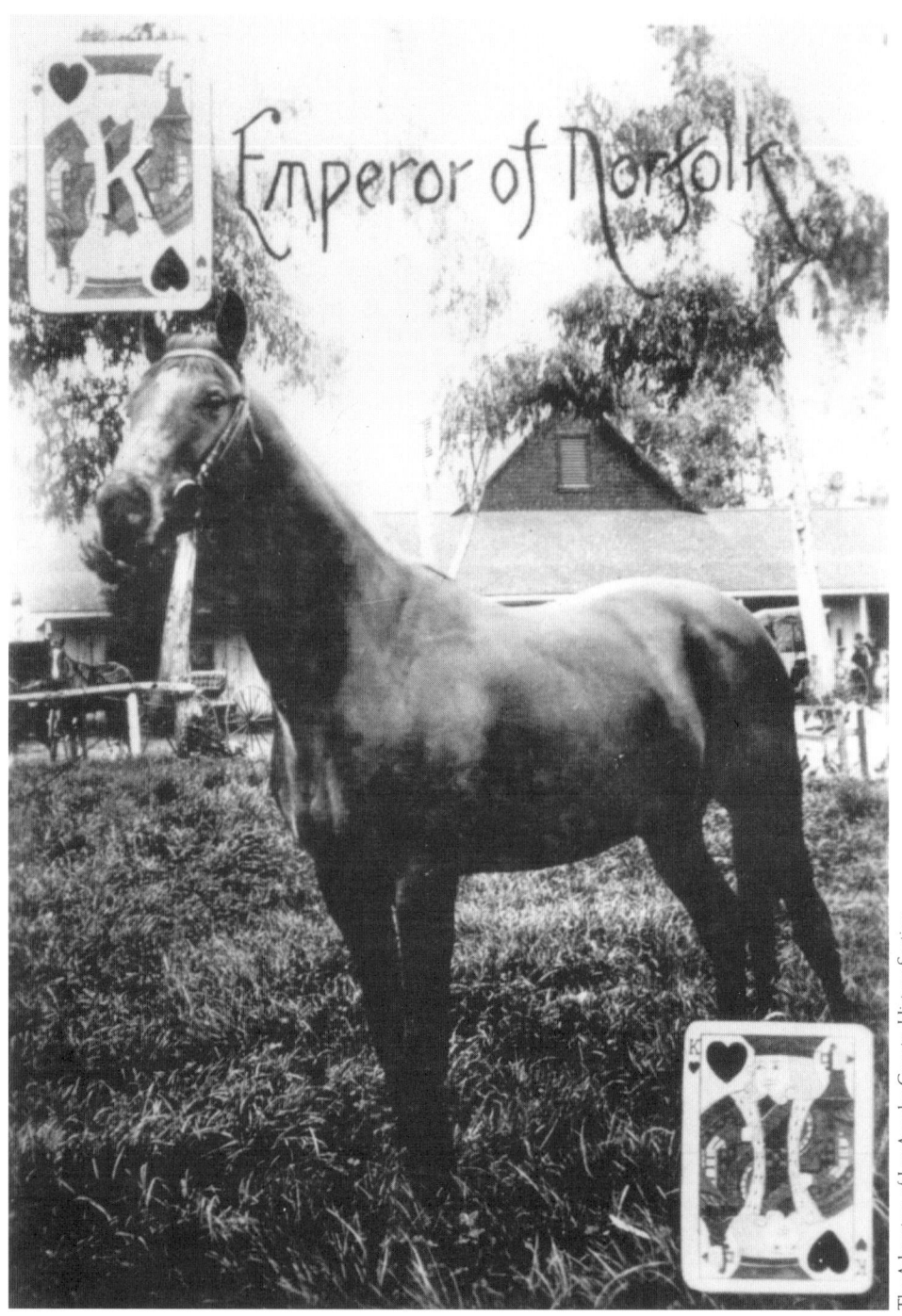

From "Lucky" Baldwin's Playing Cards, 1895, Emperor of Norfolk, Baldwin's best and favorite horse, raced only two years, but won 21 of 29 starts including the 1888 American Derby. He is the sire of eight stakes winners.

Painting of Emperor of Norfolk owned by E. J. "Lucky" Baldwin.

Americano, a full brother to Cruzados, proved to be a great disappointment who Baldwin refused $50,000 for. He turned out to be only a mediocre sprinter.

Americus was sent to England. The horse took Lexington's bloodlines and Woodburn's influence to Europe.

The Maltese Cross and grave site of Baldwin's four American Derby winners, Volante, Emperor of Norfolk, Silver Cloud and Rey El Santa Anita.

E. J. "Lucky" Baldwin's home at Rancho Santa Anita. This picture shows the old Hugo Reid Abode, (found on the ranch when Baldwin purchased it), on which he built.

THE OWENSBORO
✠ FAIR ✠
SEPT. 18, 19, 20, 21 and 22,

Will be the Best Fair ever held in Kentucky.

MAGNIFICENT HORSES

THE BEAUTIES OF THE EQUINE WORLD, WILL BE SEEN IN THE SHOW RINGS. THE RACES WILL BE THE BEST EVER RUN IN WESTERN KENTUCKY.

THE OWENSBORO DERBY, FIRST DAY,

OF 1¼ MILE, FOR $700, WILL BE THE BEST RACE OF THE YEAR. FRANK JAMES, THE NOTED REFORMED OUTLAW AND BANDIT, WILL BE HERE TO START THE HORSES IN THE "DERBY" AND ALL OTHER RACES THE FIRST DAY—HE WILL ONLY BE HERE THE FIRST DAY.

AUTOMOBILE RACES

WILL BE RUN EVERY AFTERNOON. THESE HORSELESS CARRIAGE RACES, THE FIRST EVER RUN IN THE SOUTH OR WEST, WILL BE VERY EXCITING; THE MACHINES THAT WILL BE HERE WILL BE FASTER THAN ANY OF THE HORSES. THIS FEATURE IS ONE YEAR AHEAD OF ANY OTHER FAIR OR EXHIBITION IN THE COUNTRY.

THE WORLD'S HIGH DIVER,

PROF. MATT GAY, WILL DAILY MAKE A FEARFUL PLUNGE FROM THE TOP OF HIS 100-FOOT TOWER.

KEMP'S Wild West and Roman Hippodrome

WILL EVERY MORNING GIVE A REALISTIC FRONTIER EXHIBITION OF WESTERN LIFE, INCLUDNG DARING EXAMPLES OF RDING, LASSOEING, CAPTURING A HORSE THIEF AND OTHER THRILLING ACTS. THEIR ROMAN HIPPODROME REVIVES THE SPORTS OF OLD ROME; CHARIOT RACES AND STANDING RACES ARE RUN IN FAST TIME.

THERE WILL BE A PUBLIC MARRIAGE FROM PLATFORM WITH MANY WEDDING PRESENTS; A WHITE BABY SHOW; A COLORED BABY SHOW; THE GENTLEMAN'S CUP RACE; THE DAVIESS COUNTY ROAD RACE; SOMETHING GOING ON ALL THE TIME.

THE FIRST DAY WILL BE THE BEST.

ADMISSION—ADULTS, 25cts.; CHILDREN UNDER 12 YEARS, 15cts., UNDER 6 YEARS, FREE.

For premium list or speed program apply to
L. FREEMAN LITTLE, Secretary, Owensboro.

Advertisement from 1900 mentioning Frank James as a race starter.

CHAPTER FOURTEEN

Frank James ● Race Starter

"As tough an outfit as ever drew the
breath of life, and a gang that would have
ridden into hell, if there was loot to be found there."
Quantrill Raider and James-Younger Gang Member, Kit Dalton.[1]

In the early days of racing, fraternities and tight friendships were made among trainers, riders, drivers, bookies, turf followers and sportsmen. Through a careful and thorough investigation it has been discovered that a close bond existed during the 1890s between "Lucky" Baldwin, Josephine and Wyatt Earp, "Colonel Jack" Chinn, Frank James and the renown Missouri trainer, Sam Hildreth, who for a brief time trained Baldwin's horses.[2]

In *I Married Wyatt Earp*, Josephine Sarah Marcus Earp tells of attending the races with Baldwin watching Wyatt race his trotters.[3] Baldwin also gave old Katy, a very valuable gray driving mare, to "Colonel Jack" Chinn as a present. Frank James worked as the Assistant Starter at the St. Louis Fairgrounds under Jack Chinn, the Chief Starter, and Frank would visit Chinn's "Leonatus" farm at Harrodsburg, Kentucky, every year.[4] In 1902 Frank James also worked for trainer, Sam Hildreth, at the Fairgrounds Race Track at New Orleans.

At E.J. "Lucky" Baldwin's famous Baldwin Hotel,
"the finest hotel west of New York City," there was a $25,000 clock from Tiffany's that, as Mark Twain [another noted Missourian] described it, told "not only the hours, minutes and seconds, but the turns of the tides, the phases of the moon, the price of eggs and who's got your umbrella.... The hotel vault, by Herring Brothers was the envy of bankers. Carpets at $30 a yard were ordered from Europe quite literally by the mile."[5]
Attached to the hotel was the Baldwin Theater, a place where "Lucky" could meet actors, actresses and famous people of the day who would partake of his offer of hospitality among the wild peacocks and guinea hens at Rancho Santa Anita.[6]

"Colonel Jack" Chinn is the father of the first State Racing Commission of Kentucky and in this country and served as its first Chairman. It was Chinn who drew up the rules and reg-

Goldsmith Maid 2:14. Frank James was recognized by a witness at his Gallatin Missouri trail as having seen this great mare at the Kansas City Fair. Her sire was the great Alexander's Abdallah.

ulations which served as the model that dictated American Thoroughbred racing (with few changes) in nearly every state today. He served as a starter and presiding judge at many race tracks throughout the United States.[7] Chinn was a noted horse breeder, who owned the 1883 Kentucky Derby winner, Leonatus, by Longfellow, and was"...one of the most celebrated men in Kentucky."[8] In the 1890's while in St. Louis, Frank worked as an Assistant Starter under Colonel Jack Chinn.

After winning the Derby, Chinn bought Shawnee Farm at Harrodsburg, Mercer County, in 1884, and renamed it after his Derby winner. He was a good friend of E.J. "Lucky" Baldwin. Baldwin ran his horses at many of the tracks Chinn started over, and after 1894, in St. Louis or at Saratoga Springs, New York, Baldwin undoubtedly met Frank James.[9]

The racing career of Frank James, or his involvement with racing, goes back to the Woodburn Raid of 1865. Abdallah was taken and died as a result of this raid. In October 1882 Frank James, in a dramatic surrender to Missouri Governor Thomas T. Crittenden, in his office at the Capitol Building in Jefferson City, Missouri, brought his outlaw career to an end. After his sensational trials for murder and robbery and acquittals in 1883-84, he moved his family to Nevada, Missouri, and then to Dallas in 1887 where he worked in several clothing stores.[10]

Frank's knowledge of trotters also goes back to his Civil War and outlaw days, a fact verified by witness Jonas Potts during James' Gallatin, Missouri, trial in 1883. Jonas Potts, a blacksmith, testified, under cross-examination, that he believed he had seen Frank James before, when Goldsmith Maid trotted at the Kansas City Fair and again at the Hamilton Fair. At that time the mare had become the first 2:14 trotter. This horse lowered the Worlds' Record seven times and at the time Frank saw her, possibly in 1877, when she retired, she had won more times, more heats and more money than any other harness performer that had ever lived. She retired with a Worlds' Record of 2:14. When this great horse appeared, the fences surrounding the race track would be torn down by people who wanted to see the champion. Therefore, there is no question that Frank saw her and Potts recognized him at the Kansas City fair. Goldsmith Maid's sire was Alexander's Abdallah.[11]

During their outlaw careers (and in semi-retirement at Nashville, Tennessee, 1877-1881) the James Boys owned and raced thoroughbreds. Among other places Jesse raced in New York, New Jersey, Baltimore, Louisville, Chicago and St. Louis. Jesse owned three famous thoroughbred colts named Red Fox, Jim Malone and Skyrocket, who was foaled at Woodburn in 1873. Frank owned Jewel Maxey, Rebel and Jim Scott and George Rice was training for him.[12] Other horses the brothers owned include: Stonewall, Rio Grande and Col. Hull.

Frank did, however, return briefly to the East from Texas, and according to *The Kentucky Derby Story*, attended the 1889 Derby,"...one of the biggest, earliest upsets..." in its history. Reportedly, Frank laid down a heavy bet on "the 10-1 long shot, Spokane...smilingly unconcerned at the hoots of derisions from those about who felt Proctor Knott could not lose."[13]

Apparently, James "approached a bookmaker with the query, "What's the price on Spokane?" The bookmaker replied, "10-1 and the sky's the limit." Frank counted out his money and declared, "There's $5,000 here and as far as I'm concerned that's the sky."[14] In 1893 Frank returned from Texas with his wife and son and settled in St. Louis. According to *Such Was Saratoga*, Frank, "still using an alias to avoid untoward comment," attended the races at Saratoga Springs which started on July 23, 1894, and ran through August 25th.[15]

By October 1895 Frank was starting races as the Assistant Starter under "Colonel Jack" P. Chinn at the St. Louis Fair Grounds Race Course, a large complex located at Kossuth Avenue.[16] During the off season, Frank worked for the City Boss and boodler of St. Louis, Colonel Ed Butler. Butler was a master farrier by trade, eventually owning a patent on a horse shoe which he sold to the city of St. Louis's railways. This gave him a blanket contract for all the mules and the horses owned by the city. Butler also owned The Standard (burlesque) Theater where James worked as the ticket-taker at the front door. Frank and his family lived at 4279 Laclede Avenue. He worked for Butler until 1901 when Frank joined an acting touring

This rare old photograph shows Col. Jack Chinn in the buggy with William Jennings Bryan, who was holding a revival meeting at High Bridge, Kentucky, in 1899. Frank James, brother of Jesse James, is standing at the left and little Dickie Bryan at the right. The horse is old Katy, a favorite of Col. Chinn, given him by "Lucky" Baldwin.

company.[17] In 1897 Frank worked the races at the Boone County Fair in Columbia, Missouri.[18] In May of 1898 he was still working at the Fairgrounds Race Course as an Assistant Starter.[19] In 1896 a:

> "severe financial depression swept over the country. The abundance of crops and the low prices for farm products reduced purchasing power; overinvestment in railways stopped further expansion; the economic distress in Europe left its mark on the American market. The gold reserve of the treasury, tapped by withdraws by England and other European countries, and by financiers and speculators, dwindled. While gold was scarce, silver was abundant."[20] This huge over production in the U. S., coinciding with the failure of the crop market, influenced by the Liverpool market, sent the country into a deep econimic and crippling depression which started in 1894 and lasted until 1897. It shook the foundations of the financial structure of the country. Hundreds of thousands of workers were out of work. The amount of money that was in circulation was becoming inadequate for the daily necessities, and the country was having difficulty maintaining commercial stability. Many in the west felt that the U. S. was a silver producing country and silver became the answer to the depression crisis.

The abundance of silver was due to the Sherman Silver Purchase Act which committed the U.S. Treasury to buy a large amount of silver annually:

"But as the silver certificates were redeemable in gold, the speculators exchanged them for the much sought after metal, shipping the gold bullion to Europe where high premiums were paid. Thus the gold resources of the Treasury were drained until the reserve was under the crucial hundred million mark."[21]

President Grover Cleveland:

"believed in the sound-monies policy that the notes of the Treasury had to be backed by gold. Cleveland wanted Congress to repeal the Silver Purchase Act. A great number of Democrats [,however,] were for the free coinage of silver. Cleveland had to employ the help of the gold standard Republicans, and with their assistance the repeal was passed. The silver Democrats were enraged; they denounced the President as a tool of Wall Street financiers. From then on, Cleveland faced hostile opposition from an influential segment of his own party."[22]

Because of the scarcity of gold the economy slowed:

"Under this the farmers suffered most. The prices for their products were low, their mortgages and loans heavy; more grain and more livestock were needed to buy one gold dollar. It was argued that if the government would allow the coinage of silver, the money situation could be eased; the resulting inflation would drive prices up, and mortgages and loans could be paid off in cheaper money."[23]

The Democrats in the West were convinced that:

"the gold standard meant bankruptcy and the Democratic Convention, held in Chicago, would declare for the free coinage of silver at 16 to 1 (the present legal ratio) and damn the consequences."[24]

The gold standard delegation from Nebraska was unseated by the Silverites who admitted the free silver delegation headed by William Jennings Bryan.[25] It was at this Convention that Bryan gave his stirring *Cross of Gold* speech and overnight became a contender for the Democratic Presidential Candidate nomination, which he won, but only to lose the Presidency to William McKinley.[26]

In October 1896 Frank James, now a celebrity, was interviewed on the Nation's silver matter by *The Chicago Chronicle*. The interview was reprinted in *The New York Times*:

"I am willing to confess that I don't like Bryan, and I think I have good cause. He made some speeches several years ago in which he referred in a very uncomplimentary manner to my dead brother, Jesse and myself, but I can afford to be generous and return good for evil.

We are not going to vote for individuals in November but for a cause that is right, and that

Reunion of Quantrill's Guerrilla Band, circa mid 1890's. Frank James is pictured sitting in middle foreground.

must prevail. Silver is the stuff, and the money barons can't stop us from having it. This country has been governed too long by Wall Street and the West is about due to make a change.

I don't believe in permitting any foreigners to dictate our financial policy and if necessary, I am willing to shoulder a gun and do my share toward effecting our release from the bonds of the monopolists. They are going too far with the squeezing process, and the masses are not going to stand it much longer. Money is a power and the man with it can do a lot of things that would get a poor beggar into trouble. These Tariff Barons and Trust Kings have things their own way. They can roll right and left without taking a chance of getting the worst of it.

Even in my old profession we never had such a good thing. Holding up trains usually pans out rich when you happen to stop one with an express car well filled with the 'long green,' but it's not so nice when some messenger or conductor takes a shot at you from behind. We used to take long chances of being filled with lead at my old business, but these foreign money sharks can hold up a nation and suck it dry, and then a lot of fools are made to believe that they actually got the best of the bargain.

The only sincere gold advocates are the money drones and financial sharks. The snobbish aristocracy of the country should go over to England, where they belong. We don't want any Princes or Dukes over here. The poorest hard-working American is their superior, and if I were a millionaire several times over and had a daughter who wanted to marry one of them for his title, she would have to do it without my consent.

I am no Anarchist or revolutionist, but like hundreds of thousands of Americans I am good and tired of the existing state of affairs. Look at the decreased interest taken in horse racing. When I first landed in St. Louis, three or four years ago, twenty and thirty books were unable to handle the ring. Now what a contrast presents itself! Half as many books can handle the coin and the attendance is not half what is was formerly."[27]

Frank was aware of what the bookmakers and tracks had been making, and the profits they were losing at the time of the interview. It is interesting to note that Frank would again compare what was happening at the race tracks to what he was doing in a few short years.

By 1899 William Jennings Bryan was the leader of the Democratic Party and would again be the party's Presidential Candidate in 1900. In 1899 Colonel Chinn entertained Frank James and William Jennings Bryan at Leonatus when Bryan was holding a revival meeting at High Bridge, Kentucky. Someone even offered to take a picture of Chinn, James and the Bryan brothers and they obliged. Chinn's "parties lasted as long as the guest could stay" or stand. No man in Kentucky could boast..."better bourbon, superior fox hounds, thoroughbreds or game cocks."[28] We may never know if Frank's opinion of Bryan had changed by 1899, but one thing is very clear, Frank certainly agreed with Bryan's politics on the nation's silver matter.

On September 18, 1900, Frank worked the races for the Owensboro, Kentucky Fair.[29] He also worked the races at Guthrie, Kentucky (Todd County) on September 19-22, 1900, taking the train from Owensboro, and after the races visiting his old outlaw haunts at nearby Adairville.[30] On October 12, 1900, he attended the two–day barbecue and reunion of Quantrill's Guerrillas at Oak Grove near Independence, Missouri. He was always the center of attention.[31]

On Monday, September 23, 1901, Frank again attended the Quantrill's Guerrillas reunion in Jackson County at Little Blue Church, three miles from Blue Springs. That evening Frank left on the Chicago & Alton train for Bedford, Indiana, where he started the horse races.

"He was dressed in a natty business suit and his high collar and dressy fedora hat were a striking contrast to the garb of other survivors. That Frank James was near to the hearts of [the] old guerrillas was shown when the date of the reunion was changed solely to accommodate the ex-bandit who was under contract to start horses in Indiana. The date was changed to a day earlier than originally intended."[32]

At Bedford (in Lawrence County) while officiating the races, Frank was interviewed by *The Republican* newspaper while a guest at the Hotel Burton. Referring to the condition of the track at the fair grounds, he said that it was one of the best half mile tracks he ever "started over. The various turns are almost perfect, and the surveyor who laid it out certainly knew his business.[33]

"The presence of Frank James of St. Louis as starter, added interest to the races. Mr. James has the reputation of being one of the fairest and most capable starters in the country, and his reputation was born out by his actions of yesterday. Mr. James plays no favorites, and riders and drivers soon find this out."[34]

The Fair Grounds were located in the north end of town.[35] Bedford was on the Central Indiana Fair Circuit.[36] He proved to be a great drawing card. Many of the tracks Frank started at were 1/2-mile tracks.

In late 1901 Frank left his job as the ticket-taker at the Standard Theater in St. Louis to join H. Walter Van Dyke's melodrama, *Across The Desert*, which lasted ten weeks. James first appeared with the troupe on November 30th in Zanesville, Ohio. In a *St. Louis Post-Dispatch* interview, Frank explained his reasons for going on the stage:

"My thorough knowledge of horses fitted me for an honorable place in connection with race meetings, and that enabled me to piece out my income so that I was to live comfortably and provide a modest education for my boy. In the past three years, when I officiated at the races in smaller cities of Ohio and Kentucky, it was plain that a large number of those who attended came for the especial purpose of seeing me. It finally dawned on me that as much as I dislike the idea of appearing on exhibition where I appeared as a race starter; and I was doing it too, without any financial benefit to myself."[37]

In 1902 Frank worked as a Sheet Writer for one of the book makers (he knew most of them) at the New Orleans Fair Grounds Race Course. While there he became a betting commissioner for the renowned thoroughbred trainer, Sam Hildreth.[38] Hildreth was a native of Independence, Missouri. His horses were doing so well on the race tracks that he found he could not bet on his own horses because the bookmakers "were afraid to offer any kind of price on the horses from [his] stable."[39] The books would offer only the shortest odds, and the runners working for the bookies would be told to follow Hildreth around to see if he was placing any bets down.

James realized what was happening and one day at New Orleans he approached Mr. Hildreth with the situation and offered to help by making his bets for him. Therefore, James became a betting agent for a year and a half for the trainer. Hildreth stated that James was a very loyal friend and Hildreth received the best odds Frank could get for him on his horses.[40] In 1909 Frank James (then living at Fletcher, Oklahoma) returned to Louisiana, most likely New Orleans, for a week to attend the horse races.[41]

James also worked the horse races for the Queen City Fair Association at Springfield, Missouri. They also presented him with a starter's medal adorned with a picture of the painting, *Pharaoh's Horses* on the front and two crossed American flags on the back.[42] On August 15, 16, 17, 1903, James returned to Lexington, Louisville and Bardstown, Kentucky, with his and Cole Younger's *Wild West Show*, which performed in Louisville with an additional long street parade before the shows.[43]

In 1907

"James assisted in celebrating the birth of the new state [of Oklahoma] on Saturday and carried the U.S. flag with the new star. During the celebration, he [was quoted to have] said: 'God bless the new state. Boys, we live under the Best government the world has ever seen. Some of my old friends are yet thinking that General Lee is [still] in the field in front of Richmond, but that's gone by with me [now]. It's time to close up [ranks] and all stand by Roosevelt.'"[44]

In 1904 Frank changed from the Democratic to the Republican Party, as did his native state Missouri, to support Theodore Roosevelt for President. This support for Roosevelt would continue until the day he died. In 1914 a reporter, on a visit to the James' farm in Kearney, Missouri, noted that painted on James' chicken coop was "Bull Moose-T.R."[45]

Between 1907-1909 Frank worked the horse races at Duncan and Commanche, Oklahoma, and at the Texas State Fair in Dallas.[46] Frank continued to travel throughout the South during these later years where he was popular and really loved by the people. On July 4, 1910, Frank James and Kit Dalton (then living in Memphis) attended a barbecue picnic together at Summit, Mississippi. They were the guests of honor. The *Summit Sentinel* published an unusual greeting to Frank James with his picture at the top of the column in his necktie and high collar:

"Frank James is now making his last call. If you fail to see him now you will never have the privilege again. He wants to say farewell to his beloved Southland and his friends. He will be at the opera house door to collect your ticket and shake your hand if the first, no doubt for the last time. His most bitter enemies have said to him: 'Frank you never broke a promise or mislead a friend.' You have lived a life guarded by every newspaper reporter from infancy to your present age; and for the record, aside from dime novels, and your devotion to the South, none can say other than well done. You are welcome in our midst, and when you leave us for your most comfortable home, hope you may have a long life yet ahead of you, and that a green spot in memory shall remain with you during all your future days for Summit, Godbold Wells and Mississippi."[47]

After his mother died in 1911, Frank rented his Oklahoma farm and returned to Missouri. He died on February 18, 1915, in Kearney, at age 72.[48] Frank James had a very long and somewhat distinguished career in the racing business.

Katherine Brewer Collection.

Wounded Lexington

CHAPTER FIFTEEN

Woodburn's Legacy

In 1874, one year before Lexington died, a visitor to Woodburn noted:
"Lexington was running out in his paddock enjoying the ripe summer sun, but the groom caught him and led him to the stable. The blind old horse came forward with a competent, springy step. He had been rolling in the dust, but soiled as he was we could see at a glance the rich, healthy luster of his coat. Upon the left side of his neck and running down to the goiter, there was a fresh wound, and Mr. Broadhead informed us that it was received in a fight over the fence with a mule. ...He is doing very well however.... The old horse has to be cared for very tenderly now. His stomach is delicate, his teeth bad, and he is subject to colic."[1]

To help put Lexington's and Australian's influence as sires in these thoroughbred families bred at Woodburn more into perspective here is a list of what they produced. This also helps show Woodburn's consistency in lowering the times on the racetracks by the produce of these two stallions, and consistency lowering them in subsequent generations.

"Lexington was the first horse that carried time for four miles below 7:20, and since then two of his daughters have produced horses that have beat his performance. He wrought a wonderful change in the time records, and for the past twenty years he and his get have occupied the highest positions on the American turf. If we examine the *Racing Calendars*, we find the fastest and best time on record at all distances, from a half-mile to four miles, have been made by Lexington and his sons, or else by horses out of Lexington or his son's mares. Besides all this [one] cannot lay [his] finger upon a sire of any note, imported or native, whose reputation as a stallion does not rest upon Lexington blood. The best of these stallions get are out of Lexington mares, or daughters of his sons. Such is the case with Bonnie Scotland, Leamington [foaled 1853 and died at age 26 in May 1878] (except in the case of Longfellow), Phaeton, King Alfonso, Glenelg, Waverley, Longfellow, Virgil, Buckden, Australian, Alarm, Billet, John Morgan, Revolver, King Ernest, Catesby, Enquirer (whose dam is by Lexington), Hiawatha, Melbourne, Jr., Glengarry, Lelaps, Saxon, [winner of the 1874 Belmont Stakes] Dickens, Star Davis, Harry O'Fallon, and a number of others, to say nothing of what his sons have sired. It is in the light of such facts

Harold, sire of Maud S.

Alix 2:03:3/4, "That sweet little mare."

as these that we must judge of the worth and merit of this great horse's produce."[2]

Lexington, Australian and Planet's breeding records speak for themselves. See Appendix, Stakes Winners. Lexington and Planet died in 1875 and Australian, the great-great-grandsire of Man O'War, who produced his own immortal family, died in 1879. Australian was succeeded by Pat Malloy as the head of the Woodburn Stud.[3] By the 1890's Falsetto (sent to England to race on August 30, 1879, by Pierre Lorillard) and imported Hermance were at the head of the stud, and both were sold with 49 Woodburn broodmares in 1897.[4] To understand this influence on breeding, one must look at the stallions and bloodlines of that era.

WOODBURN STALLIONS–TROTTERS

The best descriptions of these stallions and family builders come from John H. Wallace (founder of *Wallace's Monthly* racing magazine). During the time he wrote his book, *The Horse of America* in 1896-97, Wallace was in a rift with Lucas Broadhead, then Woodburn Farm's manager. Despite this rift however, Mr. Wallace gives great credit to these Woodburn stallions, realizing their importance and influence in the harness racing industry. Therefore, his accounts are given.

HAROLD

"Harold became very famous when Maud S. became queen of the turf with the then marvelous record of 2:08 3/4, a record that stood unequaled from 1885 till 1891."[5] This horse was bred by Charles S. Dole (owner of Lakeland Farm in Crystal Lake, Illinois, near Chicago), who sold him, in an exchange of horses, to Woodburn Farm as a yearling. Harold, by Hamilbetonian, was foaled in 1864, and went to Woodburn as an early two-year-old. He had been purchased in 1866 to replace Alexander's Abdallah, who had been killed the year before.[6]

"Harold was six years old when he made his first service and from the five [mares] bred to him that year were produced the three foals, Hermes (2.27 1/2), Bicara [dam, Belle] and Childe Harold. ...Bicara became a broodmare at Woodburn and Childe Harold was taken to England as a colt. Bicara has to her credit 3 sires, Pancoast (2:21 3/4), the most successful of his sons, Ponce de Leon (2:13), Patrou (2:14 1/4) and Patronage, the latter being the sire of the champion race mare Alix 2:03 1/4."[7]

Alix, Worlds' Record holder in 1894, was foaled in 1888 and was by Patronage out of Atalanta. Atalanta was by Attorney 1005, a son of Harold (by Hambletonian) and Attorney's dam was Maud by Abdallah who died in 1865. Atalanta was also the grandam of Minor Heir 1:58 1/2, once holder of the World's race record for pacers, as was Alista (a daughter of Attorney) the grandam of Minor Heir.[8] Patronage was by Pancoast, 2:21 3/4, who was by

Robert J. 2:01 1/2 (1894 World's record holder for Pacers).

Woodford Mambrino. 2:21 1/2

Woodford Mambrino, 2:21 1/2, (by Mambrino Chief out of Woodbine, who stood at Woodburn), and his (Woodford Mambrino) entire stud service was done at Woodburn Farm.[9] "In addition to Alix, Patronage sired Pactolus 2:12 3/4, whose daughter Izetta 2:13 1/2 produced the pacing champion Directum I. 1:56 3/4, holder of many World's Records and one of the greatest performers of all time."[10] One note of interest is Pancoast's dam Bicara, (by Harold out of Belle), who was foaled in 1857, by Mambrino Chief, her dam Belle Lupe being by Brown's Bellfounder. Bicara was one of the premier matrons of her day. In addition to this breeding is Patronage's dam Beatrice, who was by Cuyler (by Hambletonian), out of Mary Mambrino by Mambrino Patchen (by Mambrino Chief). This shows that Alix was closely inbred on both side of her family tree.[11]

In Harold's entire career he was bred to but 594 mares, or an average of about 26 for each of his 23 seasons. At 11 years old Harold had produced only 19 foals because only mares bred to him were difficult to get in foal or otherwise considered undesirable for breeding:

"It is now a matter of history that the breeding of several thoroughbred mares to Pilot Jr. was an experiment for the purpose of getting brood mares, the first of their offspring were not considered at all superior, which was the real reason Miss Russell, Midnight and several others were bred in 1873 to Harold.

From these services came the champion trotter, Maud S (2:08 3/4), Noontide (2:20 1/2), which many... claimed had much natural speed, and several others [who] helped to make the Pilot Jr. Mares famous. Notwithstanding, the superiorty of these and others which were foaled later, at no time has Harold ever received full patronage, and only one year did he make even a fairly full season[.] Consequently his total number is small; in fact only half as great as that of his more popular stable companion, Belmont and only about a third as large as that of Almont."[12]

With the exception of Maud S., Harold got nothing of the first class, but in the second generation the family holds better rank in respect to extreme speed production. Beuzetta, 2:06 3/4, Early Bird, 2:10, The Conqueror, 2:13, and the great three-year-old Impetuous, 2:13, are out of daughters of Harold, while Kremlin, 2:07 3/4, Io, 2:13 1/2, Rizpah, 2;13 1/2, Russellmont, 2:12 3/4, and the great pacer Robert J., 2:01 1/2, are among the produce of his sons, and the trotting queen, Alix, 2:03 3/4, who is out of a daughter of Attorney, by Harold. Harold died at Woodburn, October 6, 1893, at age 29. This horse never trotted in public, but he was worked sometimes at Woodburn for speed. As a six-year-old he is said to have once trotted the farm track in 2:40 1/2, and in this mile "grabbed a quarter" and therefore, was not worked again. He is the sire of 44 standard performers, 43 of his sons produced 181 standard performers, and 45 of his daughters produced 67 standard performers.

Belmont, the great son of Alexander's Abdallah.

Almont, F. V. R. L. Hull up.

'There is little doubt that it was the Harold cross that has made the Pancoast strain so far superior to nearly all others of the Mambrino Chief family and the fact that such a famous trotter and campaigner as the race mare Alix is so closely inbred to Harold, and possessed so many of his characteristics is strong evidence of the value of this blood. Individually, and as a sire, Lord Russell, sire of the famous Kremlin, is decidedly superior to any other trotting stallion. Another son of Harold is the sire of the famous pacer, Robert J."[13]

Again, the influence of Woodburn Farm emerges through the pacer, Robert J., 2:01 1/2 (1894). He was strictly trotting bred, being by Hartford, 2:22 1/4, a son of Harold and Judith, by Mambrino Chief. His dam, (Robert J.'s), Geraldine, was by Jay Gould, 2:21 1/2, out of an American Star mare, one of the best sons of Rysdyk's Hambletonian and the sire of Pixley 2:08 1/4. Robert J. was a very well bred colt and a great Worlds' champion.

BELMONT

Abdallah's "two great sons, Almont and Belmont rose to pre-eminent places in the list of great sires. Other sons of this remarkable progenitor have taken rank as sires, and his daughters proved of the highest excellence as broodmares; but Almont and Belmont established large, important, and popular sub-families...."[14]

"Belmont was a bay horse of very superior form and finish, bred at Woodburn Farm, and foaled there in 1864. He was by Alexander's Abdallah, out of Belle (that produced McCurdy's Hambletonian, 2:26 1/2, and Bicara, the dam of Pancoast, 2:21 3/4) by Mambrino Chief; grandam Belle Lupe, by Brown's Bellfounder. [See Harold] Belmont and Almont were of the same age, and perhaps because of his finer appearance, Belmont seems to have been the preferred one at Woodburn, and was retained while Almont was sold. [See Appendix Sons of Almont] Though Belmont was a successful horse and established a great family, no thinking man can contend that he was an equal to Almont as a sire... Almont spent almost his entire stud career at Fairlawn Farm, [owned by W.T. Withers of Lexington, Kentucky], where there never were five mares worthy in blood to be in a great trotting stud[.] Where scores of mares were of all kinds of poor and freakish pedigrees, even to Arabs, and where none of the stock was ever trained. Belmont, on the other hand, was all his life at the head of the most famous [stud], and, in his younger years, unquestionably [where there were] the best collection of trotting brood mares in the world, and where a training department was always maintained.

Belmont, besides having the advantage of excellent individuality, was also a trotter of no mean speed. He was driven a mile over the working track at Woodburn in 2:28 1/2, and was, therefore, quite well-developed. [Since Belmont] never appeared in the public, he has no public history. The most successful of his sons was Nutwood, whose dam was Miss

Swigert.

Russell, the dam of Maud S. This horse was himself a fast trotter in his day, taking a record of 2:18 3/4, and rose to great popularity and success in the stud. Daughters of Belmont, being nearly all out of producing mares, are greatly and justly esteemed as broodmares. Belmont died at Woodburn November 15, 1889. Belmont got fifty-eight standard performers, sixty-three of his sons sired four hundred and eighty-nine standard performers, and forty-eight of his daughters produced seventy-one standard performers."[15] See Appendix, Sons of Belmont.

SWIGERT

"Swigert was a brown horse, foaled 1866, got by Alexander's Norman, son of the Morse Horse; dam Blandina, by Mambrino Chief; grandam the Burch Mare, by Brown Pilot, son of Copper Bottom, pacer. He was bred at Woodburn, Kentucky, and when young became the property of Richard Richards, of Racine, Wisconsin, where he remained many years and passed to F.J. Ayers, of Burlington, Wisconsin. As a prepotent sire this horse stands high in the list of great horses. This may be accounted for in great part by the speed-producing qualities which he inherited from his dam.... He placed forty-four trotters and two pacers in the 2:30 list. Thirty-three of his sons became the sires of sixty-one trotters and fourteen pacers. Twenty-three of his daughters produced twenty-one trotters and six pacers. From the number of his sons that have already shown their ability to get trotters, it is fair to presume that his name will be perpetuated."[16]

Swigert's most successful campaigner was Moody 2:18 1/2, got when Swigert was seven years old and before his speed was developed. He was not as successful as a perpetuator of uniform standard speed as Blackwood. He is credited with 39 sons that sired a total of 94 standard performers, 65 of which were trotters. He is also credited with 30 daughters that have produced 32 trotters and 11 pacers which made standard records. Swigert ceased to perpetuate standard speed through the male line.[17] He died in 1892.

BLACKWOOD

"Blackwood was a black horse, foaled 1866, got by Alexander's Norman, son of the Morse Horse; dam by Mambrino Chief; grandam a fast trotting dun mare, brought from Ohio, pedigree unknown. He was bred by Daniel Swigert, Spring Station, Kentucky. His dam was sold in foal to Andrew Steele, of Scott County, Kentucky, at auction in 1865. At five years old he was sold to John W. Conley, and by him to Harrison Durkee, of New York, and was afterward owned at Ticonderoga, New York. He made a record of 2:31 when three years old, which, at that day, was considered phenomenal for a colt of that age. His opportunities in the stud were not the best, but nine of his progeny entered the 2:30 list;

Blackwood.

eleven of his sons got twenty performers, and twenty-five of his daughters produced thirty-seven performers."[18]

Among the most notable of his get was Blackwood Jr., who as a three-year-old held a record of 2:33 3/4 and a record of 2:32 as a four-year-old. Rosewood, out of a Mambrino mare, who as a 5-year-old held a record of 2:27; Freshman, out of a Ned Forrest mare, held a record of 2:36 1/2 as a 4-year-old; Blackwood Belle held a 3-year-old record of 2:46 3/4; and Proteine, who as a yearling trotted in 3:23 1/4-3:23 3/4, the fastest record at that time. Proteine as a three-year-old trotted a trial doing his last mile in 2:33 3/4. Blackwood is regarded as the representative stallion of the Norman family. He reigned over Spring Hill Stock Farm at Flushing Long Island, New York, owned by Harrison Durkee.[19]

THE MOOR

Unfortunately, research on The Moor has provided very little new information. Several sources have just repeated the same information. It appears that unique information on the stallion is rare and for this reason the following account is given in its entirety. This great horse came through the Belle of Wabash:

"This Indiana mare, known by only one son, whose foals in time made him famous, occupies a unique position among the great broodmares of the country. Without absolute certainty as to her sire, [the bay thoroughbred Bassinger, owned by Mr. Weisiger] with only sufficient opportunity to show that she had speed, soundness and endurance, and to secure a local reputation, she passed out of sight to become an object of curiosity and investigation when her descendants in the first and second generations revealed extraordinary merit[.] Now that the lineage not only of the stallion king, Stamboul (2:07 1/2), but of Sable Wilkes and his swift youngsters, of Bow Bells (2:19 1/4) Chimes, sire of seven, and many more, must end in one line of search, Belle of Wabash[.] The individuality of this Indiana product is still a matter of interest...."

[Through the Belle of Wabash's] "son The Moor, bred by George Stephens of Milwaukee, she was a queen of a splendid line. There was something in the atmosphere and circumstances of California to develop very showy and elegant and popular lines of trotters. The felicity of the nomenclature adopted in naming the colts and fillies, not equaled elsewhere, may have had a little to do with attracting attention and popularizing some of the California families. Though of course true merit also belonged to Minnehaha, Beautiful Bells and their happily named offspring.

There is quite an Oriental picturesqueness in the names of The Moor, Sultan, Stamboul, Alcazar (Spanish from the Arabic word), Amurath, Kismet, Othello, Saladin, [referred to as a "mixed gaited horse" (he both trotted and paced) held records for both gaits. His trotting record of 2:03 1/2 was made in July 1893]. Bell Boy, [full brother to Hinda Rose, was foaled at Palo Alto and not yet 3 years old when he sold for $35,000 in February 1888. He was sold again on July 31, at Lexington, Kentucky to C. C. Seaman for $50,000. He died in a stable fire at Versailles, Kentucky on January 11, 1890.] Moonstone, et al, and a tinkling rhythm in Minnehaha, Beautiful Bells, Chimes, Bell Bird, St. Bel, Bow Bells, Midnight Chimes. [This] graceful naming was suggested by the Indiana men who gave Belle of Wabash her name.

The Moor, the black son of the ebony-coated mare, must have transmitted some of his dam's attributes to his small but very select family, which contained the great Beautiful Bells, Black mare (dam of seven), Bell Boy, 2:19 1/4, Bell Bird, (1), 2:26 1/4, Belleflower, (2), 2:24 3/4, [sold at Madison Square Garden on May 12, 1896 for $3,700 as a 7-year-old] Hinda Rose, 2:19 1/2, Polo Alto Belle 2:22 1/2, St. Bel, (4), 2:24 1/2, Bow Bells, 2:19 1/4, and of Chimes 2:30 3/4, (sire of seven), and superb Sultan (sire of Stamboul, 2:07 1/2), Sable, black mare, dam of Sable Wilkes (3), (2:18), black horse (nine in the list), Leo Wilkes (2:29 3/4), Ulee Wilkes (4) (2:23), black filly, and dam of Rupee (2:11).

Of Minnehaha's great brood of trotters and of producing dams, the only foal by The Moor was the wondrous black mare Beautiful Bells, undoubtedly the greatest of the band. Another broodmare whose story is not fully told is Sable, granddaughter of Belle of Wabash, whose son Sable Wilkes may outstrip the remarkable sire of early and extreme speed; Guy Wilkes, since at eight years old he has on the list the speedy juveniles, Freedom (1) (2:29 3/4), Macleay, (2) (2:22 1/4), Sabina (2) (2:27 1/2), Ora Wilkes (2:21 1/2), brown colt, Lon Wilkes (3) (2:20 3/4), Lallah Wilkes (3) (2:26), brown filly, Wilkes Blanche (2:26 1/2), brown colt (formerly called Native Son) Sabledale (2) (2:18 1/2) and Puritan (2:29 1/2); surely an unequaled list. Sable has also to her credit Leo Wilkes (2:29 3/4), Ulee Wilkes (4) (2:23), black colt, and the dam of Rupee (2:11).

The roll of the descendants of The Moor, son of Clay Pilot, and Belle of Wabash has a sumptuous look, as it covers Beautiful Bells and her progeny, St. Bel and his get, Chimes and his seven, Sable Wilkes and his phenomenal nine, Stamboul (2:07 1/2), "and he shall be king," with his 10; Sultan, his greater sire, and his 28 performers; Alcazar 2:20 1/2 and his five, and the list can be extended to monotony, in honor of the unmarked, unregistered mare from Wabash."[20]

It is difficult to find early information on Mr. Leonard. J. Rose and mostly what we do know comes from his son, Leonard J. Rose, Jr.'s book, *L.J. Rose of Sunny Slope*. Mr. Rose Sr.'s reputation as a breeder was well known and the information that has been found speaks very highly of him, which proves that he was an influential California breeder of trotters. What we do know is that in Milwaukee, Wisconsin, Rose purchased six head, one a two-year-old black stallion, Beau Clay (later changed to The Moor); Overland, a yearling bay stallion; Pilot, a yearling gelding; Barbara, Maggie Mitchell and Minnehaha (bought for $200), all yearling fillies.

"They were shipped by rail to San Francisco, then transferred to a coast steamer for San Pedro. The landing facilities were meager, and each horse had to be hoisted from the steamer's hold to the wharf in a box. The horses were then led overland to San Gabriel, a distance of about forty-five miles, taking two days for the trip.... The Moor (Beau Clay) was very beautiful. Being a stallion and two years old, he showed to better advantage than the others, who were but yearlings and suffered more from the wear and tear of the long trip. The Moor was jet black with a shield-shaped white spot about the size of a small apple in the center of his forehead."

Early in the spring of 1870 Rose started on an eastern trip, which consumed three months. From New York he went directly to "Kentucky and bought ten mares and fillies, eight of trotting and two of running breed." Part of them were purchased from Woodburn Farm.

"The others, including the two running fillies, were purchased from General (William Hicks) Jackson, of [Belle Meade Stock Farm in Tennessee]. One of the running fillies had been named Lulu Jackson for a daughter of the general, the other, Irene Harding for the daughter of General (William Giles) Harding (father-in-law to General Jackson).

The animals were at once shipped by rail to San Francisco, then by steamer to San Pedro, then overland, and finally arrived at Sunny Slope in good condition after a long tedious trip. They were a choicely lot and all fine [stock]. Four of them—Gretchen, Sea Foam, Kate Tabor, and Belle View Maid—were of matronly age, the remaining six, including the two running fillies, were two years old. Sea Foam and Gretchen had been to the court of Woodford Mambrino, and Kate Tabor to that of Mambrino Patchen, both of these stallions being held in favor."[21]

WEDGEWOOD

Wedgewood was bred at Woodburn and foaled in 1871, by Alexander's Belmont, out of Woodbine by Woodford. Woodbine was a most prolific mare, producing 15 foals from 1861 to 1878. In 1863, to the cover of Mambrino Chief, she produced:

"...that great trotter and sire of trotters, Woodford Mambrino (2:21 3/4). [Woodbine] was a prime favorite at Woodburn, and in 1870, was bred for the second time to the head of the stud there, Alexander's Belmont, and the result was Wedgewood.

Woodbine infused into Wedgewood's composition an abundance of the stoutest thoroughbred blood, and she would need no certificate of merit beyond being also the dam of Woodford Mambrino, who sired Abbottsford, (2:21 1/2); Mambrino Dudley (2:22), Convoy

Wedgewood.

(2:22 1/2), Magenta (2:24 1/2), Rachel (2:26 3/4), Inca (2:27), Lady McFatridge (2:29), Dacia (2:29 1/2) and George A. Ayer (2:30).

Wedgewood first appeared on the turf at Cynthiana, Ky. in 1877 beating a field of four in 2:39 1/4, 2:38 1/4, 2:38 1/4, although he trotted over the Woodburn track in 2:25 that same year."[22]

Wedgewood, however, would later hold a record of 2:19.

"The first full season of this great stallion was made in 1882, at the Bates Farm, Watertown, Mass., a few miles from Boston. At Woodburn he had been obscured by Belmont and Harold and his opportunities with good mares were few. At the Bates Farm, the public appreciation of his excellencies brought fast and highly bred mares, such as has never before been know in the history of any trotting stallion. Others have served more mares in a season, but no horse was ever visited by a company of matrons averaging so high in speed and breeding."[23]

The great John R. Gentry's bloodlines go back to Kentucky and Woodburn Farm through Woodbine, dam of Wedgewood, sire of Damewood who is the dam of John R. Gentry. John Hervey's *The American Trotter* is the best source to explain and to clarify this:

"Woodford Mambrino was bred by Mason R. Henry, of Woodford County, Kentucky, and was one of a few foals got by Mambrino Chief just before his death in March 1862, Woodford Mambrino being a 1863 colt."[24]

His dam, Woodbine, also bred by Henry, was by Woodford, a thoroughbred son of Kosciusko, by Sir Archy; grandam, known as the Singleton Mare, of unknown blood but always understood as well-bred.

"That Woodbine was considered a choice mare for breeding purposes is shown by the fact she was bought for Woodburn stud by R.A. Alexander with Woodford Mambrino at foot and became one of its great producers. Her long list of foals bred there includes Wedgewood, 2:19, by Belmont, whose campaign of 1880 along the Grand Circuit, in which he was unbeaten, included a series of five-, six-, and seven-heat races that as a test of gameness, stamina, and ruggedness never has been surpassed. Later, Wedgewood became a celebrated sire and is memorable as having got Damewood, the dam of John R. Gentry, 2:00 1/2, the first horse to approach the 2:00 mark in single harness."[25]

John R. Gentry was gaited like a champion, smooth, frictionless and light; was called "a brainy race horse," and as stoutly bred in trotting line as any horse on the turf at that time. He was bred by H.G. Toler at Wichita, Kansas, by Ashland Wilkes, 2:17 1/4, (trotter) a son of Red Wilkes, 2:40, out of Daisy B., by Administrator, 2:29 1/2, second dam by Knight of St. George, thoroughbred. Gentry's dam was Damewood, by Wedgewood, 2:19, second dam Fancy 2:30, a chestnut mare of untraced breeding, who won her record at Philadelphia on October 3, 1878. Damewood is also the dam of Myron McHenry, 2:18 1/4, (trotter) and Theodore Shelton, (pacer), who as a 2-year-old was a close second to Directly in 2:13, 2:15, at the Terre Haute Fair meeting on August 16, 1894.[26] A truly great family came from this line with Alexander's Belmont at its head. This collection of great trotting stallions carried the fame of the Woodburn trotting department, and continued to produce some of the finest Standardbreds that the American turf had ever seen.

A handsome photograph portrait of Alexander John Alexander. It is through him that the family descended into the twentieth century.

CHAPTER SIXTEEN

The Alexanders Extended Family

"A large part of the legacy is the fact that, although R.A. had no progeny of his own, he created such a strong identity of place and love of the land that his extended family has never left the original land grant. He created a bond between blood and earth that reaches far beyond the thoroughbred and which would have the descendants of the original Scotsman who settled there fight literally to the death before abandoning the land made precious by a man named R.A. Alexander."[1]

Although Woodburn Farm no longer stands as a great singular breeding establishment, its heritage survives. All of the 2,700 acres in Robert Alexander's original land grant continue to be owned and occupied by his family. Upon R.A.'s death his brother, Alexander John Alexander, inherited Woodburn Farm in accordance with the "express dying wish of his brother."[2] A.J. Alexander had been living and working in Chicago for ten years prior to R.A.'s death. He had left Kentucky after the deaths of his first wife, Lucy Humphreys, and their three children, David, Mary and Robert, in an epidemic, and the subsequent loss of his home by fire. These losses devastated him, and he first went to Texas for a brief time, and then to Chicago to oversee the family's properties in the North. Prior to his return to Woodburn, he married Lucy Fullerton of Chillicothe, Ohio, a cousin to his first wife.[3]

At R.A.'s death, his brother, A.J., sold the Airdrie Ironworks to former Union General Don Carlos Buell for the price of the tax lien against the property. Buell, then President of Airdrie Petroleum Company, was looking for oil, but found coal. Muhlenburg County, Kentucky, later became one of the major coal producing areas in the United States. Buell was unsuccessful in his mining venture since the Green River Navigation Company charged him a prohibitive cost to move the coal on the Ohio River.[4]

Although A.J. Alexander inherited the farm, he did not share his brother's passion for horses and did not personally possess a deeply committed interest in the breeding or racing of thoroughbreds and standardbreds. His personal preference was the breeding of sheep and cattle. A.J. initially left the responsibility of the horses to Daniel Swigert, and began the publication of *The American Short Horn Registry* simply as a means of keeping records of his own herd.[5] It quickly expanded, however, to include many of the finest cattle of that breed in the nation. After two years Swigert resigned (1869) to start his own farm, the 300–acre Stockwood Stud. In 1881 Swigert bought the famed Preakness Stud near Lexington and renamed the farm, Elmendorf, after the maiden name of his wife's paternal grandmother. Swigert, however, remained loyal to Woodburn Farm and continued to be a regular customer at the farm's yearling sales.

After the loss of Daniel Swigert, A.J. promoted Lucas Broadhead to farm manager. Broadhead, who had been working at the Airdrie Mill in Montgomery, Illinois, was Swigert's 25–year–old brother-in-law and a cousin by marriage to A. J. Among Broadhead's duties was the decision as to which horses were bought and sold and which were chosen as studs for the farm's broodmares. According to Dan Bowmar, III, "...his record was outstanding, particularly in the early years of his tenure, when he had Lexington and Australian."[6] Under Broadhead's direction Woodburn Farm flourished from 1880-1892 and Broadhead developed into "a man of great ability who became one of the most distinguished figures in the breeding world."[7] "The make-up of the stud [,however,] remained as it had been, except that as death removed stallions and broodmares they were replaced by others, of which King Alfonso was one, Falsetto another, and so on. The mares used were for the most part descendants of the original Woodburn strains."[8]

By 1874 Woodburn was 3,200 acres and besides the racing stock, the farm was still involved in breeding Shorthorn and Alderney cattle, as well as Southdown sheep.[9] (R.A. had first introduced Durham and Alderney cattle and Southdown sheep imported from England in 1853. Later he introduced Ayrshire and Shorthorn cattle and helped to establish these breeds in the United States.)[10]

In April 1878 it was anticipated that 51 thoroughbred foals would be dropped during that season, which was "...a large increase over 1877. Mr. F.V.R.L. Hull [had] some 22 head of trotters up at Woodburn, most of them youngsters running from two to three years old."[11] During the 1880s the Woodburn Stud produced its two greatest trotters, Jay-Eye-See and Maud S. Jay-Eye-See lowered the World's Record to 2:10 in 1884 and Maud S. lowered it further in 1886 when she trotted the mile in 2:08 3/4. By 1887 Woodburn's leading trotting stallions were: Harold, Belmont and Lord Russell. Woodburn's stud also produced, in addition to the above, "Nutwood, Noontide, Mambrino Gift [2:20, died at 10-years-old at Flint Michigan on September 1, 1877], Indianapolis, Dick Moore, Hylas, Tattler, Almont, Abdallah Pilot, Woodford Mambrino, Pancoast, King Rene, Hermes, Princeps, Wedgewood, Mambrino Dudley, Voltaire, and Swigert."[12]

The thoroughbred stud of Woodburn included the stallions Glen Athol, Lisbon, King Alfonso, Pat Malloy, Powhatan, and Falsetto. In addition, Woodburn claimed a "large and very superior herd of Shorthorn cattle, a fine flock of purebred Southdown sheep, and a small but select herd of Jerseys...."[13] It is this influence that helped in building Woodburn's national reputation as a great breeding establishment.

In 1893, during the great panic and the ensuing economic depression, the thoroughbred and standardbred operations at Woodburn Farm were largely discontinued and "...in a series of sales the entire stud was dispersed, the last one being held in 1901."[14]

In October 1897 an announcement proclaimed that the Woodburn stock was to be dispersed. It stated:

"...the broodmares of Woodburn have been among the greatest in the land, and their daughters have also given to the racing world many of its best race horses. A large percentage of the best native thoroughbreds trace to Woodburn bred mares and stallions....The get of the Woodburn thoroughbred stallions have won nearly $3,000,000, and the winners of many of the classic events of both America and England have come from its paddocks."[15] In this sale the stallions, Falsetto, imported Hermence, and a big band of thoroughbred broodmares were also sold.[16]

In 1896 Lucas Broadhead:

"...compiled a table which showed that, beginning in 1866 and up to the date, Woodburn had sold 744 head of trotters at either public or private sales, for the sum of $747,254, an average of $1,000 per head, of which all but 174 head were sold privately. [Bowmar lists the number at 950 head, the cost at $823,161 with an average of $866 per head.]"[17] Unlike the thoroughbreds, most of the harness horses at Woodburn were sold privately, often in large lots. The farm conducted auctions several times, but the results were never as good as those of thoroughbred auctions. Woodburn's best thoroughbreds were bred between 1861 and 1882, but there were several good ones in the last years of the farm's horse operations, including the Belmont Stakes' winners Burlington and Patron."[18]

Woodburn's dominance in thoroughbred breeding began its decline at the death of Lexington and Australian, although Woodburn still stood King Alfonso, who was "...one of the stallions selected to succeed Lexington and Australian after their passing." King Alfonso produced Foxhall who was sent to England and won the Grand Prix de Paris at Longchamp, France. [19] He also won the Ascot Gold Cup on June 8, 1882.

After an illustrious career, Lucas Broadhead died at age 70 of double pneumonia at his country home "Okalee" in early October of 1914.[20] Alexander John Alexander died on December 2, 1902, at the age of 78, having owned Woodburn Farm for 35 years. The lega-

Alexander John Alexander with his children at Woodburn. It is the house where A. J. lived after his return to Kentucky. A. J. inherited Woodburn in 1867 and had owned it for 35 years when he died in 1902.

cy continued, however, and Woodburn was subsequently divided among his three living children: Alexander John Aitcheson, Kenneth Deedes and Lucy. A thousand acres, more or less, on the north side of the Old Frankfort Pike passed to the eldest son, Dr. Alexander John Aitcheson Alexander. This included the large brick house (Woodburn Mansion) where A.J. Alexander lived after his return to the Bluegrass, and it was this portion of the farm that maintained the name "Woodburn." The remainder of the estate, south of the road, which contained the rambling one–and–a–half story structure that had been the home of R.A. Alexander, was inherited by Kenneth and Lucy.

Dr. Alexander John Aitcheson Alexander was born on August 5, 1875, and became a medical missionary in Kunsan, Korea, in 1902-1903.[21] Because of his strict religious beliefs, he did not participate in the racing industry. He did, however, continue the breeding of cattle at Woodburn and, dedicated to the Presbyterian Church, he supported a number of worthy causes. He was the first National Chairman of Mary Breckinridge's Frontier Nursing Service in Leslie County and was an active member on the Board of Centre College in Danville, Kentucky. Dr. A.J.A. Alexander died in 1928 and Woodburn passed on to his two sons, Alexander John Alexander, who married Jean Preston of Lexington, Kentucky, and James H. Alexander, who married Lucy Multhrop of Montgomery, Alabama.

Once again the estate bearing the name Woodburn was divided. A.J., the eldest son, inherited Woodburn House along with 500 acres, more or less, and the residual of the estate became the property of A.J.'s brother, James.

A.J. Alexander graduated from Princeton and received his medical degree from Johns Hopkins University in 1934. He entered the practice of pediatrics in 1938, only to have it interrupted by World War II. He served as an officer in the Army Medical Corps. He subsequently returned to Woodburn where he raised a family of three children while continuing to practice medicine in Lexington on Bullock Street, in 1940 on Short Street, and later on Esplanade.

In 1955 he acquired his first thoroughbred broodmare and continued to breed and race a few horses over the ensuing years. None, however, achieved national notoriety.

Kenneth Deedes Alexander, brother of Lucy and Dr. A.J.A., inherited a portion of the land south of the Old Frankfort Pike which contained the original Woodburn House. He subsequently sold his acreage to Lucy and her husband, William E. Simms, in 1919. They named all the land south of the Pike (which had been contained in the original land grant) Airdrie Farm after the town in Scotland where the Alexander estate was located.

Kenneth married Molly King of New York and had two sons, Kenneth Deedes, Jr., and Robert Aitcheson, III. During the decade of 1915-1925, Kenneth Sr. bred and raced thoroughbreds with significant success. According to Dan Bowmar III's book, *Giants Of The Turf*, Kenneth Alexander's best horses were Stakes winners Star Voter, Billy Watts, Trevisco (bought in England) and Escoba. Star Voter, by Ballot, raced in 1920-1921 and in 18 starts earned a total of $23,587. Escoba by Broomstick, started 19 times and earned a total of $23,200 and finished second against Exterminator in the 1918 Kentucky Derby. Kenneth disposed of his horses prior to his untimely death at age 46 in Hot Springs, Arkansas, on July 2, 1935.[22]

Lucy and Will Simms had three children: William who died as a small child, Elizabeth, and Lucy. Mrs. Elizabeth Simms Gay, the granddaughter of Alexander John Alexander, together with her husband, Augustus Benjamin (A.B. or Gus) Gay, inherited a portion of Airdrie Farm and renamed it "Lanark" after Lanarkshire, the county in Scotland where the town of Airdrie is located.

The Gays owned and bred race horses from the mid-1930s, and produced a very impressive index of winners. The most notable of the fine stock bred and raced by the Gays included Porter's Cap (winner of the 1941 Santa Anita Derby and the 1940 Washington Park Futurity) and Stakes winners Waller (winner of the 1942 Queens County Handicap), Woodford Lad (winner of the 1942 Hawthorne Juvenile Handicap), John Doe (winner of the 1958 Yearlings Sale Stakes), as well as Bring Back, Gay Lothario, Genteel Gus, Viking Spirit

Original house on Lanark Farm, the original Woodburn Farm.

Woodburn, home of Robert and Katherine Brewer.

(bred and sold for $7,700 in 1961), By to Market, Tim's Stingray (sold for $16,500 in 1963), El Fantastico (sold for $30,500 in 1976), and Atop, dam of the $399,981 money winner Top Avenger. At the September 1980 Keeneland yearling sales, the Gays sold a Best Turn colt for $155,000.[23]

Augustus B. Gay was the last surviving member of the original Board of Directors of the Keeneland Association, having served for 48 years. He held the position of second Vice-President for 20 years. He was also a member of the Kentucky State Racing Commission and the Thoroughbred Club of America. Augustus B. Gay is survived by his son, Dr. James G. Gay, and his daughter, Mrs. Lucy Gay Bassett. Dr. James G. Gay served in the North Atlantic as a line officer with the U.S. Navy before earning his medical degree. Dr. Gay married Anne Pinkney of Richmond, Virginia. They live in the beautiful home, "Mansfield," located on Richmond Road in Lexington and have four children: Elizabeth Gay Freeman, Charlotte Gay Stites, "Teddy", and Anne.

Upon her father's death, Mrs. Lucy Gay Bassett inherited an undivided half interest in Lanark Farm, (subsequently delineated from the portion owned by her brother) including a lovely home with pristine and manicured grounds and pastures. She bought her first mare, Hunt the Thimble (in foal to Star de Naskra) in 1984, who foaled the subsequent Stakes winner, Astraeus. Mrs. Bassett bred Linden Lime by Green Dancer (grandson of Northern Dancer) by Nijinsky II. In 1994 Linden Lime earned a total of $311,278, with total career earnings in the U.S. of $627,808. She also raced in England.[24] Mrs. Bassett is also the breeder of Secrage by Secreto (son of Northern Dancer) out of Wayage by Mr. Prospector (by Raise a Native). In 1992 Secrage earned a total of $228.715.[25] Records show that in 1994 Mrs. Bassett owned nine mares. Records for 1995 show her owning Winnowing Wind, White Reason, Wayage, Separate Issue, Jamilleah, Hunt the Thimble and Daydream.[26]

Her husband, James E. "Ted" Bassett III, served with distinction as a Marine Corps officer in the 4th Marine Regiment from 1943-1946. At one time he was President of Keeneland Association. On March 27, 1986, he was elevated to Chairman of the Board.[27] Under Mr. Bassett's guidance as President, Keeneland Association became a pioneer in Kentucky racing, preparing for the 21st century as one of the premier race tracks in the country. In 1988 he became the first President of the *Breeders Cup Ltd.*, and has been a great asset to the sport of racing and its promotion. He is always ready to take up a cause which he feels is valuable to the sport. He owns Falconese (bred by Mrs. Bassett) by Imperial Falcon by Northern Dancer.[28] In 1995 Falconese had a total earnings of $106,605, with total career earnings of $168,080.

At Alexander John Alexander's (Dr. A.J.A. Alexander's son) death in 1969, his estate was passed on to his two daughters: Katherine (Mrs. Robert Brewer) and Jean (Mrs. Roger

Photograph by William H. Strode

Airdrie Farm.

Gilcrest), and to his son, Dr. Alexander John Alexander V. Dr. Alexander served as Battalion Surgeon with the 5th Marines in Viet Nam, and, among other decorations, was awarded the Bronze Star for valor. Despite the temptation to breed and race thoroughbreds, Dr. Alexander has played a supportive role in the breeding and racing industry by publishing one of the first papers on the molecular genetics of the horse.[29]

The name Woodburn still endures, surrounded by the old stone fences, as the beautiful home of Robert M. and Katherine (Alexander) Brewer. Mrs. Brewer has owned several broodmares and takes an active interest in fox hunting. Robert Brewer was decorated as a Naval line officer during the Korean conflict, and subsequently became Commander of the Kentucky Naval Reserve with the rank of Captain. In 1985 Mr. Brewer was recognized with the prestigious state award, "Man of the Year In Service to Kentucky Agriculture" from *Progressive Farmer* magazine for excellence in farming. He is also a member of the Kentucky Cattleman Association and serves on the Kentucky Horse Park Commission. From 1987-1994 he was the "Master of Hounds" at the Iroquois Hunt Club in Lexington and has been actively involved in numerous civic organizations. Mr. and Mrs. Brewer have three children: Jean, Juliet, and Robert Aitcheson Alexander Brewer.

A short time after the death of their father, Dr. Alexander and Katherine Brewer bought equal portions of their sister's interest in the estate. Today Jean Gilcrest lives in Mishawaka, Indiana. Her children are: William Alexander Gilchrist, Gretchen Burud and Anne Guillen.

History is full of ironies and it seems only fitting that R.A.'s namesake, R.A. Alexander III (Kenneth Alexander's son), enjoyed a long and distinguished career breeding thoroughbreds as the owner of the 135-acre Bosque Bonita Farm, the home of R.A.'s ancient rival, General Abe Buford. Robert served with the 10th Mountain Division in Italy and was decorated for valor in World War II. He sold the original Bosque Bonita in 1976 (his current farm is also Bosque Bonita), but continues to breed and race horses and he goes to the race track daily.

The most notable of his stock was Bally Ache (by Ballydam out of Celestial Blue) who was syndicated in 1960 for $1,250,000.[30] Bally Ache finished second in the Kentucky Derby to Venetian Way, and won a 4-length decision in the Preakness, after which he won the Jersey Derby over Tompion. The day before the Belmont, one of his ankles filled and he did not race for 2 1/2 months. He returned to defeat Royal Native in the United Nations Handicap, running third to the great T.V. Lark and Sword Dancer by only 2 1/2 lengths back from the winner. He broke down in Chicago on October 8th, in a "9-furlong tune up" while preparing for the $100,000-added Hawthorne Gold Cup on the 15th, "...finishing unplaced for only the second time in a 31–race career."[31] The injury was a partial dislocation of the right fetlock joint, with damage to the collateral ligaments, the sesamoid bone, and the long

Airdrie, home of former Governor Brereton C. and Elizabeth Lloyd Jones.

pastern bones. Bally Ache retired as a 3-year-old to Bosque Bonita, arriving there on October 23rd "...wearing a blanket given him by Garden State Park."[32] Bally Ache's earnings for his last year were $455,045, "...leading all horses in 1960 in this department (T.V. Lark is second with $393,900)."[33]

Unfortunately, just five days later Bally Ache died of an acute inflammation of the digestive tract, ending the life of a great horse and an outstanding career of 16 victories and 13 placings, with total career earnings of $758,522.[34] He was buried at Bosque Bonita where his grave is simply marked by a stone with a bronze plaque.[35]

R.A. Alexander III's daughter, Lucy Deedes Lloyd, and her husband, Duncan Lloyd, run a successful breeding operation at Village View Farm, located at the edge of Versailles. His other daughter, Brownell, also has had a life–time interest in horses. R.A. III's brother, Kenneth, served with distinction in the Royal Canadian Air Force, and was Senator in the territorial Senate of the U.S. Virgin Islands..

Elizabeth ("Libby") Lloyd Jones, (daughter of General Arthur Y. and Lucy Simms Lloyd and granddaughter of William "Will" and Lucy Alexander Simms) married Brereton C. Jones on October 31, 1970, and at that time was the sole heir to Airdrie Farm. Arthur Y. Lloyd rose to the rank of Major General as Adjutant General of Kentucky after a distinguished career in the Pacific and in the European theater during World War II. In 1970 Airdrie was approximately 1,200 acres and..."had not been a race horse operation for more than seventy years."[36]

Former Governor and Mrs. Jones co-own Airdrie Farm and have expanded the original farm. Today the farm is approximately 2,000 acres, much of which is the old Woodburn land.[37] Like R.A. Alexander, Brereton Jones has raced horses of his own breeding with marked success. In 1975 he bought, for a world record price of $730,000, the stallion Key to the Kingdom for Airdrie Stud.[38] Key to the Kingdom is the half brother of Key to the Mint, both out of the mare Key Bridge.

Desert Wine, bred by Brereton Jones and Warnerton Farm, brought Airdrie great fame when he finished second in the 109th Kentucky Derby in 1983. Desert Wine also placed second in the Preakness two weeks later. Another participant, Highland Park, co-owned by Brereton Jones, also ran in the Derby, but finished unplaced.[39] Tragedy struck Airdrie on January 5, 1985, when a barn fire killed 15 horse at an estimated loss of $1 million. Airdrie quickly recovered and has produced several of today's outstanding and world-class champions.[40] Dansil, bred by Jones, ran in the 1989 Kentucky Derby against Sunday Silence and Easy Goer, and finished fourth.[41]

In 1991 Brereton C. Jones was elected Governor of Kentucky, an accomplishment rivaled only by his success in breeding and racing thoroughbreds. Airdrie has enjoyed great success in recent years with such stallions as: Hawkster, Silver Hawk, Naevus, Ghazi, Mi Cielo, Slew City Slew, Irish Open, Technology (winner of the 1992 Florida Derby) and El Prado. In 1992 Airdrie stood 17 stallions and some 130 broodmares (of which Jones owned about 75) and ranks as one of the top 10 stud farms by stallion income.[42] Together, the Joneses continue the tradition of breeding thoroughbreds, which may well be carried on by their children: Lucy and Bret.

Lucy Alexander Breathitt, daughter of Lucy Multhrop and James H. Alexander (brother of Dr. Alexander John Alexander), inherited a portion of the original Woodburn Farm located near Spring Station. James H. Alexander ("Uncle Jimmy" to all of his extended family), owned several farms and an automobile dealership at the corner of Eastern and Vine Street, in Lexington. Mrs. Breathitt lives in Lexington with her husband, former Governor Edward T. "Ned" Breathitt, a second marriage for each.

During the Eisenhower administration Lucy was hired by Ambassador Henry Cabot Lodge to serve as Protocol Officer at the United States Mission to the United Nations. She was later moved to the visitors service of the United Nations Headquarters where she held public briefings. Lucy served as personal secretary to President and Mrs. Richard M. Nixon

Photograph by William H. Strode

Airdrie Stud — The legacy lives on....

in the Whitehouse. Later she served in the same capacity for President and Mrs. Gerald Ford. She was also Assistant Chief of Protocol for Ceremonial Affairs under Secretary of State Henry Kissinger. She has actively managed her farm since her days in Washington, DC.

Former Governor Edward T. "Ned" Breathitt served in the U.S. Army Air Corps during World War II. After his discharge he returned to the University of Kentucky where he earned a B.S. in Commerce and an L.L.B in law. He practiced law in Hopinsville, Kentucky and served three terms in the State Legislature. During the Lyndon B. Johnson's administration (1963-67) he was elected governor of Kentucky. After his term as governor, Breathitt returned to Hopkinsville to practice law. In 1968, he became director of the Institute of Rural America which continued the work he had begun as chairman of the Commission of Rural Poverty. In 1972, he was appointed vice-president of The Southern Railway System. He presently chairs The University of Kentucky Board of Directors. He has four children from a previous marriage and four grandchildren.[43]

Mrs. Breathitt has a daughter, Mrs. Lucy Parrish, by her first marriage to the late William Winchester. She is married to William "Willy" Parrish of Bourbon County. She will inherit James Alexander's part of Woodburn Farm. She and her husband live in Clark County with their two children, William Hockaday, Jr. and Lucy Alexander "Alex" Parrish.

The Alexanders and extended family have faithfully carried on the tradition of the land and the horse.

"The model for the American breeding farm is Woodburn Stud...which dominated American breeding from the 1860s through the 1890s...making Woodburn a mecca for owners looking for [fast horses]. It was Lexington's success and Woodburn's success as a commercial breeding farm that made the Lexington, Kentucky area the center of North America's and ultimately the world's thoroughbred breeding industry."[44]

By 1887 R. A. Alexander's dream seemed to have been realized when *Turf, Field and Farm* stated that his farm now had:

"A choice stud of trotters and the nucleus of the grandest and largest nursery of thoroughbred horses in the world, which did much to solve the breeding problem, and laid the foundation which has largely advanced the thoroughbred interest of America, and placed it upon a solid and enduring footing."[45] "For about [fifty] years the fame of Woodburn, as the greatest of all breeding establishments, has been as wide as the boundaries of the nation."[46]

Not much is left of Spring Station, and today, it sits quietly among the trees and rolling pasture lands. The depot was a combination of station and residence, "a one-story building with verandas, neatly painted yellow with red trimming. Right beside this building was a store, blacksmith shop and corn bin."[47] The post office is no longer open, nor do passenger trains stop, or even run on the old Louisville and Nashville railroad (now the C.S.X.), which carried buyers to the annual Woodburn yearling sales. But one can still imagine just how busy the little station must have been during the sales and its glory days, with carriages parked along the lane and the tracks waiting patiently to take guests to the farm. Many famous turfmen and sportsmen of the 1870s, 1880s, and gay 90s stepped off the train here. It is also easy to imagine Lexington being lifted into the stock car when the great stallion was moved to Illinois in 1865 from this very spot. The daydream comes easily to those who know.

APPENDIX

ALEXANDER'S THOROUGHBRED BROODMARES LISTED IN 1864

Sally Morgan, Fanny G., Utilla, Minnie Mansfield, Little Peggy, Penola, Marchioness, Heads, I See, Tokay, Miss Lightfoot, Miss Morgan, Nebula, Bay Leaf, Margaret Morris, Kitty Clark, Novice, Lightsome, Kate Hayes, Lavender, Alabama, Volga, Lilla, Zoe, Lindora, Charlotte Buford, My Lady, Weather Witch, Target, Sybilla, Luna, Bay Flower, Anna Clark, Cairn-Gorm, Wenona, Eltham Lass, Britannia 4th, Clifton Lass, Bonnet, Kate Clark, Selina, Heiress (also listed as a harness mare), Linda (also listed as a harness mare), Canary Bird, Aerolite, Nannie Butler, Marseillaise, Salvia, Mazurka, Maria, Heliotrope, Ida, Ear Ring, Penelope, Coral, Maiden, The Widow, Sapphire, Blue Bonnet, Levity, Emma Wright, Ann Watson, Sally Polk, Ann Hanley, Flora G. and Miriam. Several of these mares were sold, several died, and some were "lost." List compiled from *The Woodburn Stud Farm*, Lexington, Kentucky, J. Dunlop, Book & Job Printer, January 1864.

ALEXANDER'S THOROUGHBRED BROODMARES LISTED IN 1865

Nahmioka, Grisetta, Schottische, Verona, Gloriana, Fay, Rescue, Blonde, Lulu Horton, Alice Jones, Daisy, Iodine, Kate Quinn, Maria Innis, Amanda, Banner, Dance, Miss Pattie, Laura White. Other mares owned by Alexander included: Ann Watson, Miriam, Emma Wright, Blue Bonnet, Idlewild, Ardelle, Hilario, Levity, Mattie Gross, Miss Myrtle, Zone, and Flora G. List compiled from *Catalogue of Woodburn Farm Stock Sale, Sept. 5th & 6th, 1866*, Lexington, Kentucky, Gazette Printing Company, 1866; *Catalogue of Woodburn Farm Stock Sale, June 12, 1867*, Lexington, Kentucky, Gazette Printing Company, 1867; R. A. Alexander's *Ledger Book of Stakes Entries*. 1864-1867.

KENTUCKY GUERRILLAS

Guerrillas known to have operated in the Central Kentucky region were: Frank James, "One Arm" Sam Berry,[1] Sid Mitchell, Jim Davis (who burned the Bloomfield Masonic Hall), Captain Isaac Coulter, William "Billy" Henry Magruder, Dick Mitchell, Billy Merriman, Henry Turner, Thomas Henry, Jim Henry,[2] Ben Wigginton (also recorded as Wiggington, who is believed to have raided Elizabethtown on March 7, 1865),[3] Dick Taylor (who surrendered to General Candy at Memphis),[4] Thomas Martin (convicted in Cincinnati by court martial on April 3, 1865, and executed there on May 11, 1865),[5] Dave Downs, Wash Carter, King (an accomplice of Sam Berry who was captured December 9, 1865 near Mount Washington),[6] Major Sam Jones, Henry Metcalf (also Medkiff), Marshall Stuart (executed in Louisville on June 13, 1865),[7] Captain Dave Martin (who raided Shelbyville, Shelby County, August 26, 1864),[8] Captain Dick Yates,[9] Captain McCarroll (killed October 15, 1864, at Hardinsburg, Breckinridge County),[10] Lycrgus Morgan (killed November 19, 1865, near Oceola, Green County),[11] Bill Smith and Witcher (who raided Peach Orchard, Lawrance County November 5, 1865),[12] Captain Bowling (who raided Cadiz, Trigg County, on June 18, 1864),[13] Captain Basham (who raided

APPENDIX

Hardinsburg with 20 guerrillas and burned the courthouse on December 28, 1864),[14] Tingle, Warford, Pratt (killed in Hardin County in late December of 1865),[15] Richardson (who destroyed a train at New Hope in Nelson County October 8, 1863),[16] Colonel William Hughes (who, with a small force of guerrillas, captured and burned a freight train on the Lebanon Branch Railway on February 29, 1865),[17] Colonels Hamilton and Dougherty (who, along with Colonel Hughes, captured Scottsville in Allen County December 27, 1863),[18] Davidson and Porter (who burned the courthouse and public records at Owensboro January 8, 1865),[19] (Courthouses were often targeted by guerrillas to create havoc and confusion.) Theodore Goulder (who was wounded and caught in late June 1865 and taken to the military prison hospital in Louisville),[20] Captain Morrow (who was reportedly wounded when he derailed a train on the Memphis branch of the Louisville and Nashville Railroad one-and-one-half miles from Allensville with 18 guerrillas on April 26, 1865)[21] and Harper (who, with 30 guerrillas, derailed and burned a freight train on the Louisville and Nashville Railroad, three miles from Franklin.[22] Harper should not be confused with the Harpers of Nantura Farm). Captain George Carter (who was killed at Saltsville, Va. on October 2, 1862), Champ Furguson (hanged on October 20, 1865, in Nashville), W.S. Bledsoe and Colonel John M. Hughes (both killed in March 1864) along with John Gatewood operated together throughout the Kentucky area.[23] Captain McDougal (killed 30 miles from Paducah on March 22, 1865),[24] Pomp Curry, a noted guerrilla in East Tennessee (killed on July 24, 1864, in DeKalb County),[25] Jake Bennett (along with 17 men raided Owensboro in August 1864 as well as Lewisport and Hawesville and camped four miles from Cloverport),[26] the guerrilla, "Jesse," (Federals encountered him and 300 men at Mud Lick Spring near Owningsville in October 1864[27] and he was driven out of New Castle by Bridgewater and 125 men in December 1864 who chased him through Port Royal),[28] Captain Blackwell (who burned the railway depot at Shelbyville, Tennessee, on September 30, 1864, and shot ten Federal prisoners at Fayetteville) and Duval McNairg.[29]

HORSES LOST DURING THE SECOND RAID: 1865

Alexander's letter to Deedes did not list all of the horses taken, but provided a partial list. This information, along with other records from the *Racing Calendars* for 1861 through 1869, the *American Stallion Register*, *The American Stud Book*, Volumes I and II, *Chester's Complete Trotting And Pacing Record*, issues of *Wallace's Monthly Magazine*, *The Harness Horse Magazine*, *Wilkes' Spirit of the Times*, *The Lexington Kentucky Morning Herald*, *The Louisville Courier-Journal* and the Woodburn Farm records presented the most complete inventory to date:

*Bay Chief (a.k.a. "The Bald Horse," a.k.a. "Bald Chief"); trotter.
*Abdallah 15 (a.k.a. Edsall's Hambletonian, Love's Abdallah and Alexander's Abdallah); trotter.
*Norwich, runner (Also taken in the October 22, 1864, raid).
*Nannie Butler; runner.
*Lindora's 1862 brown colt by Star Davis (unnamed and not recovered); runner.
*Darkness; (a.k.a. "Big Black" and "Woodburn American"); trotter.
*Edwin Forrest 49; trotter. (Traditionally listed as taken, but is controversial and a subject of much debate as detailed in this book.)

Other horses included:
*one unidentified 4-year-old thoroughbred mare from the training stable;[30]
**two thoroughbred brood mares, which Spirit of the Times, only identified as "purchased from Mr. Dudley" and which were recovered by March 18th;[31]
*one unidentified horse which was likely a thoroughbred;
**"a pair of thoroughbred mares well broken to harness;
*a thoroughbred horse...used as a saddle horse;
***and some 2 or 3 others of less value."[32]

APPENDIX

Turf, Field and Farm later identified one of these thoroughbred brood mares as Nebula, the dam of Asteroid,[33] but listed Nebula as purchased from a W.A. Dudley. Nebula was not purchased from W.A. Dudley, but was bred by W.W. Boyden. Nebula, owned by Colonel Jack Chinn at the beginning of the war, was also 13 years old and heavily in foal by Lexington at the time (she foaled on March 29, 1865).[34] Therefore, it is doubtful that the guerrillas would have taken a horse in her condition. Nebula, like Pilot Jr., however, would later become a victim of the War as told in this book.

Mares that were purchased from W.A. Dudley as listed in *The American Stud Book* included Vogla, 9 years old and in foal to Lexington, Levity, 20 years old and barren in 1864 and 1865 and Lightsome, 10 years old and whose 1864 filly had died, but was in foal to Abdallah in 1865.[35] Other mares purchased from Dudley included Britannia IV, Cairn-Gorm, Eltham Lass, Weatherwitch and Zone.[36] Therefore, it could have been any of the above, but it is very doubtful that Nebula or Levity would have been chosen by guerrillas looking for fast mounts.

WOODBURN HORSES MOVED TO ILLINOIS 1865
THOROUGHBRED BROODMARES

Thoroughbred broodmares owned by R.A. Alexander known to have been part of the group moved to Illinois included some of the great matrons of the greatest runners that ever raced upon the turf up to that day.

Among the Glencoe mares were: Novice (the dam of Norfolk who at the time had a foal at her side), Nebula (the dam of Asteroid with a foal at her side), Ann Watson (the dam of Rhinodine and Florida), Kitty Clark (the dam of Maiden, with a foal at her side), Miriam (the dam of Mammona and Magenta), Old Prunella (the dam of Lizzie W. and Sympathy by imported Scythian), Emma Wright by imported Margrave (the dam of Mollie Jackson), Blue Bonnet by imported Hedgeford (the dam of Lightning and Thunder), Bay Leaf (the dam of Bayflower and Beacon who had a foal at her side) and Idlewild by Lexington out of a Glencoe mare. List compiled from "Proposed Sale of Mr. Alexander's Horses", *The Spirit of the Times*, April 15, 1865, page 105.

WOODBURN TROTTING BROODMARES WHO FOALED IN
MONTGOMERY, ILLINOIS 1865

In the back of the stud book for Edwin Forrest's 1865 season, a list was found of the mares that foaled from April 3 to August 14, 1865, while at Montgomery, Illinois. They included: Charles Young Clipper, Bay York, Fanny Henry, Brown Martha William, Ellesler, Forty Cents, Fanny Hill, Brown Haughton Mambrino, Indiana Mambrino, Miss Myrtle, Tweedle-Dum, Mary Temple, Little Meg, Madam Dudley, Grey Goose, and one other that is unclear. Black Rose also appears on this list, but according to a record journal titled, "Trotting Foals from 1859 to 1869 Inclusive", Black Rose is listed as foaling a "bay filly, large star, left fore and hind ankle white" on February 24, 1865 which indicates that she foaled at Woodburn and was moved to Montgomery with the foal at her side. Also listed are the mares Blandina, R.A.'s gray saddle mare, Woods Mare, Monroe Mare, Cora, Pauline, Twilight, Madam Temple, Sally Russell, Bacchante and Mother Hubbard. Three thoroughbred mares were used as broodmares for trotters and include: Heiress (by Scythian, out of Heads I See), Linda (by Scythian, out of Lightsome), and Slipper (by Yorkshire, out of Clipper by American Eclipse). These three broodmares, noted by "Story of Woodburn" *Lexington, Kentucky Morning Herald*, (27 January 1898), p. 3, were sent to Montgomery on May 2, 1865.

APPENDIX

WOODBURN TROTTING BROODMARES FROM THOROUGHBRED DAMS

	2:30 Descendants	2:20 Descendants	Sires	Dams
Miss Russell	53	10	8	2
*Midnight	2	1	0	0
Vanity Fair	3	1	1	0
Heiress	3	0	0	0
Total:	61	12	9	2

* Midnight died at 19 years old on January 19, 1884 at Sen. Leland Stanford's Palo Alto Farm. Stanford bought her in 1882 from David Bonner.

WOODBURN TROTTING BROODMARES NOT FROM THOROUGHBRED DAMS

	2:30 Descendants	2:20 Descendants	Sires	Dams
Black Rose	75	8	19	6
Madam Dudley	15	2	2	4
Waterwitch	24	2	4	4
Belle	164	19	36	22
Total	278	31	61	36 [37]

WOODBURN TROTTING BROODMARES IN 1864

By 1864 Alexander's stock of trotting broodmares included: Madame Temple, Fanny Hill, Susan, Iris, Hedgeford Mare, Black Rose, Grey Goose, Catallpa, Dolly, Ducatoon, Cora, Fanny Henry, Madame Dudley, Bay Mare, Nelly Morgan, Sally Russell, Young Clipper, Young Ellsler, Tell Tale, Glencona, Bay Hook, Bay York, Grey York, Juliet, Little Meg, Gray Bacchante, Forty Cents, Slipper, Herr Mare, Lame Mare, Norma, Ripton Membrino, Missouri, Mattie Williams, Mother Hubbard, Snowflake, Belle, The Duchess, Twilight, Houghton Mare, Sue Dudley, Bacchante Membrino, Clay Forrest, Paria, Miss Myrtle, Tweedle-Dum, Brunette, Sally Anderson, Indiana, Bay-Hall, Mary Temple, Medoca, Pilot Celia, Brown-York, Georgia, Little Miss, Miss Carter, Houghton Filly, Kate Anderson, Hermosa, Quena and Bland Temple. List compiled from *The Woodburn Stud Farm*, Lexington, Kentucky, J. Dunlop, Book & Job Printer, January 1864.

WOODBURN TROTTING BROODMARES FROM 1864-1866

Trotting broodmares owned by R.A. Alexander and believed to have been part of the group moved to Illinois include: Ducatoon, Sally Anderson, Catacpa, Bay Mare, Glencona, Grey Bacchante, Lame Mare, Norma, Ripton Membrino, Mattie Williams, Snow Flake, Belle, The Duchess, Houghton Mare, Sue Dudley, Georgia, Little Miss, Young Ellsler, Dolly, Kate Anderson, Hermosa, Bland Temple, Susan, Juliet, Missouri, Tell-Tale and Brunette. List compiled from *The Woodburn Stud Farm*, Lexington, Kentucky, J. Dunlop, Book & Job Printer, January 1864.

> "The trotting department has never exceeded forty-five broodmares, the object being rather quality than [in] number. As evidence of the wisdom of this course Woodburn bred forty-one animals with records from 2:30 to 2:10 and 2:08 3/4, ... Twenty nine Woodburn bred mares have produced thirty-one horse with records of 2:30 or better, including the dams of two of the fastest, Maud S. and Jay-Eye-See. Twenty-seven Woodburn bred stallions are sires of one hundred and forty-eight horses with records of 2:30 or better, fourteen of them with records with better than 2:20. These three Woodburn bred trotting stallions, Nutwood, Pancoast and Wedgewood, sold for $75,000."[38]

APPENDIX

LEXINGTON AS SIRE

Many of Lexington's foals continued to race over the next few years after his death in 1875. "When the last retired, some 200 runners had amassed earnings of $1,1159,000...."

Year	Rank	Starters	Races Won	Money Won
1859	Seventh	7	10	$6,700
1860	Second	12	37	$22,295
1861	First	13	27	$22,245
1862	First	5	14	$9,700
1863	First	10	25	$14,235
1864	First	13	38	$28,440
1865	First	31	87	$58,750
1866	First	34	112	$92,795
1867	First	33	86	$54,030
1868	First	36	62	$68,340
1869	First	36	81	$56,375
1870	First	35	82	$120,360
1871	First	40	102	$109,095
1872	First	28	82	$71,515
1873	First	23	71	$71,565
1874	First	23	70	$51,899
1875	Third	30	33	$32,245
1876	First	21	34	$90,570
1877	Second	20	29	$32,815
1878	First	16	36	$60,195
1879	Seventh	15	19	$17,439
1880	Seventeenth	9	12	$9,297
1881		6	7	$1,055
1882		3	1	$255
TOTALS:		499	1,157	$1,102,210 [39]

"Lexington sired at Woodburn 533 reported foals from a reported 963 mares bred to him. He led the American sire's list from 1861-1874 without a break."[40]

LEXINGTON'S STAKES WINNERS:

Acrobat	Harry Bassett	Niagara
Annette	Invermore	Preakness
Bay Final	Judge Durrell	Ratan
Bayonet	Kentucky	Salina
Belle of Nelson	Kingfisher	Shirley
Charley Howard	Lancaster	Shylock
Chesapeake	La Polka	Spartan
Chilicote	Loadstone	Sultana
Duke of Magenta	Madam Dudley	The Banshee
Fiddlesticks	Maiden	Tom Bowling
Finesse	Mary Clark	Tom Ochiltree
Finework	Merrill	Ulrica

APPENDIX

Garrick
General Duke

Monarchist
Neecy Hale

Uncas
Wanderer
Watson[41]

AUSTRALIAN'S STAKES WINNERS

Abd-el-Kader
Albert
Alroy
Ascension
Attila
Maggie B.B.
Fanchon

Flower Girl
Helmbold
Joe Daniels
Lizzie Lucus
Madge
Barricade
Pride of the Village

Red Coat
Rutherford
Spendthrift
Springbok
Baden Baden
Mate
Springbranch[42]

PLANET'S STAKES WINNERS

Bombay
Brigand
Checkmate
Classmat
Plenty

Katy Pease
La Favorita
Minnie W.
Plantaganet
Hubbard

Steel Eyes
Tallulah
Vespucius
Grey Planet
Sarah
Whisper[43]

WOODBURN FARM CLASSIC WINNERS

"The number of classic winners bred by Woodburn out of all proportion to the farm's production. Never did Woodburn breed more than 5% of the country's thoroughbreds foals in a year, and the usual figure was about 3%. Yet from 1868 to 1880, the farm bred 57% of the Belmont and Saratoga Cup winners, 55% of the Dixie winners and 50% of the Jerome and Travers winners."[44]

The major stakes winners that Woodburn produced during this time were:

Maiden	1865 Travers Stakes
Merrill	1866 Travers Stakes
General Duke	1868 Belmont Stakes
Lancaster	1868 Saratoga Cup
Bayonet	1868 Jerome Stakes Stakes
	1869 Saratoga Cup
Kingfisher	1870 Belmont Stakes
	1870 Travers Stakes
	1870 Jerome Stakes
Helmbold	1870 Saratoga Cup
Preakness	1870 Dixie Stakes
Harry Bassett	1871 Belmont Stakes
	1871 Travers Stakes
	1871 Jerome Stakes
	1871 Dixie Stakes
Joe Daniels	1872 Belmont Stakes

APPENDIX

	1872 Travers Stakes
	1872 Jerome Stakes
Harry Bassett	1872 Saratoga Cup
Hubbard	1872 Dixie Stakes
Springbok	1873 Belmont Stakes
Joe Daniels	1873 Saratoga Cup
Attila	1874 Travers Stake
Acrobat	1874 Jerome Stakes
Springbok	1874 Saratoga Cup
Springbok/Preakness	1875 Saratoga Cup (Dead Heat)
Tom Ochiltree	1875 Dixie Cup
	1876 Saratoga Cup
Baden-Baden	1877 Travers Stake
	1877 Kentucky Derby
Duke of Magenta	1878 Belmont Stakes
	1878 Travers Stakes
	1878 Jerome Stakes
	1878 Dixie Stakes
Spendthrift	1879 Belmont Stakes
Grenada	1880 Belmont Stakes
	1880 Travers Stakes
	1880 Jerome Stakes
	1880 Dixie Stakes
Fonso	1880 Kentucky Derby
Bob Miles	1885 Saratoga Cup
Joe Cotton	1885 Kentucky Derby
Burlington	1890 Belmont Stakes
Patron	1892 Belmont Stakes
Chant	1894 Kentucky Derby[45]

TROTTERS
Leading Sons of Alexander's Abdallah

Name & Record Year Foaled-Died	Stand. Performs.	Prod. Sons	Prod. Daughters.	Stand. Performs. Sons & Daughters.	Total prod. in two generations
Almont, 2:39 3/4 1864-1884	37	95	72	609	646
Belmont 1864-1889	58	63	48	560	618
Hambletonian (Wood's) 1858-1885	24	12	13	49	73

205

Major Edsall, 2:29					
1859-1886	3	6	3	87	90
Thorndale, 2:22 1/4					
1865-1894	10	8	14	47	57
Jim Munro					
1861-1882	8	5	17	38	46
Abdallah Pilot					
1865-1881	3	1	1	17	-[46]

Leading Sons of Almont

Name Foaled					
Almont Jr.					
F. 1872	44	7	20	39	83
Altamont					
F. 1875	39	7	1	10	49
Atlantic					
F. 1878	24	6	12	22	46
Piedmont					
F. 1871	19	3	8	18	37
Almont Jr					
F. 1871	19	11	11	51	70
King Almont					
F. 1874	14	-	1	1	15
Pasacas					
F. 1870	14	4	6	13	37
Almonarch					
F. 1875	13	2	3	7	20
Allie Gaines					
F. 1875	12	5	8	17	29
Harbinger					
F. 1879	10	1	2	3	13
Allie West					
1870-1877	7	4	10	24	31
Abdallah Mambrino					
F. 1870	13	1	11	24	37 [47]

Leading Sons of Belmont

Name Foaled					
Nutwood, 2:18 3/4					
F. 1870	136	90	69	432	568
King Rene, 2:30 1/2					
F. 1875	35	17	16	55	90
Egmont					

F. 1873 Wedgewood, 2:19	34	13	11	38	72
F. 1871 Vatican, 2:29 1/4	31	12	9	60	91
F. 1879 Warlock	14	-	-	-	14
F. 1880 Monaco	12	-	-	-	12
F. 1878 Waterloo, 2:19 1/4	11	1	4	7	18
F. 1882 Meander, 2:26 1/2	10	-	1	1	11
F. 1879 Mambritonian, 2:20 1/2	10	3	1	7	17
F. 1883 Herschell	10	-	-	-	10
F. 1883	10	-	-	.	10 [48]

YEARLING SALES AT WOODBURN: THOROUGHBREDS

August 22, 1860

Colts:	$965
Mares and fillies:	$2,450
Total of Sale:	$3,415 [49]

June 17, 18, 1863

Colts:	$5,541
Fillies:	$5,068
Mares:	$4,190
Total of Sale:	$14,799 [50]

November 14, 1863*

Colts:	$200
Fillies:	$925
Mares:	$1,355
Total of Sale:	$2,480

*Note: Sale took place at Lexington, Kentucky.[51]

1866

Colts:	$10,830
Fillies:	$5,435
Total of Sale:	$16,265 [52]

APPENDIX

Special Sale:(not a Catalogue sale)

"Mr. W.W. Boyden, who was interested in a portion of the blooded stock on the Woodburn Stud Farm, died, and Mr. Alexander became the full owner of the same. At the time of his death, Mr. Boyden was indebted to parties for thirty thousand dollars. Mr. Price McGarth prosecuted this claim in the Circuit Court of Fayette Co., Ky. A compromise was the result, in which Mr. Alexander paid ten thousand dollars to have the claim settled. By order of the court, however, the half interest in the stock dispute was sold at public auction. It was a queer case, and as other parties were not disposed to bid against Mr. Alexander, the horses were knocked down to him at a mere normal price, we observed, even under these peculiar circumstances that $8,000 were paid for a half interest in Asteroid. His owner certainly regards him as a valuable animal."[53]

June 12, 1867

Colts:	$1,580
Fillies:	$1,870
Total of Sale:	$3,450 [54]

June 18, 1868

Colts:	$10,465
Fillies:	$11,697.50
Broodmares:	$3,005
Total of Sale:	$25,167.50 [55]

1869

Colts:	$11,040
Fillies:	$9,325
Broodmares:	$1,100
Total of Sale:	$21,465 [56]

1870

Colts:	$8,490
Fillies:	$9,490
Broodmares:	$1,365
Total of Sale:	$19,345 [57]

1871

Colts:	$10,985
Fillies:	$11,790
Total Sale:	$22,775 [58]

APPENDIX

1872

Colts:	$20,355
Fillies:	$16,615
Total of Sale:	$36,970 [59]

June 25, 1873

Colts:	$16,240
Fillies:	$8,960
Total of Sale:	$25,200 [60]

June 24, 1874

Colts:	$18,955
Fillies:	$12,160
Total of Sale:	$31,115 [61]

June 23, 1875

Total of Sale:	$24,155 [62]

June 28, 1876

Colts:	$23,310
Fillies:	$17,125
Total of Sale:	$40,435 [63]

June 27, 1877

Colts:	$11,380
Fillies:	$ 4,025
Total of Sale:	$15,405 [64]

June 26, 1878

Colts:	$4,640
Fillies:	$3,800
Total of Sale	$8,440 [65]

June 18, 1879

Colts:	$8,615
Fillies:	$4,695
Total of Sale:	$13,310 [66]

APPENDIX

May 26, 1880

Colts:	$10,410
Fillies:	$5,130
Total of Sale:	$15,540 [67]

May 25, 1881

Colts:	$25,920
Fillies:	$10,295
Total of Sale:	$36,215 [68]

May 13, 1882

Colts:	$22,975
Fillies:	$15,420
Total of Sale:	$38,395 [69]

May 21, 1883

Colts:	$10,425
Fillies:	$7,010
Total of Sale:	$17,435 [70]

May 15, 1884

Colts:	$8,025
Fillies:	$6,910
Total of Sale:	$14,935 [71]

May 14, 1885

Colts:	$20,950
Fillies:	$18,570
Total of Sale:	$39,520 [72]

May 13, 1886

Colts:	$52,800
Fillies:	$17,410
Total of Sale:	$70,210 [73]

May 10, 1887

Colts:	$14,247
Fillies:	$14,353
Total of Sale:	$28,600 [74]

APPENDIX

May 3, 1888

Total of Sale: 35 belonging to Mr. Alexander sold for a total of $24,620 (an average of $703). Fifteen animals bred at Woodburn from mares belonging to other owners brought $5,300. [75]

April 30, 1889

Colts:	$5,775
Fillies:	$8,420
Total of Sale:	$14,195 [76]

July 12, 1890

Colts:	$34,750
Fillies:	$10,475
Total of Sale:	$45,225 [77]

July 11, 1891

Colts:	$28,950
Fillies:	$10,875
Total of Sale:	$39,825 [78]

May 21, 1892*

Colts:	$23,625
Fillies:	$16,500
Total of Sale:	$40,125

*Note: This sale was not held at Woodburn Farm, but at the salesroom of the American Horse Exchange and conducted by Col. S.D. Bruce. [79]

May 17, 1893

Colts:	$20,625
Fillies:	$14,600
Total of Sale:	$35,225 [80]

1894*

Colts:	$7,450
Fillies:	$4,000
Total of Sale:	$11,450 [81]

*Note: Sale did not take place at Woodburn Farm, but in New York.

1895
First night
Colts: $3,370

APPENDIX

Fillies: $1,940
Total of Sale: $5,310
Second night
Colts: $570
Fillies: $610
Total of Sale: $1,180

Two Day Total of Sale: $6,490 [82]

1896*

Colts: $575
Fillies: $440
Total of Sale: $1,015 [83]

*Note: Sale did not take place at Woodburn, but in St. Louis.

1896*

Colts: $3,950
Total of sale: $3,950 [84]

*Note: Sale did not take place at Woodburn, but at Sheepshead Bay in New York.

1897*

Colts: $200
Fillies: $325
Stallions: $3,000
Mares: $6,705
Total of Sale: $10,230 [85]

*Note: Sale did not take place at Woodburn, but in New York.

YEARLING SALES AT WOODBURN
TROTTERS

1860

Colts: $1,179
Fillies: $975
Mares: $1,180
Total of Sale: $3,334 [86]

1866

Colts: $1,200

APPENDIX

Fillies: $215
Mares: $385
Total of Sale: $1,800

Sales from the Supplementary Catalogue

2 Colts: $490
4 Fillies: $640
3 Mares: $515 (Thoroughbreds and Trotters)
2 Geldings: $155

Miscellaneous Not in Catalogue

Colts: $130
Fillies: $155
Mares: $1,050 (Thoroughbreds and Trotters) [87]

1867

Colts: $700
Fillies: $1,357
Mares: $3,955
Total of Sale: $6,012 [88]

June 18, 1868

Colts: $465
Fillies: $187
Stallions/Geldings: $2,810
Mares: $1,090
Total of Sale: $4,552 [89]

June 23, 1869

Colts: $1,275
Fillies: $2,107
Broodmares: $257
Total of Sale: $3,639 [90]

1870

Colts/Geldings: $1,390
Fillies: $2,275
Broodmares $480
Total of Sale: $4,145 [91]

1871

Colts: $1,855
Fillies: $1,430
Total of Sale: $3,285 [92]

APPENDIX

June 23, 1875

29 trotters: $7,300 averaging ($900 less per head than the thoroughbreds). [93]

June 28, 1876

Colts:	$2,220
Fillies:	$1,655
Broodmares:	$1,080
Total of Sale:	$4,955 [94]

December 1877

"Messrs Baker and Harrigan, of Comstock's, Washington County, New York bought all the Woodburn yearlings." This sale was the "largest sale of trotting stock that has ever been made in this country, and the only sale in which the entire produce of the trotting-bred mares has been made in a body, to one firm." [95]

October 25, 1888

W. H. Allen of St. Louis bought 14 head aggregating $23,000. This was the largest private sale of trotting stock in Kentucky to this date for colts: 2 fillies: 9 broodmares: 3. [96]

AMERICUS

Richard "Boss" Croker purchased Glencairn estate near Leopardstown, located six miles form Dublin, Ireland and made it into a breeding and racing stud. According to records provided by the Registry Office of the Turf Club, the Curragh, County Kildare, the following information was found on Americus who Croker owned, and Americus' outstanding colts and one filly named Americus Girl.

Americus - bay colt, by Emperor of Norfolk - Clara D.

Ran in Ireland at Cork Park (racecourse) in September 1900 finished 2nd in the 'Pegasus Cup.'

Americus Boy - bay gelding, by Americus - Saucy Lass

Ran twice in 1903 but was unplaced in both races
Won his only six races in 1904 as follows:

The Wellington Plate in April at the Curragh
The April Plate in April at Leopardstown
The Lawn Plate in April at Leopardstown
The Howth Plate in May at Baldoyle
The Hilltown Plate in July at Bellewstown
The Bellewstown Plate in July at Bellewstown
Ran three times in 1905 but was unplaced.
Won the April Stakes in 1906 at the Curragh in his only race that year

Young Americus - bay colt, by Americus - Saucy Lass

Ran four races in 1904 but was unplaced in each race
Won the Lisburn Plate at Down Royal (racecourse) in July 1905

Americus Girl - chestnut filly, by Americus - Palotta

APPENDIX

Won her only five races in 1907 as follows:

The Drogheda Memorial Stakes in July at the Curragh
The Baldoyle Foal Stakes in August at Baldoyle
The Leopardstown Grand Prize in August at Leopardstown
The Phoenix Plate in August at Phoenix Park
The National Produc Stakes in October at the Curragh

Won the May Plate in 1908 at Phoenix Park in her only race of the year.
Won the Drogheda Memorial Stakes in July 1909 at the Curragh in her only race of the year.

FOOTNOTES

CHAPTER ONE: THE ALEXANDERS OF SCOTLAND

1. John Burke, *Burke's Peerage, Baronetage and Knightage*, (London, England: Burke's Peerage Limited, 1967), pp. 52-53.

2 The custom of the time was to name sons after their fathers and grandfathers without the distinctive Jr. or Roman numerals. Therefore, to assist the reader in following the genealogy, Roman numerals have been assigned to duplicated names. Thus, the first John becomes John (I). When titles were bestowed, they have been used to differentiate between names.

3 Jacob M. Price, *France and the Chesapeake*, (Ann Arbor, Michigan, The University of Michigan Press: 1973), Vol. 1, p. 606.

4 Ibid.

5 Ibid., p. 614.

6 Ibid., Vol. 2, p. 696.

7 Ibid., Vol. 1, p. 615.

8 Ibid.

9 Ibid., Vol. 2, p. 697.

10 Ibid., Vol. 2, p. 694.

11 Ibid., Vol. 2, p. 694.

12 "The Alexanders of Woodburn," *Woodford Sun*, newspaper, (Versailles, Ky.: 21 September 1983), N.P.; Samuel M. Wilson and Temple Bodley, *History of Kentucky From 1803-1928*, 4 Vols., (Chicago, Ill.-Louisville, Ky.: S.J. Clarke Publishing Company, 1928), Vol. II, pp. 78-80.

13 John Burke, *Burke's Peerage, Baronetage and Knightage*, (London, England: 1967), pp. 52-53; Rev Charles Rogers, LLD, *Memorials of the Earl of Sterling and of the House of Alexander*, (Edinburgh, Scotland: William Patterson, 1977), Vol. II, pp. 33-37.

14 Z.F. Smith, *History of Kentucky*, (Louisville, Ky.: Courier Journal Job Printing Company, 1886), p. 544.

15 "The Alexanders of Woodburn," *Woodford Sun*, (Versailles, Ky.: 21 September 1983), N.P.

16 Z.F. Smith, *History of Kentucky*, (Louisville, Ky.: 1886), p. 544; Susan Rhodemyre, "Woodlawn Stud," *Thoroughbred Record*, weekly newspaper, formerly *Kentucky Live Stock Record* until 26 January 1895, (Lexington, Kentucky: 7 January 1981) p. 34.

17 Z.F. Smith, *History of Kentucky*, (Louisville, Ky.: 1886), p. 544; Susan Rhodemyre, "Woodburn Stud," *Thoroughbred Record*, (Lexington, Ky.: 7 January 1981), p. 34.

18 "Woodburn Stud," *Thoroughbred Record*, (Lexington, Ky.: 7 January 1981), pp. 34, 36.

19 Dan M. Bowmar, III, "Gen. Abe Buford Made Reputation as a Kentuckian Soldier," *Lexington Leader*, (Lexington, Ky.: 19 August 1970); *Autobiographical sketch, 1877, by General Abraham Buford,*

Woodford County Historical Society, Versailles, Kentucky; "Gen Buford's Unhappy End," *Turf, Field and Farm*, weekly newspaper,(New York: 13 June 1884), p. 445; William E. Railey, *History of Woodford County*, (Versailles, Ky.: Woodford Improvement League, 1968), pp. 90-93; "Gen Abraham Buford," *Woodford Sun*, (Versailles, Ky.: 4 May 1989), p. A9; Susan Rhodemyre, "Woodburn Stud," *Thoroughbred Record*, (Lexington, Ky.: 7 January 1981), pp. 34-36.

20 "Story of Woodburn," *Lexington, Kentucky Morning Herald*, daily newspaper, (27 January 1898), p. 3; by A.A. Austin, reprinted from the *Boston Herald*; Complied by J.A. Venn, Litt D., F.S.A. *Alumni Cantabrigieneses Part II From 1752 to 1900*, (Cambridge, England: The University Press, 1940), Vol. I, p. 30.

21 "The Alexanders of Woodburn," *Woodford Sun*, (Versailles, Ky.: 21 September 1983), N.P.

22 Ibid.

23 Ibid.

24 Z.F. Smith, *History of Kentucky*, (Louisville, Ky.: 1886), p. 544.

25 "Woodburn and Other Gossip," *Turf, Field and Farm*, (New York: 16 October 1874), p.287; ibid., "Robert Aitcheson Alexander," (16 November 1867), p. 312; "The Story of Woodburn," *Lexington, Kentucky Morning Herald*, (27 January 1898), p. 3. In 1867, Woodburn consisted of 5,000 acres, but by 1874 this acreage was reduced to 3,200 acres. In 1898 the acreage had grown to 3,300 acres.

26 Samuel M. Wilson and Temple Bodley, *History of Kentucky From 1803-1928*, (Chicago, Ill.: 1928), Vol. II, pp. 72-73.

27 Original receipt, dated 17 April 1857, between R.A. Alexander and Richard Ten Broeck for the purchase of Lexington: "Received of R.S.C.A. Alexander Esq. by the hands of Lees and Waller the sum of Seven thousand and five hundred dollars being balance due me on the Horse Lexington, $7,500," Woodburn Farm Records, Woodburn Farm, Lexington, Ky. (hereafter Woodburn Farm Records, Woodburn Farm). See also Rhodemyre, "Woodburn Stud," p. 36.

28 Complied by J. A. Venn, Litt D., F.S.A., *Alumni Catabrigieneses Part II, From 1752 to 1900*, (Cambridge, England: 1940), Vol. I, p. 30; Susan Rhodemyre, "Woodburn Stud," *Thoroughbred Record*, (Lexington, Ky.: 7 January 1981), p. 34; "Story of Woodburn," *Lexington, Kentucky Morning Herald*, (27 January 1898), p. 3; Dan Bowmar, III, *Giants of the Turf*, (Lexington, Ky.:The Blood-Horse, 1960), pp. 3-4; "Story of Woodburn," *Lexington, Kentucky Morning Herald*, (27 January 1898), p. 3.

CHAPTER TWO: WOODBURN FARM-THE BEGINNING

1 *Federal Writers Project: Kentucky-A Guide to the Bluegrass State*, (New York: Hastings House, 1954), p. 357. Evidence found in a letter shows that R.A. was at Airdrie on the night of March 25 through the 27th, 1857 trying to get a new furnace working properly. R.A. Alexander's letter, 25-27 March 1857, Woodburn Farm Records, Special Collections, Margaret I. King Library, University of Kentucky, Lexington, Ky. (hereafter Woodburn Farm Records, King Library.)

2 James B. Waller's letter to R.A. Alexander in London, England, 26 September and postmarked Lexington, Ky., Woodburn Farm Records, Woodburn Farm.

3 "Tell Mary I have no news of interest except that Mrs. Buford *(the old lady)* is dead & that I am to get possession of [untranslatable]... land in September. My possession should have begun on her death, but I have consented to give Miss Mary Buford the use of the house until September to enable her to make proper arrangements to remove." Letter, dated, 19 July 1866, Woodburn Farm Records, King Library; Telephone conversation/interview with Dr. A.J. Alexander, 18 November 1992, Lexington, Ky.

4 Susan Rhodemyre, "Woodburn Stud," *Thoroughbred Record*, (Lexington, Ky.: 7 January 1981), pp. 34-36.

5 "Memories of Distinguished Kentucky Turfmen-R. Aitcheson Alexander," *Kentucky Live Stock Record*, (Lexington, Ky.: 23 April 1875), p. 185.

FOOTNOTES

6 "Death of Robert Aitcheson Alexander," *Turf, Field and Farm*, (New York: 7 December 1867), p. 360. An eloquent tribute to him appeared in the *Chicago Tribune* which concluded that he was "the soul of integrity and honor." See "Death of An Useful Man," *Chicago Tribune*, (6 December 1867), p. 2.

7 "The Woodlawn Stud," *Turf, Field and Farm*, (New York: 23 December 1887), p. 514; "Memories of a Distinguished Kentucky Turfmen," *Kentucky Live Stock Record*, (Lexington, Ky.: 23 April 1875), p. 185.

8 "Robert Aitcheson Alexander," *Turf, Field and Farm*, (New York: 16 November 1867), p. 312; "Robert Aitcheson Alexander. His Claim to Rank As America's Most Successful Breeder," *Thoroughbred Record*, (Lexington, Ky.: 21 May 1938), p. 334.

9 "Memories of Distinguished Kentucky Turfmen-R. Aitcheson Alexander," *Kentucky Live Stock Record*, (Lexington, Ky.: 23 April 1875), p. 185.

10 Dan M. Bowmar, III, *Giants of the Turf*, (Lexington, Ky.: 1960), p. 21.

11 Alexander Mackay-Smith, *The Race Horses in America, 1832-1872, Portraits and Other Paintings by Edward Troye*, (Saratoga Springs, New York: The National Museum of Racing, 1981), p. 204.

12 R.A. Alexander's letter to Merwin & Bray, sole agents for Ballard's Breech Loading Rifles, 262 Broadway, New York and Merwin & Bray's reply to letter, dated 1863; Woodburn Farm Records, Woodburn Farm.

13 Chemical formulas from R.A. Alexander's personal notebook, Woodburn Farm Records, Woodburn Farm; translated on November 18, 1993 by Maurice M. Bursey, Professor of Chemistry, University of North Carolina, Chapel Hill, North Carolina.

14 Personal ledger of R.A. Alexander, property of Keeneland Association Library, Lexington, Ky., p. 67. Letter is inserted into ledger.

15 S.R. Scholarly Resources, Inc., *The Horse of America*, (Wilmington, Delaware: reprint 1973); First published by John H. Wallace, *The Horse of America*, (New York: John H. Wallace, 1897), pp. 415-416.

16 James Sinclair, *History of Shorthorn Cattle*, (London, England: Vinton & Company Ltd., 1907), p. 604.

17 James Sinclair, *History of Shorthorn Cattle*, (London, England: 1907), p. 605; Paul C. Henlein, *Cattle Kingdom In the Ohio Valley 1783-1860*, (Lexington, Ky.: University of Kentucky Press, 1959), p. 92.

18 Paul C. Henlein, *Cattle Kingdom In the Ohio Valley 1783-1860*, (Lexington, Ky.: 1959), p. 93.

19 *1854 Woodburn Stock Farm Catalogue For Cattle*, p. "Introduction," Woodburn Farm Records, Woodburn Farm; James Sinclair, *History of Shorthorn Cattle*, (London, England: 1907), p. 605.

20 James Sinclair, *History of Shorthorn Cattle*, (London, England: 1907), p. 605.

21 *1856 Woodburn Stock Farm Catalogue for Cattle*, (Lexington, Ky.: 1856), Woodburn Farm Records, Woodburn Farm; James Sinclair, *History of Shorthorn Cattle*, (London England, 1907), p. 605.

22 James Sinclair, *History of Shorthorn Cattle*, (London, England: 1907), p. 611.

23 Paul C. Henlein, *Cattle Kingdom In the Ohio Valley 1783-1860*, (Lexington, Ky.: 1959), p. 92.

24 Ibid., p. 91.

25 James Sinclair, *History of Shorthorn Cattle*, (London, England: 1907), pp. 605-606.

26 Ibid.

27 "Great Sale of Breeding Stock in Kentucky," *Porter's Spirit of the Times*, weekly newspaper, (New York: 26 September 1856), p. 36.

28 "R.A. Alexander's Sale of Short-Horned Cattle," *Spirit of the Times*, (New York: 4 July 1857), p. 249.

29 "Sale of Fine Cattle and Sheep," *Tri Weekly Commonwealth*, newspaper (Frankfort, Ky.: 25 May 1860), p. 3.

30 Paul C. Henlein *Cattle Kingdom In the Ohio Valley 1783-1860*, (Lexington, Ky.: 1959), p. 93; "The show herd composed of Mazurka 3rd and 4th, Duchess of Athol, 2nd Duchess of Airdrie, Vellum,

FOOTNOTES

Forget-me-Not, and the bulls El Hakim and Sirius as the most notable animals won great reputation, Vellum, Mazurka, Duchess of Athol and Forget-me-Not, with Sirius at their head, winning the great herd prize at the United States Agricultural Society's Show at Louisville, Ky. in 1857." James Sinclair, *History of Shorthorn Cattle*, (London, England: 1907), p. 606.

31 "The American Stud Book-New 'Spirit' and Stock Agency-Purchasers from New York and Other Parts-Visit to Capt A. Buford's-Zeb. Ward's-Jas. Ford's-Etc.," *Wilkes' Spirit of the Times*, (New York: 7 July 1860), p. 255; *1860 Census*, "Free Inhabitants," Woodford County, Kentucky, pp. 93-94; *1860 Census*, "Slave Schedule," Woodford County, Kentucky, pp. 43, 44, 45.

32 R.A. Alexander's *Woodford County Revenue Tax and County Levy* receipt; Woodburn Farm Records, Woodburn Farm.

33 R.A. Alexander's "Slave Leases," Woodburn Farm Records, Woodburn Farm; See *1860 Census*, "Slave Schedule," Woodford County, Kentucky, pp. 43-45. One lease for a young woman noted that Alexander was responsible for her health, teeth and clothing.

34 Kenneth M. Stampp, *The Peculiar Institution; Slavery in the Ante-Bellum South*, (New York: Alfred A. Knopf, 1956), p. 72.

35 "Robert Aitcheson Alexander," *Turf, Field and Farm*, (New York: 16 November 1867), p. 312.

36 "The American Stud Book-New 'Spirit' and Stock Agency-Purchasers From New York and Other Parts-Visit to Capt. A. Buford's-Zeb. Ward's-Jas. Ford's-Etc.," *Wilkes' Spirit of the Times*, (New York: 7 July 1860), p. 254.

37 *1860 Census*, "Free Inhabitants," Woodford County, Kentucky, pp. 93-94.

38 "Robert Aitcheson Alexander," *Turf, Field and Farm*, (New York: 16 November 1867), p. 312.

39 Alexander Mackay-Smith, *The Race Horse of America, 1832-1872 Portraits and Other Paintings by Edward Troye*, (Saratoga Springs, New York: The National Museum of Racing, 1981) pp. 204, 424, 425.

40 Ibid., pp. 215, 427.

41 Telephone conversation/interview with former Governor Brereton C. Jones, Midway, Kentucky, 20 October 1990.

42 "Robert Aitcheson Alexander," *Turf, Field and Farm*, (New York: 14 December 1867), p. 369.

CHAPTER THREE: THE CORNERSTONES OF THE KINGDOM

1 "Robert Aitcheson Alexander. His Claim to Rank as America's Most Successful Breeder," *Thoroughbred Record*, (Lexington, Ky.: 21 May 1938), pp. 334, 343; "The Woodburn Stud," *Turf, Field and Farm*, (New York: 23 December 1887), p. 514; Dan M. Bowmar, III, *Giants of the Turf*, (Lexington, Ky.: 1960), p. 3.

2 Alexander Mackay-Smith, *The Race Horses of America, 1832-1872, Portraits and Other Paintings by Edward Troye*, (Saratoga Springs, New York: 1981), p. 221; John Hervey, *The American Trotter*, (New York: Coward-McCann, Inc., 1947), pp. 294-295. Hervey was Dean of American turf writers, a competent judge of racing and breeding, a recognized historian and authority on American horse racing. According to Hervey, "the principal authorities for the history of the Standard breed of American light-harness horses were the official U.S.T.A. (formerly *Wallace's Register* and *Year Book*, of which 35 volumes of the former and 58 of the latter have been issued. Supplementing these the most important are the files of the turf journals of past years, beginning with the first to be published in America, the *Turf Register* (1829) and coming down to date, of which those principally useful have been *Wallace's Monthly; Spirit of the Times; Turf, Field and Farm; Horseman* and *Horse Review*. For data upon the Thoroughbred breed, the official *American Stud Book*, in 18 volumes, is the standard authority, the periodicals above-named being also indispensable...it is to be understood that in all cases the statements made rest upon carefully checked authorities and that where conflicts of evidence have supervened the data accepted were thoroughly examined and tested and the temptation to incorporate an attractive legend or tradition

FOOTNOTES

rather than a more prosaic fact steadfastly abjured." According to *The Blood-Horse*, Hervey was the historian most thoroughly acquainted with the beginning of the American Thoroughbred. "With no exception, he was the leading historical writer of the Turf in his time."

3 John Hervey, *The American Trotter*, (New York: 1947), pp. 294-295; Alexander Mackay-Smith, *The Race Horses of America, 1832-1872, Portraits And Other Paintings by Edward Troye*, (Saratoga Springs, New York: 1981), p. 221; "Aurelius" (Pseudonym),"Woodburn Farm And Thoroughbred Blood," *Wallace's Monthly*, magazine, (New York: 19 Vols., 1875-1894, June 1890), Vol. 16, No. 4, pp. 241-247.

4 John Hervey, *The American Trotter*, (New York: 1947), pp. 294-295.

5 John H. Wallace, *The Horse of America*, (Wilmington, Del.: 1973), p. 516.

6 John Hervey, *The American Trotter*, (New York: 1947), pp. 293, 295.

7 Alexander Mackay-Smith, *The Race Horses of America, 1832-1872, Portraits And Other Paintings by Edward Troye*, (Saratoga Springs, New York: 1981), p. 221; John Hervey, *The American Trotter*, (New York: 1947), pp. 295-296.

8 Alexander Mackay-Smith, *The Race Horses of America, 1832-1872, Portraits and Other Paintings by Edward Troye*, (Saratoga Springs, New York: 1981), p. 221; John Hervey, *American Trotter*, (New York: 1947), pp. 92, 295.

9 "The Story of Woodburn," *Lexington, Kentucky Morning Herald*, (27 January 1898), p. 3; John Hervey, *The American Trotter*, (New York: 1947), pp. 295-296; John H. Wallace, *The Horse of America*, (Wilmington, Del.: 1973), p. 419.

10 "The Woodburn Stud," *Turf, Field and Farm*, (New York: 23 December 1887), p. 514.

11 John Hervey, *The American Trotter*, (New York: 1947), p. 293.

12 Kent Hollingsworth, *The Great Ones*, (Lexington, Ky.: The Blood-Horse, 1970), p. 172; B.G. Bruce, *Memoir of Lexington*, (Lexington, Ky.: *Kentucky Live Stock Record*, N.D), p. 39; "Memoir of Lexington," *Kentucky Live Stock Record*, (Lexington, Ky.: 29 January 1881), Vol. 13. No. 5, p. 72.

13 Kent Hollingsworth, *The Great Ones*, (Lexington, Ky.: 1970), pp. 170, 172; "Memoir of Lexington," *Kentucky Live Stock Record*, (Lexington, Ky.: 1 January 1881), Vol. 13, No. 1, pp. 8-9.

14 "The Get of Lexington," *Thoroughbred Record*, (Lexington, Ky.: 12 April, 1927), Vol. 105, p. 466.

15 Contract, 1857, between R.A. Alexander and Richard Ten Broeck; The contract is in the Woodburn Farm Records, Woodburn Farm; "Robert Aitcheson Alexander. His Claim to Rank as America's Most Successful Breeder," *Thoroughbred Record*, (Lexington, Ky.: 21 May 1938), p. 334.

16 Woodburn Farm Records, Woodburn Farm; "Memoir of Lexington," *Kentucky Live Stock Record*, (Lexington, Ky.: 29 January 1881), Vol. 13, No. 5, p. 72.

17 "More Kentucky Horses for England," *Wilkes' Spirit of the Times*, (New York: 25 August 1860), p. 393.

18 Alexander Mackay-Smith, *The Race Horses of America, 1832-1872, Portraits And Other Paintings by Edward Troye*, (Saratoga Springs, New York: 1981), p. 215; "The Sire of Daniel Boone-Sovereign-Sale of Blood Horses in Woodford Co., Ky.," *Wilkes' Spirit of the Times*, (New York: 8 September 1860), p. 10.

19 B.G. Bruce, *Memoir of Lexington*, (Lexington, Ky.: N.D.), p. 39; "The Get of Lexington," *Thoroughbred Record*, (Lexington, Ky.: 12 April 1927), Vol. 105, p. 466; "Memoir of Lexington," *Kentucky Live Stock Record*, (Lexington, Ky.: January 29, 1881), Vol. 13, No. 5, p. 72.

20 "The Get of Lexington," *Thoroughbred Record*, (Lexington, Ky.: 12 April 1927), p. 466.

21 "Memoir of Lexington," *Kentucky Live Stock Record*, (4 December 1880), p. 360.

22 "Export of British Cattle To The United States," *London Times*, daily newspaper, (London, England: 13 October 1856), p. 10; "Arrival of Fine English Cattle and Blood Stock," *Porter's Spirit of the Times*, (New York: 22 November 1856), p. 193.; "The Stallion Scythian," *Porter's*, (29 November 1856), p. 208.

23 "Death of Mr. R.A. Alexander of Kentucky," *Wilkes' Spirit of the Times*, (New York: 7 December

FOOTNOTES

1867), p. 293; "Memoir of Lexington," *Kentucky Live Stock Record*, (Lexington, Ky.: 29 January 1881), Vol. 13, No. 5, p. 72.

24 "Robert Aitcheson Alexander," *Turf, Field and Farm* (New York: 16 November 1867), p. 312.

25 "Death of Imported Australian," *Kentucky Live Stock Record*, (Lexington, Ky.: 18 October, 1879), Vol. 16, No. 10, p. 248; John Hervey, *Racing In America, 1665-1865*, (New York: 1944), p. 329; "Imported Australian Died at Woodburn Stud Ky., Oct. 15, 1879 In His 22d. Year," *Spirit of the Times*, (New York: 25 October 1879), Vol. 98, No. 12, p. 1; List of mares from R. Aitcheson Alexander, *Woodburn Stud Farm 1864 Catalogue*, (Lexington, Ky.: January 1864), pp. 7-26; Woodburn Farm Records, Woodburn Farm; R. Aitcheson Alexander, *Woodburn Stud Farm Catalogue for Stock Sale, 5-6 September 1866*; R. Aitcheson Alexander, *Woodburn Stud Farm Catalogue for Stock Sale, 12 June 1867*; R.A. Alexander's *Ledger Book* of Stakes Entries, 1864-1867, Keeneland Association Library; "Proposed Sale of Mr. Alexander's Horses," *Wilkes' Spirit of the Times*, (New York: 15 April 1865), p. 105.

26 "Death of Asteroid," *Thoroughbred Record*, (Lexington, Ky.: 6 November 1886), p. 297. (Information quoted from the *Kentucky Live Stock Record*); H.G. Crickmore, *Racing Calendars*, (New York: H.G. Crickmore, 1901), 3 volumes by years 1986-1869.

27 "Death of Asteroid," *Thoroughbred Record*, (Lexington, Ky.: 6 November, 1886), p. 297; (Information quoted from the *Kentucky Live Stock Record*.)

28 (New reference)George Waller, *Saratoga Saga of an Impious Era*, (Englewood Cliffs, New Jersey: Prentice-Hall, Inc., 1966), pp. 127-128; Dan M. Bowmar, III, *Giants of the Turf*, (Lexington, Ky.: 1960), p. 12.

29 "The Woodburn Stud," *Turf, Field and Farm*, (New York: 23 December 1887), p. 514.

30 "Lexington and His Dynasty," *Thoroughbred of California*, (Arcadia, California: Thoroughbred Breeders Association, October 1975), p. 65.

31 G. Glenn Clift, *Events of the Civil War In Kentucky*, (Unpublished manuscript arranged by counties located in the Kentucky Historical Society, Frankfort, Ky.: 1961), p. "Woodford County," under 22 May 1864; Lewis Collins, *History of Kentucky*, (Frankfort, Ky.: The Kentucky Historical Society, 1966), Vol. I, p. 133; B.K. Beckwith, *Step and Go Together*, (Cranbury, New Jersey: A.S. Barnes and Company, Inc., 1967), pp. 230, 231; William H.P. Robertson, *The History Of Thoroughbred Racing In America*, (Englewood Cliffs, New Jersey: Prentice, Inc., 1964), p. 120.

32 Letter from R.A. Alexander's personal ledger, property of Keeneland Association Library, Lexington, Ky., p. 67.

33 *Thoroughbred of California*, (Arcadia, Ca.: March 1978), p. 175.

34 H.G. Crickmore, *Racing Calendars, 1866,1867*, (New York: 1901), pp. 28, 30, 35.

35 John Hervey, *The American Trotter*, (New York: 1947), p. 223; "The Whole Truth About The Pedigree of Pilot, Jr.," *Wallace's Monthly*, (New York: February 1879), Vol. V, pp. 49-50; Joseph Battell, *American Stallion Register*, (Middlebury, Vt.: American Publishing Company, 1935), Vol. IV, pp. 134-141; Dan M. Bowmar, III, *Giants of the Turf*, (Lexington, Ky.: 1960), p. 16.

36 John Hervey, *The American Trotter*, (New York: 1947), p. 223; "The Whole Truth About The Pedigree of Pilot, Jr.," *Wallace's Monthly*, (New York: February 1879), Vol. V, pp. 49-50.

37 "Descendants of Pilot Jr.," *American Horse Breeder*, magazine, (Boston, Mass.: American Horse Breeder Association, 7 April 1903), p. 306.

38 *Woodburn Stud Farm Catalogue*, Woodburn Farm Records, Woodburn Farm.

39 "Memoir of Col. George Elliott," *Spirit of the Times*, (New York: 23 June 1860), Vol. XXX, No. 20, pp. 229, 230; "The American Stud Book-New 'Spirit' and Stock Agency-Purchasers From New York and Other Parts-Visit to Capt. A. Buford's-Zeb. Ward's-Jas. Ford's-Etc.," *Spirit*, (7 July 1860), p. 255.

40 "Edwin Forrest 49," *Harness Horse Magazine*, (Harrisburg, Pa.: 8 March 1939), Vol. 4, No. 19, pp. 503-505; Alexander Mackay-Smith, *The Race Horses of America, 1832-1872, Portraits and Other Paintings by*

FOOTNOTES

Edward Troye, (Saratoga Springs, New York: 1981), p. 221; Joseph Battell, *American Stallion Register*, (Middlebury, Vt.: 1911), pp. 186-191.

41 Alexander Mackay-Smith, *The Race Horses of America, 1832-1872, Portraits and Other Paintings By Edward Troye*, (Saratoga Springs, New York: 1981), p. 221.

42 "Edwin Forrest 49," *Harness Horse Magazine*, (Harrisburg, Pa.: 8 March 1939), Vol. 4, No. 19, p. 503.

43 "Breeding of Mambrino Patchen," *American Saddlebred Registry*, (Louisville, Ky.: American Saddle Horse Breeders Assn., Inc., 1930, revised series), Vol. 4, pp. vii-xii.

44 R. Aitcheson Alexander, *Woodburn Stud Farm 1864 Catalogue*, (Lexington, Ky.: 1864), p. 49; James C. Harrison, *Care & Training of the Trotter & Pacer*, (Columbus, Ohio: The United States Trotting Assoc., 1968), pp. 22, 40-41; John Hervey, *The American Trotter*, (New York: 1947), pp. 200-201.

45 John H. Wallace, *The Horse of America*, (Wilmington, Del.: 1973), p. 350.

46 S. W. Parlin, *The American Trotter*, (Boston, Mass.: Horse Breeder Publishing Company, 1905), pp. 206-207.

47 W.T. Chester, *The Complete Trotting And Racing Record 1884*, (New York: Chester, 1884), p. 1; Joseph Battell, *American Stallion Register*, (Middlebury, Vt.: 1909), Vol. I, pp. 6-9. Information quoted from the *American Cultivator*, (Boston, Mass.: 11 July 1885), p. 8; John Hervey, *American Trotter*, (New York: 1947), p. 93.

48 John Hervey, *The American Trotter*, (New York: 1947), p. 295.

49 John H. Wallace, *The Horse of America*, (Wilmington, Del.: 1897), p. 294.

50 "Abdallah," *American Cultivator*, formerly *Boston Cultivator*, weekly newspaper, (Boston, Mass.: 11 July 1865), N.P.; John Hervey, *The American Trotter*, (New York: 1947), p. 92; John H. Wallace, *The Horse of America*, (Wilmington, Del.: 1973), pp. 294-295; Woodburn Farm Records, Woodburn Farm.

51 "Bay Chief," *American Horse Breeder*, (Boston, Mass.: 1910), p. 1072; Hiram Wooddruff, *The Trotting Horse of America*, (New York: J.B. Ford and Company, 1868), p. 73.

52 Hiram Woodruff, *The Trotting Horse of America*, (New York: 1868), p. 73; John H. Wallace, *The Horse of America*, (Wilmington, Del.: 1973), p. 418.

53 Alexander Mackay-Smith, *The Race Horses of America, 1832-1872, Portraits And Other Paintings by Edward Troye*, (Saratoga Springs, New York: 1981), p. 221; John Hervey, *The American Trotter*, (New York: 1947), p. 295; John Hervey, *Racing In America, 1665-1865*, (New York: Jockey Club, 1944), p. 326; R. Aitcheson Alexander, *Woodburn Stud Farm 1857 Catalogue*, (Lexington, Ky.: Kentucky Statesman Print, 1857), N.P.

54 Alexander Mackay-Smith, *The Race Horses of America, 1832-1872, Portraits And Other Paintings by Edward Troye*, (Saratoga Springs, New York: 1981), p. 221; John Hervey, *Racing In America, 1665-1865*, (New York: 1944), p. 329; John Hervey, *The American Trotter*, (New York: 1947), p. 295.

55 "The Lessons of Twenty Years At Woodburn Farm Kentucky," *Wallace's Monthly*, (New York: May 1879), Vol. V, p. 241.

56 Alexander Mackay-Smith, *The Race Horses of America, 1832-1872, Portraits And Other Paintings by Edward Troye*, (Saratoga Springs, New York: 1981,) p. 221.

57 John Hervey, *Racing in America, 1665-1865*, (New York: 1944), p. 330; John Hervey, *The American Trotter*, (New York: 1947), p. 295; R. Aitcheson Alexander, *Woodburn Stud Farm 1864 Catalogue*, (Lexington, Ky.: J. Dunlop, Book & Job Printer, 1864 January), pp. 37-45; Woodburn Farm Records, Woodburn Farm.

58 "The Lessons Of Twenty Years At Woodburn Farm Ky.," *Wallace's Monthly*, (New York: May 1879), Vol. V, pp. 242-243; John Hervey, *The American Trotter*, (New York: 1947), p. 296; "Descendants Of Pilot Jr.," *American Horse Breeder*, (Boston, Mass.: 7 April 1903), p. 306, Vols. 26, 27, 28; *Western Sportsman and Live Stock News*, newspaper, (Indianapolis, Ind.: 12 September 1890), N.P.

FOOTNOTES

59 John Hervey, *Racing In America, 1665-1865*, (New York: 1944), p. 328.

60 "The Kentucky Stock Book, A Search For the Elusive," *Filson Club Historical Quarterly Journal*, (Louisville, Ky.: July 1974), Vol. 48, No. 3, pp. 217-227. Early efforts through committee had been made to publish the Kentucky Stock Book between 1837-1841 of the pedigrees of fine stock in the state, but the attempt had been unsuccessful. Alexander, however, was the first individual breeder to ask for the pedigrees.

61 Temple Bodley and Samuel M. Wilson, *History of Kentucky*, (Chicago and Louisville: 1928), Vol. 3, p. 79.

62 Mary E. Wharton and Ellen F. Williams, *Peach Leather and Rebel Gray, Bluegrass Life and the War 1860-1865*, (Lexington, Ky.: Helicon Company, 1986), p. 21; Ken McCarr, *The Kentucky Harness Horse*, (Lexington, Ky.: University Press of Kentucky, 1978), p. 117.

63 Alexander Mackay-Smith, *The Race Horses of America, 1832-1872, Portraits And Other Paintings by Edward Troye*, (Saratoga Springs, New York: 1981), p. 221.

64 "Robert Aitcheson Alexander. His Claim to Rank as America's Most Successful Breeder," *Thoroughbred Record*, (Lexington, Ky.: 21 May 1938), p. 343.

65 "The Woodburn Stud," *Turf, Field and Farm*, (New York: 23 December 1887), p. 514.

66 John Hervey, *The American Trotter*, (New York, 1947), p. 194.

67 Richard Ulbrich, *The Great Stallion Book*, (Libra: 1986), pp. 124-125.

68 Joseph Battell, *American Stallion Register*, (Middlebury, Vt.: 1911), Vol. II, pp. 84, 87; "Diomed," *The Horseman and the Spirit of the Times*, (Chicago-New York: 22 December 1903), pp. 1252-1253; "The American Trotter," *American Horse Breeder*, (Boston, Mass.: 21 June 1904), p. 584.

69 "Messenger and Diomed," *American Horse Breeder*, (Boston, Mass.: 28 September 1910), N.P.

70 "The American Trotter," *American Horse Breeder*, (Boston, Mass.: 21 June 1904), p. 584.

71 "Diomed," *The Horseman and the Spirit of the Times*, (Chicago-New York: 22 December 1903), p. 1253.

72 Richard Ulbrich, *The Great Stallion Book*, (Libra: 1986), p. 125.

73 "Imported Diomed," *American Horse Breeder*, (Boston, Mass.: 1 June 1909), Vol. XXVII, No. 2, N.P.

74 John Hervey, *The American Trotter*, (New York: 1947), p. 102.

75 "Imported Diomed," *American Horse Breeder*, (Boston, Mass.: 1 June 1909), Vol XXVII, No. 2, N.P.

76 "Messenger and Diomed," *American Horse Breeder*, (Boston, Mass.: 28 September 1910), N.P.

77 Ibid.

78 Joseph Battell, *American Stallion Register*, (Middlebury, Vt.: 1911), Vol. II, pp. 84-87; "The American Trotter," *American Horse Breeder*, (Boston, Mass.: 21 June 1904), p. 584.

79 Fairfax Harrison, *Early American Turf Stock, 1730-1830*, (Richmond, Va.: The Old Dominion Press, 1935), Vol. 2, pp. 342-343.

80 Jeanne Mellin, *The Morgan Horse*, (Brattlesboro, Vt.: The Stephen Green Press, 1961), p. 45.

81 John Hervey, *The American Trotter*, (New York: 1947), pp. 267-268; Fairfax Harrison, *Early American Turf Stock, 1730-1830*, (Richmond, Va.: 1935), p. 341.

82 "The Woodburn Stud," *Turf, Field and Farm* (23 December 1887), p. 514.

CHAPTER FOUR: FELLOW HORSEMEN AND FRIENDS

1 *The Biographical Encyclopaedia*, (Cincinnati, Ohio: J.M. Armstrong and Company, 1878), p. 516.

2 "Gen. Abraham Buford," *Woodford Sun*, (Versailles, Ky.: 4 May 1989), p. 149; "The American Stud Book-New 'Spirit' and Stock Agency-Purchasers From New York and Other Parts-Visit to Capt. A. Buford's-Zeb. Ward's-Jas. Ford's-Etc.," *Wilkes' Spirit of the Times*, (New York: 7 July 1860), p. 254.

3 "Leamington Slept Here-At Alexander's Bosque Bonita," *The Blood-Horse*, monthly magazine,

FOOTNOTES

(Lexington, Ky.: 1 July 1961), pp. 13, 57.

4 "The American Turf Congress," *Turf, Field and Farm*, (New York: 16 June 1866), p. 372.

5 "Gen. Buford's Unhappy End," *Turf, Field and Farm*, (New York: 13 June 1884), p. 455; "Gen. Abe Buford Made Reputation as a Kentuckian-Soldier," *Lexington Leader*, (Lexington, Ky.: 8 August 1970), N.P.; "Gen. Abraham Buford," *Woodford Sun*, (Versailles, Ky.: 4 May 1989), p. 149; William E. Railey, *History of Woodford Country*," (Versailles, Ky.: Woodford Improvement League, 1968), pp. 92-93; William C. Davis, Julie Hoffman, *The Confederate General*, (Hicksville, N.Y.: The National Historical Society, 1991), pp. 145-146; *The Biographical Encyclopaedia*, (Cincinnati, Ohio: 1878), p. 516; M.B. Buford, *History and Genealogy of the Buford Family in America* (privately compiled), pp. 327-331.

6 William E. Railey, *History of Woodford County*, (Versailles, Ky.: 1968), pp. 29, 85.

7 William E. Railey, *History of Woodford County*, (Versailles, Ky.: 1968), p. 29; George B. Leach, *The Kentucky Derby Jubilee, 1875-1949*, (Louisville, Ky.:Gibbs-Inman Company, 1949), pp. 19, 21; "Rebel Outrages By Guerrillas in Kentucky-Murder of John Harper [actually it was Adam Harper]-Asteroid Recovered," *Wilkes' Spirit of the Times*, (New York: 12 November 1864), p. 169; "John Harper," *Kentucky Live Stock Record*, (Lexington, Ky.: 23 July 1875), p. 57.

8 "Lexington at Bosque Bonita Stud Farm—Explanation by Gen. Buford," *Turf, Field and Farm*, (Lexington, Ky.: 21 March 1873), Vol. 26, No. 12, p. 178. According to General A. Buford, Lexington was at his farm when he was purchased by R.A. Alexander. Lexington may have been at Bosque Bonita on the day he was purchased by R.A., but if so, it was only by coincidence. Lexington had gone there for 24 hours to breed a couple of Buford's mares. "'The truth of history compels us to state that Lexington never made a season at Bosque Bonita Stud Farm.' It is evident from your assertion above quoted that you have misapprehended the purport of the notice in the National Live Stock Journal. It is not stated in that article directly or inferentially that Lexington ever made a season at Bosque Bonita. Nor was it ever so claimed by me or for me, so far as I know. It is true, however, as stated in the article commented upon, that I had selected Lexington as my choice of all the stallions in Kentucky, and had made arrangements with his then owner to stand him at Bosque Bonita, which were never consummated on account of the sale to the late R.A. Alexander. It is also true, as stated, that Lexington was at my farm (having been removed from Mr. W.F. Harper's) at the time of his sale, and he was taken by the groom, Mr. W.M. Brown, from Bosque Bonita to Woodburn where he entered the stud of Mr. Alexander...A. Buford." Buford later recounted this.

9 "Frank B. Harper Is Dead," *Thoroughbred Record*, (Lexington, Ky.: 8 April 1905), p. 220.

10 William E. Railey, *History of Woodford County*, (Versailles, Ky.: 1968), pp. 76-77.

11 "Death of Warren Viley," *Turf, Field and Farm*, (New York: 1902), p. 79; Martineete Viley Witherspoon, "The Viley Family," Viley Papers (1907); property of Woodford County Historical Society, Versailles, Kentucky.

12 Martineete Viley Witherspoon, "Willa Viley's Horses," Viley Papers, (1907); property of the Woodford County Historical Society, Versailles, Kentucky.

13 Sanders D. Bruce, *The American Stud Book*, (New York: 1884), Vol. I, p. 242.

14 "Willa Viley," *Kentucky Livestock Record*, (Lexington, Ky.: 2 April 1875), Vol. I, No. 9, p. 136; Martineete Viley Witherspoon, "Willa Viley's Horses," Viley Papers, (1907); property of Woodford County Historical Society, Versailles, Kentucky.

15 Thomas A. Knight and Nancy Lewis Greene, *Country Estates of the Bluegrass*, (Lexington, Ky.: Henry Clay Press, 1973), p. 160; "Death of Warren Viley," *Turf, Field and Farm*, (New York: 24 January 1902), p. 79.

16 "Black Bess Given To Morgan," *Woodford Sun*, (Versailles, Ky.: 4 May 1989), p. B-2, found in Woodford County Historical Society Vertical Files, "Black Bess," p. 141; "Death Of Warren Viley," *Turf,*

FOOTNOTES

Field and Farm, (New York: 24 January 1902), p. 79.

17 "Residence of A. Keene Richards, Georgetown," *Spirit of the Times*, (New York: 28 July 1860), Vol. XXX, No. 25, pp. 229, 300.

18 "Death of Col. A. Keene Richards," *Kentucky Live Stock Record*, became *Thoroughbred Record*, (Lexington, Ky.: 26 March 1881), Vol. 13, No. 13, p. 200. The dates and length of time spent in Arabia changes from source to source, but he "is reported to have been the first American to go directly to the source to import pure-bred Arab stallions to the United States." George H. Conn, *The Arabian Horse in America*, (New York: A.S. Barnes and Company, 1957), pp. 103, 225.

19 Alexander Mackay-Smith, *The Race Horses of America, 1832-1872, Portraits and Other Paintings by Edward Troye*, (Saratoga Springs, New York: 1981), pp. 203, 222.

20 "Robert Aitcheson Alexander," *Thoroughbred Record*, (Lexington, Ky.: 21 May 1938), p. 334.

21 "Death of Colonel A. Keene Richards," *Kentucky Live Stock Record*, (Lexington, Ky.: 26 March 1881), p. 200.

22 John Hervey, *Racing in America, 1665-1865*, (New York: 1944), Vol. II, p. 145.

CHAPTER FIVE: WAR COMES TO KENTUCKY

1 "The Cincinnati Press on the Position of Kentucky Neutrality," *Frankfort Commonwealth*, daily newspaper, (Frankfort, Ky.: 30 April 1861), p. 2.

2 "Memorial, to the Senate and House of Representatives in the Congress of the United States," *Daily Commonwealth*, (Frankfort, Ky.: 19 January 1861), p. 3.

3 R.A. Alexander's letter to Mary Belle Alexander Deedes, dated 31 May 1861, Woodburn Farm Records, King Library.

4 David Greenspan, *American Heritage, Battle Maps of the Civil War*, (Tulsa, Ok.: Council Oak Books, 1992), "Railroads of the Confederacy and the Border States," pp. 14-15.

5 R.A. Alexander's personal journal, Woodburn Farm Records, Woodburn Farm.

6 John Ellis, *A Short History of Guerrilla Warfare*, (New York: St. Martin's Press, 1976), p. 86.

7 Lowell H. Harrison, *The Civil War in Kentucky*, (Lexington, Ky.: The University of Kentucky, 1975), pp. 76-77; Ezra J. Warner, *Generals In Blue*, (Baton Rouge, La.: Louisiana State University Press, 1964), pp. 54-55.

8 "Innocent Confederates Shot in Retaliation for Jones's Death," *Kentucky Standard*, weekly newspaper, (Bardstown, Ky.: 7 September 1988), p. A-8; E. Merton Coulter, *The Civil War and Readjustment In Kentucky*, (Chapel Hill, N.C.: University of North Carolina Press, 1926), pp. 232-236.

9 Captain Thomas Speed, *The Union Cause in Kentucky, 1860-1865*, (New York and London, England: G.P. Putman's Sons, The Knickerbocker Press, 1907), p. 245.

10 E. Merton Coulter, *The Civil War and Readjustment In Kentucky*, (Chapel Hill, N. C.: 1926), p. 232.

11 Lowell H. Harrison, *The Civil War In Kentucky*, (Lexington, Ky.: 1975), p. 77.

12 Ibid., p. 75.

13 "Innocent Confederates Shot In Retaliation For Jones' Death," *Kentucky Standard*, (Bardstown, Ky.: 7 September, 1988), p. A-8.

14 Lewis Collins, *History of Kentucky*, (Frankfort, Ky.: 1966), Vol. I, p. 144.

15 Ibid., p. 146.

16 "Innocent Confederates Shot In Retaliation For Jones's Death," *Kentucky Standard*, (Bardstown, Ky.: 7 September, 1988), p. A-8; Lewis Collins, *History of Kentucky*, (Frankfort, Ky.: 1966), Vol. I, p. 144.

17 Lewis Collins, *History of Kentucky*, (Frankfort, Ky.: 1966), Vol. I, p. 149.

18 Dan M. Bowmar, III, *Giants of the Turf*, (Lexington, Ky.: 1960), p. 15; John Hervey, *Racing In America, 1665-1865*, (New York: 1944), p. 329.

19 Dan M. Bowmar, III, *Giants of the Turf*, (Lexington, Ky.: 1960), p. 15; Mary E. Wharton and Ellen

FOOTNOTES

F. Williams, *Peach Leather and Rebel Gray, Bluegrass Life and the War 1860-1865*, (Lexington, Ky.: 1986), p. 88; John Hervey, *Racing In America, 1665-1865*, (New York: 1944), pp. 321-324, 329; Abram S. Hewitt, *The Great Breeders And Their Methods*, (Lexington, Ky.: Thoroughbred Publishers, Inc., 1982), p. 21; *The Alexander Genealogy* (privately compiled) property of Dr. A.J. Alexander, Lexington, Kentucky; The Lady Pamela Head, Guildford, Surrey England; Sir Claud Hagart-Alexander of Kingencleugh House, Mauchline, Ayrshire, Scotland.

20 "Stories of Maj. Warren Viley," *Woodford Sun*, (Versailles, Ky.: 30 January 1902), p. 1.

21 John Hervey, *Racing In America, 1665-1865*, (New York: 1944), p. 330.

22 "Death of Imported Australian," *Kentucky Live Stock Record*, (Lexington, Ky.: 18 October 1879), Vol. 16, No. 10, p. 248; John Hervey, *Racing In America, 1665-1865*, (New York: 1944), p. 329.

23 "Colonel Jack" P. Chinn," *Thoroughbred Record*, (Lexington, Ky.: 16 May 1931), p. 469.

24 "Breeding of Mambrino Patchen," *American Saddlebred Registry*, (Louisville, Ky.:, 1930, revised series), Vol. 4, pp. viii-xii; Mary E. Wharton and Ellen F. Williams, *Peach Leather and Rebel Gray, Bluegrass Life and the War 1860-1865*, (Lexington, Ky.: 1986), pp. v, vi, 20, 67, 88, 158, 159; Herbert T. Krum, Short Stories About Famous Horses, (Herbert T. Krum, 1910), p. 371; Louis Taylor, *The Horse America Made*, (Louisville, Ky.: American Saddle Horse Breeders Assn., Inc., 1944), pp. 9, 10, 12, 74, 235; Susanne Emily Ellen Scharf, *Famous Saddle Horses*, (Louisville, Ky.: The Farmer's Home Journal Company, 1932), pp. 45, 46, 49, 50. The number 61 is Gaines' Denmark's registration number in the *American Saddlebred Registry*. *The American Saddlebred Registry* was created in 1891, but revised around 1900. There was no formula or procedure dictating how the horses would be listed in the *Registry*.

25 Mary E. Wharton and Ellen F. Williams, *Peach Leather and Rebel Gray, Bluegrass Life and the War 1860-1865*, (Lexington, Ky.: 1986), pp. v, vi, 88, 158.

26 Ibid., p. vi, 88.

27 "Was Mambrino Patchen A Saddlebred? Old Photo Is New Evidence," *American Saddlebred Magazine*, monthly magazine, (Lexington, Ky.: The American Saddle Horse Association, Inc., July/August 1988), p. 34; "Breeding of Mambrino Patchen," *American Saddlebred Registry*, (Louisville, Ky.: 1930, revised series), Vol. 4, pp. viii-xii.

28 Telephone conversation/interview with Lynn Weatherman, Cynthiana, Kentucky, 8 October 1993.

29 Mark Mayo Boatner, III, *The Civil War Dictionary*, (David McKay Company, Inc., New York: 1976), p. 568.

30 Ibid., pp. 568, 569.

31 Louis Taylor, *The Horse America Made*, (Louisville, Ky.: 1944), p. 73.

32 Mark Mayo Boatner, III, *The Civil War Dictionary*, (New York: 1976), p. 569; James A. Ramage, *Rebel Raider, The Life of John Hunt Morgan*, (University Press of Kentucky, Lexington, Ky.: 1986), pp. 220, 223.

33 Herbert T. Crum, *Short Stories About Famous Horses*, (1910), p. 371.

34 Telephone conversation/interview with Lynn Weatherman, Cynthiana, Kentucky, 8 October 1993.

35 R. Aitcheson Alexander, *Woodburn Stud Farm 1864 Catalogue*, Woodburn Farm Records Woodburn Farm, (Lexington, Ky.: 1864), p. 37.

36 Mary E. Wharton and Ellen F. Williams, *Peach Leather and Rebel Gray, Bluegrass Life and the War 1860-1865*, (Lexington, Ky.: 1986), p. 159.

37 Old Woodburn Farm record books, "Fillies 1864," "Colts 1864," *Woodburn Farm Ledgers*: "List of Mares bred to Denmark 1864," *Woodburn Stud Book*: "Denmark Fall season 1865," *Woodburn Stud Book*; Woodburn Farm Records, Woodburn Farm; Mary E. Wharton and Ellen F. Williams, *Peach Leather and Rebel Gray, Bluegrass Life and the War 1860 1865*, (Lexington, Ky.: 1986), pp. vi, 20, 67, 88, 158, 159.

FOOTNOTES

38 "Breeding of Mambrino Patchen," *American Saddlebred Registry*, (Louisville, Ky.: 1930, revised series), Vol. 4, pp. viii-xii; Mary E. Wharton and Ellen F. Williams, *Peach Leather and Rebel Gray, Bluegrass Life and the War 1860-1865*, (Lexington, Ky.: 1986), pp. 158, 159; Herbert T. Krum, *Short Stories About Famous Horses*, (1910), p. 371; Louis Taylor, *The Horse America Made*, (Louisville, Ky.: 1944), pp. 9, 10, 12, 73, 74, 235; Susanne Emily Ellen Scharf, *Famous Saddle Horses*, (Louisville, Ky.: 1932), pp. 45, 46, 49, 50.

39 R. Aitcheson Alexander, *Woodburn Stud Farm 1864 Catalogue*, Woodburn Farm Records Woodburn Farm, (Lexington, Ky.: January 1864), p. 15.

40 "The Racers of Kentucky-Morgan's Men Among The Horses," *Wilkes' Spirit of the Times*, (New York: 2 July 1864), p. 281; "Asteroid Stolen By Guerrillas," *Wilkes'*, (5 November 1864), p. 156.

41 R.A. Alexander's letter to A.J. Alexander, 22 June 1864, Woodburn Farm Records, King Library; *1860 Census*, "Free Inhabitants," Woodford County, Kentucky, p. 93.

42 John Hervey, *Racing in America, 1665-1865*, (New York: 1944), p. 330.

43 "Fine Weather and Exciting Sport Mark Morris Park," *Turf, Field and Farm*, (New York: 25 October, 1902), p. 1026; "Rebel Outrages by Guerrillas in Kentucky-Murder of John Harper [actually it was Adam Harper]-Asteroid Recovered," *Wilkes' Spirit of the Times*, (New York: 12 November 1864), p. 169; John Hervey, *Racing In America, 1665-1865*, (New York: 1944), p. 330. See Appendix for list of Kentucky guerrillas.

44 "The Stealing and Recovery of Asteroid," *Wilkes' Spirit of the Times*, (New York: 19 November 1864), p. 185; "Rebel Outrages by Guerrillas in Kentucky-Murder of John Harper [actually Adam Harper]-Asteroid Recovered," (New York: 12 November 1864), p. 169. Sue Mundy's name is found in several references including *The War of the Rebellion; A Compilation of the Official Records of the Union and Confederate Armies*, spelled Munday.

45 R.A. Alexander's letter, Thursday 24th, Woodburn Farm Records, King Library; "The Stealing and Recovery of Asteroid," *Wilkes' Spirit of the Times*, (New York: 19 November 1864), p. 185.

46 "The Stealing and Recovery of Asteroid," *Wilkes' Spirit of the Times*, (New York: 19 November 1864), p. 185.

47 R.A. Alexander's letter, Thursday 24th, Woodburn Farm Records, King Library. R.A. named the guerrillas who allegedly participated in the raid although he did not reveal how he learned their names. The men he mentioned were: Jim Davis, John Parkhurst, Henry Warford, ("One-Arm") Berry and Ben Froman.

48 "The Stealing and Recovery of Asteroid," *Wilkes' Spirit of the Times*, (New York: 19 November 1864), p. 185; "Fine Weather and Exciting Sport Mark Morris Park," *Turf, Field and Farm*, (New York: 25 October 1902), p. 1026; "Stories of Maj. Warren Viley," *Woodford Sun*, (Versailles, Ky.: 30 January 1902), p. 1; "Asteroid Stolen by Guerrillas," *Wilkes' Spirit of the Times*, (New York: 5 November 1864), p. 156; "The Story of Woodburn," *Lexington, Kentucky Morning Herald*, (27 January 1898), p. 3; Dan M. Bowmar, III, *Giants of the Turf*, (Lexington, Ky.: 1960), p. 16.

49 Letter, dated Thursday 24th, by R.A. Alexander, Woodburn Farm Records, King Library.

50 H.G. Crickmore, *Racing Calendars-3 volumes by years, 1861-1865*, (New York: 1901), pp. 132, 161, 168; *Calendars, 1866-1867*, p. 18; "Death of Bay Dick," *Thoroughbred Record*, formally *Kentucky Live Stock Record*, (Lexington, Ky.: 15 December 1883), p. 393.

51 "Stories of Maj. Warren Viley," *Woodford Sun*, (Versailles, Ky.: 30 January 1902), p. 1; "The Stealing and Recovery of Asteroid," *Wilkes' Spirit of the Times*, (New York: 19 November 1864), p. 185.

52 "The Stealing and Recovery of Asteroid," *Wilkes' Spirit of the Times*, (New York: 19 November 1864), p. 185.

53 "Asteroid Stolen By Guerrillas," *Wilkes' Spirit of the Times*, (New York: 5 November 1864), p. 156.

54 R. Aitcheson Alexander, *Woodburn Stud Farm 1864 Catalogue*, (Lexington, Ky.: January 1864), p. 45; Woodburn Farm Records, Woodburn Farm. This catalogue was published annually, the first of its

FOOTNOTES

kind in the country. In Swigert's own copy he made handwritten notes and comments on the horses. As the farm's Superintendent, it was his job to keep track of what happened to the horses. See also "Kentucky's Most Famous Breeder Living in Obscurity in a Lexington Log Cabin," *Louisville Courier-Journal*, (23 December 1900), p. 9.

55 "Rebel Outrage by Guerrillas in Kentucky-Murder of John Harper [actually Adam Harper]-Asteroid Recovered," *Wilkes' Spirit of the Times*, (New York: 12 November 1864), p. 169.

56 "A Patch of Rumor-Horse Stealing for Some Purpose," *Chicago Tribune*, (31 October 1864), p.1.

57 "A Patch of Rumor-Horse Stealing for Some Purpose," *Chicago Tribune*, (31 October 1864), p. 1; "Rebel Guerrilla Bands-A Freight Train Thrown From Tracks and Burned by Guerrillas," *Tribune*, (25 October 1864), p. 2.

58 R.A. Alexander's letter, Thursday 24th, Woodburn Farm Records, King Library.

59 "Stories of Maj. Warren Viley," *Woodford Sun*, (Versailles, Ky.: 30 January 1902), p. 1; William E. Railey, *History of Woodford County*, (Versailles, Ky.: 1968), p.77; Martineete Viley Witherspoon, "The Viley Family," Viley Papers (1907), property of Woodford County Historical Society, Versailles, Kentucky.

60 R.A. Alexander's letter, Thursday 24th, Woodburn Farm Records, King Library.

61 "Fine Weather and Exciting Sport Mark Morris Park," *Turf, Field and Farm*, (New York: 25 October 1902), p.1026.

62 William E. Railey, *History of Woodford County*, (Versailles, Ky.: 1968), p. 171; "Stories of Maj. Warren Viley," *Woodford Sun*, (Versailles, Ky.: 30 January 1902), p. 1; "The Stealing and Recovery of Asteroid," *Wilkes' Spirit of the Times*, (New York: 19 November 1864), p. 185; "Local Turf News," *Thoroughbred Record*, (Lexington, Ky.: 25 January 1902), p. 40.

63 William E. Railey, *The History of Woodford County*, (Versailles, Ky.: 1968), p. 172.

64 Mary Rogers Clay, *The Clay Family*, (Louisville, Ky.: John P. Morton & Company, 1899), pp. 120-121, 172-173; William Elsey Connelley and E.M. Coulter, *History of Kentucky*, (Chicago, Ill. and New York: The American Historical Society, 1922), Vol. III, pp. 56-57.

65 Dan M. Bowmar, III, *Giants of the Turf*, (Lexington, Ky.: 1960), p. 16; "Fine Weather and Exciting Sport Mark Morris Park," *Turf, Field and Farm*, (New York: 25 October 1902), p. 1026; "From Louisville," *Chicago Tribune*, (2 November 1864), p. 1.

66 "The Stealing and Recovery of Asteroid," *Wilkes' Spirit of the Times*, (New York: 19 November 1864), p. 185.

67 Dan M. Bowmar, III, *Giants of the Turf*, (Lexington, Ky.: 1960), p. 16; "Stories of Maj. Warren Viley," *Woodford Sun*, (Versailles, Ky.: 30 January 1902), p. 1; "The Story of Woodburn," *Lexington, Kentucky Morning Herald*, (27 January 1898), p. 3; John Hervey, *Racing In America, 1665-1865*, (New York: 1944), p. 330; "The Stealing and Recovery of Asteroid," *Wilkes' Spirit of the Times*, (New York: 19 November 1864), p. 185. The guerrilla "who rode him [Asteroid] through the river and the woods, when Mr. Alexander's friend told him that he was a three-year-old [said] 'that be dammed! He's no three-year-old colt, but the stoutest horse I ever put my leg over.'" "The American Jockey Club," *Wilkes' Spirit of the Times*, (New York: 22 September 1866), p. 57. See also "Rebel Outrages by Guerrillas in Kentucky-Murder of John [actually Adam] Harper-Asteroid Recovered," *Wilkes' Spirit of the Times*, (New York: 12 November 1864), p. 169; "Fine and Exciting Sport Marks Morris Park," *Turf, Field and Farm*, (New York: 25 October 1902), p. 1026; "More Guerrilla Atrocities-Southern Finale of the Period of Prompt Retaliation," *Chicago Tribune*, (5 November 1864), p. 1.

68 Dan M. Bowmar, III, *Giants of the Turf*, (Lexington, Ky.: 1960), p. 16; "Stories of Maj. Warren Viley," *Woodford Sun*, (Versailles, Ky.: 30 January 1902), p. 1; "Rebel Outrages by Guerrillas in Kentucky-Murder of John Harper [actually Adam]-Asteroid Recovered," *Wilkes' Spirit of the Times*, (New York: 12 November 1864), p. 169.

FOOTNOTES

69 R.A. Alexander's letter, Thursday 24th, Woodburn Farm Records, King Library.

70 "From Louisville," *Chicago Tribune*, (2 November 1864), p. 1.

71 Report by Major Samuel Martin to Captain John S. Butler, *The War of the Rebellion; A Compilation of the Official Records of the Union and Confederate Armies*, (Harrisburg, Pa.: The National Historical Society, 1971), Series I, Vol. XXXIX, Part I, pp. 898-899. (Hereafter referred to as O.R., with volume number supplied.)

72 "General News," *New York Times*, (14 December 1864), p. 4.

73 R.A. Alexander's letter, 27 January 1865, Woodburn Farm Records, King Library.

74 R.A. Alexander's letter to Henry Charles Deedes, March 4, 1865, Woodburn Farm Records, King Library.

75 "Sue Munday Was A Confederate Captain," *Kentucky Standard*, (Bardstown, Ky.: 3 February 1966), p. 789.

76 "The Racers of Kentucky-Morgan's Men Among The Horses," *Wilkes' Spirit of the Times*, (New York: 2 July 1864), p. 281.

77 "Fine Weather and Exciting Sport Mark Morris Park," *Turf, Field and Farm*, (New York: 25 October, 1902), p. 1026; "More Guerrilla Atrocities-Southern Finale of the Period of Prompt Retaliation," *Chicago Tribune*, (5 November 1864), p. 1; "Stories of Maj. Warren Viley," *Woodford Sun*, (Versailles, Ky.: 30 January 1902), p.1; "Frank B. Harper Is Dead," *Thoroughbred Record*, (Lexington, Ky.: 8 April 1905), p. 220; "John Harper," *Record*, (22 June 1929), p. 630; "Rebel Outrages By Guerrillas in Kentucky-Murder of John Harper [actually Adam Harper]-Asteroid Recovered," *Wilkes' Spirit of the Times*, (New York: 12 November 1864), p. 169; "Asteroid and Lodestone-Who Bred Them?," *Wilkes'*, (1 July 1865), p. 281.

78 G. Glenn Clift, *Events of the Civil War in Kentucky*, (arranged by counties, 1961), p. "Woodford County," under 9 November 1864, Kentucky Historical Society, Frankfort, Ky.; (Lewis Collins, *History of Kentucky*, (Frankfort, Ky.: 1966), Vol. I, p. 146; "More Guerrilla Atrocities-Southern Finale of the Period of Prompt Retaliation," *Chicago Tribune*, (5 November 1864), p. 1.

79 Inscription on marker in Midway cemetery.

CHAPTER SIX: QUANTRILL'S ARRIVAL INTO THE BLUEGRASS

1 Mark Mayo Boatner, III, *The Civil War Dictionary*, (New York: 1976), p. 670.

2 Thomas Goodrich, *Bloody Dawn, The Story of the Lawrence Massacre*, (Kent, Ohio and London, England: Kent State University Press, 1991), p. 180; Edward E. Leslie, *The Devil Knows How to Ride*, (New York, Random House: 1996), p. 343.

3 James D. Horan, *The Authentic Wild West, The Outlaws*, (New York: Crown Publishers, Inc., 1977), p. 122.

4 "The Borderland," *Collier's Magazine*, (Springfield, Ohio: 26 September 1914), Vol. 54, pp. 18, 19, 24, 26; Telephone interview with Carl Breihan, 30 December 1994. Although some believe there was a family connection between the Jameses and Quantrill, there is no evidence to support that claim. See "Mrs. Samuel's Will," *Liberty [Missouri] Tribune*, weekly newspaper, (Liberty, Mo.: 17 February 1911), p. 3.

5 "Gathering of Old Guerrillas," *Booneville [Missouri] Weekly Advertiser*, newspaper, (Booneville, Mo.: 19 October 1901), p. 2.

6 "Sketch of the Marauder Quantrell and His Operations," *New York Times*, (26 March 1865), p. 3.

7 James D. Horan, *The Authentic Wild West, The Outlaws*, (New York: 1977), p. 122; Mark Mayo Boatner, III, *The Civil War Dictionary*, (New York: 1976), p. 134.

8 James D. Horan, *The Authentic Wild West, The Outlaws*, (New York: 1977), p. 123; Mark Mayo

FOOTNOTES

Boatner, III, *The Civil War Dictionary*, (New York, 1976), pp. 134-135.

9 Donald R. Hale, *We Rode With Quantrill*, (Clinton, Mo.: The Printery, 1975), p. 64.

10 Mark Mayo Boatner, III, *The Civil War Dictionary*, (New York: 1976), p. 670.

11 Ibid., pp. 669-671.

12 Donald R. Hale, *We Rode With Quantrill*, (Clinton, Mo.: 1975), p. 64; "William Clarke Quantrill and His Lieutenants," *Western Frontier Magazine*, bi-monthly magazine, (New York: G.Z. London Publishing Company, November 1977), p. 39.

13 Donald R. Hale, *We Rode With Quantrill*, (Clinton, Mo.: 1975), p. 64; "William Clarke Quantrill and His Lieutenants," *Western Frontier Magazine*, (New York: November 1977), p. 51; Michael Fellman, *Inside War*, (New York: Oxford University Press, 1989), p. 187; Thomas Goodrich, *Bloody Dawn, The Story of the Lawrence Massacre*, (Kent, Ohio: 1991), p. 180.

14 William Elsey Connelley, *Quantrill And the Border Wars*, (New York: Pageant Book Company, 1956), pp. 457-458; Mark Mayo Boatner, III, *The Civil War Dictionary*, (New York: 1976), pp. 669-671, 675; Jay Monaghan, *Civil War on the Western Border, 1854-1865*, (Toronto, Canada and Boston, Mass.: Little, Brown and Company, 1955), p. 346; Richard S. Brounlee, *Gray Ghost of the Confederacy*, (Baton Rouge: Louisiana State University Press, 1968), pp. 230-231.

15 Albert Castle, *William Clarke Quantrill-His Life and Times*, (Columbus, Ohio: reprinted by The General's Books, 1992), p. 201; Duane Schultz, *Quantrill's War*, (St. Martins Press, New York: 1996), p. 293.

16 "Guerrilla Quantrell," *Daily Capital*, (Topeka, Kansas: 14 April 1881), Information provided by the manuscript department of the Kansas State Historical Society, Topeka, Kansas; "Sketch of the Marauder Quantrell and His Operations," *New York Times*, (26 March 1865), p. 3.

17 Letters of A.D. Donnie Pence, 14 December 1887 and others not dated, to William W. Scott, written from Samuel's Depot, Kentucky, Regional History, Manuscripts Collection 75, Box 2, folder 57 (not dated) and folder 14a (1887), Kansas Collection, University of Kansas, Topeka, Kansas (hereafter Kansas Collection).

18 Albert Castel, *William Clarke Quantrill-His Life and Times*, (Columbus, Ohio: 1962), p. 203; Account of Ben R. Kirkpatrick, Hodgenville, Kentucky, 10 October 1936, describing *The Career of William Clark[e] Quantrill in Kentucky and his Ending*, manuscript collection, miscellaneous "Kirkpatrick," Kansas State Historical Collection, Topeka, Kansas. In *The War of Rebellion; A Compilation of the Official Records of the Union and Confederate Armies*, (Harrisburg, Pa.: 1971), Quantrill is identified as "Clarke." Among the specific references, see "Report of Gen. E. Hobson, written by Lieutenant and Acting Assistant General Thomas A. Howes, Series I, Vol. XLIX, Part 1, pp. 17-18, 35, 612, 616, 634, 635, 657, 684, 694, 698. See also James Wakefield's letter to William W. Scott, 13 June 1888, Manuscripts Collection 75, Box 2, folder 21, *Kansas Collection*.

19 "Quantrill The Guerrilla," *Louisville Courier-Journal*, (29 April 1874), p. 2.

20 Hon. Dr. J.A. Dacus, *Illustrated Lives and Adventures of Frank and Jesse James and the Younger Brothers, The Noted Western Outlaws*, (New York and St. Louis: N.D. Thompson & Company, 1882), p. 70.

21 O.S. Barton and John McCorkle, *Three Years With Quantrill*, (Norman, Ok.: University of Oklahoma Press, 1992), p. 190.

22 Hon. Dr. J.A. Dacus, *Illustrated Lives And Adventures of Frank And Jesse James And The Younger Brothers, The Noted Western Outlaws*, (New York and St. Louis: 1882), p. 70.

23 Letter of Alex Anderson, Danville, Ky.: 10 July 1888, Box 2, folder 24, Kansas Collection, "Guerrilla Quantrill," *Daily Capital*, (Topeka, Kansas: 14 April 1881), N.P. Information provided by the manuscript department of the Kansas State Historical Society, Topeka, Kansas.

24 "Guerrilla War in Kentucky," *Chicago Tribune*, (1 February 1865), p. 2.

25 "Guerrilla War in Kentucky," *Chicago Tribune*, (1 February 1865), p. 2; O.R., "Report of Captain

FOOTNOTES

William .L. Gross," Series I, Vol. XILX, Part I, p. 18; ibid., "Report of Thomas H. Howes to Mahoney," p. 615; ibid., "Report of General Speed S. Fry," p. 612.

26 O.S. Barton and John McCorkle, *Three Years With Quantrill*, (Norman, Ok.: 1992), p. 194.

27 "Guerrilla War in Kentucky," *Chicago Tribune*, (1 February 1865), p. 2.

28 Letter of Alex Alexander, Danville Ky.: 10 July 1888, box 2, folder 24, "Kansas Collection" of the University of Kansas Library.

29 "Quantrill the Guerrilla," *Louisville Courier-Journal*, (29 April 1874), p. 2; William Elsey Connelley, *Quantrill And The Border Wars*, (New York: 1956), p. 461; O.R. "Report of William L. Gross," Series I, Vol. XILX, Part I, p. 18; ibid., "Report of Thomas H. Howes," p. 615; "Guerrilla War in Kentucky," *Chicago Tribune*, (1 February 1865), p. 2; "Guerrilla Quantrill," *Daily Capital*, (Topeka, Kansas: 14 April 1881), N.P. Information provided by the manuscript department of the Kansas State Historical Society, Topeka, Kansas.

30 O.R., "Report of Major Mahoney," Series I, Vol. XILX, Part I, p. 18.

31 "Quantrill The Guerrilla," *Louisville Courier-Journal*, (29 April 1874), p. 2.

32 J.P. Burch, *A True Story of Chas. W. Quantrill And His Guerrilla Band*, (Vega, Texas: J. P. Burch, 1923), p. 243; "Bardstown Hotel, Rural Residence, Associated With Outlaws Frank And Jesse James Go, But Interesting Stories Remain," *Kentucky Standard*, (Bardstown, Ky.: 24 July 1969), N.P.; "Frank James The Intellectual Outlaw," *Salt River Arcadian*, monthly newspaper, (Taylorsville, Ky.: November issue 1988), p. B-6; "Jackman Recalls Serving With Frank And Jesse James," *Kentucky Standard*, (Bardstown, Ky.: 2 November 1988), N.P.; Sarah B. Smith, *Historic Nelson County*, (Louisville, Ky.: Gateway Press, 1971), p. 58. Most of this local information of the area comes from the collection of Hattie Clements, Bloomfield, Kentucky.

33 "The Life and Trial of Frank James," *Wide Awake Library*, monthly magazine, (New York: 28 September 1883 issue), p. 18.

34 "Quantrill's Last Fight," *Spirit of Kansas*, daily newspaper, (Lawrence, Kansas: 26 July 1873), N.P. Information provided by the Kansas State Historical Society, Topeka, Kansas.

35 "Quantrill The Guerrilla," *Louisville Courier-Journal*, (29 April 1874), p. 2; "Quantrill's Last Fight," *Spirit of Kansas*, (Lawrence, Kansas: 26 July 1873), N.P.

36 "From Louisville," *New York Times*, (1 January 1865), p. 8.

37 "From Louisville," *New York Times*, (1 January 1865), p. 8; "Movements of the Rebels in Kentucky," *Times*, (8 January 1865), p. 8.

38 Thomas Shelby Watson, *The Silent Riders*, (Louisville, Ky.: 1970), p. 25.

39 "News of the Day," *New York Times* (12 January 1865), p. 4.

40 Lewis Collins, *History of Kentucky*, (Frankfort, Ky.: 1966), Vol. I, p. 153.

41 "Guerrilla War in Kentucky," *Chicago Tribune*, (1 February 1865), p. 2.

42 "Affairs In Kentucky," *New York Times*, (1 February 1865), p. 5; "From Kentucky," *Chicago Tribune*, (2 February 1865), p. 1.

43 Sarah B. Smith, *Historic Nelson County*, (Louisville, Ky.: 1971), p. 61; "Guerrilla War in Kentucky," *Chicago Tribune*, (1 February 1865), p. 2.

44 Lewis Collins, *History of Kentucky*, (Frankfort, Ky.: 1966), Vol. I, p. 154.

45 "Guerrilla War in Kentucky," *Chicago Tribune*, (1 February 1865), p. 2.

46 Ezra J. Warner, *Generals In Blue*, (Baton Rouge, La.: 1964), pp. 231-232; Mark Mayo Boatner, III, *The Civil War Dictionary*, (New York: 1976), p. 403.

47 O.R., "Report of Colonel Harvey M. Buckley," Series I, Vol. XILX, Part I, p. 625.

48 Ibid., "Report of Brigadier General Edward H. Hobson," p. 626.

49 Ibid., "Report of John S. Butler," p. 626; ibid., "Report of Captain Emzy W. Easley," [February 2, 1865], p. 633.

50 Ibid., "Report of Captain Harvey M. Buckley," p. 635.

51 Ibid., "Report of Thomas A. Howes," p. 634.

52 "Quantrill the Guerrilla," *Louisville Courier-Journal*, (29 April 1874), p. 2; O.R., "Report of A.G. Hamilton," Series I, Vol. XILX, Part I, p. 635; ibid., "Answer to Maj. Hamilton by Thomas A. Howes," p. 635.

53 Ibid., "Report of Colonel Simeon B. Brown," p. 634.

54 "Affairs In Kentucky," *New York Times*, (5 February 1865), p. 1; "From Kentucky," *New York Daily Tribune*, (4 February 1865), p. 1; "From Kentucky," *Chicago Tribune*, (5 February 1865), p. 2; "Guerrilla Warfare in Kentucky," *Richmond Daily Examiner*, daily newspaper, (Richmond, Va.: 8 February 1865), p. 1; Edward E. Leslie, *The Devil Knows How to Ride*, (New York: 1996), pp. 354-355. Willa Viley was taken hostage. See R.A. Alexander's 4 March 1865 letter, Woodburn Farm Records, King Library.

55 Lewis Collins, *History of Kentucky*, (Frankfort, Ky.: 1966), Vol. 1, p. 154; "Guerrilla Warfare in Kenucky," *Richmond Daily Examiner*, (Richmond, VA.: 8 February 1865), p.1; R.A., Alexander's letter, Thursday 24th, Wookburn Farm Records, King Library.

CHAPTER SEVEN: DISASTER AT WOODBURN

1 "Willa Viley," *Kentucky Live Stock Record*, (Lexington, Ky.: 2 April 1875), pp. 136-137.

2 R.A. Alexander's letter to Henry Charles Deedes, March 4, 1865, Woodburn Farm Records, King Library. The ensuring description of the final raid on Woodburn Farm is derived almost entirely from R.A.'s letter to his brother-in law, Henry Charles Deedes, 4 March 1865, from Chicago. The letter is in the King Library at the University of Kentucky, Lexington, Kentucky, and Dr. A.J. Alexander has kindly permitted the author to transcribe its contents. The letter is Alexander's personal account of the February 2, 1865, raid on Woodburn Farm. Although the wording was altered to provide continuity and clarity, R.A.'s own words were used whenever possible.

3 "The Story of Woodburn," *Lexington, Kentucky Morning Herald*, (27 January 1898), p. 3.

4 R.A. Alexander's letter to his brother, "Alec" J. Alexander, 27 January 1865, Woodburn Farm Records, King Library. Also he mentions this in his 4 March 1865 letter to Henry Deedes, Woodburn Farm Records, King Library. The person who wrote the letter was never identified.

5 "The Story of Woodburn," *Lexington, Kentucky Morning Herald*, (27 January 1898), p. 3; *1860 Census*, "Free Inhabitants," Woodford County, Kentucky, p. 94. "Almont was trained early at Woodburn, and, like his sire, [Abdallah] started but once and distanced his competitor in 2:39 3/4, this being in his four-year-old form. He soon after showed 2:32 over the slow Woodburn track, and was sold to Colonel Richard West for $8,000 and put in the stud." John H. Wallace, The *Horse of America*, (Wilmington, Del.: 1973), p. 297. See Appendix, "Sons of Almont."

6 Dan M. Bowmar, III, *Giants of the Turf*, (Lexington, Ky.: 1960), p. 9; "The American Stud Book-New 'Spirit' and Stock Agency-Purchasers from New York and Other Parts-Visit to Capt. A. Buford's-Zeb. Ward's-Jas. Ford's-Etc.," *Spirit of the Times*, (New York: 7 July 1860), p. 255; *1860 Census*, "Free Inhabitants," Woodford County, Kentucky, p. 94.

7 Hull interview in "Story of Woodburn," *Lexington Kentucky Morning Herald*, (27 January 1898), p. 3.

8 Telephone conversations with Dr. A.J. Alexander, Lexington, Kentucky, 27 June 1983. The family history claims that the gun was discharged during the struggle.

9 "Another Raid on Mr. Alexander's Farm-Nannie Butler and Fourteen Other Horses Carried Off," *Wilkes' Spirit of the Times*, (New York: 18 February 1865), p. 393.

10 "The Story of Woodburn," *Lexington Kentucky Morning Herald*, (27 January 1898), p. 3.

11 Ibid.

12 "Quantrill the Guerrilla," *Louisville Courier-Journal*, (29 April 1874), p. 2; Thomas Shelby Watson,

FOOTNOTES

The Silent Riders, (Louisville, Ky.: 1970), p. 35.

13 Dan M. Bowmar, III, *Giants of the Turf*, (Lexington, Ky.: 1960), p. 16; R.A. Alexander's letter to Henry Charles Deedes, March 4 1865, Woodburn Farm Records, King Library.

14 "Mr. Alexander's Horses," *Wilkes' Spirit of the Times*, (New York: 18 March 1865), p. 41.

15 R.A. Alexander's letter to Henry Charles Deedes, March 4, 1865, Woodburn Farm Records, King Library.

16 Lewis Collins, *History of Kentucky*, (Frankfort, Ky.: 1966), Vol. I, p. 154; "Guerrilla Warfare in Kentucky," *Richmond Daily Examiner*, (Richmond, Va.: 8 February 1865), p. 1; "Affairs in Kentucky," *New York Times*, (5 February 1865), p. 1.

17 O.R., "Report of Harvey M. Buckley," Series I, Vol. XILX, Part I, pp. 625,635; ibid., "Report of Peter T. Swain to John S. Butler," p. 626; ibid., "Report of Edward H. Hobson," pp. 615-616.

18 "Survivors of Quantrill's Band," *Confederate Veteran Magazine*, November issue 1923, (Wendell, N.C.: 1923), Vol. XXXI, p. 438.

19 "Quantrill The Guerrilla," *Louisville Courier-Journal*, (29 April 1874), p. 2; William Connelley, *Quantrill and the Border Wars*, (New York: 1956), p. 461; O.R., "Report of George W. Alexander," Series I, Vol. XILX, Part I, p. 18; ibid., "Report of Edward H. Hobson," pp. 615-616; "Guerrilla War in Kentucky," *Chicago Tribune*, (1 February 1865), p. 2.

20 "Stories of Maj. Warren Viley," *Woodford Sun*, (Versailles, Ky.: 30 January 1902), p. 1.

CHAPTER EIGHT: THE RECOVERY OF THE HORSES

1 "Willa Viley," *Kentucky Live Stock Record*, (Lexington, Ky.: 2 April 1875) Vol. I, No. 9, pp. 136-137. "Topographical Map of the counties of Bourbon, Fayette, Clark, Jassamine, and Woodford, Ky. From actual Surveys and corrected by E.A. & G. W. Hewitt Published by Smith Gallup & Co. New York," (1861), original at the Kentucky Historical Society, Frankfort, Kentucky.

2 "Another Raid on Mr. Alexander's Farm-Nannie Butler and Fourteen Other Horses Carried Off," *Wilkes' Spirit of the Times*, (New York: 18 February 1865), p. 393.

3 "Stories of Maj. Warren Viley," *Woodford Sun*, (Versailles, Ky.: 30 January 1902), p. 1.

4 "Affairs In Kentucky," *New York Times*, (5 February 1865), p. 1; "From Kentucky," *Chicago Tribune*, (5 February 1865), p. 2; "Guerrilla Warfare In Kentucky," *Richmond Daily Examiner* (Richmond, Va.: 8 February 1865), p.1; G. Glenn Clift, *Events of the Civil War In Kentucky*, (Unpublished manuscript arranged by counties, Kentucky Historical Society: 1961), p. "Woodford County," 1865; Lewis Collins, *History of Kentucky*, (Frankfort, Ky.: 1966), Vol. I, p. 154; O.R., "Report of Brigadier General Edward H. Hobson, written by Thomas. A. Howes," Series I, Vol. XILX, Part I, p. 634; ibid., "Report to Commanding Officer Crab Orchard from Brigadier General Edward H. Hobson," p. 633; ibid., "Report to Major Thomas Mahoney, Lebanon, Ky.," p. 635; Albert Castel, *William Clarke Quantrill, His Life and Times*, (New York : 1962), p. 205.

5 Dan M. Bowmar, III, *Giants of the Turf*, (Lexington, Ky.: 1960), p. 16.

6 O.R., "Report to Commanding Officer Crab Orchard from Brig. Gen. Edward H. Hobson," Series I, Vol. XILX, Part I, p. 633; ibid., "Report to Brig. Gen. Speed Smith Fry," p. 633; ibid., "Report of Brig. Gen. Edward H. Hobson, written by Thomas A. Howes," p. 633; ibid., "Report of Lt. Col. John .G. Rogers," p. 635; ibid., "Report to Maj. Thomas Mahoney, Report to Brig. Gen. Edward H. Hobson, written by Thomas Howes," p. 635.

7 Ibid., "Report of Brig. Gen. Edward H. Hobson, written by Thomas A. Howes to Lt. Col. John G. Rogers," p. 364.

8 Ibid., "Report to commanding at Officer Crab Orchard from Brig. Gen. Edward H. Hobson," p. 633.

9 Ibid., "Report to Maj. Thomas Mahoney," p. 635.

FOOTNOTES

10 Ezra J. Warner, *Generals In Blue*, (Baton Rouge, La.: 1964), pp. 163-164.

11 O.R., "Report to Brig. Gen. Edward H. Hobson from John S. Butler," Series I, Vol. XILX, Part I; p. 641.; ibid., "Report to General Daniel W. Lindsey from Brig. Gen. E.H. Hobson;" ibid., "Report to Brig. Gen. Speed Smith Fry from Brig. Gen. E.H. Hobson;" p. 641; ibid., "Report to Lt. Col. Robert Henry Bentley from Brig. Gen. Hobson, written by Thomas A. Howes;" ibid., "Report to Captain John S. Butler from Major George F. Barnes;" ibid., "Report to Major George F. Barnes from Brig. Gen. E.H. Hobson, written by Thomas A. Howes;" ibid., "Report to Captain John S. Butler from Major George F. Barnes," p. 642.

12 Ibid., "Report of John S. Butler to Brig. Gen. E.H. Hobson," p. 641.

13 Ibid., "Report of Major George F. Barnes," p. 642.

14 Ibid., "Report of Thomas A. Howes to Major George F. Barnes;" ibid., "Report Major George F. Barnes to Captain John S. Butler," p. 642.

15 William Elsey Connelley, *Quantrill And the Border Wars*, (New York: 1956), p. 464; "Quantrill the Guerrilla," *Louisville Courier-Journal*, (29 April 1874), p. 2; O.R., "Report of Brig. Gen. E.H. Hobson written by Thomas A. Howes to Lt. Col. John G. Rogers," Series I, Vol. XLIX, Part I, p. 634.

16 Dan M. Bowmar, III, *Giants of the Turf*, (Lexington, Ky.: 1960), p. 16.

17 Herbert T. Krum, *Short Stories About Famous Saddle Horses*, (1910), pp. 370-371; *American Cultivator*, (Boston, Mass.: 11 July 1865), N.P.; "The Story of Woodburn," *Lexington Kentucky Morning Herald*, (27 January 1898), p. 3; Joseph Battell, *American Stallion Register*, (Middlebury, Vt.: 1909), p. 170; John H. Wallace, *The Horse of America*, (Wilmington, Del.: 1973), p. 295; O.R., "Report of Gen Edward H. Hobson," Series I, Vol. XILX, Part I, pp. 650-651; S.W. Parlin, "The American Trotter," *American Horse Breeder*, (Boston, Mass.: 19 July 1904), p. 670; R.A. Alexander's letter dated Thursday 24th, Woodburn Farm Records, King Library.

18 Herbert T. Krum, *Short Stories About Famous Saddle Horses*, (1910), pp. 370-371; "Quantrill the Guerrilla," *Louisville Courier-Journal*, (29 April 1874), p. 2; John H. Wallace, *The Horse of America*, (Wilmington, Del.: 1973), p. 295-296, 418; S.W. Parlin, *The American Trotter*, (Boston, Mass.: 1905), p. 77. Alexander reported that Bay Chief suffered another wound in his back. See Alexander to Deedes, 4 March 1865, Woodburn Farm Records, King Library. See also McCarr, *Kentucky Harness Horse*, p. 82 and Hiram Woodruff, *The Trotting Horse of America*, (New York 1868), p. 73.

19 "Another Raid on Mr. Alexander's Farm-Nannie Butler and Fourteen Other Horses Carried Off," *Wilkes' Spirit of the Times*, (New York: 18 February 1865), p. 393; John H. Wallace, *The Horse of America*, (Wilmington, Del.: 1973), p. 296.

20 "Minnehaha's Descendants," *American Horse Breeder*, (Boston, Mass.: 11 October 1911), p. "Editorial."

21 O.R., "Report to Daniel W. Lindsey-Inspector and Adjutant General from Brig. Gen. Edward H. Hobson," Series I, Vol. XILX, Part I, pp. 650-651.

22 "Guerrillas In Kentucky," *New York Times*, (7 February 1865), p. 8.

23 O.R. "Report of George G. Lott to Captain John S. Butler," Series I, Vol. XILX, Part I, p. 674.

24 Ibid., "Report of Captain John S. Butler," p. 676; ibid., "Report of Captain John S. Butler," p. 673; J.P. Burch, *A True Story of Chas. W. Quantrill And His Guerrilla Band*, (Vega, Texas: 1923), pp. 238-239.

25 O.R., "Report of Major Thomas Mahoney," Series I, Vol. XILX, Part I, p. 676; ibid., "Report of Col. Francis N. Alexander," p. 677. The number was much smaller.

26 Thomas Shelby Watson, *The Silent Riders*, (Louisville, Ky.: 1970), pp. 36, 37, 54, 62.

27 O.R., "Report of Captain William L. Gross," Series I, Vol. XILX, Part I, pp. 35-36, 674, 675, 676, 677, 684, 694, 698.

28 Thomas Shelby Watson, *The Silent Riders*, (Louisville, Ky.: 1970), p. 38.

29 O.R., "Report of Captain John S. Butler to Maj. John Clowney," Series I, Vol. XILX, Part I, p.

FOOTNOTES

698; ibid., "Report of Captain John S. Butler to Commanding Officer at Georgetown, Ky.," p. 699.

30 "A Guerrilla Gang Routed by Home Guards," *Chicago Tribune*, (16 February 1865), p. 2.

31 "Mr. Alexander's Horses," *Wilkes' Spirit of the Times*, (New York: 25 February 1865), p. 408.

32 R.A. Alexander's letter, Thursday 24th, Woodburn Farm Records, King Library.

33 R.A. Alexander's letter to Henry Charles Deedes, March 4, 1865, Woodburn Farm Records, King Library.

34 Ibid.

35 "Bay Chief," *American Horse Breeder*, (Boston, Mass.: 1910), p. 1072.

36 Joseph Battell, *American Stallion Register*, (Middlebury, Vt.: 1909), Vol. I, pp. 6-9; "Abdallah," *American Cultivator*, (Boston, Mass.: 11 July 1865); Herbert T. Krum, *Short Stories About Famous Saddle Horses*, (1910), pp. 370-371; John Hervey, *The American Trotter*, (New York: 1947), p. 92; Elizabeth Sharts, *Cradle of the Trotter, A Goshen Turf History*, (Goshen, New York: Book Mill Company, 1946), p. 47. A careful investigation into the information from Mr. Hull shows that Abdallah was found in Mr. Bush's barn at Lawrenceburg, Kentucky. See "Story of Woodburn," *Lexington, Kentucky Morning Herald*, (27 January 1898), p. 3.

37 "The Story of Woodburn," *Lexington, Kentucky Morning Herald*, (27 January 1898), p. 3.

38 Ibid.

39 Dan M. Bowmar, III, *Giants of the Turf*, (Lexington, Ky.: 1960), p. 16; S.W. Parlin, "American Trotter," *American Horse Breeder*, (Boston, Mass.: 19 July 1904), p. 670.

40 John Hervey, *The American Trotter*, (New York: 1947), p. 92; John H. Wallace, *The Horse of America*, (Wilmington, Del.: 1973), p. 296; S. W. Parlin, "American Trotter," *American Horse Breeder*, (Boston, Mass.: 19 July 1904), p. 670.

41 John Hervey, *Racing In America, 1665-1865*, (New York: 1944), p. 331.

42 John H. Wallace, *The Horse of America*, (Wilmington, Del.: 1973), p. 294.

43 "The Lessons of Twenty Years at Woodburn Farm, Kentucky," *Wallace's Monthly*, (New York: May 1879), Vol. V, No. 4, p. 248.

44 John Hervey, *The American Trotter*, (New York: 1947), p. 92.

45 H.G. Crickmore, *Racing Calendars 1866,1867*, (New York: 1901), p. 30.

46 R.A. Alexander's 4 March 1865 letter to Henry Charles Deedes; Woodburn Farm Records, King Library.

47 "Alexander's Horses," *Wilkes' Spirit of the Times*, (New York: 18 March 1865), p. 41.

48 "The Story of Woodburn," *Lexington, Kentucky Morning Herald*, (27 January 1898), p. 3.

49 R.A. Alexander's letter, Thursday 24th, Woodburn Farm Records, King Library.

50 R.A. Alexander's letter to Henry Charles Deedes, March 4, 1865, Woodburn Farm Records, King Library.

51 H.C. Crickmore, *Racing Calendars, 1861-1869*, (New York: 1901), N.P.; Saunders D. Burce *The American Stud Book*, (New York: 1882), Vol. I, II, III, under Mares.

52 R. Aitcheson Alexander, *Woodburn Stud Farm 1864 Catalogue*, (Lexington, Ky.: 1864), p. 24, Woodburn Farm Records, Woodburn Farm.

53 "Alexander's Horses," *Wilkes' Spirit of the Times*, (New York 18 March 1865), p. 41.

54 George B. Leach, *The Kentucky Derby Diamond Jubilee, 1875-1945*, (Louisville, Ky.: 1949), p. 23.

55 Sanders D. Bruce, *The American Stud Book*, (New York: 1882), Vol. I, p. 656; Ibid., Vol. III under "Mares," p. 193, under "Lindora;" "Death of Star Davis", *Kentucky Live Stock Record*, (Lexington, Ky.: 28 September 1876), Vol. 4, No. 13, p. 198; John Hervey, *Racing in America, 1665-1865*, (New York: 1944), p. 327; Joseph Battell, *American Stallion Register*, (Middlebury, Vt.: 1935), Vol. IV, p. 557.

56 "The Story of Woodburn," *Lexington, Kentucky Morning Herald*, (27 January 1898), p. 3; W.T.

FOOTNOTES

Chester, *Chester's Complete Trotting And Pacing Record*, (New York: 1884), pp. 59, 160-161, 346; "Big Black" is listed in the *Woodburn Stud Farm 1864 Catalogue* as a trotting colt in 1858 by Mambrino Chief out of Black Rose. He is also listed as "Woodburn American," Woodburn Farm Records, Woodburn Farm, *Woodburn Farm Stud Book*; Farm Records for 1864; R. Aitcheson Alexander, *Woodburn Stud Farm 1864 Catalogue*, (Lexington, Ky.: Kentucky Statesman Print., 1864), p. 49.

57 Telephone conversation/interview with Carl W. Breihan, St. Louis, Missouri, December 30, 1994: Quantrill and Frank James were not related. See "Mrs. Samuel's Will," *Liberty [Missouri] Tribune*, (Liberty, Mo.: 17 February 1911), p. 3.

58 Captioned information on the back of a print of the Edward Troye painting of Edwin Forrest. *Gribbon Graphics* in Lexington, Kentucky, was selling this print in 1981; Dr. A.J. Alexander has a print of this painting as well, and discussed with the author the information that is incorrect in the caption that is provided.

59 Joseph Battell, *American Stallion Register*, (Middlebury, Vt.: 1911), pp. 186-191.

60 "Quantrill The Guerrilla," *Louisville Courier-Journal*, (29 April 1874), p. 2.

61 R.A. Alexander's letter, Thursday 24th, Woodburn Farm Records, King Library.

62 *Woodburn Stud Book*, Edwin Forrest, N.P., Woodburn Farm Records, Woodburn Farm.

63 Ibid.

64 "Edwin Forrest 49," *Harness Horse Magazine*, (Harrisburg, Pa.: 8 March 1939), Vol. 4, No. 19, p. 505; Joseph Battell, *American Stallion Register*, (Middlebury, Vt.: 1911), Vol I, p. 187.

65 Joseph Battell, *American Stallion Register*, (Middlebury, Vt.: 1911), Vol. I, pp. 186-191; Alexander Mackay-Smith, *The Race Horses of America, 1832-1872, Portraits and Other Paintings by Edward Troye*, (Saratoga Springs, New York: 1981), p. 221.

66 Susan Rhodemyre, "Woodburn Stud," *Thoroughbred Record*, (Lexington, Ky.: 7 January 1981), p. 44.

67 John Hervey, *Racing In America, 1665-1865*, (New York: 1944), p. 331.

68 "Lexington," *Wilkes' Spirit of the Times*, (New York: 2 January 1864), p. 281.

69 R.A. Alexander's letter to Henry Charles Deedes, March 4, 1865, Woodburn Farm Records, King Library.

70 John Hervey, *The American Trotter*, (New York: 1947), pp. 92-93.

CHAPTER NINE: SECRET SANCTUARY FOR THE HORSES

1 O.S. Barton and John McCorkle, *Three Years With Quantrill*, (Norman, Ok.: 1992), p. 211.

2 R.S.C.A. Alexander's deed of ownership for the Gray-Watkins Mill, dated March 3, 1863, for deeds see Kane County Recorder Office, Geneva, Illinois, Book 80, p. 220; Book 89, p. 52; "Story of Woodburn," *Lexington Kentucky Morning Herald*, (27 January 1898), p. 3; "Proposed Sale of Mr. Alexander's Horses," Wilkes *Spirit of the Times*, 15 April 1865, p. 105; *Wilkes'*, "A Large number of Thoroughbred and Trotting Horses For Sale," (15 April 1986), p. 109. Horses believed to have been brought back to Woodburn in August 1865 by Daniel Swigert.

3 R.S.C.A. Alexander's Deed of Ownership for the Gray-Watkins Mill, dated March 3, 1863, Book 80, property of the Kane County Recorder office, Geneva, Illinois, p. 214.

4 "The Story of Woodburn," The *Lexington, Kentucky Morning Herald*, (27 January 1898), p. 3.

5 *A farm ledger* (used as a journal) kept by Alexander records a trip he made to Illinois in 1861 which includes his hand-drawn maps of some of the farms he visited. The *ledger* is in the Woodburn Farm Records, Woodburn Farm; "Story of Woodburn," *Lexington Kentucky Morning Herald*, (27 January 1898), p. 3. Alexander's affairs "extended to Chicago, where he was the owner of a very considerable landed estate which under the advice of his brother-in-law, Mr. [James] Breckinridge Waller of Lake View, he had from time to time acquired." See "Death of an Useful Man," *Chicago Tribune*, (6 December 1867),

FOOTNOTES

2; John Hervey, *Racing in America 1665-1865*, (New York: 1947) p. 331; "Mr. Alexander's Horses," *Wilkes' Spirit of the Times*, (New York: 18 March 1865), p. 41.

6 Knickerbocker & Hodder, *First Annual Gazetteer and Directory of the City of Aurora*, (Aurora, Ill.: Beacon Steam Book and Job Printer, 1868), p. 122; Thompson and Everts, *New Combination Atlas of Kane County, Illinois*, compiled, drawn and published from personal examinations and surveys by Thompson and Everts, (Geneva, Ill.: 1871-1872), N.P. This information has been helpful to the author to establish the location of the land that R.A. rented in Williamsville. The author would like to acknowledge John Robertson and Brenda O'Dell of Illiopolis, Illinois, for their research and assistance concerning the geography and layout of the area while at their Woodlawn Farm in October 1995.

7 R.A. Alexander's *Diary (Journal)*, (Chicago Trip, 18 September 1861 through 24 September 1861), Woodburn Farm Records, Woodburn Farm.

8 Susan Rhodemyre, "Woodburn Stud," *Thoroughbred Record*, (Lexington, Ky.: 7 January 1981), p. 36.

9 John Hervey, *Racing In America, 1665-1865*, (New York: 1944), p. 331; "The Story of Woodburn," *Lexington, Kentucky Morning Herald*, (27 January 1898), p. 3; "Robert Aitcheson Alexander. His Claim to Rank as America's Most Successful Breeder," *Thoroughbred Record*, (Lexington, Ky.: 21 May 1938), p. 343; "Mr. Alexander's Horses," *Wilkes' Spirit of the Times*, (New York, 18 March 1865), p. 4.

10 *Journal*, "Trotting Foals 1859 to 1869 Inclusive," Woodburn Farm Records, Woodburn Farm.

11 "The Fall Meetings of 1865. Horses Up In Training In Kentucky," *Turf, Field and Farm*, (New York: 9 December 1865), p. 89.

12 "The Story of Woodburn," *Lexington, Kentucky Morning Herald*, (27 January 1898), p. 3; Dr. D.E. Salmon, *Diseases of the Horse*, (Washington, D. C.: Government Printing Office, 1896), pp. 198-199; Margret Cabell Self, *The Horseman's Encyclopedia*, (San Diego, Calif.: A.S. Barnes And Company, Inc., 1946), p. 9.

13 John Hervey, *The American Trotter*, (New York: 1947), p. 223; "Descendants of Pilot Jr.," *American Horse Breeder*, (Boston, Mass.: 7 April 1903), p. 306; Joseph Battell, *American Stallion Register*, (Middlebury, Vt.: 1935), Vol. IV, p. 140.

14 "Descendants of Pilot Jr.," *American Horse Breeder*, (Boston, Mass.: 7 April 1903), p. 306; Joseph Battell, *American Stallion Register*, (Middlebury, Vt.: 1935), Vol. IV, p. 141; *Western Sportsman and Live Stock News*, (Indianapolis, Ind.: 12 September 1891), N.P.; "Descendants of Pilot, Jr.," *American Horse Breeder*, (Boston Mass.: 7 April 1903), p. 306.

15 "An Authority," *Turf, Field and Farm*, (New York: 21 December 1867), p. 393.

16 John Hervey, *The American Trotter* (New York, 1947), p. 92.

17 R.A. Alexander's letter to "Alec" J. Alexander, August 5, 1865, Woodburn Farm Records, King Library.

18 *Woodburn Stud Book*, Woodburn Farm Records, Woodburn Farm.

19 "A Bluegrass Letter-20 November 1865, Georgetown, Ky.," *Turf, Field and Farm*, (New York: 2 December 1865), p. 275.

20 "Woodlawn Races," *Wilkes' Spirit of the Times*, (New York: 24 June 1865), p. 261.

21 "A Large Number of Thoroughbred and Trotting Horses for Sale," *Turf, Field and Farm*, (New York: 5 August 1865), p. 15; ibid., "A Large Number of Thoroughbred and Trotting Horses for Sale," (23 September 1865), p. 127.

22 "Proposed Sale of Mr. Alexander's Horses," *Wilkes' Spirit of the Times*, (New York: 15 April 1865), p. 105; ibid., "A Large Number of Thoroughbred and Trotting Horses For Sale," p. 109.

23 "Large Sale of Thoroughbred and Trotting Stock Comprising Ninety Head on August 29th and 30th, 1866, at Woodburn Stud Farm, Spring Station, Kentucky," *Turf, Field and Farm*, (New York: 21 July 1866), p. 45; ibid., "Sale of Stock at Woodburn Farm," (28 July 1866), p. 57; ibid., "Sale at

FOOTNOTES

Woodburn Stud Farm-R.A. Alexander's, Spring Station, Woodford Co., Ky.," (15 September 1866), p. 165.

24 " Mr. Alexander's Horses", *The Spirit of the Times*, March 18, 1865, p.41. Turf, Field & Farm, January 13, 1866, p.25; *Racing Calendars, 1861-1869*, New York, W.C. Whitney, 1901.

25 H.G. Crickmore, *Racing Calendars 1861-1865*, (New York: 1901), pp. 45, 59, 60, 63, 65, 66, 71, 75, 77, 79, 85, 119.

26 "Mr. Alexander's Programme," *Turf, Field and Farm*, (New York: 13 January 1866), p. 25.

27 H.G. Crickmore, *Racing Calendars 1861-1865*, (Printed, not published, by W.C.Whitney, New York: 1901, pages 82-83), N.P.; *Calendars 1866-1867*, (New York: 1901), N.P. Information provided by *Racing Hall of Fame*, Saratoga, NY., 1998.

28 "An Interview With Napoleon Belland by Salvator," *Thoroughbred Record*, (Lexington, Ky.: 6 August 1921), p. 62. Dates do not verify his claims.

29 Ibid.

30 John Hervey, *Racing in America 1665-1865*, (New York: 1944), p. 331.

31 "The Woodburn Stud," *Turf, Field and Farm*, (23 December 1887), p. 514; "Pedigree of Ruric," *Porter's Spirit of the Times*, (New York: 31 January 1857), p. 355.

32 *Woodburn Stud Farm 1863 Catalogue*; property of Keeneland Association Library, Lexington, Ky., pp. 5, 8, 9, 10; *Woodburn Stud Farm 1867 Catalogue*; property of Keeneland Association Library, Lexington, Ky., pp. 10, 12.

CHAPTER TEN: THE FATE OF THE RAIDERS

1 O.R., "Report of Major Charles B. Leavitt to Brig. Gen. Hugh Ewing," Series I, Vol. XILX Part I, p. 49.

2 Richard S. Brownlee, *Gray Ghosts of the Confederacy*, (Baton Rouge, La.: 1958), p. 257; Carl W. Breihan, *Quantrill And His Civil War Guerrillas*, (Denver, Col.: Sage Books, 1959), p. 170; William Elsey Connelley, *Quantrill and the Border Wars*, (New York: 1956), pp. 457, 464.

3 O.R., "Report of Lt. John S. Watson to Commander Andrew Bryson," "Report of J.D. Hale to Gen. William Denison Whipple," Series I, Vol. XILX, Part I, pp. 788-789, 784.

4 Sarah B. Smith, *Historic Nelson County*, (Louisville, Ky.: 1971), pp. 293-294; Article believed to be from *Kentucky Standard*, on Donnie Pence, home is pictured, p. 256; Article on Donnie Pence. Portrait is shown, gives writer as "S.C.E.," believed to be from *Kentucky Standard*, (Bardstown, Ky.: N.D.), N.P.

5 "Guerrillas Routed-Freight Train Captured and Burned," *Chicago Tribune*, (2 March 1865), p. 4.

6 "Guerrillas Routed-Freight Train Captured and Burned," *Chicago Tribune*, (2 March 1865), p. 4; ibid., "Guerrilla War in Kentucky," (9 March 1865), p. 1.

7 "Sue Munday Was A Confederate Captain," *Kentucky Standard*, (Bardstown, Ky.: 3 February 1966), p. 789; "From Kentucky, The New Military Commandant-Capture of Guerrillas-Trial And Execution of Jerome Clark Alias Sue Munday-Spring Weather and Spring Floods," *New York Times*, (6 March 1865), p. 2; Thomas Shelby Watson, *The Silent Riders*, (Louisville, Ky.: 1970), pp. 41-43.

8 Laura Young Brown and Marie Coleman, *History of Meade County Kentucky 1824-1991*, (Utica, Ky.: McDowell Publications, 1991), p. 170; "Sue Munday and Other Guerrilla Leaders Captured," *Chicago Tribune*, (14 March 1865), p. 4.

9 "Sue Munday and Other Guerrilla Leaders Captured," *Chicago Tribune*, (14 March 1865), p. 4.

10 "From Kentucky, The New Military Commandant-Capture of Guerrillas-Trial And Execution of Jerome Clark Alias Sue Munday-Spring Weather And Spring Floods," *New York Times*, (16 March 1865), p. 2; "Execution of Sue Munday," *Chicago Tribune*, (20 March 1865), p. 2.

11 "Execution of Sue Munday," *Chicago Tribune*, (20 March 1865) p. 2; Lowell H. Harrison, The Civil War In Kentucky, (Lexington, Ky.: 1975), p. 76; "Sue Munday Hanged-A Passenger Train

FOOTNOTES

Thrown From Track by Guerrillas," *Tribune*, (16 March 1865), p. 1; "Execution of Sue Munday," *Tribune*, (20 March 1865), p. 2.

12 "From Kentucky, New Military Commandant-Capture of Guerrillas-Trial of Jerome Clark Alias Sue Munday-Spring Weather And Spring Floods," *New York Times*, (16 March 1865), p. 2; "General Palmer and the Guerrillas," *Chicago Tribune*, (15 April 1865), p. 2.

13 Edward E. Leslie, *The Devil Knows How To Ride*, (New York: 1996), p. 363.

14 Thomas Shelby Watson, *The Silent Riders*, (Louisville, Ky.: 1970), p. 25.

15 "Trial of Henry B. Magruder At Louisville-Sixteen Charges of Murder and Three of Rape," *Chicago Tribune*, (19 September 1865), p. 3.

16 "Execution of Magruder," *New York Times*, (21 October 1865), p. 4; "The Presbyterian Synod-Rebuke of the Late General Assembly-A Guerrilla Hanged," *Chicago Tribune*, (21 October 1865), p. 1; "Execution of Henry C. Magruder," *New York Times*, (25 October 1865), p.1.

17 J.P. Burch, *A True Story of Chas. W. Quantrill And His Guerrilla Band*, (Vega, Texas: 1923), pp. 239, 240, 242; Donald R. Hale, *We Rode With Quantrill*, (Clinton, Mo.: 1975), pp. 68, 75-76; Thomas Shelby Watson, *The Silent Riders*, (Louisville, Ky.: 1970), pp. 32, 53, 54, 62; William Elsey Connelley, *Quantrill And The Boarder Wars*, (New York: 1956), pp. 457, 474, 478, 479; Carl W. Breihan, *Quantrill And His Civil War Guerrillas*, (Denver, Col.: 1959), pp. 168, 169, 170, 171, 172, 173; Richard S. Brownlee, *Gray Ghosts of the Confederacy*, (Baton Rouge, La.: 1958), pp. 256, 257-261.

18 "Quantrill's Last Fight," *Spirit of Kansas*, (Lawrence, Kansas: 26 July 1873), N.P.; "Guerrilla Quantrill," *Daily Capital*, (Topeka, Kansas: April 1881), N.P. Information provided by the manuscript department of the Kansas State Historical Society, Topeka, Kansas; Duane Schultz, *Quantrill's War*, (St. Martins Press, N.Y.: 1996), pp. 298-300.

19 James Wakefield's letter, June 13, 1888, Spencer County, Kentucky, Regional History, Manuscript Collection 75, Box 2 (1888), folder 21 (1888), Kansas Collection.

20 J.P. Burch, *A True Story of Chas. W. Quantrill And His Guerrilla Band*, (Vega Texas: 1923), p. 244.

21 O.S. Castel, *Three Years With Quantrill*, (Norman, Oklahoma: University of Oklahoma Press, 1992), pp. 206-207.

22 James Wakefield's letter, June 13, 1888, Spencer County, Kentucky, Regional History, manuscript collection 75, Box 2 (1888), folder 21, Kansas Collection.

23 "Capture of Guerrilla Supposed to be Quantrill," *New York Daily Tribune*, (15 May 1865), p. 4.

24 William Elsey Connelley, *Quantrill and the Border Wars*, (New York: 1956), p. 482.

25 "Capture of Guerrilla Supposed to be Quantrill," *New York Daily Tribune*, (15 May 1865), p. 4; "Quantrill's Death Verified," *Confederate Veteran Magazine*, Frank James to O.L. Joyner (1911), (Wendell, N. C.: 1893), Vol. XIX, p. 285;. Quoted in J.P. Burch, *A True Story of Chas. W. Quantrill And His Guerrilla Band*, (Vega, Texas: 1923), pp. 243-247; "Personal," *New York Times*, (18 June 1865), p. 3; Lowell H. Harrison, *The Civil War In Kentucky*, (Lexington, Ky.: 1975), p. 76; Singleton B. Bedinger, *Missouri's Confederates, 1861-1865*, (Taylor, Texas: Merchants Press, 1967), pp. 29-32.

26 "Personal," *New York Times*, (18 June 1865), p. 3. Dates of Quantrill's birth and death (1837-1865) provided by the University of Kansas Historical Collection; It was reported that Quantrill was arrested in New York in March. Although a case of mistaken identity a man named Hamilton was arrested and jailed, and Senator Jim Lane of Kansas and his wife were telegraphed for. Upon their arrival in New York both failed to identify the prisoner as Quantrill. He was sent to Washington to the Secretary of War, to await identification. The article goes on to say that there were no less than 26 indictments for murder found by the Grand Jury against Quantrill, at Lawrence, Kansas. "Arrest of an Alleged Rebel Guerrilla. Prisoner Supposed to be Quantrill, the Kansas Raider-He is Sent to Washington," *New York Times*, (22 March 1865), p. 8.

27 "Surrender of Guerrillas," *New York Tribune*, (23 May 1865), p. 1.

FOOTNOTES

28 "Frank James Was Considered A Hero," *Kentucky Standard*, (Bardstown, Ky.: 26 October 1988), p. A-10.

29 Albert Castel, *William Clarke Quantrill, His Life and Times*, (New York: Frederick Fell, Inc. Publishers, 1962), p. 220.

30 O.S. Barton and John McCorkle, *Three Years With Quantrill*, (Norman, Ok.: 1992), p. 212.

31 William Elsey Connelley, *Quantrill and the Boarder Wars*, (New York: 1956), p. 478; Sarah Smith, Historic Nelson County, (Louisville, Ky.: 1971), p. 292.

32 Carl W. Breihan, *Quantrill and His Civil War Guerrillas*, (Denver, Col., 1959), pp. 166, 168; O.S. Barton and John McCorkle, *Three Years With Quantrill*, (Norman, Ok.: 1992), p 211.

33 "The Guerrillas," *Chicago Tribune*, (11 December 1865), p. 1.

34 "One-Arm Sam Berry Left His Mark," *Kentucky Standard*, (Bardstown, Ky.: 20 November 1983), pp. 610, 612; Thomas Shelby Watson, *The Silent Riders*, (Louisville, Ky.: 1970), p. 39.

35 "Error In Regard to 'One-Arm-Berry,'" *Confederate Veteran Magazine*, (Wendell, N.C.: 1893), Vol. XX, p. 221.

CHAPTER ELEVEN: RACING AGAIN-ASTEROID VS. KENTUCKY

1 R.A. Alexander's personal *ledger*, Keeneland Association Library, which listed entries and nominations of Woodburn race horses for races, stakes and meetings by dates and names of the race tracks from 1861-1867. From 1861-1863 entries and nominations were sent to Kentucky, Tennessee, New Jersey and New York. From 1864-1865 entries and nominations were sent to Kentucky, New Jersey, New York and Missouri. From 1865-1867 several entries in the ledger were written by Daniel Swigert and signed "R.A. Alexander" by Swigert-these entries and nominations included New York, New Jersey, Missouri, Ohio, Alabama and Louisiana. It was noted, however, that Alexander did not send horses to the Northern tracks to race.

2 "The Turf In St. Louis," *Wilkes' Spirit of the Times*, (New York: 27 May 1865), p. 201.

3 "The Race at Woodlawn-Asteroid and Loadstone," *Wilkes' Spirit of the Times*, (New York: 17 June 1865), p. 245; ibid., "Woodlawn Races" (24 June 1865), p. 261; ibid., "Asteroid and Loadstone-Who Bred Them?," (1 July 1865), p. 281.

4 R.A. Alexander's letter to Alec J. Alexander, June 23, 1865, Woodburn Farm Records, King Library.

5 Alexander Mackay-Smith, *The Race Horses of America, 1832-1872, Portraits and Other Paintings by Edward Troye*, (Saratoga Springs, New York: 1981), p. 224.

6 Death of Ansel Williamson, *Kentucky Live Stock Record*, (Lexington, Ky.: 25 June 1881), Vol. 13, No. 26, p. 409.

7 "The Georgetown Stable," *Turf, Field and Farm*, (New York: 6 January 1866), p. 9.

8 John Hervey, *Racing in America, 1665-1865*, (New York: 1944), p. 144.

9 Alexander Mackay-Smith, *The Race Horses of America, 1832-1872, Portraits and Other Paintings by Edward Troye*, (Saratoga Springs, New York: 1981), p. 223.

10 "Asteroid and Kentucky-The Saratoga Meeting," *Wilkes' Spirit of the Times*, (New York: 1 July 1865), p. 281.

11 "The Racing Problem of the Season. Will Asteroid Meet Kentucky?," *Wilkes's Spirit of the Times*, (New York: 8 July 1865), p. 296.

12 Ibid., "The Challenge to Asteroid," (15 July 1865), p. 313.

13 Ibid.

14 Ibid., "The Racing Problem. Will Asteroid and Kentucky Meet?," (New York: 22 July 1865), p. 329.

15 Roy Meredith, *Mr. Lincoln's Contemporaries*, (New York: Charles Scribner's Sons, 1951), p. 218.

FOOTNOTES

16 "Bugle Call to Asteroid," Wilkes *Spirit of the Times*, (New York: 8 July 1865), p. 297; Charles E. Trevathan, *The American Thoroughbred*, (The McMillan Company, New York and London, England: 1905), p. 314.

17 Richard Sasuly, *Bookies And Bettors*, (New York: Holt Rinehart and Winston, 1982), pp. 60, 61.

18 "Asteroid and Kentucky Controversy," *Wilkes' Spirit of the Times*, (New York: 15 July 1865), p. 309.

19 Ibid., "Response of Mr. Alexander. He Offers to Match Asteroid Against Kentucky at Three and Four-Mile Heats," (5 August 1865), p. 361.

20 Ibid., "Racing Problem of the Season-Mr. Hunter's Response to Mr. Alexander," (12 August 1865), p. 377.

21 H.G. Crickmore, *Racing Calendar, 1865*, (New York: W.C. Whitney, 1901), p. 141; "The Asteroid and Kentucky Controversy," *Turf, Field and Farm*, (New York: 2 September 1865), p. 73.

22 R.A. Alexander's letter to Alec Alexander, August 5, 1865, Woodburn Farm Records, King Library.

23 "Racing Problem of the Season. Asteroid and Kentucky," *Turf, Field, and Farm*, (New York: 5 August 1865), p. 16.

24 "Mr. Alexander's Last Proposition. The Asteroid and Kentucky Negotiation Flickers Once More and Finally Blows Out," *Wilkes' Spirit of the Times*, (New York: 2 September 1865), p. 9.

25 "The Racing Problem. New Prospects for a Meeting Between Asteroid and Kentucky," *Wilkes' Spirit of the Times*, (New York: 26 August 1865), p. 408; ibid., "The American Turf. Turf Letter from California-Norfolk, Kentucky, Asteroid, etc.-Proposals for a Great Stake, $10,000 Each," (9 December 1865), p. 228; ibid., "The Buckeye Program. A Four-Miler in the Fence," (17 February 1866), p. 385; ibid., "The Buckeye Response. Larkin, Chitty, and 'The Spirit' Reviewed," (24 February 1866), p. 401.

26 "The Georgetown Stable," *Turf, Field and Farm*, (New York: 6 January 1866), p. 9.

27 Alexander Mackay-Smith, *The Race Horses of America, 1832-1872, Portraits and Other Paintings by Edward Troye*, (Saratoga Springs, New York: 1981), p. 229; "Death of Col. A. Keene Richards," *Kentucky Live Stock Record*, (Lexington, Ky.: 26 March 1881), p. 200.

28 Alexander Mackay-Smith, *The Race Horses of America, 1832-1872, Portraits and Other Paintings by Edward Troye*, (Saratoga Springs, New York: 1981), p. 224.

29 Ibid., p. 223.

30 "Racing Problem of the Season. Asteroid and Kentucky," *Turf, Field and Farm*, (New York: 5 August 1865), p. 16.

31 Ibid., "Mr. Alexander's Programme," (13 January 1866), p. 25.

32 Letters found in R.A. Alexander's *Ledger* book, property of Keeneland Association Library Collection, Lexington, Ky. These letters are inserted into the book.

33 "Asteroid and Kentucky," *Turf, Field and Farm*, (New York: 17 March 1866), p. 168; ibid., "The Time Purse At Cincinnati," (3 March 1866), p. 9; ibid., "Letter From Larkin," (7 April 1866), p. 82.

34 Ibid., "The Woodlawn Meeting," (19 May 1866), p. 312; ibid., "An Accident To Asteroid," (19 May 1866), N.P.

35 "Asteroid Turned Out," *Wilkes' Spirit of the Times*, (New York: 26 May 1866), p. 197.

36 "The Woodland Meeting," *Turf, Field and Farm*, (New York: 19 May 1866), p. 312.

37 Ibid., "An American Turf Congress," (16 June 1866), p. 372.

38 Ibid., "Horses In Training At Paterson. Arrival of Mr. Alexander's Horses," (19 May 1866), N.P.

39 "Woodlawn Spring Meeting," *Wilkes' Spirit of the Times*, (New York: 19 May 1866), p. 181.

40 "The Paterson Races," *Turf, Field and Farm*, (New York: 16 June 1866), p. 376.

41 Ibid., "An American Turf Congress," (16 June 1866), Vol. II, p. 372.

FOOTNOTES

42 Ibid., "Visit to Kentucky," (25 August 1866), p. 118.

43 Ibid., "Saratoga.-Week After The Races," (25 August 1866), p. 115.

44 Ibid., "Asteroid Eastward Bound," (15 September 1866), p. 168.

45 "Asteroid On The Road to Fordham," *Wilkes' Spirit of the Times*, (New York: 8 September 1866), Vol. XV, No. 2, p.1.

46 "Mr. Alexander's Arrival," *Turf, Field and Farm*, (New York: 22 September 1866), p. 184; "The Turf," *Wilkes' Spirit of the Times*, (New York: 22 September 1866), p. 62.

47 "The Meeting at Jerome Park," *Turf, Field and Farm*, (New York: 29 September 1866), p. 200; ibid., "Asteroid," (29 September 1866), p. 201; R.A. Alexander's letter to Alex, September 24, 1866, Woodburn Farm Records, King Library.

48 "The Racing at Woodlawn," *Wilkes' Spirit of the Times*, (New York: 27 October 1866), p. 137; ibid., "Woodlawn Fall Meeting," (27 October 1866), p. 132.

49 "Stock Sales In Kentucky," *Turf, Field and Farm*, (New York: 11 August 1866), Vol. III, p. 88.

50 Ibid., "Large Sale of Blood Stock," (12 May 1866), N.P.

51 John Hervey, *Racing in America, 1665-1865*, (New York: 1944), p. 332.

52 "Mr. Alexander's Retirement From the Turf," *Turf, Field and Farm*, (New York: 29 December 1866), p. 409. R.A. Alexander's letter was published in its entirety.

53 H.G. Crickmore, *Racing Calendars, 1866-1867*, (New York: 1901), pp. 98-99, 107-110, 113-117, 119, 125-126, 128-129, 139-141, 143, 167-176, 178-179, 180.

54 "The Stables of Kentucky," *Turf, Field and Farm*, (New York: 13 April 1867), p. 227.

55 "St. Louis Laclede Racing Association-Fall Meeting. First Day's Racing," New York Times, (1 October 1867), p. 2; ibid., "Woodlawn Races At Louisville," (15 October 1867), p. 1.

56 Ibid., "A New Addition to the Preakness Stable," (11 May 1867), p. 296.

57 Ibid., "A Visit to Woodburn," (8 June 1867), pp. 354, 355.

58 Ibid., "Planet," (6 July 1867), p. 8.

59 Abram S. Hewitt, *The Great Breeders And Their Methods*, (Lexington, Ky.: 1982), p. 16.

60 "Death of the Race Horse Planet," *New York Times*, (8 September 1875), p. 5.

61 Abram S. Hewitt, *The Great Breeders And Their Methods*, (Lexington, Ky.: 1982), p. 16; "Sale of Blood Stock," *Turf, Field and Farm*, (New York: 26 October 1867), p. 260.

CHAPTER TWELVE: DEATH OF THE MASTER BREEDER

1 "Sale of Blood Stock," *Turf, Field and Farm*, (New York: 26 October 1867), p. 334.

2 John Hervey, *Racing In America, 1665-1865*, (New York: 1944), p. 332.

3 R.A. Alexander's letter to Henry Charles Deedes, March 4, 1865, Woodburn Farm Records, King Library.

4 "Robert Aitcheson Alexander," *Turf, Field and Farm*, (New York: 14 December 1867), p. 369.

5 Ibid.

6 Ibid.

7 Ibid., "The Woodburn Programme," (28 December 1867), p. 48. R.A. Alexander's will is a highly detailed document. See *Will of Robert Spruell [Spruel] Crawford Aitcheson Alexander*, 21 March 1860. Scottish Record Office, Edinburgh, Scotland, record number, ref: SC70/4/116, pp. 680-713; inventory number, ref: SC70/1/40, pp. 449-464. In addition to spellings given above, Spruel also appears in some documents as Spreul and Spreule. It is difficult to measure Alexander's worth, but the will does show substantial holdings in English railroads.

8 "Robert Aitcheson Alexander. His Claim to Rank as America's Most Successful Breeder," *Thoroughbred Record*, (Lexington, Ky.: 21 May 1938), p. 343.

9 John Hervey, *Racing In America, 1665-1865*, (New York: 1944), p. 328; Sanders D. Bruce, *The*

FOOTNOTES

American Stud Book, (New York: Sanders. D. Bruce, 1873), Vol. I, "Dedication."

10 "The Buckeye Response. Larkin, Chitty and 'The Spirit' Reviewed," *Wilkes' Spirit of the Times*, (New York: 24 February 1866), p. 401; Certificate for one share worth $300 of the *Louisville Association for the Improvement of the Breed of Horses*, dated 1 June 1860, Woodburn Farm Records, Woodburn Farm.

11 "Woodburn Farm and Thoroughbred Blood," *Wallace's Monthly*, (New York: 16 June 1890), p. 242.

12 "Robert Aitcheson Alexander. His Claim to rank as America's Most Successful Breeder," *Thoroughbred Record*, (Lexington, Ky.: 21 May 1938), p. 343.

13 "Mr. Alexander's Stable," *Turf, Field and Farm*, (New York: 13 January 1866), p. 24.

14 "Death of Robert Aitcheson Alexander," *Turf Field And Farm*, (New York: 7 December 1867), p. 360. An eloquent tribute to him appeared in the *Chicago Tribune* which concluded that he was "the soul of integrity and honor." See "Death of an Useful Man," *Chicago Tribune*, (6 December 1867), p. 2.

15 Ibid., "Death of an Useful Man," (6 December 1867), p. 2.

16 "Woodlawn Association-Challenge Vase, On Bits In Sporting Circles," *Wilkes' Spirit of the Times*, (New York: 18 May 1861), p. 232; "The Woodlawn Vase," *Thoroughbred Record*, (Lexington, Ky.: 17 March 1917), p. 159; ibid., "The Woodlawn Vase," (23 March 1918), p. 151; ibid., "Wilson Adds Woodlawn Vase to Preakness," (7 April 1923), p. 335; ibid., "The Preakness And the Woodlawn Vase," (3 May 1930), p. 490; ibid., "A Well-traveled Vase," (17 May 1986), p. 2477; "Woodlawn Vase," *Turf, Field and Farm*, (New York: 25 October 1902), pp. 1026-1027; "A Challenge Vase For The Woodlawn Spring And Fall Meetings," *Wilkes' Spirit of the Times*, (New York: 18 May 1861), p. 232; ibid., "A Challenge Cup," (30 June 1860), p. 269; ibid., "A Challenge Vase For The Woodlawn Spring and Fall Meetings," (10 November 1860), p. 153; "Awards of Endearment," *Town And Country Magazine*, (New York: March 1988), pp. 207-210. This article did not mention that R.A. Alexander commissioned Tiffany and Company to make the vase.

17 "Robert Aitcheson Alexander," *Turf, Field and Farm*, (New York: 14 December 1867), p. 369; John Hervey, *Racing In America, 1665-1865*, (New York: 1944), p. 332.

18 "Death of Robert Aitcheson Alexander," *Turf Field And Farm*, (7 December 1867), p. 360.

19 "Robert Aitcheson Alexander. His Claim to Rank as America's Most Successful Breeder," *Thoroughbred Record*, (Lexington, Ky.: 21 May 1938), p. 343.

20 "Memories of Distinguished Kentucky Turfmen-R. Aitcheson Alexander," *Kentucky Live Stock Record*, (Lexington, Ky.: 23 April 1875), p. 185.

21 "The Woodburn Stud," *Turf, Field and Farm*, (New York: 23 December 1887), p. 514.

22 *Trotting Horse Museum News*, Summer 1993, p. 3. I had the honor to submit R.A.'s name for induction.

CHAPTER THIRTEEN: WOODBURN'S INFLUENCE ON THE WESTERN TURF

1 "Lexington and His Dynasty," *Thoroughbred of California*, (Arcadia, Ca.: October 1975), p. 70.

2 John Hervey, *The American Trotter*, (New York: 1947), pp. 296-297. See W.J. Chesters, *The Complete Trotting And Racing Record*, (New York: 1884).

3 John Hervey, *The American Trotter*, (New York, 1947), p. 296.

4 Ibid., pp. 362-364.

5 "The Woodburn Stud," *Turf, Field and Farm*, (New York: 23 December 1882), p. 514.

6 John Hervey, *The American Trotter*, (New York: 1947), p. 54.

7 "Minnehaha's Descendants," *American Horse Breeder*, (Boston, Mass.: 11 October 1911), pp. "Editorial."

8 John Hervey, *The American Trotter*, (New York: 1947), p. 54; Ken McCarr, *The Kentucky Harness Horse*, (Lexington, Ky.: 1977), pp. 82-83.

FOOTNOTES

9 "Days of Wine and Roses," *Thoroughbred of California*, (Arcadia, Ca.: August 1991), pp. 14-15.

10 Ibid. In 1997 I had the honor to submit L.J. Rose's name to the Harness Racing Museum director for induction into the Immortal Room of the Hall of Fame. Letter from trustee member Joseph Mendelson dated August 4, 1997 informing the author of Mr. Rose's induction.

11 "Minnehaha's Descendants," *American Horse Breeder*, (Boston, Mass.: 11 October 1911), pp. "Editorial."

12 L.J. Rose, Jr., *L.J. Rose of Sunny Slope*, (San Marino, Calif.: 1959), p. 149.

13 Ken McCarr, *The Kentucky Harness Horse*, (Lexington, Ky.: The University Press of Kentucky, 1977), p. 80; John Hervey, *The American Trotter*, (New York: 1947), p. 124; "1899-1900 Witnessed the Rise of The Abbot," *Midwest Harness Horse*, (Cicero, Ill.: Pope Publications, Inc., March 1996), pp. 41-44.

14 Ken McCarr, *The Kentucky Harness Horse*, (Lexington, Ky.: 1977), p. 114.

15 "Death of L.J. Rose," *American Horse Breeder*, (Boston, Mass.: 14 May 1898), p. 502.

16 John H. Wallace, *The Horse of America*, (Wilmington, Del.: 1973), pp. 297, 332.

17 Ken McCarr, *The Kentucky Harness Horse*, (Lexington, Ky.: 1977), p. 114.

18 "The Far West Sends Tribute to Greatness of Lexington," *Thoroughbred Record*, (Lexington, Ky.: 28 May 1927), Vol. 105, p. 627.

19 Mary Fleming, *A History of the Thoroughbred in California*, (Arcadia Calif.: The California Thoroughbred Breeder Association, 1983), p. 6.

20 Ibid., p. 9.

21 "Grinstead The Grandson of Lexington," *Kentucky Live Stock Record*, (Lexington, Ky.: 1 April 1893), Vol. 37, No. 13, p. 225; Gilroy was the son of Lexington and was foaled in 1872. His dam was a sister to Ruric, who stood at Woodburn, by imported Sovereign.

22 "Grinstead, The Grandson of Lexington," *Kentucky Live Stock Record*, (Lexington, Ky.: 1 April 1893), Vol. 37, No. 13, p. 225; Mary Fleming, *A History of the Thoroughbred in California*, (Arcadia, California: 1983), p. 5.

23 "The 'Beast' of Santa Anita," *Sports Illustrated*, monthly magazine, (New York: 19 February 1962), p. 66; Mary Fleming, *A History of the Thoroughbred in California*, (Arcadia, Calif.: 1983), p. 6.

24 "Pastime of Millions," *Thoroughbred of California*, monthly magazine, (Arcadia, Calif.: March 1945), p. 32.

25 Sanders D. Bruce, *The American Stud Book*, (New York: Turf, Field and Farm, 1884), Vol. IV, p. 250.

26 Ibid., p. 321.

27 Sanders D. Bruce, *The American Stud Book*, (1889), Vol. V, pp. 584, 585.

28 Sanders D. Bruce, *The American Stud Book*, (New York: Jockey Club, 1902), Vol. VIII, p. 55. See Atalanta 2nd.

29 Sanders D. Bruce, *The American Stud Book*, (New York: Turf, Field and Farm, 1884), Vol. IV, p. 448.

30 Ibid., p. 246.

31 Sanders D. Bruce, *The American Stud Book*, (1889), Vol. V, p. 321.

32 Ibid., p. 660: See Sister Ann and Clara D.

33 Ibid., p. 275.

34 Ibid., p. 102.

35 Hubert Howe Bancroft, *Chronicles of the Builders of the Commonwealth*, (San Francisco, The History Company, 1892), Vol. III, pp. 356-357; Sanders D. Bruce, *The American Stud Book*, (New York: 1889), Vol. V, p. 368; *Woodburn Farm 1877 Catalogue*, Woodburn Farm Records, Woodburn Farm.

36 Sanders D. Bruce, *The American Stud Book*, (New York: 1884), Vol. IV, p. 448. See Santa Anita.

37 Sanders D. Bruce, *The American Stud Book*, (1889), Vol. V, p. 591. See Partisana.

38 Sanders D. Bruce, *The American Stud Book*, (1884), Vol. IV, p. 246.

FOOTNOTES

39 Sanders D. Bruce, *Bruce's American Stud Book*, (1894), Vol. VI, p. 19.

40 Sanders D. Bruce, *The American Stud Book*, (1889), Vol. V, p. 2.

41 Sanders D. Bruce, *Bruce's American Stud Book*, (1894), Vol. VI, p. 43. See Alaho.

42 "Pastime of Millions," *Thoroughbred of California*, (Arcadia, Calif.: April-May 1945) p. 17; Sanders D. Bruce, *American Stud Book*, (New York: 1902), Vol. VII, p. 55. See Alalanta 2nd.

43 "Jennie B. and Clara D.," *Kentucky Live Stock Record*, (Lexington, Ky.: 11 December 1880), p. 377.

44 "Lucky Baldwin Dead," *Thoroughbred Record*, (Lexington, Ky.: 6 March 1909, Vol. 69, No. 10, p. 134; "Luck Is What You Make It," *Spur*, monthly magazine, (Middleburg, Va.: November/December 1986), p. 64.

45 Mary Fleming, *A History of the Thoroughbred in California*, (Arcadia, Calif.: 1983), p. 6.

46 "The 'Beast' of Santa Anita," *Sports Illustrated*, (New York: 19 February 1962), p. 67.

47 "Pastime of Millions," *Thoroughbred of California*, (Arcadia, Calif.: March 1945), p. 32; ibid., "California Horse Racing Hall of Fame," (Arcadia, Calif.: November 1988), p. 18; Mary Fleming, *A History of the Thoroughbred in California*, (Arcadia, Calif.: 1983), p. 5.

48 "The 'Beast' of Santa Anita," *Sports Illustrated*, (New York: 19 February 1962), p. 67.

49 Elias Jackson "Lucky" Baldwin influenced Morgan "Horses as well as Thoroughbreds. Ethan Allen 3rd's (Borden's) foaled 1885 on his dam's side (by Cushing's Green Mountain by Charlie Watson) "brown mare" who Charlie Watson was bred to, was by Tiger by Baldwin's Black Hawk by Black Hawk 20 (by Sherman by Justin Morgan) "brown mare's" dam was a bay mare by Dr. Abel Brown Horse by Billy Root by Sherman by Justin Morgan." Jeanie Mellin, *The Morgan Horse* (The Stephen Greene Press: Brattleboro, Vermont, 1961), p. 217.

50 Lucius Beebe & Charles Clegg, *San Francisco's Golden Era*, (Berkeley, Calif.: Howell-North, 1960), p. 177.

51 Sandy Snider, The Arboretum of Los Angeles County, Arcadia, Calif., Historical Section.

52 Josephine Sarah Marcus Earp, *I Married Wyatt Earp*, (Tucson, Az.: University of Arizona Press, 1976), p. 148.

53 Kent Hollingsworth, *The Great Ones*, (Lexington, Ky.: 1970), pp. 96-97, 99.

54 "The Far West Sends Tribute to Greatness of Lexington," *Thoroughbred Record*, (Lexington, Ky.: 28 May 1927), Vol. 105, p. 627.

55 "The Far West Sends Tribute to Greatness of Lexington," *Thoroughbred Record*, (Lexington, Ky.: 28 May 1927), Vol. 105, p. 17; Mary Fleming, *A History of the Thoroughbred in California*, (Arcadia, Calif.: 1983), p. 8; "Brushing Up On Americus," *The Blood-Horse*, (Lexington, Ky.: 9 August 1971), pp. 2268-2770.

56 Kent Hollingsworth, *The Great Ones*, (Lexington, Ky.: 1970), p. 99.

57 "The Far West Sends Tribute to Greatness of Lexington," *Thoroughbred Record*, (Lexington, Ky.: 28 May 1927), Vol. 105, p. 627.

58 "A Line Not Ended," *The Blood-Horse*, (Lexington, Ky.: 27 November 1972), p. 4668.

59 Sanders D. Bruce, *The American Stud Book*, (New York: 1889), Vol. V, p. 660. See Sister Anne.

60 Ibid., p. 275.

61 "The 'Beast' of Santa Anita," *Sports Illustrated*, (New York: 19 February 1962), p. 64; "Brushing Up On Americus," *The Blood-Horse*, (Lexington, Ky.: 9 August 1971), p. 2772; "Pastime of Millions," *Thoroughbred of California*, (Arcadia, Calif.: April 1945), p. 17.

62 "Pastime of Millions," Thoroughbred of California , (Arcadia, Calif.: April 1945), p. 17; "The 'Beast' of Santa Anita,", *Sports Illustrated*, (New York: 19 February 1962), p. 62.

CHAPTER FOURTEEN: FRANK JAMES-RACE STARTER

1 "Facts and Fancies of Corinth History," *Daily Corinthian* (Corinth, Miss.: 16 May 1954), p. 1.

FOOTNOTES

2 William H.P. Robertson, *The History of Thoroughbred Racing in America*, (Englewood Cliffs, New Jersey: 1964), p. 204.

3 Josephine Sarah Marcus Earp, *I Married Wyatt Earp*, (Tucson, Az.: 1976), pp. 142-146, 149.

4 J.H. Ransom, *Who's Who and Where in Horsedom*, (Lexington, Ky.: Ransom Publishing Company, 1950), Vol. 3, pp. 123-124.

5 Lucius Beebe & Charles Clegg, *San Francisco's Golden Era*, (Berkeley, Calif.: 1960), p. 177.

6 Sandy Snider, *The Arboretum of Los Angeles County*, Historical Section; Lucius Bebe & Charles Clegg, *San Francisco's Golden Era*, (Berkeley, Calif.: 1960), p. 180.

7 *Kentucky Legislative History and Capitol Souvenir*, (Frankfort, Ky.: The Frankfort Printing Company, Inc. 1910), Vol. 1, p. 150; "Colonel Jack" Chinn," *Thoroughbred Record*, (Lexington, Ky.: 7 February 1920), pp. 101, 102; ibid., "Colonel Jack" P. Chinn," (16 May 1931), p. 469; Temple Bodley, & Samuel M. Wilson, *History of Kentucky*, 4 Vols., (Chicago and Louisville, Ky.: 1928), Vol. 3, pp. 74-78.

8 *Kentucky Legislative History and Capitol Souvenir*, (Frankfort, Ky.: 1910), Vol. 1, p. 150; "The Woodburn Stud," *Turf, Field and Farm*, (New York: 23 December 1887), p. 514.

9 J.H. Ransom, *Who's Who And Where In Horsedom*, (Lexington, Ky.: Ransom Publishing Company, 1950), Vol. 3, pp. 123-125; "Frank James As Race Starter," *Thoroughbred Record*, (Lexington, Ky.: 5 October 1895), p. 161.

10 Betty Sterett, *Scenes From The Past (of Nevada, Missouri)*, (Boulder, Col.: D.G.L. Info Write, 1985), pp. 93-97; *Dallas, Texas City Directory*, (Dallas, Tx.: 1891), printed yearly, p. 328. Frank's son, Robert, is listed and his residence is given as Frank James.

11 John D. Lawson, LL.D., *American State Trials; A Collection of the Important and Interesting Criminal Trials Which Have Taken Place in the United States From the Beginning of Our Government to Present Day*, (St. Louis: F.H. Thomas Law Book Co., 1919) p. 61-852, "The Trial of Frank James for Train Robbery and Murder. Gallatin, Missouri, 1883."

12 William P. Mangum, II., "Jesse James' Horses," *Illinois Racing News*, monthly magazine, (Burr Ridge, Ill.: Midwest Outdoors, January-1996) pp. 22-25; ibid., "Jesse James' Horses," (February 1997), pp. 70-71; ibid., "Jesse James' Horses-Nashville," (February 1996), pp. 58-62; "Jesse James' Bought Favorite Race Horse in Sumner County," *Tennessean*, newspaper, (Nashville, Tn.: 27 February 1939), N.P.; "Mr. Howard's Horses," *The Blood-Horse*, (Lexington, Ky.: 2 January 1988), pp. 52-55; William P. Mangum, II., "Frank and Jesse James Raced Horses Between Their Holdups," *National Association and Center for Outlaw and Lawman Historical Quarterly*, magazine, (Hamilton, Mt.: NOLA, Fall 1988), Vol. XIII, No. 2, pp. 8-12; Samuel C. Hildreth and James Crowell, *The Spell of the Turf*, (Philadelphia & London: J.B. Lippincot and Company, 1926), pp. 54-59; J.H. Ransom, *Who's Who and Where in Horsedom*, (Lexington, Ky.: 1950), p.124. Evidence found at the Saddle Horse Museum in Lexington, Kentucky reveals that Jesse James owned a Saddlebred mare that was bred to Flying Cloud (by Peacock, by Benton's Gray Diomed.) Uncovered is a registration application from 1900, submitted by Ike C. Chiles (of Buckner, Missouri), the son of an early gang member of the James-Younger Gang, William "Bill" Chiles. His relatives, Jim Crowe Chiles and Colonel Kit Chiles were all members of Quantrill's Raiders. See application for the registration of Rosalie 1766, by Rosewood 803, a son of Montrose 106, who was Diamond Denmark 68 (a great grandson of the pacer, Tom Hal), by Gaines', Denmark 61. This horse goes back to the great Diomed through Flying Cloud to whom Jesse James bred his mare. Also see Mary Low 1764, bred by Bill Chiles. Her sire, John Morgan, was owned by J. Lamartine Hudspeth of Lake City, Missouri, a long-time friend of Jesse James. Hudspeth would leave horses for the James' in his barn. George "Babe" and Rufus "Rufe" Hudspeth were members of Quantrill's Raiders. See also horses Lady Tenney's Jim Bland, Black Squirrel 58, Bess Osborne, all owned by T.B. Hudspeth of Sibley, Missouri (located just north of Buckner where Ike Chiles lived). William P. Mangum, II., "Pedigree of 'Jesse James' Mare' Connects Outlaws to Trotters," *Midwest Harness Horse*, (Cicero, Ill.:

FOOTNOTES

November 1995), pp. 23-27.

13 Lamont Buchanan, *The Kentucky Derby Story*, (New York: E.P. Dutton & Company, Inc., 1953), pp. 22, 23.

14 George B. Leach, *The Kentucky Derby Diamond Jubilee 1875-1945*, (Louisville, Ky.: 1949), p. 45.

15 Hugh Bradley, *Such Was Saratoga*, (Saratoga Springs, N.Y.: Arno Press, 1975), p. 222; John Burke, *Duet In Diamonds*, (New York: G.P. Putnam's Sons, 1972), p. 148; "The Racing for the Week Opening of the Racing Season at Saratoga," *New York Times*, (23 July 1894), p. 8.

16 "Frank James as Starter," *Thoroughbred Record*, (Lexington, Ky.: 5 October 1895), p. 161; "St. Louis Fair Grounds Race-Course," *Wilkes' Spirit of the Times*, (New York: 30 May 1885), p. 549.

17 "Battle At Centralia, Mo.," *Columbia [Missouri] Herald*, (Columbia, Mo.: 24 September 1897), N.P.; James D. Horan, *The Authentic Wild West, The Outlaws*, (New York: 1977), pp. 127, 141; Lincoln Steffens, *The Shame of the Cities* (New York: McClure, Phillips and Co., 1904) p.p. 72-77.

18 "Battle At Centralia, Mo.," *Confederate Veteran*, (Wendell, N.C.: 1909), Vol. XVII, pp. 30-31; Walter Williams, "Fight at Centralia," *Columbia [Missouri] Herald*, (Columbia, Mo.: 24 September 1897), N.P.

19 Picture, dated and signed by Frank James, May 18, 1898, St. Louis, Western History Collections, University of Oklahoma Library, Norman, Oklahoma.

20 Stefan Lorant, *The Presidency*, (New York: The MacMillan Company, 1952), p. 425.

21 Ibid.

22 Ibid.

23 Ibid.

24 Ibid., p. 434.

25 Ibid.

26 Ibid. pp. 425, 434.

27 "Frank James on Silver," *New York Times*, (12 October 1896), p. 4. Frank was working at the Standard Theater and the St. Louis Fair Grounds Race Course at the time.

28 J.H. Ransom, *Who's Who And Where In Horsedom*, (Lexington, Ky.: 1950), Vol. 3, pp. 122-126.

29 Advertisement for the Owensboro Fair, *Owensboro [Kentucky] Messenger*, (Owensboro, Ky.: 8 September 1900), N.P.; "Successful Inaugural of the Owensboro Fair," *Messenger*, (19 September 1900), N.P.; *Goodwin's Annual Turf Guide*, (New York: Goodwin Brothers, 1900), Vol. II, p. 7203.

30 "Well Those James Boys Were Kind To Poor Widows, Anyway-Maybe," *Louisville Courier-Journal*, (9 December 1966), p. A14.

31 "A Gathering of Old Guerrillas," *Booneville Weekly Advertiser*, weekly newspaper, (Booneville, Mo.: 9 October 1900), p. 2.

32 Ibid., "Quantrill's Men Hold Reunion," (4 October 1901), p. 2.

33 "Interesting Visitor," *Republican*, (Bedford, Ind.: 26 September 1901), N.P.

34 Ibid., "Big Fair Is Now On. The Racing Events of Wednesday Were Exceptionally Good," (26 September 1901), N.P.

35 James M. Guthrie, *Thirty-three Years in the History of Lawrence County, 1884-1917*, (James M. Guthrie, 1958), p. 137.

36 "Central Indiana Fair Circuit," *Western Horseman* (Indianapolis, Ind.: 1896), p. 528. See 1896, 1899 *Horse Review*.

37 "Frank James Is To Be An Actor," *St. Louis Post-Dispatch*, (10 November 1901), N.P.; "Frank James To Be An Actor," *Booneville Weekly Advertizer*, (Booneville, Mo.: 15 November 1901), p. 2; ibid., Advertisement, "Across The Desert," *Zanesville Signal*, (Zanesville, Oh.: 28 November 1901), N.P.; ibid., "Across The Desert, Frank James, Former Bandit Visits Zanesville," (2 December 1901), N.P.; "Frank James Once famous Outlaw In The City As a Member of the 'Across The Desert' Company," *Frankfort*

FOOTNOTES

Evening Crescent, weekly newspaper, (Frankfort, Ind.: 12 November 1901), p. 1; ibid., "Frankfort Citizen Personally Acquainted With Frank James," (18 December 1901), p. 1.

38 Louis J. Hennessey, *The Fairgrounds Race Course Diamond Jubilee* (New Orleans, La.: Fairgrounds Corporation, 1948), N.P.' "1902: James At Fair Grounds," *Time-Picayune*, weekly newspaper, (New Orleans, La.: 5 August 1990), p. F-A.

39 Samuel C. Hildreth and James K. Crowell, *The Spell of the Turf*, (Philadelphia & London: 1926), pp. 54-57; J.H. Ransom, *Who's Who And Where In Horsedom*, (Lexington, Ky.: 1950) Vol. 3, p. 24.

40 Samuel C. Hildreth and James K. Crowell, *Spell of the Turf*, (Philadelphia & London: 1926), pp. 54-55.

41 Case file for Serial Patent # 141428: Transfer of land from U.S. Government to Frank James, (Washington, D.C.: 1906-1911, Civil Archives Division, National Archives), 31 pages; *Goodwin's Official Turf Guide*, (New York: 1902), Vol. I, p. 833; Ibid., Vol. II, pp. 6958, 7084, 7246.

42 "Old Timer," *Springfield Daily News*, weekly newspaper, (Springfield, Mo.: December 1932), p. 6; Original starter's medal owned by Lee Pollock, Princeton, Illinois. Medal is marked "Queen City Fair Association, Springfield, Mo.," and was made in Newark, N.J.

43 "Wild West Leaders Will Reach Louisville For Show Today," *Louisville Courier-Journal* (17 August 1903), p. 5.

44 "Former Outlaw Will Reside At Fletcher," *Daily News Republican*, (Lawton, Ok.: 18 November 1907), p. 1.

45 "Missouri Makes Roosevelt 343," *Chicago Tribune*, (10 November 1904), p. 1; "The Borderland," *Collier's Magazine*, (Springfield, Oh.: 26 September 1914), p. 24.

46 *Chronicles of Comanche County*, (Lawton, Ok.: Comanche County Historical Society, 1958), Vol. 4, p. 25.

47 "Summit's Big Barbecue July 4th," *Summit Sentinel*, weekly newspaper, (Summit, Miss.: 30 June 1910), p. 2; ibid., "Frank James," (30 June 1910), p. 2.

48 *Chronicles of Comanche County*, (Lawton Ok.: 1958), Vol. 4, p. 25; J. Frank Dobie, *Coronado's Children: Tales of Lost Mines*, (New York: Grossett & Dunlop, 1930), N.P.

CHAPTER FIFTEEN: WOODBURN'S LEGACY

1 "Woodburn and Other Gossip," *Turf, Field and Farm*, (New York: 16 October 1874), p. 287.

2 "Memoir of Lexington," *Kentucky Live Stock Record*, (Lexington, Ky.: 12 February 1881), Vol. 13, No. 7, p. 104.

3 "Death of Imp. Australian," *Turf, Field and Farm*, (New York: 24 October 1879), p. 280.

4 "The Great Easton Sale," *Thoroughbred Record*, (Lexington Ky.: 27 November 1897), p. 255.

5 "Death of Harold," *American Horse Breeder*, (Boston, Mass.: 21 October 1893) p. 1311.

6 John Hervey, *The American Trotter*, (New York, 1947), p. 150.; John H. Wallace, *The Horse of America*, (Wilmington, Del.: 1973), pp. 305-306.

7 Ibid.

8 John Hervey, *The American Trotter*, (New York: 1947), pp. 149-150.

9 Ibid., p. 207.

10 Ibid., p. 297.

11 Ibid., p. 150.

12 "Death of Harold," *American Horse Breeder*, (Boston, Mass.: 21 October 1893), p. 1311.

13 John H. Wallace, *The Horse of America*, (Wilmington, Del.: 1973), pp. 305-306.

14 Ibid., p. 296.

15 Ibid., pp. 299-301.

16 Ibid., p. 350.

FOOTNOTES

17 S.W. Parlin, *The American Trotter*, (Boston, Mass.: 1905), pp. 206-07.

18 John H. Wallace, *The Horse of America*, (Wilmington, Del.: 1973), pp. 350-51.

19 "Blackwood: The Representative Norman Stallion," *Wilkes' Spirit of the Times*, (New York: 5 February 1876), p. 1.

20 "Belle of Wabash," *American Horse Breeder*, (Boston, Mass.: 14 January 1893), p. 39. This important and rare article explains the Moor's breeding in detail.

21 L.J. Rose, Jr., *L.J. Rose of Sunny Slope*, (San Marino, Ca.: The Huntington Library, 1959), pp. 65, 66, 68.

22 "Wedgewood," *Wilkes' Spirit of the Times*, (New York: 23 December 1882), p. 576.

23 Ibid.

24 John Hervey, *The American Trotter*, (New York: 1947), p. 206.

25 Ibid.

26 See *Chester's Complete Harness and Pacing Guide*.

CHAPTER SIXTEEN: THE ALEXANDERS-EXTENDED FAMILY

1 A.J. Alexander's letter to the author, 15 August 1995, William P. Mangum Papers, Southern Historical Collection, Chapel Hill, N.C.

2 "Memories of Distinguished Kentucky Turfmen-R. Aitcheson Alexander," *Kentucky Live Stock Record*, (Lexington, Ky.: 23 April 1875), p. 185; "The Woodburn Programme," *Turf, Field and Farm*, (New York: 28 December 1867), p. 408.

3 Telephone interview with Dr. A.J. Alexander, Lexington, Ky.: 8-10 October 1990.

4 Samuel M. Wilson and Temple Bodley, *History of Kentucky From 1803-1928*, (Chicago, Ill.-Louisville, Ky.: 1928), Vol. II, pp. 72-73.

5 Woodburn Farm Records, Woodburn Farm.

6 Dan M. Bowmar, III., *Giants of the Turf*, (Lexington, Ky.: 1960), p. 23.

7 John Hervey, *The American Trotter*, (New York: 1947), p. 297.

8 "Robert Aitcheson Alexander. His Claim to Rank as America's Most Successful Breeder," *Thoroughbred Record*, (Lexington, Ky.: 21 May 1938), p. 343.

9 "Woodburn and Other Gossip," *Turf, Field and Farm*, (New York: 16 October 1874), p. 287.

10 Dan M. Bowmar, III., *Giants of the Turf*, (Lexington, Ky.: 1960), p. 4.

11 "Woodburn Farm," *Kentucky Live Stock Record*, (Lexington, Ky.: 13 April 1878), p. 233.

12 "Three Hours At Woodburn," *Turf, Field and Farm*, (New York: 21 October 1887,) p. 334.

13 Ibid.

14 John Hervey, *The American Trotter*, (New York: 1947), p. 297.

15 "The Great Woodburn Stud To Be Dispersed," *Thoroughbred Record*, (Lexington, Ky.: 30 October 1897), p. 208.

16 "The Great Easton Sale," *Thoroughbred Record*, (Lexington, Ky.: 27 November 1897), pp. 255-257.

17 John Hervey, *The American Trotter*, (New York: 1947), p. 297; Dan M. Bowmar, III., *Giants of the Turf*, (Lexington, Ky.: 1960), p. 40.

18 Dan M. Bowmar, III., *Giants of the Turf*, (Lexington, Ky.: 1960), p. 39.

19 "Robert Aitcheson Alexander. His Claim to Rank as America's Most Successful Breeder," *Thoroughbred Record*, (Lexington, Ky.: 21 May 1938), p. 334.

20 "Local Notes," *Thoroughbred Record*, (Lexington, Ky.: 3 October 1914), Vol. 80, No. 4, p. 159.

21 George T. Brown, *Mission To Korea*, (privately published by the Korean mission, N.D.), p. 47; Telephone conversation/interview with A.J. Alexander, Lexington, Ky., 3 April 1997.

22 "Local Notes," *Thoroughbred Record*, (Lexington, Ky.: 6 April 1918), p. 187; "Death of Kenneth

FOOTNOTES

Alexander," *The Blood-Horse*, (Lexington, Ky.: 13 July 1935), p. 43; Treacy & Walker, *American Thoroughbred Stallion Register*, (Lexington, Ky.: Tracy & Walker, 1921), Vol. I, pp. 34-35.

23 "Woodburn Stud," *Thoroughbred Record*, (Lexington, Ky.: 7 January 1981), p. 44.

24 *Breeders Cup Media Guide 1994*, (Lexington, Ky.: The Blood-Horse, 1994), N.P.

25 "Stakes Annual for 1992," *The Blood Horse*, (Lexington, Ky.: 1992), pp. 265, 266.

26 *Keeneland Sales Catalogue*, (Lexington, Ky.: Keeneland Association, September 1995), See Lanark Farm, N.P..

27 "A.B. Gay (1897-1983)," *Thoroughbred Record*, (Lexington, Ky.: 6 April 1983), p. 1936; "Obituary A.B. Gay," *The Blood-Horse*, (Lexington, Ky.: 16 April 1983), p. 2758.

29 *Daily Racing Form*, (Phoenix, Az.: 5 August 1995), See Saratoga, p. 13.

29 Alexander, A.J., Bailey, E., and Woodward, J.G.: "Analysis Of the Equine Lymphocyte Antigen System by Southern Blot Analysis," *Immunogenetics* (Lexington, Ky.: 1987), pp. 25, 47-54.

30 "The Money Horse," *Sports Illustrated*, (New York: circa May 1960), N.P.; "Turfland Members Listed By Arnold," *Lexington Leader*, (Lexington, Ky.: 28 June 1960), N.P..

31 "Death of Bally Ache," *The Blood-Horse*, (Lexington, Ky.: 5 November 1960), p. 1123.

32 "News Or Not; Party for Bally Ache," *The Blood-Horse*, (Lexington, Ky.: 29 October 1960), p. 1071.

33 "Sudden, Crippling Injury to His Leg Ends Spunky Bally Ache's Career," *The Blood-Horse*, (Lexington, Ky.: 15 October 1960), p. 933.

34 "Death of Bally Ache," *The Blood-Horse*, (Lexington, Ky.: 5 November 1960), pp. 1122, 1123.

35 "Leamington Slept Here-At Alexander's Bosque Bonita," *The Blood-Horse*, (Lexington, Ky.: 1 July 1961), p. 13.

36 "The Governor's A Horseman," *Keeneland*, magazine, (Lexington, Ky.: Keeneland Association, Spring/Summer 1992), pp. 23-24; "Woodburn Stud," *Thoroughbred Record*, (Lexington, Ky.: 7 January 1981), p. 44.

37 "The Governor's A Horseman," *Keeneland*, (Lexington, Ky.: Spring/Summer 1992), p. 23.

38 Ibid., p. 24.

39 Ibid., pp. 8, 16.

40 Ibid., pp. 8, 19, 23, 24, 27; "Rosy outlook for Kentucky's man of vision," *Pacemaker International*, (Middlesex, England: April 1994), pp. 64, 65. Airdrie was the home of the World's record-holding stallion Rich Cream, sire of the 1985 Super Derby, Jockey Club Gold Cup, and 117th Belmont Stakes winner Creme Fraiche out of Likely Exchange, by Terrible Tiger. By 1980 Likely Exchange had won 2 million dollars. Creme Fraiche was trained by the renowned Woody Stephens and was the first gelding to ever win the Belmont Stakes, and Stephens' fourth consecutive Belmont win. Creme Fraiche's winning time of 2:27 flat was the fourth fastest Belmont ever. "Creme Fraiche had run second by just a neck to Spend a Buck in the Jersey Derby 13 days ago and his victory today reinforced Spend a Buck's ranking as the top 3-year-old in the country. Spend a Buck won the Kentucky Derby and then skipped the Preakness [won by Tank's Prospect] in order to run in the Jersey Derby, where victory earned him a record $2.6 million payday. Creme Fraiche did not run in the Derby or Preakness because the trainer did not consider him good enough." "Creme Fraiche Gives Stephens 4th Belmont In a Row," *New York Times*, (9 June 1985), Section 5, p. 1. Also see *Sports Illustrated*, "For The Record," (Chicago, Ill., Time-Life, Inc.: 17 June 1985), Vol. 62, No. 24, p. 101.

41 "The Governor's A Horseman," *Keeneland*, (Lexington, Ky.: Spring/Summer 1992), p. 8.

42 Ibid., p. 19; Advertisements from 1995 Issues of *The Blood-Horse*; "The Heirs of Woodburn," *Thoroughbred Times*, (Lexington, Ky.: 20 May 1993), p. 18.

43 Sponsored by The Kentucky Advisory Commission of Public Documents and the Kentucky Historical Society, *The Public Papers of Governor Edward T. Breathitt 1963-1967*, Kenneth E. Harrell, General

FOOTNOTES

Editor. (Lexington, KY: The University Press of Kentucky: 1984),pp1,2

44 "The Heirs of Woodburn," *Thoroughbred Times*, (Lexington, Ky.: 20 May 1993), p. 18.

45 "The Woodburn Stud," *Turf, Field and Farm*, (New York: 23 December 1887), p. 514.

46 John H. Wallace, *The Horse of America* , (Wilmington, Del.: 1973), p. 506.

47 "The Story of Woodburn," *Lexington, Kentucky Morning Herald*, (27 January 1898), p. 3.

THE APPENDIX

1 "Operations of One-Armed Berry and His Gang of Guerrillas Near Louisville," *Chicago Tribune*, (7 November 1865), p. 3.

2 Sarah B. Smith, *Historic Nelson County*, (Louisville, Ky.: 1971), p. 58.

3 "Guerrilla War in Kentucky," *Chicago Tribune*, (9 March 1865), p. 1.

4 "Surrender of Dick Taylor," *New York Daily Tribune*, (10 May 1865), p. 1.

5 "From Cincinnati," *Chicago Tribune*, (4 May 1865), p. 1; ibid., "The Execution of Guerrilla Postponed by Order of Secretary of War," (6 May 1865), p. 1; ibid., "Execution of Martin the Guerrilla," (12 May 1865), p. 1.

6 "From Louisville," *Chicago Tribune*, (11 December 1865), p. 2.

7 Ibid., "From Louisville," (15 June 1865), p. 3.

8 Lewis Collins, *History of Kentucky*, (Frankfort, Ky.: 1966), Vol. I, p. 139.

9 Ibid., p. 137.

10 Ibid., p. 142.

11 Ibid., p. 148.

12 Ibid., p. 146.

13 Ibid., p. 135.

14 Ibid., p. 150; Captain Thomas Speed, *The Union Cause in Kentucky, 1860-1865*, (New York and London: 1907), p. 261.

15 "From Louisville," *New York Times*, (1 January 1865), p. 8.

16 Lewis Collins, *History of Kentucky*, (Frankfort, Ky.: 1966), Vol. I, p. 128.

17 "Guerrillas Routed-Freight Train Captured and Burned," *Chicago Tribune*, (2 March 1865), p. 4.

18 Louis Collins, *History of Kentucky*, (Frankfort, Ky.: 1966), Vol. I, p. 129.

19 Ibid., p. 152.

20 Sarah B. Smith, *Historic Nelson County*, (Louisville, Ky.: 1971), p. 58; "One Arm" Sam Berry Left His Mark," *Kentucky Standard*, (Bardstown, Ky.: 20 November 1983), p. 612; Thomas Shelby Watson, *The Silent Riders*, (Louisville, Ky.: 1970), pp. 23, 25, 26, 29, 36, 37, 41; "From Louisville," *Chicago Tribune*, (30 June 1865), p. 2.

21 "From Louisville," *Chicago Tribune*, (28 April 1865), p. 1.

22 "The Late Guerrilla Outrage on the Nashville Railroad-Three Men Brutally Murdered," *Chicago Tribune*, (8 March 1865), p. 3; "Guerrilla Outrages. A Band of Cut-Throats. In Tennessee, Indiscriminate Murder-Arson and Robbery-Horrible Cruelties," *New York Times*, (28 September 1865), p. 1.

23 "Execution of Champ Furguson," *New York Times*, (21 October 1865), p. 4; Thurman Sensing, *Champ Furguson, Confederate Guerrilla*, (Nashville, Tn.: Vanderbilt University Press, 1942), pp. 166, 168, 169, 253.

24 "War in the Southwest. Guerrilla Gang Brokenup-A Notorious Leader Killed-General Guerrilla Hunt in West Kentucky," *New York Times*, (27 March 1865), p. 4.

25 Ibid., "Kentucky and Tennessee. Movements of Guerrillas," (30 July 1864), p. 1.

26 Ibid., "Rebel Atrocities. A Batallion of Negro Troops Slaughtered in Cold Blood-Murders and Outrages in Kentucky," (3 September 1864), p. 4.

27 Ibid., "Fight With the Guerrilla Jesse," (20 October 1864), p. 1.

FOOTNOTES

28 Ibid., "From Kentucky and Tennessee. Jesse's Guerrillas Routed-Affairs in Front of Nashville-Murfreesboro All Right-Advance of the Rebel Gen. Lyon," (15 December 1864), p. 8.

29 Ibid., "Guerrilla Operations in Tennessee," (7 October 1864), p. 4.

30 R.A. Alexander's personal count of the horses taken, that are mentioned in his letter to Henry Charles Deedes, Woodburn Farm Records, King Library.

31 "Mr. Alexander's Horses," *Wilkes' Spirit of the Times*, (New York: 18 March 1865), p. 41.

32 Robert A. Alexander's letter to Henry Charles Deedes, March 4, 1865, Woodburn Farm Records, King Library.

33 "Racing Problem of the Season. Asteroid and Kentucky," *Turf, Field and Farm*, (New York: 5 August 1865), p. 16.

34 Sanders D. Bruce, *The American Stud Book*, (New York: 1884), Vol. II, p. 144; R. Aitcheson Alexander, *Woodburn Stud Farm 1864 Catalogue*, (Lexington, Ky.: 1864), p. 14; Woodburn Farm Records, Woodburn Farm.

35 Sanders D. Bruce, *The American Stud Book*, (New York: 1884), Vol. II, p. 401, ibid., Vol. I, pp. 650, 652. "Colonel Jack" P. Chinn had some very fine mares when the Civil War broke out. Knowing that they would be confiscated by the Federal government he sent them to Woodburn under the protection of his friend, R.A. Alexander. Among those mares was Nebula, the dam of Asteroid. Broke Chinn lost her to R.A. after the war. "Colonel Jack" P. Chinn," *Thoroughbred Record*, (Lexington, Ky.: 16 May 1931), p. 469.

36 John Hervey, *Racing in America, 1665-1865*, (New York: 1944), pp. 269, 270.

37 "Woodburn Farm And Thoroughbred Blood," *Wallace's Monthly*, Vol. XVI, No. 4, (New York: June 1890), p. 246.

38 "The Woodburn Stud," *Turf, Field and Farm*, (New York: 23 December 1887), p. 514.

39 "Lexington and His Dynasty," *Thoroughbred of California*, (Arcadia, Calif.: October 1975), p. 70.

40 Abram S. Hewitt, *The Great Breeders and Their Methods*, (Lexington, Ky.: 1982), p. 12.

41 Clio D. Hogan, *Index to Stakes Winners 1865-1967*, Vol. II, (privately printed: 1968), p. 613.

42 Ibid., p. 533.

43 Ibid., p. 644.

44 Dan M. Bowmar, III, *Giants of the Turf*, (Lexington, Ky.: 1960), p. 43.

45 Ibid., p. 43.

46 John H. Wallace, *The Horse of America* (Wilmington, Del.: 1973), p. 297.

47 Ibid., p. 299.

48 Ibid., p. 300.

49 "The Sire of Daniel Boone-Sovereign-Sale of Blood Horses in Woodford Co., Ky.," *Wilkes' Spirit of the Times*, (New York: 8 September 1860), pp. 10-11.

50 Ibid., "Thorough-Breds and Trotters in Kentucky," (11 July 1863), p. 290.

51 Ibid., "The Kentucky Sales," (5 December 1863), p. 211.

52 Ibid., "Sale At Woodburn Stud Farm-R.A. Alexander's Spring Station, Woodford Co., Ky.," (15 September 1866), p. 165.

53 "Sale of Stock At The Woodburn Farm," *Turf, Field and Farm*, (Lexington, Ky.: 31 March 1866), N.P.

54 "Mr. Alexander's Annual Stud Sale," *Wilkes' Spirit of the Times*, (New York: 29 June 1867), p. 322.

55 Ibid., "Annual Sale of Through-Bred and Trotting Stock, by A.J. Alexander, At Woodburn Stud Farm, June 18, 1868," (27 June 1868), p. 337.

56 Ibid., "The Horse Market," (3 July 1869), p. 311; ibid., "Woodburn Sales, Lexington, Ky.," (27 June 1874), p. 493.

57 Ibid., "Sales At The Woodburn Stud Farm," (2 July 1870), p. 311; ibid., "Woodburn Sales,

FOOTNOTES

Lexington, Ky.," (27 June 1874), p. 493.

58 Ibid., "Sale of Blooded Stock At Woodburn," (8 July 1871), p. 326; ibid., "Woodburn Sales, Lexington, Ky.," (27 June 1874), p. 493.

59 Ibid., "Sale of Woodburn Yearlings," (29 June 1872), p. 320; ibid., "Woodburn Sales, Lexington, Ky.," (27 June 1874), p. 493.

60 Ibid., "Mr. Alexander's Yearlings," (28 June 1873), p. 325; ibid., "Woodburn Sales, Lexington, Ky.," (27 June 1874), p. 493.

61 Ibid., "Woodburn Sales, Lexington, Ky.,"(27 June 1874), p. 493.

62 "The Alexander Sales," *New York Times*, (7 July 1875), p. 5. One colt, the only brother to Madam Dudley, went for $4,000 and another, the son of Australian and Bonita went for $1,400. At the time it was hailed as "the most successful stock sale in America".

63 "Woodburn Yearlings-Annual Sale, Wednesday June 28, 1876," *Kentucky Live Stock Record*, (Lexington, Ky.: 1 July 1876), Vol. 4, No. 1, pp. 3-4.

64 "The Woodburn Sale. Mr. Alexander's Great Sale of Yearlings-The Horses, The Buyers and the Prices Paid," *New York Times*, (28 June 1877), p. 5.

65 Ibid., "Thoroughbreds At Auction. A.J. Alexander's Sale of Yearlings At Woodburn Farm Kentucky," (27 June 1878), p. 5.

66 Ibid., "Alexander's Sale In Lexington-The Purchasers and the Prices," (19 June 1879), p. 5.

67 Ibid., "Thorough-bred Yearlings Sold At Good Prices. Spirited Bidding At The Annual Sale Of The Woodburn Stud Farm in Kentucky-The Horses Disposed Of And Their Buyers," (27 May 1880), p. 2.

68 "Sale of Woodburn Farm Yearlings," *Kentucky Live Stock Record*, (Lexington, Ky.: 21 May 1881), p. 329; ibid., "Sale of the Woodburn Yearlings," (28 May 1881), p. 345.

69 Ibid., "Sale of Woodburn Yearlings," (Lexington, Ky.: 20 May 1882), Vol. 15, No. 201, pp. 306-307.

70 "Sale of Yearlings. A.J. Alexander's Thorough-Breds Under Hammer at Spring Station, Ky.," *New York Times*, (22 May 1883), p. 2.

71 Ibid., "Thoroughbreds At Auction. Sale of Alexander's Stock and the Prices Obtained," (16 May 1884), p. 2.

72 "Sale of the Woodburn Yearlings, Property of A.J. Alexander, Woodburn Farm, Spring Station, Ky., May 14, 1885," *Kentucky Live Stock Record*, (Lexington, Ky.: 16 May 1885), Vol. 21, No. 20, p. 311.

73 "More Youngsters Sold. A Full Brother to Foxhall Sells For $6100. Falsetto's and King Alfonso's Get Sell for a High Average-Bookmakers Among the Buyers," New York Times, (14 May 1886), p. 3.

74 Ibid., "Woodburn Yearlings. Thirty-Nine Youngsters Sold at Very handsome Prices," (11 May 1887), p. 2.

75 Ibid., "Yearlings Sell Better. The Woodburn Lot Bring High Prices. The Dwyer Brothers and the Melbourne Stables Among the Largest of the Purchasers," (4 May 1888), p. 3.

76 Ibid., "Yearlings At Auction. Kentucky Youngsters Under the Hammer. The Pick of the Lot Secured By The Dwyer Brothers As Usual-Some Good Prices Obtained," (1 May 1889), p. 5.

77 Ibid., "A Good Sale of Yearlings. A High Average Price For The Woodburn-Bred Thoroughbreds," (13 July 1890), p. 2.

78 Ibid., "Sale of Thoroughbreds. High Prices For The Yearlings From Woodburn Stock Farm," (12 July 1891), p. 2.

79 Ibid., "Sale of Thoroughbreds. Good Prices Obtained For The Yearlings From Woodburn Farm," (22 May 1892), p. 3.

80 Ibid., "Good Prices For Thoroughbreds. The Woodburn Farm Stock Sells in Lively Fashion-Mr. Daly's New Colt," (18 May 1893), p. 3.

FOOTNOTES

81 "Thoroughbred Sale In New York," *Kentucky Live Stock Record*, (Lexington, Ky.: 26 May 1894), Vol. 39, No. 21, p. 328.

82 "Prices For Blue Grass Yearlings," *Thoroughbred Record*, (Lexington, Ky.: 29 June 1895), Vol. 41, No. 26, p. 416.

83 Ibid., "The St. Louis Sale," (27 June 1896), p. 307.

84 Ibid., "The Woodburn Yearlings," (11 July 1896), p. 17.

85 Ibid., "The Great Woodburn Stud to be Dispersed," (30 October 1897), Vol. 46, No. 18, p. 208; ibid., "The Great Easton Sale," (27 November 1897), Vol. 46, No. 22, pp. 255-257.

86 "The Sire of Daniel Boone-Soverign-Sale of Blood Horses in Woodford Co., Ky.," *Wilkes' Spirit of the Times*, (New York: 8 September 1860), pp. 10-11.

87 "Sale At Woodburn Stud Farm-R.A. Alexander's Spring Station, Woodford Co., Ky.," *Turf Field and Farm*, (New York: 15 September 1866), p. 165.

88 "Mr. Alexander's Annual Stud Sale," *Wilkes' Spirit of the Times*, (New York: 29 June 1867), p. 322.

89 Ibid., "Annual Sale of Thorough-Bred and Trotting Stock, By A.J. Alexander, At Woodburn Stud Farm, June 18, 1868," (27 June 1868), p. 337.

90 Ibid., "Mr. Alexander's Sale of Blooded Stock At Woodburn, June 23," (3 July 1869), p. 311.

91 Ibid., "Sales At The Woodburn Stud Farm," (2 July 1870), p. 311.

92 Ibid., "Sale of Blooded Stock at Woodburn," (8 July 1871), p. 326.

93 "The Alexander Sale," *New York Times*, (7 July 1875), p. 5.

94 Ibid., "Woodburn Yearlings-Annual Sale, Wednesday, June 28th, 1876," (1 July 1876), p. 3.

95 Ibid., "A Great Stock Sale. Twenty-two Kentucky Weanlings. Trotters Bought by a New York State Firm," (24 December 1877), p. 8.

96 "Sale of Trotters," *New York Timews*, (26 October 1888), p. 3.

INDEX

10th Mountain Division, 193
12th Kentucky, 84
12th Kentucky Cavalry, 73
12th Ohio, 84
12th Ohio Cavalry, 83
12th U.S. Colored Heavy Artillery, 107
13th Kentucky, 84, 86
15th Kentucky Infantry, 70
17th Army Corps, 73
1860 Census, 18
1860 *Woodburn Farm Catalogue*, 91
1864 *Woodburn Farm Catalogue*, 78
1864 *Woodburn Stud Farm Catalogue*, 28, 53, 91
1865 *Racing Calendar*, 99
1867 *Woodburn Stud Farm Sale Catalogue*, 105
1st Kentucky Mounted Rifles, 57
26th Kentucky, 48
2nd Colorado Cavalry, 66, 67
2nd Duke of Atholl, 19
37th Kentucky Infantry, 59
39th Missouri Cavalry, 65
4th Marine Regiment, 191
4th Missouri Cavalry, 67, 70
54th Kentucky, 71
5th Indiana Cavalry, 109
5th Marines, 193
7th Pennsylvania Cavalry, 70
Alexander, A.J.A., 191
Abbottsford, 181
Abdallah 15, 32, 33, 36, 37, 80, 85, 87, 89, 90, 95, 101, 160,
Abdallah Pilot, 186
Abingdon, Virginia, 51
Across The Desert, (Play), 166
Ada Cheatham, 105
Adairville, Kentucky, 165
Adam Huntsman, 41
Adams, N., 61
Adbell, 32
Adelaide, 125
Adios, 145
Adjutant General of Kentucky, 194
Administrator, 183
Advertiser, 2:15 1/4, 32
Aerolite, 50
Agatha, 7
Agathia, 7
Agricultural Fair Association, 57

Airdrie, 5, 9, 11, 189
Airdrie Farm, 189, 194
Airdrie Furnace, 11, 18
Airdrie House, 5, 7, 9
Airdrie Ironworks, 9, 11, 185
Airdrie Mill, 9, 97, 186
Airdrie Petroleum Company, 185
Airdrie Stud Farm, 9, 195
Aitcheson, Christian, 5, 6
Aitcheson family, 7
Alabama, 115
Alaho, 147
Alarm, 169
Albany, New York, 78
Albany, New York penitentiary, 113
Albion, 29
Alcantara, 2:23, 139, 141
Alcazar, 143, 179
Alcyone, 141
Alderney, 19, 186
Alderneys, 124
Alex Churchill, 41
Alexander, 5, 7, 15, 18, 21, 22, 23, 25, 29, 32, 33, 34, 37, 40, 41, 42, 45, 46, 47, 49, 50, 52, 53, 54, 56, 57, 60, 75, 76, 77, 78, 79, 80, 85, 87, 89, 90, 91, 92, 95, 96, 97, 98, 99, 100, 101, 102, 103, 104, 105, 114, 115, 116, 117, 118, 119, 120, 121, 122, 123, 124, 125, 126, 127, 133
Alexander, Alexander John, 5, 185, 187, 188, 189, 191
Alexander, Alexander John "Alec" (A.J.), 8, 15, 60, 101, 130, 147, 185, 188, 189
Alexander, Anna, 3
Alexander, Bethia, 6
Alexander, Brownell, 194
Alexander, Dr. A.J., 92
Alexander, Dr. Alexander John Aitcheson, 188
Alexander, Dr. Alexander John, 195
Alexander V, Dr. Alexander John, 191
Alexander, James (I), 3
Alexander, James H., 188, 195
Alexander, Jane, 6
Alexander, Janet Cuninghame, 3
Alexander, Jean, 5
Alexander, John (I), 3, 5, 7
Alexander, John (II), 3
Alexander, Kenneth, 193

255

INDEX

Alexander, Kenneth Deedes, 189
Alexander, Robert, 3, 7, 185
Alexander, Robert Spruel Crawford Aitcheson (RA), 9
Alexander, I, R. A., 8, 9, 11, 15, 16, 17, 18, 22, 25, 27, 31, 32, 34, 37, 39, 41, 53, 73, 101, 104, 105, 123, 125, 130,131, 133, 134, 135, 137, 183, 185, 188, 189, 194, 195, 197
Alexander I, Robert, 3
Alexander II, Robert, 3
Alexander III, Robert, 5, 6
Alexander IV, Robert, 6, 7, 9
Alexander, III, Robert Aitcheson, 189
Alexander, Sir William (William III), 8
Alexander I, William, 3, 5, 7, 8
Alexander II, William, 5, 6, 7
Alexander III, William, 6, 7
Alexanders, 3, 6
Alexander's Abdallah, 28, 144, 171, 175
Alexander's Belmont, 181, 183
Alexander's Edwin Forrest, 139
Alexander's Norman, 31, 139, 177
Alhambrah, 121
Ali, Hyder, 137
Alice Carneal, 23
Alista, 171
Alix, 2:03 1/4, 37, 171, 173, 175
Alix, 2:03 3/4, 173
Alleghenies, Mountain Range, 118,
Alma Mater, 139
Almeh, 143
Almont, 78, 144, 173, 175, 186
Altho, 151
Althola, 147
America, 7, 9, 11, 15, 21, 22, 23, 36, 37, 116, 117, 130, 131, 133, 134, 143, 149, 187, 197
American, 22, 23, 27, 28, 34, 35, 36, 129, 133, 135, 150, 162, 165, 166, 197
American Citizenship, 9
American Derby, 150, 151
American Jockey Club, 124
American Saddle Horse Association, 29
American Saddle Horse Magazine, 51
American Saddle Horse Register, 30
American Short Horn Registry, The, 186
American Stallion Register, 92, 95
American Star 14, 36, 175
American stock-farm-catalogue, 32
American Stud Book, 36, 130
American Trotter, The, 139, 182
American Trotting Horse, The, 32, 34
American Turf, 117, 123, 131, 149, 151, 169
American Turf Congress, 39
Americano, 150
Americus, 36, 145, 150
Americus Girl, 150
Amigo, 147
Amurath, 179

Anayzas, 42
Anderson, Alex, 68
Anderson, Captain William "Bloody Bill", 63, 65, 66, 67
Anderson County, Kentucky, 83, 85, 87, 89, 90
Aneroid, 121
Anna, 3
Anna Mace, 39
Anne, 191
Anne Guillen, 193
Annette, 23, 147,
Anvil, 125
Arabia, 42
Arabian, 43
Arabian horses, 42
Arboretum of L.A. County, California, 149
Arcadia, California, 145, 147
Ariel, 37
Arkansas River, 63
Army Medical Corps, 189
Army of Northern Virginia, 51
Ascot Gold Cup, 187
Ashland, 49
Ashland Stud, 91
Ashland Wilkes, 183
Asterick, 99, 124, 125
Asteroid, 25, 27, 44, 50, 54, 55, 56, 57, 58, 59, 60, 75, 79, 80, 87, 90, 99, 101, 114, 115, 116, 117, 118, 119, 120, 121, 123, 124
Astraeus, 191
Atalanta, 37, 143, 171
Atalanta 2nd, 145, 147
Atlantic, 117, 121
Atop, 191
Attorney 1005, 171, 173
Aurora, Illinois, 97
Australian, 24, 25, 37, 43, 50, 53, 54, 95, 99, 101, 102, 125, 139, 141, 146, 169, 171, 186, 187
Avery, H.S., 78, 90
Ayers, F.J., 177
Ayrshire, Scotland, 3, 186
Bab, 41
Babta, 105
Bachelor of Arts, 9
Baldwin, E.J. "Lucky",145, 147, 149, 150, 151, 159, 160
Baldwin, Elias Jackson "Lucky", 145
Baldwin Hotel, San Francisco, California, 149, 159
Baldwin Theater, San Francisco, California, 159
Baldwin, Verona, 149
Ballard's Breech Loading Rifle, 12
Ballot, 189
Bally Ache, 193
Ballydam, 193
Balmorral, 121
Baltimore, Maryland, 133, 161
Bank of Kentucky, Frankfort, 8
Barbara, 181

INDEX

Bardstown, Kentucky, 60, 70, 71, 112, 166
Barker, Henry L., 31
Barnes, Major George F., 84
Baron Rose, 143
Basham, William, 112
Bassett, Lucy Gay, 191
Bassett, III, James E. "Ted", 191
Bassett, III, Mr. and Mrs. James E., 12
Bassinger, 179
Bates Farm, 182
Bath County, Kentucky, 49
Bath, England, 5
Battle at Westport, Missouri, 66
Bay Chief, 32, 80, 85, 87, 89, 95, 141
Bay Dick, 56, 99, 121, 125
Bay Flower, 53, 54, 99
Bay Kentucky Hunter, 29
Bay Leaf, 125
Bay Mare, 54
Bay Roman, 2:42, 32
Bay York, 21, 101
Bayard, 101
Bayflower, 103, 104
Bayonet, 121
Baywater, 123, 125
Baywood, 121, 125, 147
Beatrice, 173
Beau Clay, 181
Beautiful Bells, 2:29 1/2, 141, 143, 144, 145, 179, 180
Bedford, George M., 16, 17
Bedford, Indiana, 165
Bedouins, 42
Bell Bird, 180
Bell Boy, 180, Belland Jr., Napoleon, 104, 105
Belle, 171, 173, 175
Belle Anderson, 41
Belle Lewis, 105
Belle Lupe, 173, 175
Belle Meade, 134
Belle Meade Stock Farm in Tennessee, 181
Belle Meade Stud, 25
Belle of Wabash, 179, 180
Belle View Maid, 181
Belle Winnie, 139
Belleflower, 180
Bell's, Tennessee, 67
Belmont, 175, 182, 183, 186, 193
Belmont, August, 104
Belmont Stakes, 169, 187
Belvidere, 41
Belwin, 2:06 3/4, 139
Bentley, Lt. Colonel Robert Henry, 84
Bruce, Benjamin Gratz, 134
Bennett, Albert A., 149
Bennett Farm, North Carolina, 112
Bennett, Lillie, 149
Berkshire pigs, 12

Bernadello, 150
Berry, "One Arm" Sam, 49, 57, 59, 113
Berry, Captain "One Arm" Sam, 71
Berry, Richard, 48
Best Turn, 191
Bethal, Kentucky, 49,
Beuzetta, 2:06 3/4, 173
Bewleyville, Kentucky, 85, 107
Bicara, 171, 173, 175
Big Creek, Tennessee, 67
Big Springs, Kentucky, 109
Billet, 169
Billy Watts, 189
Bincoe, M., 48
Binderton, 189
Bingen, 2:06 1/4, 32
Black Bess, 41
Black Eyed Susan, 41
Black Hawk Mill, Aurora, Illinois, 97
Black Horse Tavern, (Midway-Wersailles Road), 91
Black mare, 180
Black Rose, 21, 30, 91, 99
Blackhouse, Scotland, 3
Blackwater Ford, Missouri, 65
Blackwood, 31, 177, 179
Blackwood Belle, 179
Blackwood Jr., 179
Blandina, 177
Bloomfield, Kentucky, 48, 49, 58, 59, 70, 71, 84, 88, 112, 113
Blossom, 145, 147
Blue Bonnet, 103
Blue Grass Park, 116
Blue Springs, Missouri, 165
Bluegrass, 28, 135, 188
Blunder, 146, 147
Boghall (Scotland), 3
Bonnie Scotland, 169
Boone County Fair, Missouri, 161
Bosque Bonita, 38, 39, 193
Bosque Bonita Farm, 22, 193
Boston, 25, 36, 37, 139, 182
Boudinot, E., 27
Bourbon County, Kentucky, 16, 17, 57, 58, 195
Bourbon whiskey, 65
Bow Bells, 179, 180
Bowen, 41
Bowie & Hall, 104
Bowmar III, Dan M., 18, 187, 189
Boyd County, Kentucky, 49
Boyd's Hole, Virginia, 5
Bradfordsville, Kentucky, 86
Bragg, General Braxton, 51
Brandenburg, Kentucky, 107, 109
Breathitt, Edward T. "Ned", 195
Breathitt, Lucy Alexander, 195
Breckinridge County, Kentucky, 109

257

INDEX

Breckinridge, General John C. (Vice-President, U.S.), 43
Breeders Cup Ltd., 191
Bret Hanover, 145
Brewer, Katherine (Alexander), 193
Brewer, Katherine (Mrs. Robert), 191
Brewer, Robert, 193
Bridgewater, Captain James H., 69, 85, 86
Brimmer, 28
Bring Back, 189
British, 7, 17
British citizen, 9
British Citizenship, 49
British subject, 9
British turf authorities, 150
Broadhead, Lucas,169, 171, 186, 187
Broomstick, 189
Brown, Colonel Simeon B., 73
Brown Dick (Horse), 120
Brown, Ed ("Brown Dick") Jockey, 120
Brown Pilot, 177
Brownsville, Tennessee, 67
Brown's Bellfounder, 173, 175
Bruce, Colonel Sanders D., 102, 119, 130
Brunette, 105
Bryan, William Jennings, 163, 165
Buck Elk, 41
Buckden, 169
Buckeye Race Track, 99, 120, 130
Buckley, Colonel Harvey M., 71, 72, 73
Buckner Hill, Kentucky, 48
Buell, General Don Carlos, 185
Buena Vista, Mexico, 39
Buford, Abraham "Abe",22, 39
Buford, Abraham, 11
Buford, Captain, 39
Buford, General, 115, 123
Buford, General Abe, 118, 123, 193
Buford, Henry, 11
Buford, Tom, 11, 39
Buford, William, 8, 11
Buford, William A., 39
Bufords, 11
Bull Moose Party, 167
Bullitt County, Kentucky, 70
Burbridge, Brigadier General Stephen Gano, 48, 49, 54, 61
Burbridge, George, 41
Burch Mare, 177
Burgess of Glasgow, Scotland, 3
Burlington, 187
Burlington and Quincy Railroad, 97
Burlington, Wisconsin, 177
Burnes, Dick, 67
Burud, Gretchen, 193
Butler, Captain John S., 84
Butler, Colonel Ed (City "Boss" of St. Louis), 161
By to Market, 191

Byerly Turk, 36
C.H. Todd, 145
C.S.X. Railroad, 133, 197
Cadiz, Kentucky, 67
Calf Pasture, Virginia, 7
California, 17, 27, 120, 141, 143, 146, 149, 150, 151, 179
Cameron, Sir Roderick, 105
Camp Nelson, Kentucky, 84
Campbell, John, 127
Campbells (Scotish Clan), 124
Campbellsville, Kentucky, 86
Camptown Races (Song), 21
Canada, 104, 105, 125
Canadian Hals, 35
Canadian Pacers, 35
Cane Spring Farm, 83
Canton, Tennessee, 67
Capitola, 41
Captain Bates's Home Guards, 87
Caribbean, 5
Carroll County, Kentucky, 73
Casey County, Kentucky, 86
Catch Filly, 144
Catesby, 169
Catharine, 41
Catherine Ogle, 41
Cattle Kingdom in the Ohio Valley, 1783-1860, 17
Celestial Blue, 193
Celoso, 150
Central Indiana Fair Circuit, 166
Central Kentucky, 60
Centralia, Missouri, 65
Centre College, Kentucky, 188
Challenge Vase (Woodlawn Vase), 121, 133
Chant, 150
Chaplin, Kentucky, 67
Chaplintown, Kentucky, 67, 69
Charlotte Buford, 105
Chenoweth, Colonel, 48
Chester Cup, 23
Chestnut Hills, New York, 23
Chetham, Illinois, 47
Chevalier Claussen's Method of Preparing Flax, 15
Cheviot, 147, 151
Chicago, Illinois 47, 97, 99, 101, 150, 161, 163, 171, 185, 193
Chicago & Alton Railroad, 165
Chicago Chronicle, 163
Chicago Daily Tribune, 107
Chicago Tribune, The, 59, 71, 102, 133
Chief Betting Commissioner, 118
Childe Harold (Standardbred), 171
Chillicothe, Ohio, 185
Chimes, 143, 145, 179, 180
Chinn, Colonel " Jack" John P.,50, 159, 160, 161, 165
Churchill Downs, 146

INDEX

Cincinnati, Ohio, 99, 102, 115, 116, 120, 121, 125, 130
Citizen, 28
Civil War, 17, 35, 40, 41, 42, 43, 62, 66, 92, 104, 117, 118, 120, 133, 137, 161
Clara D., 147, 149
Clarke, Captain a.k.a. (Quantrill), 67, 68, 88, 110, 111
Clarke, Marcellus Jerome a.k.a. (Sue Mundy), 54, 73, 110
Clay (Union Commander), 107
Clay, Brutus J., 16, 57
Clay, Colonel Ezekiel Field, 57
Clay County, Missouri, 65
Clay, Henry (U.S. Seantor), 91, 116
Clay, John M., 91, 116
Clay Jr, Hon. Cassius M., 57
Clay Pilot, 144, 180
Clay, U.S. Senator Henry, 91
Clerk of Session of Edinburgh, Scotland, 3
Cleveland, President Grover, 163
Clifton and Glenn's Creek roads (Kentucky), 57
Clinton, New York, 31
Clowney, Major John, 87
Cockspurs, 35
Col. Hull, 161
Colesburg, Kentucky, 107
Collins, Lewis, 80
Colter, Captain, 71
Columbia, Kentucky, 86, 162
Columbus, Ohio, 116
Commanche, Oklahoma, 167
Commissioner Foster, 41
Commodore, 141
Company B, 30th Wisconsin Infantry, 109
Confederacy, 47, 48, 49, 109
Confederate, 43, 47, 49, 50, 51, 56, 57, 58, 60, 61, 65, 66, 68, 69, 70, 88, 111
Confederate Veteran Magazine, 110
Conley, John W., 177
Consolation Stake, 123
Consternation, 37
Convoy, 181
Cook, Sidney, 48, 49
Copperbottom, 35, 177
Cordelia, 147
Cornflower, 147
Cotswold (Sheep), 12, 17
Court Exchequer, 8
Court Martial, 150
Covington, Kentucky, 67, 70
Cowden Hill (Scotland), 9
Cox Place, Kentucky, 109
Crab Orchard, Kentucky, 84, 86
Craigs, Newton, 54
Crimean War, 42
Crittenden Hospital, Louisville, 109
Crittenden, Missouri Governor Thomas T., 160

Croker, Richard "Boss" (City Boss of New York City), 150
Cross of Gold (by William Jennings Bryan), 163
Crossland, 39
Cruzados, 145, 147, 150
Cruzdos, 150
Crystal Lake, Illinois, 171
Culver Handicap, 150
Cumberland River, 67
Cuninghame, Alexander, 3
Currier & Ives, 91
Cuyler, 173
Cynthiana, Kentucky, 32, 53, 54, 58, 73, 182
Dacia, 181
Daily Commonwealth, The, 45
Daisy B., 183
Daisy Rose, 143
Dallas, Texas, 160
Dalton, Kit, 159, 167
Dame Winnie, 139
Damewood, 182, 183
Daniel Lambert (Morgan Horse), 37
Dansil, 195
Danville, Kentucky, 67, 68, 69, 71, 84, 86, 188
Danville, Indiana, 39
Daphne, 23
Darbytown Road (Virginia), 53
Darkness, 30, 91
Davis, Judge Jonathan, 70
Davison (Guerrilla), 107
Day Star, 91
Daydream, 191
Deatsville, Kentucky, 70, 110, 112
Dee Stakes, 23
Deedes, Henry Charles, 60, 79, 89, 97, 129, 189
Deedes, Kenneth, 188
Deedes, Jr., Kenneth, 189
Deedes, Mary Alexander, 45
Deedes, Mary Belle, 8, 60, 189
Deep Bottom Run, Virginia, 53
Deihl, Henry, 113
de la Croix, Marianne, 3
de la Port, Agatha, 7
de la Port, Armaund, 7
de la Port, MariaDeleware, 37
Democratic Convention, 163
Democratic Party, 165
Democratic Presidential Candidate, 163
Democrats, 163
Deputy Chief of Protocol, 195
Derby Stakes, 37
Derby Trial, 150
Desert Wine, 195
Devil's Elbow (on the Mississippi River), 67
Dick Doty, 54
Dick Johnson, 41
Dick Menifee, 41
Dick Moore, 186

INDEX

Dick Singleton, 41
Dickens, 125, 169
Dictator, 2:29 3/4, 36
Dijon, France, 6
Diomed ("Father of the American Turf"), 35, 36, 37, 141
Directly, 183
Directum I., 1:56 3/4, 173
Dole, Charles S., 171
Doll, 29
Dolly, 105
Dolly Spanker, 141
Doswell, Colonel, 127
Double Team Trot (Print), 91
Dr. Lewis, 109
Ducatoon, 23
Duchess of Athol, 16
Dudley, Nelson, 22
Dudley, W.A., 105
Duke, General Basil, 51
Duke of Airdrie, 17
Duncan, Mr., 16
Duncan, Oklahoma, 167
Duncomb, W.E., 25
Durastus (slave), 51
Durham, North Carolina, 186
Durkee, Harrison, 177
Duroc, 37
Dutch, 3, 41
Earls of Sterling, 3
Early Bird, 2:10, 173
Early Light, 41
Earp, Josephine Sarah Marcus, 149, 159
Earp, Wyatt, 149, 159
East Aurora, New York, 145
Easter, 41
Eastern and Vine Street, Lexington, Kentucky, 195
Easy Goer, 195
Edinburgh, Scotland, 3, 5, 6
Edwin Forrest, 21, 29, 32, 33, 49, 56, 91, 92, 94, 95, 102
El Arroyo Ranch, 27
El Fantastico, 191
El Prado, 195
El Relicario, 151
El Rio Rey, 145
Electioneer, 32, 139, 145
Eliza McGuffin, 57
Elizabethtown, Kentucky, 70, 71, 72, 84
Elkhart, Illinois, 47
Elliott, Colonel George, 28
Elliott, Judge, 39
Elmendorf, 186
Elmendorf Stud Farm, 147
Elwes, C.F., 104
Emelia, 25
Emily Johnson, 41
Eminence, Kentucky, 70, 73, 84

Emma Wright, 56
Emperor of Norfolk, 36, 145, 147, 149, 150, 151
England, 3, 7, 8, 12, 15, 18, 22, 23, 25, 36, 42, 60, 95, 104, 116, 133, 134, 150, 162, 164, 171, 187, 189
English, 23, 34
Enquirer, 23, 39, 169
Epsom, England, 37
Escoba, 189
Estella, 139, 141
Ethan Allen 50 (Morgan Horse), 35, 37, 91
Eugene, 124
Eureka, 33
Europe, 7, 150, 159, 162
European, 15, 31, 162
European theater, 195
Eva, 2:23 1/2, 141
Evans, Tom, 112
Eventide, 36
Ewing, General Hugh, 107
Expedition, 37
Experiment, 147, 151
Exterminator, 189
Fair Trial, 150
Fairgrounds Race Track at New Orleans, 159
Fairlawn Farm, 175
Falconese, 191
Falsetto, 171, 186, 187
Fancy, 183
Fannie G., 139
Fanny Cook, 37
Father of the American Turf (Diomed), 37
Faugh-a-Ballagh, 23
Faustus, 39
Fayette County, Kentucky, 22, 120
Federal army, 48, 57, 101
Federal Court of Winchester, Kentucky, 120
Federal forces, 73
Federal Home Guards, 71
Federal soldiers, 88, 92
Federal troops, 72, 109, 110
Federals, 69, 73, 83, 86, 110
Field, Amelia, 57
Field, Ann, 57
Field, General Charles William, 53
Fishhook, 147
FitzGerald, George (& Firm or Company), 5
Flat Rock, Kentucky, 84
Fleetwing, 123, 124, 143
Fleming County, Kentucky, 49
Flemingsburg, Kentucky, 49
Fletcher, Oklahoma, 166
Flirt, 37
Flirtilla, 37
Flood, 145
Flora Temple, 21, 29
Florida, 194
Florida Derby, 195

INDEX

Florizel, 35, 37
Flushing Long Island, New York, 179
Ford, President Gerald, 195
Forest Temple 136, 32
Fort Jones, Kentucky, 107
Fort Smily, Arkansas, 63
Forty-Niner, 117
Foster, Stephen (Song Writer), 21
Fox Creek Bridge, Kentucky, 70
Fox River, Illinois, 97
Foxhall, 187
France, 3, 6, 7, 12
Frankfort, Kentucky, 8, 9, 17, 39, 48, 54, 70, 84, 87, 89, 93
Frankfort Cemetery, Frankfort, Kentucky, 130
Franklin, Benjamin, 6, 7
Franklin-Alexander liaison, 6, 7
Fredricktown, Missouri, 63
Free Hill Farm, 11
Freeman, Elizabeth Gay, 191
Freedom, 180
French, 3, 5, 7
French & Indian War, 8
Freshman, 179
Froman, Ben, 90
Frontier Nursing Service, Kentucky, 188
Fry, Brigadier General Speed Smith, 84
Fullerton, Lucy, 185
Furguson, G.W., 95
Gadsden, Tennessee, 67
Gaines' Denmark (Saddlebred), 29, 50, 53
Gallatin, Missouri, 161
Gallatin, Tennessee, 28
Gano, 147
Garden State Park, 194
Garrard, Charles T., 16
Garrard County, Kentucky, 53
Garrett's Horse, 33
Gay, Anne, 191
Gay, Augustus B., 191
Gay, Augustus Benjamin (A.B. or Gus), 189
Gay, Dr. James G., 191
Gay, Elizabeth Simms, 189
Gay Lothario, 189
Gay, "Teddy", 191
Genteel Gus, 189
George A. Ayer, 2:30, 181
George Wilkes, 2:22, 32, 139, 141
Georgetown, Kentucky, 25, 53, 71, 73, 80, 83, 115, 116
Geraldine, 175
Germantown, 41
Germany, 41
Gertrude Russell, 2:23 1/2, 139
Ghaz, 195
Giants of the Turf, 18, 189
Gibson's Tom Hal, 35
Gilcrest, Jean (Mrs. Roger), 191

Gilchrist, William Alexander, 193
Gildersleeve, 41
Gilpatrick, 103
Gilroy, 146
Glasgow, Kentucky, 48
Glasgow, Scotland, 3, 5
Glasscock, Dick, 69
Glen Athol, 147, 187
Glencoe, 25, 37, 43, 90, 101, 115, 116
Glenelg, 105, 147, 169
Glengarry, 169
Glenita, 147
Gobbler, 41
Godbold Wells, Mississippi, 167
Godolphin Barb, 36
Goldsby, T.B., 115, 120
Goldsmith Maid, 2:14, 32, 161
Good Time, 145
Goodnight, 39
Goodwood Stakes, 23
Goshen, New York, 32, 34, 36, 134
Goslin's Lane (Missouri), 63
Gossip, 28
Graigends, Scotland, 3
Grand Circuit, 183
Grand Master, 19
Grand Prix de Paris, 187
Graves, Specner, 54
Gray, Agnes, 97
Gray, Amelia, 97
Gray, Daniel S., 97
Gray Diomed, 36
Gray Goose, 99
Gray, Margaret, 97
Grayson County, Kentucky, 85
Great Britain,5, 23, 49, 97
Great Ones, The, 22
Green Dancer, 191
Green River, Kentucky, 11
Greenville, Kentucky, 67
Gregg, Bill, 65
Grenada, 5
Gretchen, 181
Grey Goose, 21
Grinstead, 145, 151
Grinstead, J.A., 146
Gross, William L., 68
Guildmaster of Edinburgh, Scotland, 3
Guillen, Anne, 193
Guthrie, Kentucky, 165
Guy Wilkes, 180
Hackett, Captain Rowland E., 48
Hall, Bob, 112
Hall, Ike, 112
Hall of Fame, 28, 29, 34, 134
Hall, Tom, 113
Hambletonian 10, 32, 36, 37, 171, 173
Hamilton, Major, 107

INDEX

Hamilton, Major Andrew G., 73
Hamiltonian (Thoroughbred), 41
Hamlin, C.J., 145
Hamlin Patchen, 145
Hancock County, Kentucky, 109
Hanover, 58
Hardin County, Kentucky, 70, 71
Harding, General Giles William, 181
Harness Racing Museum, 28, 29, 34
Harness Racing Museum & Hall of Fame, 134
Harold, 25, 171, 173, 175, 182, 186
Harper, Adam, 61
Harper, Betsy, 41
Harper, Frank, 91, 146
Harper, Frank B., 41
Harper, Jacob, 41
Harper, John, 54, 60
Harper, W.F., 116
Harper, William, 41
Harper, William Frank, 22
Harpers, 41
Harrieta, 2:09 3/4, 139
Harriman, E. H., 143
Harris, Amanda, 39
Harris, John, 112
Harris, Tom, 67
Harrison County, Kentucky, 32, 53
Harrodsburg, Kentucky, 68, 69, 81, 159, 160
Harry O'Fallon, 169
Hartford, 2:22 1/4, 175
Haskins, Richard, 70
Hatley, Sherwood, 48
Havoc, 99
Hawesville, Kentucky, 107
Hawkster, 195
Hawthorne Gold Cup, 193
Hawthorne Juvenile Handicap, 189
Haysville, Kentucky, 86
Henlein, Paul, 17
Hennie Farrow, 145
Henrico County, Virginia, 7
Henry, Captain Zachariah "Zach" B., 57, 87, 88, 90
Henry County, Kentucky, 70, 71, 72, 73
Henry, Jim "Zac", 59
Henry, Mason, 57
Henry, Mason R., 182
Henry, Tom, 57, 85, 90
Henry, Zach, 87, 88, 90
Hermes, 2.27 1/2, 171, 186
Herod, 36
Hervey, John, 30, 101, 105, 139, 182
Hiawatha, 169
Hickman, Kentucky, 107
High Bridge, Kentucky, 165
Highland Park, 195
Highway 62 (Midway-Versailles Road), 91
Hildreth, Sam, 159, 166

Hillsboro, Kentucky, 49
Hilton, Dave, 112
Hinda Rose, 143, 180
Hindoo, 147
History of Kentucky, 80
History of Shorthorn Cattle, 16
Hobart, Walter S., 143
Hobson, Brigadier General Edward Henry, 72
Hobson, General Edward Henry, 54, 84, 85, 87
Hodgenville, Kentucky, 84, 85
Hollingsworth, Kent, 22
Hollywood, 39, 115
Holtzclaw, Clifton D., 111
Home Guard (Kentucky), 109
Honest Allen (Morgan Horse), 91
Hoomes, Col. John, 37
Hopkins, Jas. (Jasper), 49
Horses, 130
Hopkinsville, Kentucky, 67
Horse of America, The, 171
Hospodar, 41
Hot Springs, Arkansas, 189
Hotel Burton, 165
Hotspur, 101
House of Commons, 5
Howard's Hill, Kentucky, 109
Howes, General Thomas, 73
Hudson River, New York, 117
Huerta, Victoriano, 65
Huguenot, 3, 41
Hull, F.V.R.L., 78, 186
Hulse, William ("Bill"), 86, 111, 112
Humbolt, Tennessee, 67
Humphreys, Lucy, 185
Hunt the Thimble, 191
Hunter, John, 117, 118, 119, 120
Hunt's Commodore, 141
Hustonville, Kentucky, 86
Hustonville Turnpike, 67
Hylas, 186
Hymenia, 147
I Married Wyatt Earp, 149, 159
Idlewild, 50, 121, 124
Illinois, 90, 97, 99, 101, 104, 105, 129, 197
Illiopolis, Illinois, 47
Immortal Room (Hall of Fame), 134
Imperial Falcon, 191
Impetuous, 2:13, 173
imported Glencoe, 91
imported Hermence, 171, 187
imported Jolly Roger, 29
imported Margrave, 139
imported Priam, 91
imported Sovereign, 105, 146
imported Valiant, 29
Inauguration Stakes, 121, 124
Inca, 181
Independence, Missouri, 66, 68, 81, 165, 166

262

INDEX

Indian Territory (Oklahoma), 66
Indiana, 17, 51, 179, 180
Indianapolis, 2:21, 28, 186
Invalid Corps, 86
Io, 2:13 1/2, 173
Iowa, 37
Ireland, 18, 150
Irene Harding, 181
Irish Birdcatcher, 23, 42
Irish Open, 195
Iron Brigade, 67
Iroquois, 25
Iroquois Hunt Club, 193
Italy, 193
Izetta, 2:13 1/2, 173
Jackson, Andrew, 37
Jackson, General Andrew, 28
Jackson, J., 61
Jackson,. James H. "Jim", 111
Jackson County, Missouri, 67, 111, 165
Jackson, General William Hicks, 181
Jackson, M., 61
James Boys, 161
James, Frank, 63, 65, 66, 67, 70, 79, 86, 91, 92, 107, 110, 111, 112, 158, 159, 160, 161, 162, 163, 164, 165, 166, 167
James, Frank and Jesse, 57
James, Susan Lavenia, 86
James-Younger gang, 112, 159
James, Zerelda (Cole), 91
Jamilleah, 191
Jane, 6
Janet, 3
Jay Gould, 2:21 1/2, 36, 175
Jay-Eye-See, 2:10, 36, 139, 141, 186
Jefferson City, Missouri, 160
Jefferson County, Kentucky, 49, 113
Jefferson, Thomas, 37
Jefferstown, Kentucky, 49
Jennie D., 147
Jennie Dexter, 147, 149
Jerome, Leonard W., 118
Jerome Park, Fordham, New York, 121, 123, 124, 125
Jerome Stakes, 121
Jersey Cattle, 12, 134, 187
Jersey Derby, 25, 118, 193
James, Jesse, 63, 65, 66, 112
Jewel Maxey, 161
Jills Johnston, 41
Jim Allen, 41
Jim Malone, 161
Jim Scott, 161
Jockey Club Purse, 124
Joe Daniels, 147
Joe Hooker, 145
Joe Stoner, 127
John (Slave Jockey), 120

John Alcock (Slave, Jockey) Pizo, 121
John Doe, 189
John Morgan (Standardbred), 99
John Morgan (Thoroughbred), 169
John, Alexander, 5, 7
John O'Donnell, 146
John R. Gentry, 182, 183
John W. Sipple, 49
Johns Hopkins University, 189
Johnson County, Kentucky, 48
Johnson, Major A.E.V., 65, 66
Johnson, President Andrew, 112, 113, 120
Johnson's Island, Lake Erie, 58
Johnston, Joe, 112
Jones, Brereton C. (Kentucky Governor), 194
Jonesboro, 125
Jones, Captain Sam, 86
Jones, Colonel Sam, 71, 85, 109
Jones, Elizabeth ("Libby") Lloyd, 194
Jones, John R., 48
Jones, Major Sam, 71, 109
Jones, Payne, 111, 112
Jones, Willis Field, 50, 53
Josie C, 146
Judith, 175
Juliet, 21
Julius, 124
Kalida, 121
Kane County, Illinois, 97
Kansas City Fair, 161
Kansas City, Missouri, 63, 81
Kate, 144
Kate Tabor, 181
Katie Darling, 32, 80
Katy, 159
Kearney, Missouri, 65, 167
Keeneland Association, 191
Keeneland Association Library, 78, 91, 103
Kentucky, 7, 15, 16, 17, 19, 21, 22, 25, 27, 28, 31, 32, 34, 35, 41, 42, 43, 45, 48, 49, 50, 51, 54, 57, 58, 62, 64, 65, 66, 67, 72, 74, 76, 81, 89, 101, 112, 114, 115, 116, 117, 118, 119, 120, 121, 123, 124, 129, 130, 131, 134, 137, 143, 146, 165, 166, 167, 177, 181, 182, 185, 188, 191, 197
Kentucky Bourbon, 149
Kentucky Cattleman Association, 193
Kentucky Derby, 91, 150, 160, 189, 193, 195
Kentucky Derby Story, The, 161
Kentucky Horse Park Commission, 193
Kentucky Naval Reserve, 193
Kentucky Racing Association, 58
Kentucky River, 56, 73, 81
Kentucky State Legislature, 8, 48
Kentucky State Racing Commission, 191
Kentucky Whip, 145
Kentucky-Association Race Course, 41
Kentucky's Slave Codes, 17

263

INDEX

Keoku, 32
Keokuk, 32
Keokuk, Iowa Stock Breeding, 92
Key Bridge, 195
Key to the Kingdom, 195
Key to the Mint, 195
King Alfonso, 41, 169, 186, 187
King Ernest, 169
King Herod, 36
King Rene, 186
Kinkead, Frank P., 83
Kirby-Smith, General Edmund, 63
Kirk-Stief Company (Baltimore, Maryland), 133
Kirkwood, 91
Kirtley, Francis Walker, 11
Kismet, 179
Knight of St. George, 37, 124, 183
Knobs State Forest, Kentucky, 70, 111
Koger, John, 65
Korean conflict, 193
Kosciusko, 183
Kossuth Avenue, St. Louis, Missouri, 161
Kremlin, 2:07 3/4, 173, 175
Kunsan, Korea, 188
L.J. Rose of Sunny Slope, 180
La Bruna, 147
La Polka, 121
Laclede Association, St. Louis, Missouri, 115, 120, 125
Laclede Avenue, St. Louis, Missouri, 161
Lady Dan Bryant, 123
Lady Diamond, 150
Lady Josephine, 150
Lady Juror, 150
Lady McFatridge, 181
Lady Moffit, 41
Lag, 147
Lair Station, Kentucky, 73
Lake Erie, 58
Lakeland Farm, 171
Lallah Wilkes, 180
Lanark, 189
Lanark Farm, 12, 191
Lanarkshire, Scotland, 5, 189
Lancaster, 99, 121, 123, 125
Lansing, Paul, 57
Lantados, 150
Lapdog, 29
Lark, 147
Lawrence County, Indiana, 165
Lawrence, Kansas, 65, 111
Lawrenceburg, Kentucky, 71, 83, 85, 86, 87, 89, 92
Lawrenceburg Road, 83
Laynesport, Arkansas, 66
Leamington, 23, 25, 39, 146, 169
Leatherlungs, 104
Leavitt, Major Charles B., 107

Lebanon, Kentucky, 70, 84, 86
Lebanon Junction, Kentucky, 70, 107
Lecomte, 22
Lee, General Robert E., 67, 167
Leitchfield, Kentucky, 85, 86
Lelaps, 169
Leo Wilkes, 180
Leonatus Farm (Named for Kentucky Derby Winner), 159, 160, 165
Leroy, Jefferson County, New York, 31
Leslie County, Kentucky, 188
Leviathan, 29
Lexington, 19, 20, 22, 23, 24, 25, 27, 33, 34, 36, 41, 48, 51, 54, 56, 61, 66, 70, 72, 78, 79, 80, 83, 84, 86, 87, 89, 90, 91, 95, 99, 101, 102, 103, 104, 116, 119, 120, 123, 124, 125, 131, 133, 137, 139, 143, 145, 146, 147, 151, 166, 168, 169, 171, 180, 186, 187, 188, 189, 191, 193, 195, 197
Lexington Association race track, 83
Lexington Stake, 119
Lexington Trotting Club (Kentucky), 34
Lexington, Kentucky, 99, 116, 125, 175
Lilly, Jim, 112
Lincoln, President Abraham, 67
Linden, 41
Linden Lime, 191
Lindora, 80, 91
Lindsey, General Daniel W., 72, 84, 85
Lisbon, 187
Little Blue Church, 165
Little Rock, Arkansas, 63
Little South Fork, 86
Littleton, 39
Liverpool, 42, 121
Lizzie G., 39
Lizzie McDonald, 127
Lizzie W., 25
Lizzie Whipps, 39
Lloyd, 194
Lloyd, Duncan, 194
Lloyd, Lucy Deedes, 194
Lloyd, Lucy Simms, 194
Loadstone, 60, 115, 123, 147
Lon Wilkes, 180
London, 5, 22
London Times, 23
Long, Peyton, 85
Longchamp, France, 187
Longfellow, 23, 39, 41, 42, 160, 169
Lord Chief Baron(Chancellor) of the Exchequer of Britain, 8
Lord Jersey, 116
Lord John, 17, 19
Lord Provost of the City of Edinburgh, Scotland, 3
Lord Russell, 36, 175, 186
Lorillard, Pierre, 171

INDEX

Los Angeles, California, 141, 144
Louisiana, 17, 43, 120, 166
Louisville, Kentucky, 47, 60, 69, 88, 90, 92, 99, 106, 107, 109, 110, 111, 113, 115, 120, 121, 125, 133, 146, 161, 166
Louisville and Frankfort Railroad, 72, 85, 133
Louisville and Nashville Railroad, 70, 97, 197
Louisville Association for the Improvement of the Breed of
Louisville Courier-Journal, 92
Louisville Military Prison Hospital, 111
Love, Joseph, 32
Lucy, 8, 101, 188, 189
Ludwig, Ike, 71
Lula, 2:15, 31, 32
Lulu Jackson, 181
Lansing, Lydia May, 57
Lynchburg, 23, 39
Lyon, Brigadier General Hyland B., 57, 87
Mabel, 143
Macleay, 180
Madam Dudley, 21, 99
Madam Temple, 21, 32
Madeline, 25
Madison Square Garden, New York City, 180
Magdelemas, 150
Magenta, 181
Maggie, 144
Maggie B.B., 25
Maggie Emerson, 146
Maggie Mitchell, 144, 181
Magnolia, 25, 115
Magnum Bonum, 31
Magruder, Henry C., 70, 71, 73, 80, 81, 85, 86, 107, 109, 110, 111
Magruder's guerrilla band, 107
Mahmoud, 150
Maiden, 27
Maillard, A., 146
Martin, Major Samuel, 59
Mahoney, Major Thomas, 69, 84, 86
Maltese, 42
Maltese Cross, 149, 151
Mambrino Chief, 11, 28, 29, 30, 32, 33, 37, 51, 89, 91, 144, 173, 175, 177, 181, 182
Mambrino Dudley, 181, 186
Mambrino Gift, 186
Mambrino King, 143, 145
Mambrino Patchen, 29, 30, 36, 139, 145, 173, 181
Mambrinos, 125
Man of the Year In Service to Kentucky Agriculture, 193
Man O'War, 171
Mansfield, 191
Marais Des Cygens, Kansas, 66
Margaret Morris, 53, 54
Margrave, 37
Maria, 7

Maria "Mattie" Gross, 53
Marian, 145
Marianne, 6, 7
Marine Corps, 191
Marion, 39, 77, 121, 125
Marion County, Kentucky, 86
Marshall, Captain Lewis O., 109
Marshall, John, 37
Marshalltown, Iowa, 95
Martha Wilkes, 2:08, 139
Mary Breckinridge's Frontier Nursing Service, 188
Mary Brennan, 41
Mary Mambrino, 173
Mary Martin, 147
Mary Portor, 41
Mascot, 143
Master of Hounds, 193
Mattie Gross, 54
Maud S., 2:08 3/4, 36, 139, 141, 171, 173, 177, 186
May Hamilton, 48
May King, 2:20, 32, 139
May Queen, 2:20, 31, 139
McChesney, 150
McCorkle, John, 67, 68, 111, 112
McCurdy's Hambletonian, 2:26 1/2, 175
McDuffy, 41
McGuire, Andy, 69, 112
McHenry, 39
McKay, E.H., 88
McKenzie, 67
McKinley, President William, 163
McKinney, 2:11 1/4, 139, 141
McMurty, Lee, 112
McWhiriter, 39
Mead, Captain, 112
Meade County, Kentucky, 85, 107
Meadow Skipper, 145
Melbourne, Jr., 169
Meltonian, 41
Melville (English Lawyer), 97
Memphis, Tennessee, 67, 167
Mercer, 41
Mercer County, Kentucky, 69, 160
Mercer, General Hugh, 7, 41
Merrill, 99, 121, 123, 124, 125
Merry, T.B., 27
Messenger, 36
Metcalf, Henry, 70, 107, 109, 110
Mexican War, 39
Mexico, 67
Mi Cielo, 195
Miami Juvenile Stakes, 151
Michigan Stakes, 115
Middleton, Kentucky, 84
Midnight, 27, 36, 139, 173
Midnight Chimes, 180
Midway, Kentucky, 49, 51, 61, 71, 73, 76, 80, 81,

265

INDEX

83, 84, 86, 87, 93
Midway Road, 91
Midway-Versailles Road (Kentucky), 39
Milan, 67
Military Commission, 113
Military District of Kentucky, 48
Mill Street (Montgomery, Illinois), 97
Miller, James "Uncle Jimmy", 32
Millington, 25
Milwaukee, Wisconsin, 143, 179, 180
Minister from the American Colonies to France, 6
Minnehaha, 141, 143, 144, 179, 180, 181
Minor, Captain W.L., 115
Minor Heir, 1:58 1/2, 171, 173
Mishawaka, Indiana, 193
Miss Alice, 39
Miss Gallop, 41
Miss Naylor, 41
Miss Russell, 27, 36, 139, 173, 175
Miss Woodford, 58
Mississippi, 167
Mississippi River, 67, 107
Missouri, 21, 35, 63, 67, 111, 112, 159, 162, 167
Missouri Cavalry, 68, 111
Missouri River, 65, 66
Mistletoe, 41
Mobile, Alabama, 125
Mollie McCarthy, 146
Molly King, 189
Molly McCarthy, 145
Monarchist, 147
Monogram, 50
Monroe Chief 2:18 1/4, 95
Montgomery Park, Illinois, 97
Montgomery, Alabama, 188
Montgomery, Illinois, 9, 92, 97, 99, 102, 104, 186
Montreal, 42
Moody, 2:18 1/2, 177
Moonstone, 180
Morgan, 35, 37, 51, 53, 54
Morgan, General John Hunt, 41, 43, 51
Morgan horses, 34, 35, 137
Morning Star (Steamer), 109
Morris, Charlie "Pacific Place" on the Mississippi River, 67
Morrissey, John, 117, 118
Morse Horse, 31, 177
Mother Farm of the Standardbred, (Woodburn), 34
Mount Sterling, Kentucky, 73, 84
Mr. Alexander, 17, 18, 22, 27, 32, 34, 37
Mr. Barnes of Tennessee, 54
Mr. Boice of South Carolina, 50
Mr. Bush, 85, 87, 90
Mr. Grigsby, 70
Mr. Hull, 79, 80, 89
Mr. Humphrey, 47, 54
Mr. Monduit, 7

Mr. Prospector, 191
Mr. Richards, 43
Mr. Russell, 31
Mr. Weisiger, 179
Mrs. Jones, 51
Mrs. Nev Ross, 111
Muhlenburg County, Kentucky, 9, 11, 67, 185
Multhrop, Lucy, 188, 195
Mumtaz Mahal, 150
Mundy, "Sue", 44, 49, 54, 55, 56, 57, 59, 60, 61, 63, 70, 71, 72, 73, 74, 75, 76, 77, 80, 81, 83, 84, 85, 86, 106, 107, 109, 110, 133
Mundy's Way, Kentucky, 60
Murat, 41
Murdoch, Peter, 3
My Lady, 37
McMurray, N.R., 68
Myron McHenry 2:18 1/4, 183
Naevus, 195
Nancy Hanks, 2:04, 139
Nancy Pope, 99
Nannie Butler, 80, 87, 91, 123
Nantura Farm, 41, 60, 61, 91
Napoleon, 29, 103
Nashville Railroad, 57
Nashville, Tennessee, 112, 134, 161
Nasrullah, 150
National Gallery Collection, 43
National Museum of Racing, Saratoga Springs, NY, 19
Native Son, 180
Nebraska, 163
Nebula, 50, 54, 101, 115, 119
Ned Forrest, 125, 179
Nellie Gray, 39, 115
Nelson County, Kentucky, 58, 59, 67, 70, 71, 86, 88, 110
Nettie Clay, 141
Nettie King, 2:20 1/4, 145
Nettie Murphy, 145
Netty Viley, 99
Nevada, Missouri, 160
New Jersey, 25, 123, 161
New Jersey Derby, 27
New Market, Kentucky, 86
New Orleans, Louisiana, 22, 28, 166
New Orleans Fair Grounds Race Course, 166
New York, 23, 31, 32, 35, 104, 116, 117, 120, 121, 124, 130, 137, 143, 146, 150, 161, 177, 179, 181, 189
New York City, 104, 125, 143, 159
New York Daily Tribune, 111, 112
New York Times, The, 71, 73, 80, 102, 163
Newberwick, Captain R.M., 70
Newmarket Stakes, 23
Newry, 121, 125
Nijinsky, II, 191
Nixon, Pat, 195

INDEX

Nixon Whitehouse, 195
Noland, George N., 81
Nolands (Bill, Henry, Ed, and George),69, 81
Noontide, 173, 186
Norfolk, 25, 26, 27, 36, 54, 80, 87, 88, 115, 120, 123, 125, 145, 147, 150, 151
Norito, 150
Norman, 21, 31, 33, 179
North Africa, 195
North America, 197
North Atlantic, 191
Northern Dancer, 191
Norway, 99, 121, 125
Norwich, 27, 56, 80, 87, 88, 90, 121, 123, 125
Norwood, 121
Novice, 90, 115, 147
Nursery Stakes, 121
Nutwood, 139, 177, 186
Oak Grove, Missouri, 165
Oak Hill, Kentucky, 49
Oakland Park California, 147
Oglenah, 41
Ohio, 17, 51, 97, 101, 129, 177
Ohio River, 51, 185
Okalee, 187
Oklahoma, 167
Old Frankfort Pike (Kentucky), 9, 41, 91, 188, 189
Old Pilot, 34, 99
Old Woodford Church (Kentucky), 18
Ontario, 39
Onward, 37, 124
Ophir, 147
Ora Wilkes, 180
Original Rebellion Records of the Civil War, 69
Orrick, Missouri, 66
Othello, 179
Overland, 181
Overstreet Farm, 53
Owen County, Kentucky, 71
Owensboro, Kentucky, 109
Owensboro, Kentucky Fair, 165
Owingsville, Kentucky, 49
Pacific, 134
Pacolet, 28
Pactolus 2:12 3/4, 173
Paisley, Scotland, 3
Palmer, General John M., 110, 112
Palo Alto, 180
Palo Alto (the Tall Pine) Farm, 139
Palo Alto, 2:08 3/4, 139
Palo Alto Stock Farm, 143
Pancoast, 2:21 3/4 , 171, 173, 175, 186
Pantaloon, 23
Paris, Tennessee, 3, 7, 67
Paris and Cynthiana Pike (Kentucky), 58
Paris "literary supper", 6
Paris, France,3, 7

Parkhurst, John, 59
Parksville, Kentucky, 86
Parliament, 5, 8
Parmer, "One-Arm" Allen,86, 111, 112
Parole, 27
Parrish, Lucy, 195
Parrish, William "Willy", 195
Partisan Ranger, 51
Partisana, 147
Passaic County Agricultural Society, 15, 27
Passy, 7
Pat Malloy, 171, 187
Paterson, New Jersey,25, 27, 99, 103, 104, 125
Patron, 187
Patronage, 171, 173
Patrou, 2:14 1/4, 171
Pawnee, 143
Payne, Thomas, 76
Pedro, 181
Peggerty, 125
Peggot (Workman at Woodburn), 54
Pence, Bud, 67, 86, 112
Pence, Donnie, 107
Perche Hills, Missouri, 63
Perryville Pike (Kentucky), 68
Phaeton, 169
Pharaoh's Horses (Painting), 166
Philadelphia, Pennslyvania, 183
Philocea, 143
Picayune, 23
Pilot, 181
Pilot Jr., 21, 27, 28, 33, 36, 97, 99, 102, 139, 144, 173
Pilot Knob (Battle of), 63
Pilot Temple, 2:24 1/2, 28
Pilots, 125
Pincus, Jacob, 104, 121, 123
Pixley 2:08 1/4, 175
Planet, 127, 139, 171
Plato, 41
Pocahontas, Arkansas,63, 67
Polo Alto Belle, 180
Ponce de Leon, 2:13, 171
Pond Gap, Kentucky, 73
Pool, Dave, 67, 111
Pope mare, 144
Porter, Captain Henry (Guerrilla), 112
Portersville, Tennessee, 67
Porter's Cap, 189
Potomac, 37, 141
Powhatan, 187
Pratt, Brigadier General J.V., 111
Preakness Racing Stable, 125
Preakness Stakes, 133, 193, 195
Preakness Stud, 125, 147, 186
Presbyterian, 3
Presbyterian Church, 188
Presidential Candidate, 165

267

INDEX

Preston, Jean, 188
Pretty Woods (Bosque Bonita), 39
Price, General Sterling, 63, 66
Price, Major General, 63
Princeps, 186
Princeton University, 189
Princeton, Arkansas, 63
Privy Counselor, 8
Proctor Knott, 161
Progressive Farmer, 193
Proteine, 179
Provosts, 3
Puncheon Creek, Kentucky, 57
Puritan, 180
Quaker, 31
Quantrill, William C., 62, 63, 64, 65, 66, 67, 68, 69, 70, 71, 72, 73, 74, 76, 77, 78, 80, 81, 82, 83, 85, 86, 88, 89, 92, 107, 108, 110, 111, 112, 133
Quantrill, William C. Charley, 112
Quantrill, William Clarke "Charley", 63
Quantrill's Guerrillas, 165
Queen Anne Cottage, 149
Queen City Fair Association, 166
Queen Mary, 41
Queens County Handicap, 189
Rabet, Jack, 59
Rachel, 182
Racine, Wisconsin, 177
Racing Calendars, 56, 169
Racing in America, 105
Racing in America, 1830-1865, 103
Rafferty, 104
Railway, 41
Raise a Native, 191
Ralf, 41
Rancho del Rio, 27
Rancho Santa Anita, 149, 159
Rappahannock River, Virginia, 5
Rawcliffe Stud Company, England, 42
Raywick, Kentucky, 84, 85
Rebel, 161
Rebellion Records of the Civil War, 77
Red Dick, 125
Red Fox, 161
Red Wilkes, 183
Regan, 147
Reign of Terror (France), 7
Renfrewshire, Scotland, 3
Renick, Chat, 68, 69
Republican, The, 165
Republicans, 163
Reveille, 50
Revenue, 39
Revolver, 169
Rey del Caredas, 150
Rey del Caredes, 145, 150
Rey el Rio, 151

Rey el Santa Anita, 147, 151
Rey el Tierra, 151
Rhinodine, 60
Rice, George, 161
Richards, Alexander Keene, 25, 37, 39, 42, 43, 50, 54, 115, 116, 120, 123
Richards, Richard, 177
Richard "Dick" Singleton, 41
Richmond, Kentucky, 84
Richmond & Danville Railroad, 39
Richmond Road (Lexington, Kentucky), 191
Richmond, Virginia, 48, 167
Richmond, Virginia *Daily Examiner*, 80
Ringgold, 37, 56
Rissinger, G., 61
Rio Grande, 161
Rizpah, 2:13 1/2, 173
Robert J., 2:01 1/2, 173, 175
Robespierre, Maximilien, 7
Robinson, George, 69
Rochelle, France, 3
Rockbridge County, Virginia, 7
Roosevelt, Theodore, 167
Rose, Leonard J., 141, 143, 144, 180, 181
Rose, Jr., Leonard J., 180
Rose Hill, 57
Rosemead, California, 141, 143
Rosemead Stock Farm, 141
Rosewood, 179
Ross, John, 86, 111, 112
Rosslyn Castle, Scotland, 3
Rosslyn Chapel, Scotland, 3
Royal Bank, 5
Royal Bank of Scotland, 5
Royal Canadian Air Force, 194
Royal Charger, 150
Royal Native, 193
Royalist, 7
Runnymede Stud, 58
Rupee, 180
Ruric, 105, 146
Russell, Bedford, 110
Russellmont, 2:12 3/4, 173
Rutherford, 146
Rysdyk's Hambletonian, 175
Purdy, S.F., 121
Sabina, 180
Sable, 180
Sable Wilkes, 179, 180
Sabledale, 180
Sacramento, California, 27
Saint Mary's Station, Kentucky, 86
Saladin, 179
Sally Anderson, 144
Sally Hardin, 41
Sally Russell, 36, 139
Salt River, Kentucky, 110
Slocum, Samuel, 31

INDEX

Sample, W.H., 92
Samuels Depot, Kentucky, 70, 110, 111, 112
San Francisco, California, 143, 149, 181
San Gabriel, 143, 145, 181
San Gabriel Valley, California, 141
Sandusky Bay, Lake Erie, 58
Sanford, Milton H., 125, 147
Sangamon County, Illinois, 99
Santa Anita, 147
Santa Anita Derby, 189
Santa Anita Park, 151
Santa Anita Stud, 149
Saratoga Springs, New York, 19, 25, 27, 39, 116, 117, 118, 119, 121, 124, 125, 146, 149, 160, 161
Saratoga Cup Stakes, 27, 115, 118, 119, 120, 121
Saratoga of the West (Woodlawn Race Track), 133
Saratoga Stakes, 121
Sarpedon, 37
Saxon, 169
Sayer (home), 111
Sayer, Judge Alexander, 69, 110
Sayers, Finetta, 70
Scarlet, 41
Scotland, 3, 7, 8, 9, 11, 18, 19, 189
Scott County, Kentucky, 41, 42, 73, 81, 177
Scott, General Winfield, 43
Scott, William W., 112
Scythian, 23, 28, 54, 102, 125, 147
Sea Foam, 181
Seaman, C.C., 180
Searcy, Captain Wiley, 69
Sebastopol, 16
Second Duke of Athol, 16
Secrage, 191
Secreto, 191
Seely's American Star 14, 36
Selena, 39
Stanford, U.S. Senator Leland, 143
Separate Issue, 191
Sequel Stakes, 25, 121
Seven Years' War, 5
Shadowlawn Farm, 22
Shawnee Farm, 160
Shelby, Brigadier General Jo O., 63, 67
Shelby County, Kentucky, 17, 70, 72
Shelbyville, Kentucky, 73, 90
Shephard, George, 67
Shepherdsville, Kentucky, 70
Sherman, General William T., 112
Sherman Silver Purchase Act, 163
Shirke, Major John L., 70
Short Account of Shorthorn Cattle, 16
Shorthorn Cattle, 12, 15, 16, 17, 19, 39, 134, 186, 187
Shorthorns, 124
Silurian, 41
Silver Cloud, 151

Silver Eye, 29
Silver Hawk, 195
Silver Medallion, 195
Silverites, 163
Simms, William E., 189
Simms, William "Will" and Lucy Alexander, 194
Sinclair, James, 16
Singleton Mare, 183
Sipple, John W., 49
Sir Archy, 29, 36, 37, 99, 183
Sir Archy of Montorio, 41
Sir Dixon, 58
Sister Anne, 147, 151
Skyrocket, 161
Slave leases, 17
Slew City Slew, 195
Slocum, John N., 31
Smiley, Kentucky, 112
Smileytown, Kentucky, 112
Smithfield, Kentucky, 72
Sni River, Missouri, 65
Sophie, 139
Southdown sheep, 12, 17, 134, 186, 187
Sovereign, 29, 39
Spain, 3
Spectator, 35
Spencer County, Kentucky, 69, 70, 72, 110
Spencer Graves, 54
Spendthrift, 146
Spirit of the Times, 56, 87
Spokane, 161
Spring Hill Stock Farm, 179
Spring Station, Kentucky, 97, 99, 177, 195, 197
Springfield, Illinois, 47, 99
Springfield, Missouri, 166
St. Bel, 180
St. Giles, 29
St. Joseph's Catholic Hospital, Louisville, 111
St. Lager, 118, 119, 123
St. Louis, Missouri, 63, 90, 99, 104, 111, 120, 125, 160, 161, 165, 166
St. Louis Fair, 23
St. Louis Fair Grounds Race Course, 161
St. Louis Fairgrounds, 159
St. Louis Post-Dispatch, 166
St. Louis, Missouri, 99, 125
Stagville, Samuel, 49
Stamboul, 2:07 1/2, 32, 143, 144, 179
Stanford, 86
Stanford, California Governor Leland, 139
Star Davis, 33, 80, 91, 125, 169
Star de Naskra, 191
Star Voter, 189
State Department, 195
State Legislature, 39
State Racing Commission of Kentucky, 159
Steele, Andrew, 177
Stephens, George, 179

269

INDEX

Stephensport, Kentucky, 107
Stevens' Bald Chief, 141
Stevens, George C., 141, 143
Stites, Charlotte (Gay), 191
Stock-farm-catalogue (American), 32
Stockholm's American Star, 37
Stockwell and St. Simon (England), 95
Stockwood Stud, 186
Stonewall - (Horse), 161
Stonewall, 60
Stonewall Farm, 41, 83, 84
Such Was Saratoga, 161
Sudie McNair, 39
Sue Lewis, 54, 60, 101
Sultan, 2:24, 143, 144, 179
Summit Sentinel, 167
Summit, Mississippi, 167
Sunday Silence, 195
Sunny Slope, 141, 181
Sutton, Lewis J., 32
Sweepstakes Hurdle, 125
Sweetheart, 143
Swigert, Daniel, 31, 53, 54, 59, 77, 78, 90, 91, 101, 115, 177, 186
Swigert (Horse), 177, 186
Swigert, Mary, 78
Swigert, Mrs. A., 78, 79
Swope, Captain, 109
Sword Dancer, 193
Sympathy, 25
Taylor, T.B., 47
Taylor, T.G., 99
T.V. Lark, 193, 194
Tabernacle, 67
Talbot, Rev., 109
Tammany Hall (New York City), 150
Tarabine, 42
Tariff Barons, 164
Tattler, 2:26, 28, 186
Taylor County, Kentucky, 86
Taylor, G.W., 47
Taylor, General Zachary, 39
Taylor, Major Dick, 85
Taylorsville, Kentucky, 69, 70, 111
Technology, 195
Ten Broeck, 22, 41, 146
Ten Broeck, Richard, 22, 104
Tennessee, 35, 37, 47
Tennessee River, 67
Tenpenny, 41
Terms of Breeding, 34
Terre Haute, Indiana, 183
Terrell, Captain Edward, 71, 90, 110
Texas, 17, 67, 161, 185
Texas State Fair (Dallas), 167
The Abbe, 145
The Abbot, 2:03 1/4, 143, 145
The Conqueror, 2:13, 173

The Hook, 147
The Knight of St. George, 42
The Moor (Beau Clay), 143, 144, 179, 180, 181
The Nun, 147
The Standard (burlesque) Theater, St. Louis, 161, 166
The System (Paris, France), 3
Theobalion, 41
Theodore Shelton, 183
Taylor, Thomas, 47
Thomas, Morris, 17
Thompson, Samuel, 54,
Thoroughbred Club of America, 191
Thoroughbred Record, 134
Thunder, 103, 104
Ticonderoga, 177
Tiffany & Company (New York), 133, 159
Tiger, 41
Tijuana, Mexico, 150
Tilton, 49
Timoleon, 36
Tim's Stingray, 191
Tindle, 59
Tippo Saib, 28
Titcomb & Waldron, 31
Todd, Captain George (Guerrilla), 63, 66
Todd County, Kentucky, 165
Toler, H.G., 183
Tom Teemer, 91
Tompion, 193
Top Avenger, 191
Topgallant, 29, 36
Town And Country Magazine, 133
Townely, Colonel, 16
Traducer, 147
Transylvania plantation, 120
Travers Stakes, 27, 121
Travers, William R., 117, 118
Tree Hill Farm, 11
Tremont, 147
Trevisco, 189
Tri Weekly Commonwealth, 17
Trigg County, Kentucky, 67
Trinity College, Cambridge, England, 8, 9
Trotting Register, The, 27, 32
Troye, Edward, 18, 42, 43, 92, 120
Truffle, 32
Trust Kings, 164
Trustee, 37
Tudor Minstrel, 150
Turf, Field and Farm 101, 102, 119, 121, 123, 124, 125, 131, 197
Twain, Mark (Samuel Clements), 159
Twilight, 139
U.S., 119, 162, 167
U.S. Congress, 45, 163
U.S. Constitution, 45
U.S. House of Representatives, 45

270

INDEX

U.S. Military Academy at West Point, 39
U.S. Navy, 191
U.S. Senate, 45
U.S. Treasury, 163
U.S. Virgin Islands, 194
Ulee Wilkes, 180
Uncle Vic, 41
Union, 45, 47, 48, 54, 60, 65, 66, 67, 69, 73, 82, 83, 84, 86, 112
Union Club Casino, Saratoga Springs, NY, 117
Union Guards, 71
Union Jack, 49
United Nations Handicap, 193
United States, 12, 15, 16, 17, 41, 117, 119, 133, 134, 145, 160, 162, 167, 185, 186
Vandal, 41, 147
Vanderbilt, Commodore Cornelius, 117
Vanderbilt, William Henry ESQ., 139
Van Dyke, H. Walter, 166
Venable, Randall, 112
Venetian Way, 193
Verano, 147
Vermont Black Hawk,, 35
Versailles, Kentucky, 39, 44, 49, 57, 59, 71, 73, 83, 84, 85, 87, 93, 180, 194
Versailles Pike (Highway 62) (Kentucky), 83
Versailles, Kentucky, 180
Veto, 37
Viet Nam, 193
Viking Spirit, 189
Viley, Captain Willa, 22, 41, 76, 81, 83
Viley, Major Warren, 41, 57, 58, 60, 75, 76, 81, 87
Viley, Warren, 75, 76, 81, 87
Villa, Pancho, 65
Village Farm, 143, 145
Village View Farm, 194
Virgil, 145, 147, 169
Virginia, 5, 7, 18, 37, 41, 78, 127
Volante, 145, 151
Voltain, 2:21 1/4, 28
Voltaire, 186
W. Overton, 41
Wagner, 23
Wagner, Captain, 66
Wakefield farm, 110
Wakefield, Major, 111
Wakefield, Major James, 110
Wall Springs Farm, 28
Wall Street, New York City, 163, 164
Wallace, John H., 15, 171
Wallace's Grove, Missouri, 81
Wallace's Monthly, 33, 131, 171
Waller, James Breckinridge,101, 189
Walnut Hill Stud, 146
War Dance, 39
War of the Rebellion Original Records, 70, 80, 83, 107
Ward, Junius R., 22
Warford, Henry, 59

Warnerton Farm, 195
Warwick, 32
Washington, D.C., 43, 67
Washington County, Kentucky, 113
Washington Park, 150
Washington Park Futurity, 189
Watertown, Massachusetts, 182
Watkins, Catharine, 97
Watkins flour mill, Montgomery, Illinois, 97
Watkins, Vine A., 97
Watson, 121, 123, 125
Waverley, 169
Waverly, Missouri, 67
Waxy, 23
Wayage, 191
Wetherton, John, 60
Weatherman, Lynn, 23, 39, 53
Webb place, Missouri, 65
Webster, Kentucky, 109
Wedgewood, 181, 182, 183, 186
Weisiger, Eliza Richardson, 8
Weldon, J. W., 104
Wells, General Thomas Jefferson, 43
Wellswood Plantation, Louisiana, 43
West Allis, Wisconsin, 141
West Florida, 41
West Indies, 3
West Point, New York, 70
Westchester County, New York, 124
Whalebon, 23
Wheatley, Charles R., 117, 121
White Reason, 191
Wichita, Kansas, 183
Wickerman, W.F., 48
Wiggington, Ben, 70
Wigginton, George, 67, 112
Wiggington, Jim, 69
Wigginton Place, Missouri, 67
Wild West Show (Cole Younger and Frank James), 167
Wilkes Blanche, 180
Wilkes' Spirit of the Times, 17, 23, 53, 90, 95, 101, 102, 116, 117, 118, 124
Willard Hotel Stakes, 124
William Alexander and Sons (Firm), 5
William Farish's Lane's End Farm, 39
Williams Jr., Jonathan, 7
Williams, Press, 85
Winchester, William, 195
Williamson, Ansel,27, 54, 56, 79, 80, 99, 115, 120, 121, 123, 125
Williamson's Belmont, 37
Williamsville, Illinois, 23, 99
Williamsville, Sangamon County, Illinois,47, 101, 102
Wilson Lilly, 48
Winchester, Kentucky, 112
Winnowing Wind, 191

INDEX

Winters, Theodore H. ("Black T."), 27, 145
Wisconsin, 141
Withers, General W.T., 175
Woodbine, 173, 181, 182, 183
Woodburn, 17, 18, 20, 21, 22, 25, 28, 29, 32, 33, 34, 36, 37, 47, 49, 50, 51, 52, 53, 54, 55, 56, 57, 59, 63, 71, 73, 74, 75, 76, 78, 80, 81, 82, 83, 85, 86, 87, 89, 91, 92, 97, 99, 101, 102, 103, 104, 105, 115, 118, 119, 120, 121, 122, 124, 126, 127, 129, 130, 131, 133, 134, 137, 139, 145, 146, 147, 149, 150, 151, 156, 160, 161, 169, 171, 173, 175, 177, 181, 182, 183, 193
Woodburn Farm, 7, 8, 9, 15, 17, 18, 19, 22, 23, 24, 31, 33, 34, 35, 41, 49, 50, 51, 53, 54, 57, 61, 83, 86, 87, 94, 95, 97, 101, 105, 107, 121, 124, 125, 130, 136, 137, 138, 144, 147, 171, 173, 175, 181, 185, 186, 187, 190
Woodburn Farm Catalogue, 147
Woodburn Farm Sales,124, 133
Woodburn House, 8, 11, 39, 189
Woodburn mansion, 18, 188
Woodburn Raid, 81
Woodburn Stud, 21, 34, 41, 133, 171, 183, 197
Woodburn Stud Book, 53
Woodburn Stud Catalogue, 56
Woodburn Trotting Stud, 101
Woodford, 181, 183
Woodford County, KY, 7, 39, 45, 47, 73, 81, 133, 182
Woodford County Home Guards, 85, 89
Woodford County Revenue Tax and County Levy, 17
Woodford Lad, 189
Woodford Mambrino, 2:21 1/2, 173, 181, 183, 186
Woodford Sun, 81
Woodlawn, 115, 121, 123, 124, 125
Woodlawn Association Race Course, 130, 133
Woodlawn Course, 123
Woodlawn Park, 133
Woodlawn Race Course, 121, 127
Woodlawn Race Course Association, 115, 121, 123, 124, 125, 127, 130, 133, 134
Woodlawn Vase, 123, 133
Woodruff, Hirum, 32
Woodstock, 125
World War II, 189, 193, 195
Worthville, Kentucky, 73
Yearlings Sale Stakes, 189
Yo Tambien, 145
Yolo County, California, 27
Yorkshire, 91, 147
Young, Captain (Union Officier0, 112
Young Giantess, 36
Young Highlander, 29
Young, Lieutenant Thomas P., 68
Younger, Cole, 167

Younger, Jim, 67, 69
Zanesville, Ohio, 166
Zenith, 41

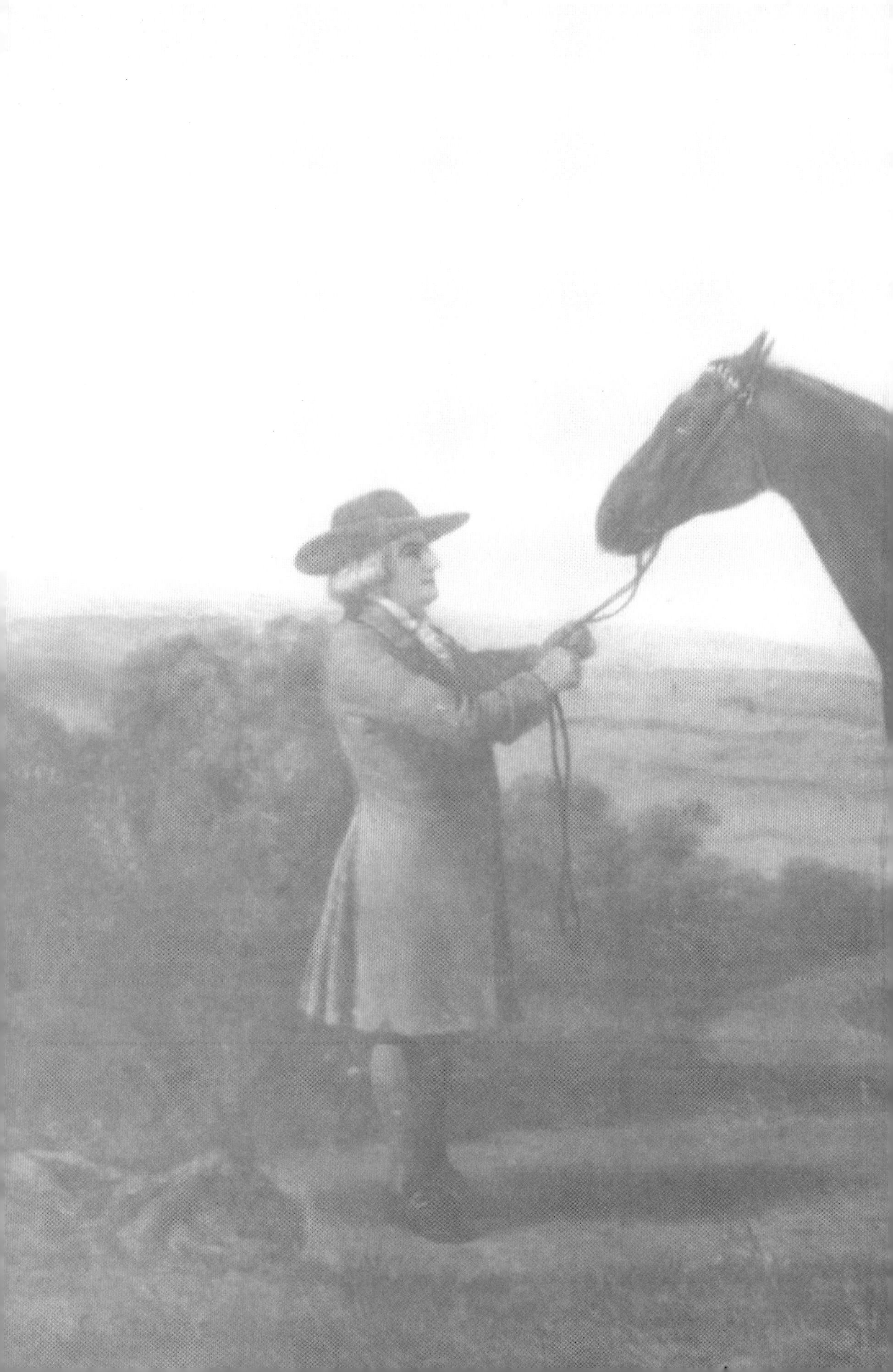